I0885401

Exploring the Dark Side of FinTech and Implications of Monetary Policy

Sheraz Ahmed
LUT University, Finland

John Agyekum Addae
LUT University, Finland & Ghana Communication Technology University, Ghana

Kwame Simpe Ofori
International University of Grand-Bassam, Côte d'Ivoire & University of Electronic Science and Technology of China, China

IGI Global
PUBLISHER of TIMELY KNOWLEDGE

A volume in the Advances in Finance, Accounting, and Economics (AFAE) Book Series

Published in the United States of America by
IGI Global
Business Science Reference (an imprint of IGI Global)
701 E. Chocolate Avenue
Hershey PA, USA 17033
Tel: 717-533-8845
Fax: 717-533-8661
E-mail: cust@igi-global.com
Web site: http://www.igi-global.com

Copyright © 2023 by IGI Global. All rights reserved. No part of this publication may be reproduced, stored or distributed in any form or by any means, electronic or mechanical, including photocopying, without written permission from the publisher.
Product or company names used in this set are for identification purposes only. Inclusion of the names of the products or companies does not indicate a claim of ownership by IGI Global of the trademark or registered trademark.

Library of Congress Cataloging-in-Publication Data

Names: Ahmed, Sheraz, 1973- editor. | Agyekum Addae, John, 1982- editor. | Ofori, Kwame, 1983- editor.
Title: Exploring the dark side of fintech and implications of monetary policy / Sheraz Ahmed, John Agyekum Addae, and Kwame Ofori, editor.
Description: Hershey, PA : Business Science Reference, [2023] | Includes bibliographical references and index. | Summary: "This book guides monetary authority on CBDC policy choices, improve upon CBDC interoperability and minimize implementation challenges overrun. Covering topics such as the digital euro, ethical implications, and sustainable development goals, this book is an essential resource for banks, high frequency traders, insurance companies, and finance professionals as they position themselves to leverage on CBDC and Fintech applications"-- Provided by publisher.
Identifiers: LCCN 2022039339 (print) | LCCN 2022039340 (ebook) | ISBN 9781668463819 (hardcover) | ISBN 9781668463826 (paperback) | ISBN 9781668463833 (ebook)
Subjects: LCSH: Finance--Technological innovations. | Monetary policy.
Classification: LCC HG173 .E976 2023 (print) | LCC HG173 (ebook) | DDC 332--dc23/eng/20220908
LC record available at https://lccn.loc.gov/2022039339
LC ebook record available at https://lccn.loc.gov/2022039340

This book is published in the IGI Global book series Advances in Finance, Accounting, and Economics (AFAE) (ISSN: 2327-5677; eISSN: 2327-5685)

British Cataloguing in Publication Data
A Cataloguing in Publication record for this book is available from the British Library.

All work contributed to this book is new, previously-unpublished material.
The views expressed in this book are those of the authors, but not necessarily of the publisher.

For electronic access to this publication, please contact: eresources@igi-global.com.

Advances in Finance, Accounting, and Economics (AFAE) Book Series

ISSN:2327-5677
EISSN:2327-5685

Editor-in-Chief: Ahmed Driouchi, Al Akhawayn University, Morocco

MISSION

In our changing economic and business environment, it is important to consider the financial changes occurring internationally as well as within individual organizations and business environments. Understanding these changes as well as the factors that influence them is crucial in preparing for our financial future and ensuring economic sustainability and growth.

The **Advances in Finance, Accounting, and Economics (AFAE)** book series aims to publish comprehensive and informative titles in all areas of economics and economic theory, finance, and accounting to assist in advancing the available knowledge and providing for further research development in these dynamic fields.

COVERAGE

- Corporate Finance
- Auditing
- Entrepreneurship in Accounting and Finance
- Fiscal Policy
- Economic Downturn
- Ethics in Accounting and Finance
- Risk Analysis and Management
- Economic Indices and Quantitative Economic Methods
- Health Economics
- E-Accounting

IGI Global is currently accepting manuscripts for publication within this series. To submit a proposal for a volume in this series, please contact our Acquisition Editors at Acquisitions@igi-global.com or visit: http://www.igi-global.com/publish/.

The Advances in Finance, Accounting, and Economics (AFAE) Book Series (ISSN 2327-5677) is published by IGI Global, 701 E. Chocolate Avenue, Hershey, PA 17033-1240, USA, www.igi-global.com. This series is composed of titles available for purchase individually; each title is edited to be contextually exclusive from any other title within the series. For pricing and ordering information please visit http://www.igi-global.com/book-series/advances-finance-accounting-economics/73685. Postmaster: Send all address changes to above address. © © 2023 IGI Global. All rights, including translation in other languages reserved by the publisher. No part of this series may be reproduced or used in any form or by any means – graphics, electronic, or mechanical, including photocopying, recording, taping, or information and retrieval systems – without written permission from the publisher, except for non commercial, educational use, including classroom teaching purposes. The views expressed in this series are those of the authors, but not necessarily of IGI Global.

Titles in this Series

For a list of additional titles in this series, please visit:
http://www.igi-global.com/book-series/advances-finance-accounting-economics/73685

Exploring Business Ecosystems and Innovation Capacity Building in Global Economics
Mihir Joshi (Banasthali Vidyapith University, Rajasthan, India) Mohsen Brahmi (University of Sfax, Tunisia) Luigi Aldieri (University of Salerno, Italy) and Concetto Paolo Vinci (University of Salerno, Italy)
Business Science Reference • © 2023 • 325pp • H/C (ISBN: 9781668467664) • US $250.00

Considerations of Territorial Planning, Space, and Economic Activity in the Global Economy
Helmuth Yesid Arias Gomez (Masaryk Institute of Advanced Studies (MIAS), Czech Technical University in Prague, Czech Republic) and Gabriela Antošová (Institute of Education and Communication, Czech University of Life Sciences in Prague, Czech Republic)
Business Science Reference • © 2023 • 356pp • H/C (ISBN: 9781668459768) • US $250.00

Transforming Economies Through Microfinance in Developing Nations
Yahaya Alhassan (University of Sunderland in London, UK) and Uzoechi Nwagbara (University of Sunderland in London, UK)
Business Science Reference • © 2023 • 263pp • H/C (ISBN: 9781668456477) • US $250.00

Advanced Machine Learning Algorithms for Complex Financial Applications
Mohammad Irfan (CMR Institute of Technology, India) Mohamed Elhoseny (American University in the Emirates, UAE) Salina Kassim (International Islamic University of Malaysia, Malaysia) and Noura Metawa (University of Sharjah, UAE)
Engineering Science Reference • © 2023 • 292pp • H/C (ISBN: 9781668444832) • US $270.00

Blockchain Applications in Cryptocurrency for Technological Evolution
Atour Taghipour (Normandy University, France)
Business Science Reference • © 2023 • 308pp • H/C (ISBN: 9781668462478) • US $250.00

For an entire list of titles in this series, please visit:
http://www.igi-global.com/book-series/advances-finance-accounting-economics/73685

IGI Global
PUBLISHER of TIMELY KNOWLEDGE

701 East Chocolate Avenue, Hershey, PA 17033, USA
Tel: 717-533-8845 x100 • Fax: 717-533-8661
E-Mail: cust@igi-global.com • www.igi-global.com

Table of Contents

Detailed Table of Contents

their regulatory regimes and continue to provide and develop guidelines to mitigate these risks. This study provides a cross-country review of fintech policy responses of developed world.

Section 2
FinTech Challenges

Many bank failures have occurred in history. The lessons learnt from past bank failures remind us that any bank can fail, and they fail for different reasons. The first step to avoid the failure of a strong bank is to identify the factors that cause the failure of a strong bank. This paper focus on strong banks and identifies the reasons why strong banks might fail. The reasons why a strong bank might fail are numerous. The insights offered in the article can help existing banks to avoid a bank failure in the future. The insights also have financial stability implications which need to be taken seriously.

This study constructed an assessment of the barriers and challenges of financial technology (fintech) and accentuated a critical research area that is relatively new and currently understudied in extant literature. A theoretical framework was developed from a blend of the technology, organization, and environment (TOE) framework and the human, organization, and technology (HOT) fit model. The best-worst method was used to analyze and rank the identified barriers and challenges of fintech according to their weighted averages. The findings of the study point to perceived risk and lack of trust; transaction cost; privacy and security issues; legal and regulatory barriers; and the human element and psychological factors as the highest ranked barriers and challenges of financial technology. This study has significant theoretical and managerial implications for academia, policy makers, and practitioners, as it would stretch their standpoints on the best practices for adoption and implementation of fintech modernisms.

The study sought to investigate the determinants of MoMo fraud perception in C2C e-commerce from a trust perspective. The research model comprises a set of relationships between constructs from empirical studies. The constructs are culture (uncertainty avoidance), perceived reputation of mobile service provider, trust in C2C trader, structural assurance, perceived usefulness, and consumer fraud perception. A quantitative research design was used for the study. The sample consisted of three hundred and eighty-seven (387) respondents. Data were analysed using PLS-SEM (partial least squares structural equation modelling) via SmartPLS 3. Culture (uncertainty avoidance) was found to have a significant negative influence on consumer fraud perception. Perceived reputation of the mobile service provider was found to have an insignificant influence on consumer fraud perception. Trust in C2C trader, structural assurance, and perceived usefulness were found to have a significant positive influence on consumer fraud perception.

Despite FinTech's considerable financial inclusions in West Africa, its unintended criminogenic features cannot be overlooked. While the region rises as the continental FinTech hub, many countries have collapsed under terrorism. It faces a unique vulnerability to terrorism financing for having a high rate of joblessness among its FinTech-savvy millennials, which overlaps another high rate of joblessness among young terrorist recruits. But by highlighting the difference between the "operational" and "networking" motives of terrorism financing, this chapter demonstrates that the natures of assaults occurring in West Africa are operational financing using rudimentary cash flow carriers across borders. But given the ingenuity with which cybercriminals operate, it conducts a comprehensive analysis of the legislative measures implemented in West Africa to prevent FinTech's terrorism financing risks. It explores futureproofing, cutting-edge, and dynamic technology-based strategy, designed explicitly on cryptocurrencies and virtual assets to anticipate and combat terrorism financing.

Mobile payment systems have created a lot of opportunities for both businesses and consumers to easily transact business. Due to the portable and interactive nature of mobile devices, mobile payment systems have aided most consumers in their daily business activities. In spite of their numerous benefits, mobile payment systems can create problems for consumers, and one such problem is impulse buying. Consumers usually make unplanned purchases spontaneously and intuitively after being exposed to exciting cues like price promotions, limited offers, and attractive product appearances; mobile payment systems facilitate these purchases. In the light of this, the current study synthesizes some scholarly works on mobile payment systems and impulse buying. The paper contributes to the growing body of literature on the dark side of financial technologies.

The financial and monetary system is transitioning into contactless payment options and digital currencies. About 90 percent of the world's central banks are engaged in CBDC research, proof of concept, pilot, development, and launch, while the remaining are overlooking CBDC offerings. Notwithstanding, many central banks have cancelled their CBDC following their launch. While learning from the past failure is extoled as a virtue, learning from failed CBDC is seldom in the CBDC ecosystem, contrary to dominant literature on CBDC development and scalability. This study explores reasons why central banks discontinued already launched CBDC's. The authors adopted criterion sampling to select failed CBDC. This multiple case content analysis shows that low levels of trust, cybersecurity concerns, inadequate digital identification infrastructure, and obsolete and uncompetitive technology are the leading triggers of failed CBDC. Through the lens of actor-network theory

(ANT), actors contributing to CBDC failure was identified

The financial system has been changing rapidly with the recent advancements in technologies underlying the money and payment systems. With the increase in the involvement of technology in the financial world and the emergence of new technologies like distributed ledger technologies (DLT), there has been a rising trend of creating private cryptocurrencies and stablecoins to replace existing currencies and assets. The increasing influence of big-tech companies in the financial systems and the usage of unregulated cryptocurrencies and stablecoins pose many challenges for financial authorities worldwide, generating the need for government intervention. As a result, numerous central banks worldwide are looking for possibilities to change their monetary systems by including central bank digital currencies (CBDCs) like the digital euro in their offerings. However, it is uncertain how these CBDCs and other digital money initiatives will impact the existing systems and provide solutions to existing problems and benefit the citizens and other stakeholders.

This chapter outlines the risks and challenges involved in implementing central bank digital currency (CBDC). Interest in CBDC is currently growing, with a number of central banks paying it serious consideration, and a number of countries are implementing or piloting CBDC. Although CBDC holds a great deal of promise, its implementation is not without difficulty. This chapter highlights the major implementation issues, such as CBDC contributing to financial exclusion, technology risks, CBDC's inability to work in an offline environment, lack of privacy, and confidential consideration, since anonymity is difficult to achieve. The chapter concludes by highlighting the need to deploy CBDC with greater attention paid to societal, economic, and political factors instead of a purely technocratic approach.

Preface

Financial Technology (Fintech), the fusion of financial innovation and technology, has revolutionized the way financial services are delivered. Fintech's objective is to make financial services more accessible, efficient, and user-friendly, while cutting costs and enhancing security. Examples of Fintech applications includes mobile wallets, mobile payments, P2P lending, crowdfunding, InsureTech, cryptocurrencies, blockchain technology, central bank digital currency and robo-advisors (Bollaert et al., 2021). The increasing prevalence of electronic commerce and the burgeoning popularity of mobile devices and applications are fueling the boom in FinTech adoption. Fintech has had a profound impact on the financial services industry, and has made many financial services more accessible, convenient, and efficient for consumers and businesses alike. Fintech multichannel is currently used by 64% of the global population (Najaf et al., 2020, p. 915). Global investment in FinTech reached $210 billion in 2021 (KPMG, 2022). According to a recent report by Accenture, the global fintech market is expected to reach $309 billion by 2022.

The fintech industry has made a substantial contribution to the COVID-19 recovery effort (Bai et al., 2021; Charaia et al., 2021; World Bank, 2020), as well as in driving SGD targets (Hinson et al., 2019) and increasing financial inclusion (Senyo & Osabutey, 2020). Moreover, comparative study conducted by Apeti and Edoh (2023) find that FinTech significantly increases tax revenue performance in FinTech countries relative to non-FinTech countries.

In spite of the numerous gains that Fintech delivers, there are also enormous "dark sides" that pose significant risks to individuals and organizations, as well as to society (Bollaert et al., 2021; I. Lee & Shin, 2018; Schwienbacher, 2019). FinTech's unintended consequences have received relatively little attention in research. On the consumer side, there are concerns regarding privacy (Yeh et al., 2020), loan default (Li et al., 2021), financial fraud exposures (Akomea-Frimpong et al., 2019; Nikkel, 2020), and techno-stress (Y. K. Lee, 2021). Ethical, moral, environmental, and social issues have been raised at the organizational and societal level (Anshari et al., 2021).

While literature on the brighter side of Fintech abounds, there is a dearth of scholarly works on the dark side of Fintech and this book fills that void. Similarly, with the increased use of digital financial services, traditional financial institutions have been disrupted, and new challenges have emerged for monetary authorities. On the policy and monetary front, to combat FinTech's dark side, policymakers and monetary authorities are devising several strategies to counteract the adverse effects of FinTech. This book sheds light on monetary policy implications which are essential to foster resilient FinTech ecosystem. As we navigate the rapidly changing world of finance, it is crucial to understand both the benefits and drawbacks of FinTech and the role of monetary policy in shaping its future.

This book, *Exploring the Dark Side of FinTech and Implications of Monetary Policy*, provides a comprehensive examination of these challenges, delving into the negative impacts of FinTech on financial inclusion, government responses, and financial stability. Through ten chapters, the book covers a wide range of topics related to the dark side of FinTech, including financial inclusion and digitalization in developed and developing countries, the risks of mobile payment systems, and the challenges of implementing central bank digital currencies. The authors provide a detailed analysis of these topics, drawing on the latest research and case studies to offer insights into the implications of FinTech for the financial industry and monetary policy. Some of the implications of FinTech for monetary policy include:

1. New challenges for monetary policy transmission: The increasing use of digital financial services has made it more difficult for central banks to transmit monetary policy effectively, as traditional channels of transmission may no longer be as relevant.
2. The role of central banks in the digital age: The rapid growth of FinTech has raised questions about the role of central banks in the digital age, particularly with regards to their ability to regulate and monitor digital financial services.
3. The impact of FinTech on financial stability: The decentralization of financial services brought about by FinTech has created new risks and challenges for financial stability, requiring central banks to adapt their policy tools to address these challenges.

Whether you are a financial professional, student, or simply interested in the world of finance, this book offers a valuable resource for understanding the challenges and risks associated with FinTech and a thought-provoking examination of the impact of FinTech on monetary policy and the future of finance. With its comprehensive coverage of the topic, *Exploring the Dark Side of FinTech and Implications of Monetary Policy* is a must-read for anyone looking to gain a deeper understanding of the current financial technology landscape and the future of finance.

The book's 10 chapters are divided into three sections. There are two chapters in the "FinTech Environment," five in the "FinTech Challenges," and three chapters are in the "Central Bank Digital Currency" sections. These chapters were authored by experts from the UK, Canada, Europe, Africa, and Asia. Below is an overview of each chapter:

In Chapter 1, "Financial Inclusion and the Dark and Bright Sides of Digitalisation in Developed and Developing Countries," the author explore the positive and negative effects that financial innovation has had on financial inclusion. The chapter further discusses government financial innovation strategies necessary to promoting financial inclusion in all classes of society.

In Chapter 2, "Government Response to FinTech: A Cross-Country Analysis," the author provides a cross-country review of FinTech policy responses.

In Chapter 3, "Why Strong Banks Fail," the author identifies the reasons why strong banks might fail and offer insights to help existing banks to avoid a bank failure in the future. Furthermore, the author emphasizes financial stability implications that must be considered seriously.

In Chapter 4, "Ratings of Barriers and Challenges of Financial Technology in a Developing Economy," the author applied best-worst method to rank barriers and challenges facing Fintech ecosystem.

In Chapter 5, "Determinants of Mobile Money Fraud on C2C E-Commerce: A Trust Perspective," the chapter employed the partial least square (PLS) approach to structural equation modelling (SEM) to examine mobile money fraud through the lens of trust theory.

Chapter 6, "Financing Terrorism With FinTech in West Africa?" investigates FinTech-based criminogenic enablers and FinTech Terrorism Financing risks. The study recommended futureproofing, cutting-edge, and dynamic technology-based strategy, designed explicitly on cryptocurrencies and virtual assets to anticipate and combat Terrorism Financing.

Chapter 7, "Mobile Payment Systems and Impulsive Buying: A Conceptual Paper," synthesizes scholarly works on mobile payment systems and impulse buying. The chapter demonstrated that mobile payment systems facilitate consumers impulsive buying behavior after being exposed to exciting cues like price promotions, limited offers, and attractive product appearances.

Chapter 8, "Learnings From Discontinued Central Bank Digital Currencies (CBDC): A Multiple Case Study Analysis," focuses on reasons why central banks discontinued already launched CBDC's. Through the lens of Actor-network Theory (ANT), the study identifies factors and actors contributed to CBDC failure.

Chapter 9, "Digital, Programmable Euro From Paper to Programmable Money," showcases how digital euro and digital money initiatives is transforming the financial landscape and the future of finance.

In Chapter 10, "Unpacking Central Bank Digital Currency (CBDC) Implementation Challenges and Risks," the author deepens our understating on the risks and challenges involved in implementing central bank digital currency (CBDC).

We are exceptionally honored to edit this book for IGI Global and are very thankful to all contributors. We believe that this book is the first in a long line of upcoming, quality texts for fintech enthusiasts. We have had a great time reading and editing the chapters, and we sincerely hope you will enjoy reading them as well.

Sheraz Ahmed
LUT University, Finland.

John Agyekum Addae
LUT University, Finland & Ghana Communication Technology University, Ghana

Kwame Simpe Ofori
International University of Grand-Bassam, Côte d'Ivoire & University of Electronic Science and Technology of China, China
9 February 2023

REFERENCES

Abbasi, K., Alam, A., Du, M., & Huynh, T. L. D. (2020, May). FinTech, SME efficiency and national culture: Evidence from OECD countries. *Technological Forecasting and Social Change, 163*, 120454. doi:10.1016/j.techfore.2020.120454

Akomea-Frimpong, I., Andoh, C., Akomea-Frimpong, A., & Dwomoh-Okudzeto, Y. (2019). Control of fraud on mobile money services in Ghana: An exploratory study. *Journal of Money Laundering Control, 22*(2), 300–317. doi:10.1108/JMLC-03-2018-0023

Anshari, M., Almunawar, M. N., Masri, M., & Hrdy, M. (2021). Financial Technology with AI-Enabled and Ethical Challenges. *Society, 58*(3), 189–195. doi:10.100712115-021-00592-w

Apeti, A. E., & Edoh, E. D. (2023). Tax revenue and mobile money in developing countries. Journal of Development Economics, 161(April 2022), 103014. https://doi.org/ doi:10.1016/j.jdeveco.2022.103014

Asamoah, D., Takieddine, S., & Amedofu, M. (2020). Examining the effect of mobile money transfer (MMT) capabilities on business growth and development impact. *Information Technology for Development*, *26*(1), 146–161. doi:10.1080/02681102.2019.1599798

Bai, C., Quayson, M., & Sarkis, J. (2021). COVID-19 pandemic digitization lessons for sustainable development of micro-and small- enterprises. *Sustainable Production and Consumption*, *27*, 1989–2001. doi:10.1016/j.spc.2021.04.035

Bollaert, H., Lopez-de-Silanes, F., & Schwienbacher, A. (2021). Fintech and access to finance. *Journal of Corporate Finance*, *68*(March), 101941. doi:10.1016/j.jcorpfin.2021.101941

Charaia, V., Chochia, A., & Lashkhi, M. (2021). Promoting fintech financing for SME in S. Caucasian and baltic states, during the COVID-19 global pandemic. *Business, Management, and Economics Engineering*, *19*(2), 358–372. doi:10.3846/bmee.2021.14755

Hinson, R., Lensink, R., & Mueller, A. (2019). Transforming agribusiness in developing countries: SDGs and the role of FinTech. *Current Opinion in Environmental Sustainability*, *41*, 1–9. doi:10.1016/j.cosust.2019.07.002

KPMG. (2022). *Pulse of Fintech H2 '21*. https://assets.kpmg/content/dam/kpmg/xx/pdf/2022/02/pulse-of-fintech-h2-21.pdf

Lee, I., & Shin, Y. J. (2018). Fintech: Ecosystem, business models, investment decisions, and challenges. *Business Horizons*, *61*(1), 35–46. doi:10.1016/j.bushor.2017.09.003

Lee, Y. K. (2021). Impacts of digital technostress and digital technology self-efficacy on fintech usage intention of Chinese gen Z consumers. *Sustainability (Switzerland)*, *13*(9). Advance online publication. doi:10.3390u13095077

Li, Z., Zhang, J., Yao, X., & Kou, G. (2021). How to identify early defaults in online lending: A cost-sensitive multi-layer learning framework. *Knowledge-Based Systems*, *221*, 106963. doi:10.1016/j.knosys.2021.106963

Lin, H. J., Chen, C. C., & Chiu, Y., & Lin, T. Y. (2021). How financial technology (fintech) can improve the business performance of securities firms by using the dynamic data envelopment analysis modified model. *Managerial and Decision Economics*, (April), 1–20. doi:10.1002/mde.3443

Lorenz, E., & Pommet, S. (2021). Mobile money, inclusive finance and enterprise innovativeness: An analysis of East African nations. *Industry and Innovation*, *28*(2), 136–159. doi:10.1080/13662716.2020.1774867

Luo, S., Sun, Y., Yang, F., & Zhou, G. (2022). Does fintech innovation promote enterprise transformation? Evidence from China. *Technology in Society*, *68*, 101821. doi:10.1016/j.techsoc.2021.101821

Najaf, K., Schinckus, C., & Chee Yoong, L. (2020). VaR and market value of Fintech companies: An analysis and evidence from global data. *Managerial Finance*, *47*(7), 915–936. doi:10.1108/MF-04-2020-0169

Nikkel, B. (2020). Fintech forensics: Criminal investigation and digital evidence in financial technologies. *Forensic Science International: Digital Investigation*, *33*, 200908. doi:10.1016/j.fsidi.2020.200908

Papadimitri, P., Pasiouras, F., & Tasiou, M. (2021). Financial leverage and performance: The case of financial technology firms. *Applied Economics*, *53*(44), 5103–5121. doi:10.1080/00036846.2021.1915949

Phan, D. H. B., Narayan, P. K., Rahman, R. E., & Hutabarat, A. R. (2019). Do financial technology firms influence bank performance? *Pacific-Basin Finance Journal*, *101210*(September). doi:10.1016/j.pacfin.2019.101210

Pizzi, S., Corbo, L., & Caputo, A. (2021). Fintech and SMEs sustainable business models: Reflections and considerations for a circular economy. *Journal of Cleaner Production*, *281*, 125217. doi:10.1016/j.jclepro.2020.125217

Schwienbacher, A. (2019). Equity crowdfunding: Anything to celebrate? *Venture Capital*, *21*(1), 65–74. doi:10.1080/13691066.2018.1559010

Senyo, P. K., & Osabutey, E. L. C. (2020). Unearthing antecedents to financial inclusion through FinTech innovations. *Technovation*, *98*(March), 102155. doi:10.1016/j.technovation.2020.102155

WorldBank. (2020). The Global Covid-19 FinTech Market Rapid Assessment Study. *World Economic Forum*, 28–32. https://www3.weforum.org/docs/WEF_The_Global_Covid19_FinTech_Market_Rapid_Assessment_Study_2020.pdf

Yeh, K. H., Deng, R. H., & Kikuchi, H. (2020). Special Issue on FinTech Security and Privacy. *Future Generation Computer Systems*, *112*, 1172–1173. doi:10.1016/j.future.2020.07.057

Section 1

FinTech Environment and Financial Inclusion

Chapter 1
Financial Inclusion and the Dark and Bright Sides of Digitalisation in Developed and Developing Countries

Faris Nasif Alshubiri
Dhofar University, Oman

ABSTRACT

This chapter explores the relationship between financial inclusion and the dark and bright sides of digitalisation in ten developed and developing countries over the period of 2008 to 2020. An analysis of panel data for the studied countries revealed a significant positive relationship between financial inclusion and technology, especially in terms of secure servers and financial innovation in the developing countries. These findings indicate that technology fosters access to and usage of financial services. In addition, the analysis revealed significant negative relationships between financial inclusion and secure servers and financial innovation in the developed countries as well as a significant positive relationship between financial inclusion and technology growth. The chapter concluded that the governments should adopting low-cost and easy-to-access technology and promoting financial inclusion in all classes of society.

DOI: 10.4018/978-1-6684-6381-9.ch001

Copyright © 2023, IGI Global. Copying or distributing in print or electronic forms without written permission of IGI Global is prohibited.

INTRODUCTION

The COVID-19 pandemic has caused many long-term disturbances around the world. For example, to slow the spread of the disease, many institutions have adopted lockdown procedures that have affected their revenue (Demirguc-Kunt et al., 2022). Furthermore, the unemployment rate increased, which negatively impacted society and contributed to a 4.3% decline in global economic growth (World Bank, 2021). Access to financial services has become extremely important in light of crises such as the COVID-19 pandemic, especially for the poor class, which requires financing to complete daily transactions (Emara & Moheildin 2021). Therefore, financial inclusion is an important consideration during such crises and a requirement for development (Auer et al., 2022). Meanwhile, the acceleration of the spread of COVID-19 led to the acceleration of digitisation in financial services and prompted governments to adopt digitisation, resulting in the emergence of various Internet- and telephone-based banking and financial services of the progress of digitalisation, especially for people with limited income (Shen et al., 2021).

Consequently, financial inclusion plays a prominent role in mitigating social and economic, increasing financial access for low-income families and small enterprises, increasing financial recovery. However, digitisation may negatively in the use of digitisation, as it may negatively affect economic sectors and introduce various risks (Shen et al., 2021). Therefore, the principles of sustainable development promote progress in financial inclusion at different stages of development and achieve meaningful progress in economic growth (Lutfi et al., 2021). The purpose of the present study was to present the dark and bright sides of digitisation within digital financial ecosystems (Kanungo and Gupta 2021). It also aimed to identify the mechanism for supporting digital financial inclusion and its link to digitisation (Aziz & Naima, 2021).

Digital financial inclusion involves providing all individuals with easy access to the financial services digital technology so that they can obtain formal financial services that are appropriate for their needs and sustainable for service providers (Ayyagari et al., 2013). Digital financial inclusion also involves deploying cost-effective digital means to reach excluded and underserved populations through a range of formal financial services that are affordable and appropriate for clients' needs, delivered responsibly and sustainable for service providers (Pal et al., 2021).

It is important to address financial inclusion in developing and developed economies because many challenges, including those related to education, poverty and industry, impact economic activities. At the global level, the increased interest in bridging income gaps between individuals to reduce inequality and the increased focus on providing stable political systems have been highlighted (Levine, 2002). Furthermore, citizens and governments have significantly modified their consumption patterns based on changing needs due to the COVID-19 pandemic. For example, the more people need Internet access to complete transactions, increasing financial flexibility and facilitating relationships between customers and banks (Beck and Levine, 2002). Since financial inclusion has become a global priority for all generations it can be considered a general benefit that satisfies individuals and improves their quality of life (Ayyagari et al., 2013). In fact, the World Bank and the G20 countries stated that digital financial inclusion was important to achieve these goals of the sustainable development goals (Mahalle et al., 2021).

Mobile payment technologies are spreading around the world; however, their expansion has not been uniformed. Political leaders are concerned about this lack of standardisation as well as financial exclusion, and they see mobile payment technologies as a way to promote it. Payment technologies are still developing and are spreading through mobile phone technologies in a non-uniform way, prompting many decision makers to be concerned about the spread (Pal et al., 2021).

Many studies have identified a causal relationship between financial development and economic growth (World Bank, 2007; Beck & Levine, 2002; Demirguc-Kunt & Maksimovic, 2002; Levine, 2002). However, for inclusive economic growth, a country needs inclusive financial systems and applications that confirm the accessibility, availability, and usage of formal financial services for its entire population. According to the United Nations (2006), financial inclusion has two primary dimensions: 1) customer access to many formal financial services through credit tools and savings accounts as well as more complex services, such as insurance services and pensions, and 2) customer access to many financial service providers, which enhances competition.

Financial inclusion is important for reducing poverty (Ayyagari et al., 2013) and helping poor people pay for their children's education (Jacoby, 1994). Furthermore, financial inclusion has an indirect effect on the structural effects of financial deepening (Ayyagari et al., 2013). Diniz et al. (2012) reported that financial inclusion promotes the socio-economic in different sectors. Dermiguc-Kunt and Klapper (2012) argued that the poor depend on their limited savings to invest in education or attract entrepreneurs. Furthermore, financial inclusion allows individuals with low incomes to pay for education and health care (Kempson 2006; World Bank, 2008). In addition, small companies rely on a low profit to pursue promising growth opportunities.

Inequality appears in all societies and negatively affects technological growth. The theory of standard growth assumes that digital investments and technological innovations contribute to a long-run increase in per capita income (Ngo and McCann, 2019(. According to the depository destruction theory, technological progress contributes to financial and economic development by supporting production (Schumpeter, 1912). Meanwhile, the creative destruction theory suggests that the main catalyst for economic growth is the replacement of existing institutions with innovative organisations (Barefoot, 2020).

Financial access concerns the ability of individuals and institutions to obtain financial services, including credit, deposit, insurance, and risk management services (Diniz, et al., 2012). Financial access helps many companies receive all kinds of credit, which increases investment opportunities in information technology (Wagner, 2019). Therefore, financial access supports the economies of countries, enhances competition and increases employment opportunities (Kerr & Nanda, 2015; Yoshino & Morgan, 2016). Financial access also enhances income and increases the chances of benefiting the customers from internal sources of income. However, in the present climate of intense competition, small and medium enterprises face challenges in obtaining access to finance. Moreover, if companies lose economic opportunities, their social networks will decline, reflecting the dark side of financial technology (FinTech) (Tarafdar, et al., 2015; Yang et al., 2020).

Although technology brings many benefits, it can also be associated with negative effects for many projects and entrepreneurs due to risks related to financial applications (Ozili, 2018; Helm, Low, & Joshua, 2019). This dark side of digitalisation is known among a literal community of information systems (technostress), which represents the negative direct and indirect effects of technology on institutions (Weil & Rosen, 1997). In addition, the burden of individual actions when using information systems or continually trying to obtain the latest technologies leads to behavioural and psychological responses opposite to the adoption of digitalisation (Owusu-Ansah et al., 2016). Thus, when individuals feel tired of the use of digitalisation, their dissatisfaction with information technology increases, and the dark side appear as a result of the use of technology (Harris et al., 2014). Since the increasing spread of digital technology in the financial sector may lead to positive and negative effects, countries must work to correct the digital network in order to achieve progress and competition at the international level (Fanta & Makina 2019).

This chapter describes a study that aimed to investigate the bright and dark sides of digitalisation, especially the relationship between financial inclusion and digitalisation. To address the research gap, the following question was raised: Does the use of digitalisation for financial access and the ICT trade balance increase or decrease ethical, technological growth and technological innovation proxies? To answer this question, we used a panel data methodology to study 10 developed and 10 developing countries over the period of 2008–2020. Since, few studies have investigated factors that encourage companies to invest in technology (Yang et al., 2020), the originality of this chapter is that it provides important insights for researchers and practitioners regarding digitalisation and financial inclusion and whether financial access has a positive (bright) or a negative (dark) effect.

The rest of this chapter is structured as follows. Section 2 explains the literature review. Section 3 presents the methodology and data specifications. Section 4 describes the empirical results, and Section 5 discusses those results. Section 6 presents conclusions and policy implications.

LITERATURE REVIEW

Digitisation is defined as the introduction of technology into financial, industrial or other services. As such, it involves converting all economic activities, including infrastructure and transportation activities, into a digital format (Aziz & Naima 2021). A few empirical studies have attempted to measure the relationship between technological developments and access to financial services; however, more studies are needed on this topic to measure causal relationships. Although studies have expressed caution about the use of technology in financial services, it is considered beneficial because it has a low cost and because it has helped financial services become more efficient and effective.

Technological developments, such as the Internet and mobile phones, have enhanced access to financial services and increased their widespread use. Modern technologies were able to break the barrier to entry into the financial services market, which had been monopolised by banks (Birch & Young 1997). Internet use by individuals has increased worldwide in recent years, and it has become a channel for financial services. Andrianaivo and Kpodar (2012) found that mobile phone use increased economic growth in African countries via increased financial inclusion. Financial inclusion measures private credit as a percentage of GDP and deposits.

Sarma and Pais (2008) identified three indicators of financial inclusion: the accessibility, availability, and usage of banking services. Accessibility is measured by the number of bank accounts per 1,000 people, while availability is measured by the number of bank branches and ATMs and the number of ATMs. Usage is measured by the amount of credit and the size of deposits relative to GDP. The main findings of Sarma and Pais's study is that financial inclusion is observed using telephone and Internet variables.

Meanwhile, financial inclusion and digitalisation have an ethical indicator, a technological growth indicator and a technological innovation indicator. First, regarding the ethical indicator, financial inclusion includes access to services at a low and reasonable cost, especially for people with low incomes (Diniz, et al, 2012). Financial inclusion supports poverty strategies and boosts economic growth through technological innovation and new communication tools that enhance financial systems. Digital technology is making access faster to financial services, protecting communities and shaping a new way of life (Boskov & Drakulevski, 2017). However, it is necessary to comprehend the caution of digital technology users, especially in terms of the use of electronic systems for financial services (Caruana, 2016; Ozili, 2018; Gollapudi et al., 2019). Some studies have referred to financial inclusion in terms of the number of web servers and secure online transactions (Diniz, Birochi & Pozzebon, 2012; Caruana, 2016; Gollapudi et al., 2019; Helm, Low and Joshua, 2019).

Second, the technological growth indicator reflects the extent to which mobile phone technologies and the Internet can support financial services (Abubakar & Handayani, 2018). Fanta and Makina (2019) found a significant positive relationship between financial inclusion and technology (Fanta and Makina, 2019). Meanwhile, Boskov & Drakulevski (2017), Boshkov (2016), Gonzalez et al. (2014), Burjorjee & Scola (2015), Helm, Low, & Joshua (2019) and Yang et al. (2020) support an economic revolution, small-scale projects or technology exports. According to Xing (2014) and Kabaklarli et al., (2017), technological exports are a main tool of technological growth indicators of ICT trade.

Third, regarding the technological innovation indicator, financial innovation helps promote financial inclusion, as technological inventions, such as mobile banking services, have enhanced access to low-cost and rapid financial services and reduced the financial movements used in financial services (Beck, Senbet & Simbanegavi, 2015; Yoshino & Morgan, 2016). Kerr and Nanda (2015) indicated that internal finance sources support technological innovation investments. In addition, patent, design and trademark applications are considered tools of technological innovation (Caruana, 2016; Agoba, et al., 2017; Kabaklarli, et al., 2017; Nemoto and Koreen, 2019). Understanding financial inclusion and its relationship to financial innovation requires a high understanding of financial products and how they are used (Agoba, et al, 2017). In recent years, the Fourth Industrial Revolution has played a vital role in technological innovation as well as in achieving the sustainable development goals (SDGs). From this perspective, technological innovation improves environmental quality.

A limited number of studies have measured financial inclusion in emerging economies or examined financial inclusion's impacts on technology and different population groups in developing and developed economies. The McKinsey Global Institute (2016) has examined several studies on financial inclusion, including a study on regional digital finance in Russia (Lapina et al., 2021), a study on digital finance in rural areas in Colombia (Van Klyton et al., 2021) and studies on gender and financial inclusion in India (Jariwala 2017, Lal 2019). Tay et al. (2022) indicated that many developing countries have become more interested in improving financial inclusion in order to reduce poverty; however, individuals at different income levels do not have the same access to digital financial services. Meanwhile, Aziz and Naima (2021) found that access to Internet services in urban areas was associated with low-cost commercial transactions, indicating that digitisation contributed to building investment in infrastructure. Emara and Moheildin (2021) found that financial inclusion development is commensurate with the needs of society in terms of education, health and various economic sectors. Kanungo and Gupta (2021) indicated that financial inclusion has a long-term impact on economic growth, especially in the information and communication technology sector. Lutfi et al. (2021) indicated that there is a great dependence on informal financial resources in the field of development? In developing countries due to individuals' low confidence in financial institutions. Shen et al. (2021) that a positive viewpoint on adopting financial services helps build a strong economic system.

Digital financial services play a vital role in financial inclusion. In fact, Auer et al. (2022) indicated that the digitisation of financial services is enhanced through digital payments in which credit, insurance, savings, and other products are developed. Keister and Sanches (2022) highlighted the need for banks to focus on reducing profit margins in order to increase the attractiveness of deposits based on the banks' market power and competition. Meanwhile, Demirguc-Kunt et al. (2022) pointed to the importance of adopting digital services and indicated that more than 24% of the world's population does not have a bank account with digital financial services; in developing countries, that figure rose to 29%.

The methodological literature indicates that digitisation is used to try to achieve digital financial inclusion, and current research questions focus on the extent of the development of digital financial inclusion and its dark and bright sides. This chapter adds to the literature clarifying the stages of financial inclusion development in order to enable policy and decision makers to promote digitisation in the implementation of existing policies and practices and reduce digital financial inclusion disparities in light of current and future digital financial service gaps created by financial crises and the pandemic. Thus, an opportunity was given to institutions to increase the supply of customised digital financial products and promote digital financial inclusion.

The study model was chosen because digital financial services act as an indicator of sustainability and the broader ecosystem and promote financial inclusion, which creates value for customers and enhances market competition. Moreover, positive competition necessitates the use of digital technologies to enhance productivity and efficiency and increase profit margins. Furthermore, digitisation has many advantages, including awareness of increased efficiency and productivity, reduced operational costs, an improved customer experience, speedy access to financial services and enhanced morale.

The dark and bright sides of digitalisation can help expand financial inclusion. Therefore, the present study sought to address the following main question: How does financial inclusion affect the dark and bright sides of digitalisation? To determine the main indicators of digitalisation related to financial inclusion, the following hypotheses were examined:

- H-1: Is there a significant relationship between financial inclusion and ethical indicators, as measured by the use of Internet servers
- H-2: Is there a significant relationship between financial inclusion and technological growth indicators, as measured by high-technology exports?
- H-3: Is there a significant relationship between financial inclusion and technological innovation indicators, as measured by industrial design, patent and trademark applications?

METHODOLOGY AND ECONOMETRIC MODEL

This chapter highlights the dark and bright sides of digitalisation and how financial inclusion affects it and supports public policy objectives. The panel data technique was used to examine data collected from the World Development Indicators for the period of 2008–2020 (World Bank, 2022). The relationship between financial inclusion and the dark and bright sides of digitalisation in 20 developed and developing countries was examined. Appendix A lists the countries included in the study.

The variables were selected based on the importance of financial inclusion in enhancing digitalisation for economic growth. Financial inclusion was measured by the number of commercial bank branches (per 100,000 adults) (LOGNCBB). Three control variables were used: GDP per capita growth (annual %) (GDPG); inflation, GDP deflator (annual %) (IGDP); and trademark applications, direct resident (LOGTRD).

The dependent variable measured dark and bright digitalisation and was divided into three proxies. The ethical proxy was measured by secure Internet servers (LOGSES), the technological innovation proxy was measured by patent applications, residents (LOGPAT) and the technological growth proxy was measured by high-technology exports (% of manufactured exports) (LOGHTEE). Definitions of all of the variables are available in Appendix B. The studied period covered 13 years and included the financial crises in 2007–2008, which remark that, in most economic sectors, digitalisation supports economic growth and financial services. The 13 -year period examined in this study includes the financial crisis of 2008, which was a very critical period for the countries around the world, which are focused on how to realise the immense promises of digital technologies for economic growth and financial markets.

The main econometric model was developed based on the following equation:

$$Dep_{i,t} = \beta_0 + \beta_0 IV_{i,t} + \beta_0 control\ variables_{i,t} + \varepsilon_{i,t}$$

where $Dep_{i,t}$ refers to $LOGSES_{it}$, $LOGPAT_{it}$ and $LOGHTEE_{it}$ as proxies of the dark and bright sides of digitalisation of country i at time t; these variables are the dependent variables. The $IV_{i,t}$ is the independent variable and refer to the proxy of financial inclusion of country i at time t. The $control\ variables_{i,t}$ are GDPG, IGDP and LOGTRD.

The descriptive statistics for all variables of the main econometric model as well as the correlation matrix were analysed. The augmented Im-Pesaran-Shin (IPS) (1997, 2003) and Levin-Lin-Chu (LLC) unit root tests were used to show the stationarity of the variables at each level. Regarding the main estimators, Panel least squares (PLS) was used as the basic requirement for regression, followed by Fxed effect (FE), Random effect (RE), Driscoll-Kraay standard errors for FE and Feasible general least squares (FGLS).

For more robustness, diagnostic tests, including the Wooldridge test for autocorrelation and the modified Wald test for groupwise heteroskedasticity, were used. Cross-sectional independence was examined using the Pesaran CD test and the Breusch-Pagan (B-P) Lagrangian multiplier (LM) test of independence. To determine whether to use FE or RE, the Hausman test was employed. Both time series and cross-sectional panel data were used to minimize the multicollinearity problem (De Hoyos and Sarafidis, 2006). The endogeneity problem in the panel data was solved by using dynamic intertemporality, the individuality of the entities and the degree of freedom (Hsiao, 2007). Additionally, the heterogeneity of the microunit of the panel data (Baltagi, 2012) was managed based on time and country observations.

Initially, PLS was used to examine the hypotheses, as this estimator ignores the possibility of group structure and supposes that different periods are in the same trend. The Hausman test was used to overcome the problems of heterogeneity and endogeneity (Wooldridge, 2010) and determine whether FE or RE was the best estimator for the study (Johnston and Dinardo, 1997). FE indicates the coefficients as one time intercept for each subject in a regression model, and independent variables are correlated with individual-specific effects. Furthermore, FE is related to each group as non-random and of a specific fixed quantity. Meanwhile, RE refers to the distribution of values that are interpreted as predictor variables. Furthermore, it shows the variance at different levels of values to overcome unobserved heterogeneity, which resolves the heterogeneity issue as a constant during the time period and uncorrelated with independent variables. If FE reveals cross-sectional dependence, Hoechle (2007) suggested using regression with Driscoll-Kraay standard errors. FGLS is used to solve serial correlation and/or heteroscedastic issues in a model. FGLS estimates the coefficients under a multiple linear regression model. Furthermore, the covariance matrix is in the presence of non-spherical innovations with an unknown covariance matrix.

RESULTS

The nine subsections in this section explain how the study hypotheses were tested.

Descriptive Statistics

Table 1 shows the descriptive statistics of seven variables for 10 developed and developing countries over the period of 2008 to 2020. The data included 65 observations of these countries. Specifically, Table 1 shows that the mean and median values for LOGGHTEE were lower in the developing countries than in the developed ones. In addition, IGDP and LOGTRD were higher in the developing countries, while LOGSES was higher in the developed ones. The standard deviations for most variables were higher in the developing countries than in the developed ones.

Skewness is a measure of a lack of symmetry. There was positive skewness in LOGSES, IGDP, LOGTRD and LOGNCBB and negative skewness in LOGPAT, LOGHTEE and GDPG. Kurtosis is a measure of heavy-tailed (high kurtosis) or light-tailed (low kurtosis) data relative to a normal distribution. The Jarque-Bera test results showed that the probability for all variables of the model was insignificant for the developed and developing countries, which means that the data followed the normal distribution.

Table 1. Descriptive statistics

Developing Countries							
	LOGSES	**LOGHTEE**	**LOGPAT**	**IGDP**	**GDPG**	**LOGTRD**	**LOGNCBB**
Mean	4.057	0.872	3.062	4.806	3.192	4.543	1.274
Median	4.139	0.864	3.111	4.288	3.293	4.402	1.229
Maximum	5.893	1.410	3.912	16.48	11.20	5.477	1.661
Minimum	2.117	0.268	2.100	-0.053	-5.285	4.100	1.115
Std. Dev.	0.925	0.323	0.526	3.306	2.672	0.383	0.140
Skewness	0.111	-0.135	-0.109	1.341	-0.294	0.512	0.972
Kurtosis	2.333	2.218	1.674	5.166	5.230	2.014	2.598
Jarque-Bera	1.338	1.854	4.886	32.19	14.40	5.478	10.67
Probability	0.512	0.395	0.086	0.000	0.000	0.064	0.004
Sum	263.7	56.71	199.0	312.4	207.5	295.3	82.82
Sum Sq. Dev.	54.84	6.703	17.73	699.8	457.0	9.424	1.263
Observations	65	65	65	65	65	65	65
Developed Countries							
Mean	5.093	1.256	3.878	1.772	1.656	4.568	1.412
Median	5.018	1.261	4.150	1.663	2.008	4.669	1.460
Maximum	6.811	1.470	4.692	6.252	4.179	4.978	1.805
Minimum	3.181	0.944	2.410	-0.549	-5.693	3.907	1.040
Std. Dev.	0.831	0.154	0.616	1.264	1.731	0.348	0.181
Skewness	0.087	-0.656	-0.358	0.992	-2.007	-0.892	-0.469
Kurtosis	2.386	2.269	2.029	4.823	8.667	2.402	2.409
Jarque-Bera	1.084	6.019	3.878	19.37	128.6	9.446	3.281
Probability	0.581	0.049	0.143	0.000	0.000	0.008	0.193
Sum	325.9	80.39	248.2	113.4	106.0	292.4	90.42
Sum Sq. Dev.	43.53	1.500	23.96	100.7	188.8	7.670	2.065
Observations	65	65	65	65	65	65	65

Correlation Matrix

Table 2 shows the coefficients of correlation for all regressors as well as the significance of all variables. The findings for the developed and developing countries were compared. For the developing countries, there were negative relationships between LOGNCBB and IGDP (-.261), LOGNCBB and LOGTRD (-.324) and LOGTRS and GDPG (-.057). In addition, there were positive relationships between LOGNCBB and GDPG (.124), LOGTRD and IGDP (.602) and GDPG and IGDP (.045). For the developed countries, there were negative relationships between LOGTRD and IGDP (-0.032), LOGNCBB and IGDP (-.252), LOGTRD and GDPG (-0.006), LOGNCBB and GDPG (-.187) and LOGNCBB and LOGTRD (-.101). In addition, there was a positive relationship between GDPG and IGDP (.039). These results are consistent with financial and economic theories. Most of the variables had low values, which were considered significant. Furthermore, the results demonstrated the strength of the coefficients. This pre-test indicated that there was no multicollinearity between predictor and response as two variables of independent and/or control variables (Evans, 1996).

Table 2. Correlation matrix

VARIABLES	LOGSES	LOGHTEE	LOGPAT	IGDP	GDPG	LOGTRD	LOGNCBB
Developing Countries							
LOGSES	1.000						

LOGHTEE	-0.024	1.000					
	0.843	-----					
LOGPAT	0.546	-0.190	1.000				
	0.000	0.129	-----				
IGDP	0.169	-0.531	0.270	1.000			
	0.176	0.000	0.029	-----			
GDPG	0.024	-0.295	0.130	0.045	1.000		
	0.846	0.016	0.299	0.718	-----		
LOGTRD	0.151	-0.069	0.397	0.602	-0.057	1.000	
	0.228	0.584	0.001	0.000	0.646	-----	
LOGNCBB	0.356	-0.016	0.528	-0.261	0.124	-0.324	1.000
	0.003	0.898	0.000	0.035	0.323	0.008	-----
	Developed Countries						
LOGSES	1.000						

LOGHTEE	0.472	1.000					
	0.000	-----					
LOGPAT	0.407	0.601	1.000				
	0.000	0.000	-----				
IGDP	-0.121	-0.202	-0.232	1.000			

Continued on following page

Table 2. Continued

VARIABLES	LOGSES	LOGHTEE	LOGPAT	IGDP	GDPG	LOGTRD	LOGNCBB
			Developing Countries				
	0.340	0.108	0.064	-----			
GDPG	0.147	-0.222	-0.359	0.039	1.000		
	0.246	0.077	0.003	0.755	-----		
LOGTRD	0.500	0.809	0.742	-0.252	-0.187	1.000	
	0.000	0.000	0.000	0.044	0.138	-----	
LOGNCBB	-0.380	0.155	-0.343	-0.032	-0.006	-0.101	1.000
	0.001	0.219	0.005	0.797	0.961	0.425	-----

Unit Root Tests

Table 3 shows the IPS and LLC unit root test results for the developed and developing countries. The tests of level and first difference order were run to show the stationarity of the variables. The results indicated that all variables were integrated in the order I(0). Therefore, all variables were considered stationary at this level.

Table 3. Panel unit root IPS test and LLC test

	ICTTB	LOGCBB	GDPG	IGD	LOGATM	LOGIUI	LOGPA
				Developing Countries			
IPS (Level)	0.751	0.439	-1.387*	-2.906***	-2.468***	2.995	-0.470
IPS (1St Difference)	-2.700***	-5.836***	-1.248	-6.174***	-7.602***	-0.074	0.523
LLC test t (Level)	-1.741**	-0.727*	-1.86**	-4.187***	-4.553***	6.032*	7.540*
LLC test (1St Difference)	-3.85***	-8.12***	-1.109	-9.315***	-10.91***	3.097**	22.35**
				Developed Countries			
IPS (Level)	1.855*	-0.694	0.665	-7.090***	-8.766***	-0.741	-1.164*
IPS (1St Difference)	-4.63***	-1.762**	-2.754***	-9.578***	-10.68***	-0.089	-4.289***
LLC test t (Level)	-0.882	-1.506*	2.592*	-10.31***	-7.50***	-0.731*	-1.564
LLC test (1St Difference)	-6.698***	-1.419*	-4.040***	-13.26***	-14.43***	-0.659**	-0.590
Note: The significance levels refer to $p < 0.01$ (***), $p < 0.05$ (**) and $p < 0.1$ (*).							

Note: The significance levels refer to $p < 0.01$ (***), $p < 0.05$ (**) and $p < 0.1$ (*).

Panel Least Squares (PLS)

The PLS test results for all six models for the developed and developing countries are presented in Table 4. Models 4 and 5 revealed significant negative relationships between LOGNCBB and LOGSES and LOGNCBB and LOGPAT in the developed countries. A 1% increase in LOGNCBB led to decreases of -.123 and -.930 in LOGSES and LOGPAT, respectively. Models 1, 2 and 6 revealed significant positive relationships between LOGNCBB and LOGSES and LOGNCBB and LOGPAT in the developing countries and between LOGNCBB and LOGHTEE in the developed countries. A 1% increase in LOGNCBB led to 2.49 and 1.64 increases in LOGSES and LOGPAT, respectively, in the developing countries, while a 1% increase in LOGNCBB led to a .080 increase in LOGHTEE in the developed countries. The control variables were significant in all models except Models 1, 2 and 6, in which IGDP and LOGSES, IGDP and LOGPAT and IGDP and LOGHTEE were insignificant. Furthermore, GDPG and LOGSES, LOGPAT and LOGHTEE were insignificant.

Table 4. Panel least squares

	Model (1)	Model (2)	Model (3)	Model (4)	Model (5)	Model (6)
	Developing Countries			Developed Countries		
VARIABLES	LOGSES	LOGPAT	LOGHTEE	LOGSES	LOGPAT	LOGHTEE
LOGNCBB	2.49***	1.64***	-.108	-.123***	-.930***	.080***
	(.163)	(.271)	(.174)	(.383)	(.207)	(.026)
IGDP	-.013	.008	-.027**	.126***	-.083***	-.011
	(.029)	(.018)	(.011)	(.047)	(.025)	(.007)
GDPG	.063*	.044**	-.074***	.013	-.030	-.008
	(.037)	(.017)	(.011)	(.064)	(.034)	(.006)
LOGTRD	.137**	.161*	.320***	1.44***	1.17***	.257***
	(.067)	(.084)	(.054)	(.117)	(.063)	(.007)
R-squared	.210	.486	.441	.405	.682	.649
Cross-sections	5	5	5	5	5	5
Note: The significance levels refer to $p < 0.01$ (***), $p < 0.05$ (**) and $p < 0.1$ (*).						

Note: The significance levels refer to $p < 0.01$ (***), $p < 0.05$ (**) and $p < 0.1$ (*).

FE and RE Regressions

As shown in Table 5, we ran FE and RE to overcome the heterogeneity issue and used the Hausman test to select which one was the best estimator. Regarding the results, Models 1 and 4 were consistent with the PLS estimator. Model 5 was consistent with the PLS estimator but had a positive signal. Model 4 of the control variable indicated a significant negative relationship between IGDP and LOGSES, and Model 6 identified a significant negative relationship between LOGTRD and LOGHTEE in the developed countries. Furthermore, Models 2, 3 and 4 revealed significant positive relationships between LOGTRD and LOGPAT and LOGHTEE and LOGSES. Meanwhile, the probability of the Wald chi2(4) value was significant in all six models, implying that all models were appropriate and fit.

Table 5. Fixed effect and random effects regression

	Model (1)	**Model (2)**	**Model (3)**	**Model (4)**	**Model (5)**	**Model (6)**
	Developing Countries			**Developed Countries**		
VARIABLES	**LOGSES**	**LOGPAT**	**LOGHTEE**	**LOGSES**	**LOGPAT**	**LOGHTEE**
	RE	**FE**	**RE**	**RE**	**FE**	**FE**
LOGNCBB	3.09***	-.400	.212	-1.50***	.300**	.018
	(.799)	(.300)	(.208)	(.459)	(.145)	(.046)
IGDP	.049	-.010	-.008	-.008**	.000	-.004
	(.040)	(.008)	(.006)	(.067)	.014	(.004)
GDPG	-.010	.001	-.004	.115	-.004	.004
	(.039)	(.006)	(.005)	(.048)	(.011)	(.003)
LOGTRD	.474	.629***	.223**	1.21***	.039	-.182***
	(.352)	(.165)	(.109)	(.250)	(.197)	(.063)
Constant	-2.24	.759	-.337	1.49	3.27***	2.06***
	(2.00)	(.632)	(.450)	(1.43)	(.963)	(.310)
R-squared	0.566	0.320	0.195	0.460	.078	0.796
Wald chi2(4)	17.55	-	9.07	42.10	-	-
Prob > chi2	.000	-	.044	.000	-	
Cross-sections	5	5	5	5	5	5-
Modified Wald test for groupwise heteroskedasticity -chi2 (6)	207.82	169.29	55.31	57.97	21007.58	30.02
Prob.	.000	.000	.000	.000	.000	.000
Wooldridge test for autocorrelation - Prob	.002	.067	.146	.025	.004	.019
Hausman test	.195	.000	.853	0.087	0.001	.000

Note: The significance levels refer to p < 0.01 (***), p < 0.05 (**) and p < 0.1 (*).

Note: The significance levels refer to p < 0.01 (***), p < 0.05 (**) and p < 0.1 (*).

FGLS Estimator

As shown in Table 5, some of the study models had problems with heteroskedasticity and serial correlation. To overcome these problems, the FGLS estimator was used. This estimator confirmed the PLS results in all models and the FE and RE results in some models. The probability of Wald chi2(4) was significant in all six models, implying that all models were appropriate and fit.

Table 6. Feasible generalized least squares regression

	Model (1)	Model (2)	Model (3)	Model (4)	Model (5)	Model (6)
	Developing Countries			Developed Countries		
VARIABLES	**LOGSES**	**LOGPAT**	**LOGHTEE**	**LOGSES**	**LOGPAT**	**LOGHTEE**
LOGNCBB	3.09***	2.75***	-.162	-.150***	-.958***	.204***
	(.768)	(.291)	(.227)	(.441)	(.241)	(.057)
IGDP	-.010	.013	-.028**	.115**	-.084***	-.006
	(.038)	(.014)	(.011)	(.046)	(.025)	(.006)
GDPG	.049	.018	-.073***	-.008	-.032	.002
	(.038)	(.014)	(.011)	(.065)	(.035)	(.008)
LOGTRD	.474	.782***	.290***	1.21***	1.15***	.365***
	(.338)	(.128)	(.100)	(.240)	(.131)	(.031)
Constant	2.24	4.13***	.201	1.49	.158	-.693***
	(.192)	(.730)	(.571)	(.139)	(.752)	(.177)
Wald chi2(4)	19.01	123.00	51.69	45.67	137.64	78.08
Prob > chi2	0.000	0.000	0.000	0.000	0.000	0.000
Cross-sections	5	5	5	5	5	5
Panels:	All models showed no autocorrelation					
Correlation	All models showed homoscedastic					
Note: The significance levels refer to $p < 0.01$ (***), $p < 0.05$ (**) and $p < 0.1$ (*).						

Note: The significance levels refer to $p < 0.01$ (***), $p < 0.05$ (**) and $p < 0.1$ (*).

Diagnostic Tests

Many diagnostic tests were used to increase the robustness of the study models. The test results showed that all estimators were appropriate, fit, consistent and unbiased. As shown in Table 3, all variables were stationarity. And were confirmed using unit root tests; all of the variables Were integrated at order I(0). Table 5 shows the results of the Hausman test, which was conducted to determine whether FE or RE was the best fit for the models. Based on the results, FE was selected for three models because the *p*-value was below 0.05. RE was selected for the other three models.

As shown in Table 5, the results of the modified Wald test for groupwise heteroskedasticity and the Wooldridge test for autocorrelation indicated the presence of heteroskedasticity in all models and serial correlation in all models except Models 2 and 3. The FGLS estimator was used to overcome these issues; the results shown in Table 6 indicate that the panels were homoscedastic and that there was no autocorrelation in the six study models.

DISCUSSION

As shown in Tables 4, 5, 6 and 7, financial inclusion had a significant positive impact on the digitalisation proxies and reflected the bright side of digitalisation in most estimators in the developing countries in terms of the relationships between LOGNCBB and LOGSES and LOGPAT. Meanwhile, financial inclusion had a significant negative impact on the digitalisation proxies and reflected the dark side of digitalisation in most of estimators in the developed countries in terms of the relationships between LOGNCBB and LOGSES and LOGPAT. However, there was a significant positive relationship between LOGNCBB and LOGHTEE in the developed countries. Decision makers try to find the best ways to link financial services with technology and electronic systems to support individuals and protect their rights and simultaneously increase the benefits of using digitisation in various financial services.

The dark side of digitalisation reflects a lack of trust and awareness among customers, which has led to a decrease in efforts to access financial services. The studies fear data safekeeping among customers (Ozili, 2018; Caruana, 2016). Others have doubts about digitalisation (Boskov and Drakulevski, 2017). Agoba et al. (2017) found a negative relationship between the well-being of individuals and technological innovation, while Tarafdar et al. (2015) and Helm et al. (2019) found that the risk of information technology had a negative impact on financial inclusion. According to Corbett (1987) and Carayon (1993), there is a high risk that manufacturing activities will negatively affect the adoption of customers. Meanwhile, Kling (1996) found that, while less privacy, intellectual piracy had a negative effect on financial services. Markus and Mentzer (2014) showed that trading firms' use of a high-speed IT network negatively affected financial services operations.

The bright side of digitalisation can be interpreted as a high level of awareness about digitalisation, which increases the safety of servers and the growth of technology. Parham et al. (2001) found a positive effect on the growth of digitalisation. Yang et al. (2020) confirmed that information technology has a positive effect on investment activities. Furthermore, financial inclusion has been positively related to innovation technology (Lazonick, 2009; Diniz, Birochi and Pozzebon, 2012; Yeo et al., 2014). In addition, Kabaklarli et al. (2017) found that patent applications offer a bright picture of the growth of high-technology exports.

The global expansion of financial and digital technologies has allowed many individuals in specific job roles to increase financial inclusion, especially for the low-income class, through digital financial services that are more efficient, affordable and widely available. Even though developed and developing countries prioritise financial inclusion and digital technology in order to reduce poverty and strengthen the global economy through global economic bodies, developing countries still face challenges. For example, many people in developing countries do not use banks. In addition, low acceptance rates for digital banking transactions due to the absence of a technological framework and a broad financial inclusion policy can lead to fears about data security problems.

CONCLUSION

Policy Implications

Financial inclusion plays a vital role in all developed and developing economies. In recent years, there has been increased interest in the extent to which companies and individuals can access financial products. However, they face obstacles in the form of limited income or high-risk financial conditions that are inconsistent with customers and banks.

The present study aimed to show the impact of financial inclusion and digitalisation in 10 developed and developing countries over the period of 2008–2020. The main findings were consistent and confirmed by PLS, FE, RE and FGLS estimators. Financial inclusion had a significant negative impact on the digitalisation proxies and reflected the dark side of digitalisation in all estimators in the developed countries. Meanwhile, the results for the developing countries reflected the bright side of digitalisation. This indicates that consumers' lack of trust in financial service systems hinders financial inclusion efforts, reducing the positive side of digitalisation and reflecting the dark side of digitalisation. These negative effects increase uncertainty in complex environments.

The present study's findings indicate that digital financial services have a low cost if all members of society have easy access to them within effective financial systems that encourage new and existing company growth. In addition, access to financial services stimulates economic growth, thereby developing and strengthening demand. As such, when financial inclusion in a country is weak, economic growth decreases and the possibility of vulnerable groups increases. Therefore, governments have a constant need for regulators for financial institutions that operate with clear procedures regarding financial inclusion and benefit from the positive aspects of financial technology.

We recommend that financial institutions establish an individual financial services agent to target vulnerable groups and educate them on the use of digital financial services in order to combat digitisation-related financial fraud. Financial institutions also need to encourage the largest segment of society to adopt financial digitisation by reducing associated costs. We also recommend the re-evaluation of banking rules to ensure that all customer segments have easy access to financial services.

In response to COVID-19 pandemic-related restrictions, the world expanded the use of technology to facilitate communication and provide services in various areas of life. Moreover, digital access to financial services increased and became a special priority. The large discrepancy between developing and developed countries in the field of technological acceptance has led to the provision of financial services at varying levels. Cooperation between policy makers and regulatory and financial agencies has become an urgent necessity. Furthermore, we suggest that policy makers work on the following issues. Since interest in digital inclusion is still low, governments must examine the factors that contribute to the degree of digital financial exclusion in each country and implement a systematic plan for digital financial inclusion. In addition, governments should do goods and services in light of systematic policies that help the poor benefit from technology. Policy makers should prioritise digital initiatives that ensure rapid access to services and reduce costs in low-income areas. Policy makers should also acknowledge the importance of digital inclusion and promote the development of digital skills and financial literacy because having such skills as well as a firm understanding of financial services can increase financial opportunities, leading to increased savings and positive economic growth.

Therefore, policy makers should establish safety regulations and flexible laws and maintain awareness of the different types of financial products and services delivered through digital business. More attention by policy makers? between countries on technology-intensive equipment requires adequate knowledge of the rights to adopt the bright side of digitalisation. Furthermore, policy makers should encourage digital financial transactions and they should promote the importance of financial access in a low-risk framework. Future studies should consider more critical variables related to environmental quality and socioeconomic indicators as factors determining the dark and bright sides of digitalisation.

Note: Developed countries: Australia, France, Germany, New Zealand and the United Kingdom. **Developing countries**: Chile, Colombia, Mexico, Poland, and Turkey.

Compliance with ethical standards

Availability of data and material: Source of data sets are available in:

- World Development Indicators (WDI) 2008-2020, World Bank, retrieved on 01-10-2022 Available at the link: https://data.worldbank.org/

Conflict of interest: The author declare that they have no conflict of interest.

Ethical standard: The author declare that this research article is in compliance with the ethical standards of this journal.

Informed consent: This article does not contain any information that requires informed consent.

Funding: There is no funding for this manuscript.

Author's contributions: The author read and approved the final manuscript.

REFERENCES

Abubakar, L., & Handayani, T. (2018) Financial Technology: Legal Challenges for Indonesia Financial Sector. In *IOP Conf. Ser.: Earth Environ. Sci. 175 IOP Conf. Series: Earth and Environmental Science*, (p. 12204). IOP. 10.1088/1755-1315/175/1/012204

Agoba, A. M., Sare, Y. A., & Bugri-Anarfo, E. (2017). Financial Inclusion and Monetary Policy: A Review of Recent Studies. *Ghana Journal of Development Studies*, *14*(1), 231. doi:10.4314/gjds.v14i1.12

Andrianaivo, M., & Kpodar, K. (2012). Mobile phones, financial inclusion, and growth. *Revista de Economia Institucional*, *3*(2), 1–30.

Auer, R., Banka, H., Yaa Boakye-Adjei, N., Faragallah, A (2022) J. Frost, H. Natarajan, & J. Prenio. (eds) *Central bank digital currencies: a new tool in the financial inclusion toolkit?* FSI Insights 41

Ayyagari, M., Demirgüç-Kunt, A., & Maksimovic, V. (2011). ' Firm Innovation in Emerging Markets: The Role of Finance, Governance, and Competition'. *Journal of Financial and Quantitative Analysis*, *46*(6), 1545–1580. https://www.jstor.org/stable/41409661. doi:10.1017/S0022109011000378

Aziz, A., & Naima, U. (2021). Rethinking digital financial inclusion: Evidence from Bangladesh. *Technology in Society*, *64*, 101509. doi:10.1016/j.techsoc.2020.101509

Baltagi, B. H. (2012). *Econometric Analysis of Panel Data* (4th ed.). Wiley.

Barefoot, J. A. (2020) *Digital Technology Risks for Finance: Dangers Embedded in Fintech and Regtech*. 151. Harvard Kennedy School. https://www.hks.harvard.edu/centers/mrcbg/publications/awp/awp151

Beck, T., & Levine, R. (2002). Industry growth and capital allocation: Dose having a market- or bank-based system matter? *Journal of Financial Economics*, *64*(2), 147–180. doi:10.1016/S0304-405X(02)00074-0

Beck, T., Senbet, L. and Simbanegavi, W. (2015) 'Financial Inclusion and Innovation in Africa: An Overview', *Journal of African Economies*, *24*(suppl_1), pp. i3–i11. doi: . doi:10.1093/jae/eju031

Birch, D., & Young, M. A. (1997). Financial services and the Internet - what does cyberspace mean for the financial services industry? *Internet Research*, *7*(2), 120–128. doi:10.1108/10662249710165262

Boshkov, T. (2016) Growing the Global Economy through SMEs International Aspirations. LAP LAMBERT Academic Publishing.

Boskov, T., & Drakulevski, L. (2017). Addressing the Role of Risk Management and Digital Finance Technology on Financial Inclusion. *Quality - Access to Success*, *18*(161), 113–115. http://eprints.ugd.edu.mk/18591/

Burjorjee, D. M., & Scola, B. (2015) *A Market Systems Approach to Financial Inclusion Guidelines for Funders*. CGAP. www.cgap.org

Carayon, P. (1993). *'Effect of electronic performance monitoring on job design and worker stress: Review of the literature and conceptual model', Human Factors*. SAGE PublicationsSage CA. doi:10.1177/001872089303500301

Caruana, J. (2016) 'Financial inclusion and the fintech revolution: implications for supervision and oversight', in M. Gamser (eds) *Third GPFI-FSI Conference on Standard-Setting Bodies and Innovative Financial Inclusion: New Frontiers in the Supervision and Oversight of Digital Financial Services.*

Corbett, J. M. (1987). A psychological study of advanced manufacturing technology: The concept of coupling. *Behaviour & Information Technology*, *6*(4), 441–453. doi:10.1080/01449298708901855

De Hoyos, R. E., & Sarafidis, V. (2006). Testing for cross-sectional dependence in panel-data models. *The Stata Journal*, *6*(4), 482–496. doi:10.1177/1536867X0600600403

Demirguc-Kunt, A., & Klapper, L. (2012). Measuring Financial Inclusion: The Global Findex Database. *Policy Research Working Paper 6025*. World Bank: Washington, D.C

Demirguc-Kunt, A., Klapper, L., Singer, D., & Ansar, S. (2022). *The Global Findex Database 2021: Financial Inclusion, Digital Payments, and Resilience in the Age of COVID-19*. World Bank Publications. doi:10.1596/978-1-4648-1897-4

Demirguc-Kunt, A., & Maksimovic, V. (2002). Funding growth in bank-based and market-based financial system: Evidence from firm-level data. *Journal of Financial Economics*, *65*(3), 337–363. doi:10.1016/S0304-405X(02)00145-9

Diniz, E., Birochi, R., & Pozzebon, M. (2012). Triggers and barriers to financial inclusion: The use of ICT-based branchless banking in an Amazon county. *Electronic Commerce Research and Applications*, *11*(5), 484–494. doi:10.1016/j.elerap.2011.07.006

Emara, N., & Moheildin, M. (2021). Beyond the digital dividends: Fintech and extreme poverty in the Middle East and Africa. *Proceedings of Middle East Economic Association*, *23*(2), 41–73.

Evans, R. H. (1996). An analysis of criterion variable reliability in conjoint analysis. *Perceptual and Motor Skills*, *84*(3), 988–990. doi:10.2466/pms.1996.82.3.988

Fanta, A., & Makina, D. (2019). The Relationship Between Technology and Financial Inclusion: Cross-Sectional Evidence. In *Extending Financial Inclusion in Africa* (pp. 211–230). Elsevier. doi:10.1016/B978-0-12-814164-9.00010-4

Gollapudi, S. P. V., Choppella, V., Sanagavarapu, L. M., Chimalakonda, S., & Reddy, Y. R. (2019). Promoting better financial inclusion through web page transformation—A systematic literature review. *Journal of Banking and Financial Technology*, *3*(2), 131–147. doi:10.100742786-019-00010-0

Gonzalez, A. (2014). *Exporting Financial Services in Latin America and the Caribbean, Economic Modelling*. Elsevier. doi:10.1016/j.econmod.2014.04.013

Gupta, A., Li, H., & Sharda, R. (2013). Should I send this message? Understanding the impact of interruptions, social hierarchy and perceived task complexity on user performance and perceived workload. *Decision Support Systems*, *55*(1), 135–145. doi:10.1016/j.dss.2012.12.035

Harris, J. K., Moreland-Russell, S., Tabak, R. G., Ruhr, L. R., & Maier, R. C. (2014). Communication About Childhood Obesity on Twitter. *American Journal of Public Health*, *104*(7), e62–e69. doi:10.2105/AJPH.2013.301860 PMID:24832138

Helm, T., Low, A., & Joshua, T. (2019). *The positive impact of technology on the financial services sector in the United Kingdom is unprecedented globally*. UK FinTech–- State of the Nation.

Hsiao, C. (2007). Panel data analysis-advantages and challenges. *Test*, *16*(1), 1–22. doi:10.100711749-007-0046-x

Im, K., Pesaran, M., & Shin, Y. (1997). *Testing for Unit Roots in Heterogeneous Panels. Department of Applied Economics, University of Cambridg Johnston, J. and Dinardo, J. (1997) Econometric Methods*. McGraw-Hill.

Im K, M., Pesara, H., Shin Y (2003) Testing for unit roots in heterogeneous panels. *Journal of Econometrics, 115*, 53ñ74.

Jacoby, H. G. (1994). Borrowing constraints and progress through school: Evidence from Peru. *The Review of Economics and Statistics*, *76*(1), 151–160. doi:10.2307/2109833

Jariwala, H. V. (2017). Financial literacy: one step ahead of financial inclusion. *Prestige International Journal of Management and Research, 9/10*(2), 59-65. https://0-searchproquest-com.bibliotecails.tec.mx/docview/2013606469?accountid511643

Kabaklarli, E., Duran, M. S., & Üçler, Y. T. (2017) The Determinants Of High-Technology Exports: A Panel Data Approach For Selected Oecd Countries. *DIEM : Dubrovnik International Economic Meeting*, *3*(1), pp. 888–900.

Kanungo, R. P., & Gupta, S. (2021). Financial inclusion through digitalisation of services for well-being. *Technological Forecasting and Social Change*, *167*, 120721. doi:10.1016/j.techfore.2021.120721

Keister, T., and Sanches, D (2022). Should central banks issue digital currency? *The Review of Economic Studies*. doi:/ rdac017 doi:10.1093/restud

Kempson, E. (2006). *Policy level response to financial exclusion in developed economies: lessons for developing countries*. Paper for Access to Finance: Building Inclusive Financial Systems Conference, World Bank, Washington, D.C.

Kerr, W. R., & Nanda, R. (2015). Financing Innovation. *Annual Review of Financial Economics*, *7*(1), 445–462. doi:10.1146/annurev-financial-111914-041825

Kling, R. (1996) Computerization and Controversy. Elsevier. doi:10.1016/b978-0-12-415040-9.x5081-7

Lal, T. (2019). Measuring impact of financial inclusion on rural development through cooperatives. *International Journal of Social Economics*, *46*(3), 352–376. doi:10.1108/IJSE-02-2018-0057

Lapina, E. N., Orazaliev, A. A., Kalnaya, A. Y., Kiseleva, I. N., & Oseledko, I. V. (2021). Increasing the availability of financial services as a factor in ensuring socio-economic stability in the region. *Lecture Notes in Networks and Systems*, *206*, 715–724. doi:10.1007/978-3-030-72110-7_78

Lazonick, W. (2009) What is New, and Permanent, about the" New Economy"? Sustainable Prosperity in the New Economy? Business Organization and High-Tech Employment in the United States. Upjohn Institute for Employment Research.

Levine, R. (2002). Bank-based or market-based financial systems: Which is better? *Journal of Financial Intermediation*, *11*(4), 398–428. doi:10.1006/jfin.2002.0341

Lutfi, A., Al-Okaily, M., Alshirah, M. H., Alshira'h, A. F., Abutaber, T. A., & Almarashdah, M. A. (2021). Digital financial inclusion sustainability in Jordanian context. *Sustainability*, *13*(11), 6312. doi:10.3390u13116312

Mahalle, A., Yong, J., & Tao, X. (2021). Regulatory challenges and mitigation for account services offered by FinTech. Proceedings of the 2021 IEEE 24th International Conference on Computer Supported Cooperative Work in Design, 2021. CSCWD. www.scopus.com, doi:10.1109/CSCWD49262.2021.9437631

Markus, M. L., & Mentzer, K. (2014). Foresight for a responsible future with ICT. Information Systems Frontiers. Kluwer Academic Publishers. doi:10.100710796-013-9479-9

Mckinsey Global Institute. (2016). *Digital Finance for All: Powering Inclusive Growth in Emerging Economies. September 2016. MGI-Digital-Finance-For-All-Executive-summary-September2016.Ashx (mckinsey.Com)*. McKinsey & Company.

Nemoto, N., & Koreen, M. (2019) *Digital Innovation Can Improve Financial Access for SMEs*. Japan. https://www.rieti.go.jp/en/projects/t20japan/tf9/pb1.html

Ngo, C. N., & McCann, C. R. Jr. (2019). Rethinking rent seeking for technological change and development. *Journal of Evolutionary Economics*, *29*(2), 721–740. doi:10.100700191-018-0591-3

Ozili, P. K. (2018). Impact of digital finance on financial inclusion and stability. *Borsa Istanbul Review*, *18*(4), 329–340. doi:10.1016/j.bir.2017.12.003

Parham, D., Roberts, P., & Sun, H. (2001). Information Technology and Australia's Productivity Surge. *Development and Comp Systems*. https://ideas.repec.org/p/wpa/wuwpdc/0110006.html

Ragu-Nathan, T. S., Tarafdar, M., Ragu-Nathan, B. S., & Tu, Q. (2008). The consequences of technostress for end users in organizations: Conceptual development and validation. *Information Systems Research, 19*(4), 417–433. doi:10.1287/isre.1070.0165

Sarma, M., & Pais, J. (2008). Financial Inclusion and Development: A Cross Country Analysis. Working Paper: Indian Council for Research in International Economic Relations Tarafdar, M. *et al.* (2011) 'Crossing to the dark side: Examining creators, outcomes, and inhibitors of technostress'. *Communications of the ACM, 54*(9), 113–120. doi:10.1145/1995376.1995403

Schumpeter, J. (1912). *Theorie der Wirtschaftlichen Entwicklung [Theory of Economic development]*. Duncker und Humblot.

Shen, Y., Hu, W., & Hueng, C. J. (2021). Digital financial inclusion and economic growth: A cross-country study. *Procedia Computer Science, 187*, 218–223. doi:10.1016/j.procs.2021.04.054

Tarafdar, M., Gupta, A., & Turel, O. (2015). Introduction to the special issue on "dark side of information technology use. Information Systems Journal. Blackwell Publishing Ltd. doi:10.1111/isj.12076

Tarafdar, M., Pullins, E. B., & Ragu-Nathan, T. S. (2015). Technostress: Negative effect on performance and possible mitigations. *Information Systems Journal, 25*(2), 103–132. doi:10.1111/isj.12042

Tay, L., Tai, H., & Tan, G. (2022). Digital financial inclusion: A gateway to sustainable development. *Heliyon, 8*(6), e09766. doi:10.1016/j.heliyon.2022.e09766 PMID:35785228

The World Bank. (2021). *Digital Financial Inclusion*. World Bank. https:/ www.Worldbank.Org/En/Topic/Financialinclusion/Publication/Digital-Financial Inclusion. .

The World Bank. (2022) *World Development Indicators*. DataBank. https://databank.worldbank.org/source/world-development-indi
cators

Turel, O., Serenko, A., & Giles, P. (2011). 'Integrating technology addiction and use: An empirical investigation of online auction users', MIS Quarterly: Management. *Information Systems*, *35*(4), 1043–1061. doi:10.2307/41409972

United Nations. (2006). *Building Inclusive Financial Sectors for Development*. United Nations.

Van Klyton, A., Tavera-Mesıas, J.F. & Castano-Munoz, W. (2021). Innovation resistance and mobile banking in rural Colombia. *Journal of Rural Studies, 81*, pp. 269-280. doi:. jrurstud.2020.10.035. doi:10.1016/j

Wagner, J. (2019). Access to Finance and Exports – Comparable Evidence for Small and Medium Enterprises from Industry and Services in 25 European Countries. *Open Economies Review*, *30*(4), 739–757. doi:10.100711079-019-09534-w

Weil, M. M., & Rosen, L. D. (Eds.). (1997). *Technostress : coping with technology @work @home @play*. Wiley. https://lib.ugent.be/en/catalog/rug01:000826059

Wooldridge, J. M. (2010). *Econometric Analysis of Cross Section and Panel Data* (2nd ed.). The MIT Press. https://mitpress.mit.edu/books/econometric-analysis-cross-section-and-panel-data-second-edition.

Xing, Y. (2014). China's high-tech exports: The myth and reality. *Asian Economic Papers*, *13*(1), 109–123. doi:10.1162/ASEP_a_00256

Yang, S., Milner, C., Lancheros, S., & Gunessee, S. (2020). Access to Finance, Technology Investments and Exporting Decisions of Indian Services Firms. *Open Economies Review*, *31*(5), 1009–1036. doi:10.100711079-020-09595-2

Yeo, Y. H.. (2014). The assessment of information and communication technology (ICT) policy in South Korea. In *Lecture Notes in Electrical Engineering* (pp. 1241–1249). Springer Verlag. doi:10.1007/978-3-642-41674-3_172

Yoshino, N., & Morgan, P. J. (2016) *Overview of Financial Inclusion, Regulation, and Education, ADBI Working Papers*. 591. Asian Development Bank Institute. https://ideas.repec.org/p/ris/adbiwp/0591.html

Chapter 2
Government Response to FinTechs:
A Cross-Country Analysis

Amir Manzoor
https://orcid.org/0000-0002-3094-768X
Karachi School of Business and Leadership, Karachi, Pakistan

ABSTRACT

Technological innovations in the financial sector are transforming the provision of financial services. Fintech is one such innovation that not only provides opportunities (such as financial development and inclusion) but also brings various potential risks to consumers and investors. These risks also threaten the stability and integrity of global financial system. As such, financial regulators across the globe are adjusting their regulatory regimes and continue to provide and develop guidelines to mitigate these risks. This study provides a cross-country review of fintech policy responses of developed world.

INTRODUCTION

Technology advancements, coupled with easier internet access and increased bandwidth has resulted in the birth of new applications in the financial sector. Some of these applications include new approaches to credit extension, new payment methods, new ways of channeling funds etc. Fintech is one of these new applications that has great potential to enhance financial inclusion and reduce poverty. At the same time, fintech has its associated risks for consumers, investors, and stability/integrity of the global financial system (IMF, 2018). The global bodies that set standards for the

DOI: 10.4018/978-1-6684-6381-9.ch002

Copyright © 2023, IGI Global. Copying or distributing in print or electronic forms without written permission of IGI Global is prohibited.

financial industry have continued to issue guidelines aimed at keeping consumers and industry abreast of developments in fintech sector and its implications. The Financial Stability Board (FSB) is an international body that monitors and makes recommendations about the global financial system. A study of the FSB found that financial system is not systematically influenced by fintech innovations (Financial Stability Board, 2017, 2019).

The biggest challenge is balancing the risks and benefits of fintech. This balance is crucial for realizing the benefits of fintech for society without compromising the integrity of financial system. The various fintech regulations introduced by regulators aims to address those vulnerabilities of financial system that can result in market failures (Tourpe, 2017). Even with fintech use in traditional financial services, regulators need to ensure that fintech does not provide opportunities for criminals to misuse financial system and consumers have fair and easy access to use fintech services. This is important given some massive scandals e.g., crowdfunding fraud by Ezubao which was a peer-to-peer lending scheme based in in China (Reuters, 2017).

Regulators face various new challenges and trade-offs when it comes to fintech. Fintech may present regulators with issues not covered under the traditional financial regulatory regime. As such, dealing with these challenges required broader cooperation among various government bodies (such as consumer protection and anti-competition). Technological innovations, such as fintech, also pose a serious challenge for regulators because of lack of in-house expertise (Alaassar, Mention, & Aas, 2022). Due to this resource constraint, regulators may find it difficult to respond in a timely fashion to developments that are taking place in fintech sector. The timely response is important because fintech sector is not obliged to wait for regulators' actions before proceeding to utilize fintech (Buckley, Arner, Veidt, & Zetzsche, 2020). Another challenge is that use of fintech may lead to increased decentralization of the financial sector. This increased decentralization means that regulators would need to change their regulatory/supervisory frameworks (Financial Stability Board, 2019).

Financial regulators have come up with various responses to fintech developments. One such response is a license regime specific to fintech (Financial Stability Board, 2019a, February 14). Under this regime, fintech firms are required to obtain prior authorization to offer fintech services. Another response is issuance of fintech-specific requirements. These requirements may be a modified version of existing requirements or new requirements that are built on old regulatory frameworks. Some financial regulators decided to develop guidelines aimed to inform consumers, investors, and fintech firms how the existing regulatory frameworks can be applied on fintech and what are regulatory expectations. This study provides a cross-country review of developed world's regulatory response to fintech developments. The developed world consists of high-income countries with well-developed industrial bases and infrastructural facilities, enabling an environment for businesses and a high human capital index including strong governmental institutions (Raimi, Kah, & Tariq, 2022). This overview is structured around three key components of fintech environment: fintech activities, enabling technologies and policy enablers.

THE FINTECH ENVIRONMENT

Fintech is still in its nascent stages of development. As such, there still exist no clear definition of fintech. Consumers, users, and industry use many terms (such as fintech credit, peer-to-peer lending, or crowdlending) interchangeably (Havrylchyk, 2018). For this study, we have used the definition of fintech from Financial Stability Board (2017). According to this, fintech is defined as an innovation that is enabled by the use of technology and capable to provide new business models, applications, and products that are beneficial for financial industry and provision of financial services.

There exist various global classifications and frameworks that regulators use to analyze fintech. For example, the framework of FSB categorizes the fintech innovations based on the primary economic function (Financial Stability Board, 2017). On the similar lines, Basel Committee on Banking Supervision has developed their framework that categorizes fintech innovations into three sectors. These three sectors are related to core banking services i.e. credit/deposit, payments/clearing/settlement, and investment management (Basel Committee on Banking Supervision, 2018).

The fintech environment consists of three elements: fintech activities, enabling technologies, and policy enablers (Ehrentraud et al., 2020). Fintech activities are the ways technology can be used to provide financial services. Fintech activities can be of various forms. Enabling technologies are the backbone of fintech. These are the technologies that make fintech services possible. Policy enablers are measures/initiatives that support fintech activities and fintech development. By defining the fintech environment in this way, we can classify the regulatory response to fintech in three categories. In first category, there are regulatory bodies that have changed their regulatory framework and/or provide direct interventions for fintech sector. In second category, the responses of regulatory bodies are focused on use of new technologies to provide financial services. In third category, the regulatory regime is providing broader responses to facilitate/promote technology innovations in provision of financial services.

Fintech Activities

There exist different fintech activities that are performed in different financial services such as raising capital, trading, payment, and asset management. Some of the most important fintech activities include digital banking, fintech platform financing, robo-advisors, electronic money services, digital payment services, insurtech and cryptoassets fintech (Ehrentraud et al., 2020).

Digital Banking

The regulatory regime for banks varies from country to country. As such, it is not necessary that an entity recognized as a bank in one country will also be recognized as a bank in other countries. In this study, digital bank is defined as an institution that accepts deposits but delivers its services through electronic means. A digital bank does not maintain any physical branches. Since, a digital bank has no physical presence, its business model is heavily reliant on technology (Dubey, 2019). There exist many examples of digital banks e.g., KakaoBank of Korea, MyBank of China, Nubank of Brazil etc.

Fintech Platform Financing

Electronic platforms are used to facilitate many fintech activities. These platforms heavily deponent on technology and work as an intermediary to provide financing to consumers. There are two important platforms: fintech balance sheet lending and crowdfunding. In fintech balance sheet lending, internet-based platforms are used to facilitate provision of credit from lenders to borrowers. These platforms are not operated by banks. Rather, they use their own balance sheet. These platforms use their equity or debt as sources of their funding. These platforms enter in direct credit facility arrangement with their borrowers. The credit risk here is assumed by the platform because the credit (or loan) stays on their balance sheet until it is sold to some investors. Some popular examples of fintech balance sheet lenders include WeLend in Hong Kong (Bloomberg, 2022) and Quicken Loans in USA (nerdwallet, 2022). The term crowdfunding refers to businesses that provides matching services. This matching services match two types of entities: first the people looking to raise funds and second the investors looking to invest their funds. These investors are interested in getting a return on investment but not willing to use traditional banks. There are two major forms of crowdfunding: equity crowdfunding and loan crowdfunding. In equity crowdfunding, the investors provide equity as the form of funding. In loan crowdfunding, the crowdfunding platform facilitate a loan contract between borrower and lender. The crowdfunding platforms does not involve in risk transformation (FSB, 2017). The regulatory regimes of fintech balance sheet lending vary greatly (FSB, 2017; Ehrentraud et al., 2020; Adrian & Griffoli, 2019). Therefore, this study does not include fintech balance sheet lending in the definition of loan crowdfunding.

Robo-advisors

Robo-advisor is a digital platform that provides automated advice on financial products. Robo-advisors rely on little to no human intervention. Robo-advice is enabled by extensive use of technology. Using robo-advice, fintech companies can automate the process of many investment tasks such as retirement planning (Belanche et al., 2019; Madir, 2021).

Digital Payment Services

The digital payment service providers facilitate payments between payee and payer. These payments are digital and require no use of physical cash (Committee on Payment and & Settlement Systems, 2004). These service providers can either handle the funds themselves or facilitate payment on behalf of payer whose account can be at another financial institution (Horn et al., 2020).

Electronic Money Services

Electronic money service providers utilize facilitate payments by using debt-like instruments (Chaves, 2019). When an electronic money services provider issues electronic money, the service provider creates a pre-established but fixed face-value claim on its own balance sheet. This claim is dominated in fiat currency. This claim guarantees that the issued electronic money can be redeemed in future at the pre-established face value. However, there are certain pre-requisites before this claim can be considered electronic money. This claim must be acceptable by other parties and created only after receiving the cash (Madir, 2021).

Insurtech Business Models

Insurtech refers to fintech designed to improve the efficiency of the insurance industry. Note that insurtech can refer to either use of digital technology or technology-driven innovative business models for insurance industry (The International Association of Insurance Supervisors, 2017). For this article we define insurtech as the use of new transformative business models for insurance industry. These business models are emerging in two major areas of insurance i.e., distribution and underwriting. In distribution, we see companies like digital brokers and in underwriting companies like peer-to-peer insurance providers (Yan et al., 2018; Madir, 2021).

Cryptoassets Fintech

Cryptoassets are an emerging field of finance and as such there exist no common definition and classification of cryptoassets (Madir, 2021). For this article, we use the cryptoassets definition provided by FSB (Financial Stability Board, 2019). According to this definition, a cryptoasset is a private asset. A cryptoasset utilizes two technologies for its functioning: cryptography and distributed ledger. Some of the important financial activities related to cryptoassets related to their creation/distribution/exchange and their use for investments/payments.

Enabling Technologies

Enabling technologies are technologies that fuel innovations in financial sector. Some of the most important enabling technologies include artificial intelligence, cloud computing, machine learning, distributed ledger, application programming interface, and biometrics. These technologies have a vast variety of applications. For example, application programming interface help non-banking companies to gain secure and regulated access to customer information held in financial institutions. Cloud computing provides an efficient, scalable, and flexible processing of large amounts of data. Distributed ledger is used to increase efficiency and lessen the reliance on intermediaries for financial transactions. Biometrics are being used for customer authentication. Artificial intelligence and machine learning is being used for robo-advisors and automated trading (Ehrentraud et al., 2020).

Policy Enablers

Policy enablers are policies and initiatives developed by government bodies to enable digital infrastructure required for provision of stable and efficient fintech products/services. The policy enablers can cover a broad range of policies and initiatives including but not limited to national broadband infrastructure, digital identity and authentication management systems, and data protection/cyber security frameworks, and policies to promote innovations in financial sector (Ehrentraud et al., 2020). Regarding adoption of innovations in financial sector, various initiatives have been taken in many countries. These initiatives include innovation hubs, regulatory sandboxes, and innovation accelerators. An innovation hub is a physical arrangement in which researchers, and innovators work together under a single roof to develop ideas into products/services that could transform the industry. A regulatory sandbox, as the name implies, is a system in which innovations are tested under regulator's watch. This testing is live and conducted in a specified time frame. An innovation accelerator is designed to support innovators in validation of their business ideas. The purpose is to accelerate the scaling of their business. Besides promoting innovations, these initiatives also help governments to understand technology applications, the new business models, and assess the changes required in existing regulatory regime (Buckley et al., 2020; Alaassar et al., 2022).

REGULATORY RESPONSES TO FINTECH ACTIVITIES

In a broad sense, the regulatory response to fintech activities can be divided into three categories: a) no response or no change in existing regulatory regime b) developing fintech-specific regulatory regime and c) not allowing certain fintech activities. In the first category, governments are still not clear how the existing regulatory regime can be applied to fintech. In the second category, the governments have developed fintech-specific laws/regulations/guidelines or amended the existing regulatory regime to include fintech activities. In third category, governments are working to modify the existing regulatory regime to include fintech activities. In the last category, the regulatory regime does not permit certain fintech activities (World Bank, 2020; IMF, 2022).

Digital Banking

In most cases, the countries are using existing regulatory regime of banking to regulate digital banking as well (Ehrentraud et al., 2020). Very few countries, such as Hong Kong and Singapore have developed specific regulatory regime for digital banks. In Hong Kong, regulators issued guideline on authorization of virtual banks in 2019 (Hong Kong Monetary Authority, 2019). These guidelines describe the principles used to authorize operations of virtual banks in Hong Kong. These guidelines provide some basic minimum requirements to be fulfilled before a digital bank can be authorized to operate. For example, the virtual bank has to operate as a locally incorporated bank, have a committed support from a parent company, and no branches are allowed. The digital banking framework of the Monetary Authority of Singapore provides two types of licenses for digital banks: digital full bank and digital wholesale bank. Both types of banks serve different types of customers. The digital full bank serves retail customers while digital wholesale bank serves small and medium-sized enterprises. The applicant of digital bank license must fulfill certain requirements such as physical place of operation /headquarter in Singapore, control by a Singaporean, track record of operating a technology-oriented business, and clear value proposition.

In Europe, European Central Bank (ECB) amended the existing regulatory regime for fintech companies. The guidelines provided by ECB in this regard were technology-neutral (European Banking Authority, 2018). While the regulatory regime applies the authorization standards of conventional banks on fintech business models, the supervisory considerations are different. For example, the supervisory considerations for fintech business models require that the management of the fintech firm must have suitable background in technology and finance. The shareholders must be reputed and financially sound. The fintech company must have a robust organizational structure. The firm must have a sound business plan and pass the required capital, liquidity, and solvency assessment.

Some countries do not have a regulatory regime specific to digital banking. In such cases, these countries have taken measures to facilitate establishment of new digital banks. In Australia, a new regulatory regime allows authorized digital banks to operate on limited scale for 2 years without satisfying complete prudential regulations. To be eligible, the business must be a low-risk business with a total balance sheet size not greater than100 million (Peterson & Mallesons, 2021). In UK, the regulatory bodies established a new unit to guide and support applicants of digital bank license (Bank of England, 2022). The guide is frequently updated to keep applicants abreast of the latest developments in the regulatory regime. Both these initiatives allowed potential applicants to understand the licensing regime and give them some time to prepare for full compliance with prudential regulations.

Fintech Platform Financing

Broadly speaking, the regulatory regime for fintech platform financing considers multiple factors such as types of activities performed and entities involved, which entity performs which activity and bears which type of risk (International Organization of Securities Commissions, 2017). A banking license is required if the business model of fintech platform financing involves accepting deposits from public and combining it with its own equity. Some countries also require a license even if the firm only grants loans without accepting deposits from public. In such cases, fintech firms uses other banks as third party to originate and assign loans to investors (FSB, 2017). Fintech platforms dealing with securities, providing investment advice, or acting as intermediaries for loans/investments need a license as per securities regulation. Fintech platforms providing payment services are subject to the licensing regime applicable to payments industry. It applies whether the platform uses its own accounts to transfer payments between clients or make payments on behalf of clients.

Fintech platform-specific regulatory regime are focused on a particular business model (Ehrentraud et al., 2020) e.g., fintech balance sheet lending, loan crowdfunding and equity crowdfunding. Regulatory regimes specific to fintech balance sheet lending are few. In most cases, the regulators treat it as an extension of credit. Some countries (e.g., Austria and Germany) require a banking license for any entity making loans to consumers or investors. Other countries have specific regulations for such non-bank entities. For example, Hong Kong regulators require a money lender license for any entity making loans. The existing regulations do not distinguish whether the consumer obtains loan from a digital platform or a physical conventional bank.

For fintech balance sheet lending, few countries have introduced a dedicated licensing mechanism. The Brazil's National Monetary Council issued a declaration to establish direct credit companies. These companies are a new type of financial institution that exclusively operate digitally and require a license to run their operations. Their only source of funding is their own equity and authorized to provide loans and financing. The activities involved in loan and equity crowdfunding are similar. Both platforms facilitate direct connect between lenders and borrowers. Both use digital platforms to target public but do not take any risk or do balance sheet intermediation. Both earn their profits from fees they charge from their clients. Many countries have introduced a dedicated licensing mechanism for both equity and loan crowdfunding models. Most regulatory regimes are focused on customer protection and financial stability. In many cases, a license or registration is required before a crowdfunding platform can start its operations. In many countries, specific regulations exist for equity crowdfunding. The policy objectives behind these regulations are generally enhanced investor protection and expansion of direct financing channels. Few countries have specific regulations for loan crowdfunding. In 2018, Brazil's National Monetary Council introduced peer-to-peer loan companies. This new type of financial institution required a license to operate. Under Chinese regulation for internet finance, loan crowdfunding platforms act as brokers between lenders and borrowers (OECD, 2021). Under Australian regulations, the crowdfunding platforms are under existing regulatory regime and require a license to operate. The policy objectives behind most regulatory regimes are consumer/investor protection, anti-money laundering, operational resilience, and prohibit terror financing. The crowdfunding platforms may also be required to fulfill other requirements such as risk management, governance, business continuity etc.

Robo-Advisors

Typically, robo-advisors falls under the existing regulatory regime. Robo- advisors are providers of financial advice. As such, they fall under securities regulation for authorization of their business and subsequent operations. Regulatory regimes for financial advice are not technology-specific to ensure the customers of robo-advisers received similar level of protection and quality of advice provided by conventional providers of financial advice. In majority of countries, no specific regulations exist for robo-advisors and existing regulatory and licensing requirements are applied. These requirements may vary depending on different factors (e.g., type of advice and advisor, type of client, purpose of investment, type of product, and type of activities performed). The regulatory regimes in many countries only consider personalized advice. The regulatory requirements are less stringent if the advice limited in scope or adviser is restricted and not independent. Regulatory requirements are typically more stringent if the client is a retail client. Different types of investments have different types of requirements. For example, robo-advice for retirement plans falls under tougher regulations. Type or complexity of product also affects the applicable regulations. The extent of the robo-adviser's activities also affects licensing regime (Huang et al., 2022; Abraham et al., 2019).

Many countries have developed specific guidelines and supervisory requirements for robo-advisors. The policy objectives of these guidelines and requirements were customer protection and provision of level-playing field for all companies. In Singapore, robo-advisors need a financial adviser's license. Robo-advisors are expected to collect sufficient and reliable information using clear and self-explanatory automated tools. This could be a significant challenge. As such, some regulatory regimes require involvement of human advisor to provide suitable advice. The heart of robo-advisor's business model is the algorithm that transforms information into actionable advice. If the algorithm has a coding error or bias, then the advice generated could be inaccurate and results in unexpected losses. Therefore, regulators require that robo-advisors put in place a governance mechanism for their algorithm. The ultimate responsibility falls on the shoulders of company board or senior management. Under this mechanism, robo-advisors should perform frequent assessment of their algorithm to monitor the quality of advice and any changes made in the algorithm. The robo-advisor is responsible to inform the client of limitations of the advice and the potential consequences. Robo-advisors could do that by issuing a risk disclosure statement. Robo-advisors are expected to provide simple, sufficient, easily understandable, and clear information to their clients for making informed decisions. Some regulatory regimes require robo-advisors disclose the information on scope of advice provided and conflicts of interest. In some countries, specific regulations for robo-advisors do not exist. These countries rely on existing regulatory requirements to guide robo-advisors of compliance and other requirements under securities laws. One example is Markets in Financial Instruments Directive (MIFID) in the European Union (Huang et al., 2022).

Electronic Money and Digital Payments

Both banks and non-banks provide digital payment services. Non-bank fintech companies have established a strong foothold in payments industry once dominated by conventional banks. Customers now have the option to make payments using their bank account or electronic money account operated by a non-bank payment service provider. Non-bank providers of digital payment services use technology to assist payments. Categorization of the non-bank payment service providers is difficult because of differences in business models and because they provide services at different stages. One categorization is done based on whether the payment service overlaps the existing payment infrastructures or use its own proprietary standalone system. Famous standalone payment service providers include Alipay and WeChat Pay. Some important examples of overlay include PayPal and Calibra. Electronic money is monetary value that can be stored on a physical device or specialized software. The issuer of electronic money treats it like a pre-paid debt claim denominated in the currency issued by central bank and redeemable in fiat currency at face value. Due to risks involved, electronic money has separate regulations. For example, in European Union, the electronic money providers are subject to the regulations provided in Electronic Money Directive 2 (EMD2). Electronic money providers are generally subject to more stringent regulatory requirements (Advapay, 2021).

Digital Payment Services

Regulations specific to digital payment services exist in many countries. However, the policy objectives of these regulations vary. In general, payment services dealing with customers' funds are subject to different regulations. In some countries, regulatory regimes facilitate non-banks to do business in the payments industry. For example, European Union introduced two new categories of regulated payment service providers: payment initiation service providers and account information service providers. Both can access clients' accounts held by other financial institutions but cannot operate their own payment accounts. Regulators in South Africa and Chile require non-bank payment service providers to team up with a conventional bank to offer their services. In Japan, non-bank firms are allowed to make fund transfers up to JPY 1 million. Some regulatory regimes have more stringent requirements for non-banks. In Canada, retail payment systems were put under regulatory regime with oversight by Bank of Canada. In Turkey, licensing requirements for non-bank payment services were introduced in 2013. In Singapore, Payment Services Bill was enacted by parliament to provide separate legislation for payment services. The legislation offers different types of licenses based on the type of activities and size of business.

Electronic Money Services

Regulations specific to electronic money services exist in many countries. These regulations are either in the form of specific licensing or other specific requirements. Many countries are still in the process of developing specific regulatory regime for. Argentina is an exception that has no specific regulation for electronic money but allow these services under existing regulatory regime.

In general, there are two broad classes of licensing regimes for electronic money. Under first regime, the electronic money providers are considered a bank and subject to regulations applied to conventional banks. One example is South Africa. Under second regime, electronic money providers are classified as a special bank that requires a separate license and comply with specific requirements. One example is Colombia. Both regimes require insurance of customers' deposits. Electronic money providers are typically not allowed to engage in financial intermediation or make loans. They are also not allowed to earn interest.

There exist common requirements for the float. Most regulatory regimes require 100% reserve requirement to safeguard against risks of insolvency of electronic money provider. All regulatory regimes require holding clients' funds in safe and liquid assets. Requirements for protection of customers' funds are common. Often, regulatory regimes require separation of customers' funds from the e-money provider's assets. Regulators choose various means to implement this requirement e.g., holding clients' funds in a separate account of a bank (e.g. Turkey) or the central bank (e.g. China), in a trust (e.g. Hong Kong and Peru), or an insurance policy (e.g. EU).

Insurtech Business Models

There exist few specific licensing regimes for insurtech business models. Existing licensing regimes and regulatory requirements are considered sufficient to adequately address the underlying risks of such business models. In many countries, regulators are assessing the feasibility of issuing new requirements to address the potential risks when the insurtech business models are scaled up. Many authorities are either issuing new requirements or modifying existing requirements relating to insurtech business models.

Cryptoassets Financial Services

There is a lack of a common categorization of cryptoassets. As such, regulators face challenges in deciding the appropriate regulatory approach for cryptoassets. There exist various terms and classifications such as virtual/crypto-/digital asset. According to Blandin et al., (2019), when regulators define cryptoasset, they consider some common and shared distinctive elements of cryptoasset. Some of these elements include a) form of the asset (i.e., currencies, commodities, real estate, securities etc.), b) properties of the asset, c) function of the asset, d) nature of issuer (i.e., whether cryptoasset was issued by non-regulated or regulated businesses, or the public sector e) economic function (i.e., payment or exchange, source of investment etc.).

In general, regulators use the economic function as the criterion to classify cryptoassets and establish the applicable regulatory perimeter. In case the economic function and purpose are the same, then cryptoassets are subject to the same regulatory regime. Similarly, activities of cryptoassets provider are like those performed by regulated financial entities then they are subject to the same regulatory regime. The regulators also use the underlying assets criterion to determine regulatory requirements. Switzerland has published a suggestive classification of cryptoassets that classifies cryptoassets according to the asset to which they are linked. Regulators' attention is mostly focused on cryptoassets issued by non-regulated businesses because risks associated with cryptoassets increases when the issuer is not subject to regulatory requirements.

There is a great variation in regulatory regime for cryptoassets. These regimes vary depending on many factors such as market maturity, kind of the judicial procedure etc. There are many categories of regulatory approaches to cryptoassets. These categories are not mutually exclusive, and they may cover regulations from other authorities. In general, regulators opt to provided published warnings to inform consumers and investors the risks associated with cryptoassets. Various regulatory regimes have published policy instruments regarding the regulatory framework for cryptoassets. Due to criminal uses of cryptoassets, various regulatory regimes are modifying their corresponding frameworks to combine international guidelines for anti-money laundering and combating the financing of terrorism. Some of the important guidelines include Fifth Anti-Money Laundering Directive (AMLD5) and recommendations issued by the Financial Action Task Force (FATF) (Landerer, 2022).

Few countries have developed specific regulatory regime for cryptoassets. In UAE, a cryptoasset business needs financial services permission to operate. France requires mandatory registration for some of the cryptoasset services. In Germany, Japan, USA, and Singapore cryptoasset businesses require a separate license. Other countries, such as Mexico, Netherlands, and the Philippines require cryptoassets institutions to obtain authorization to deal with cryptoassets. Various countries implement prohibitions on crypto-related activities. For example, Belgium, Colombia, Mexico, and Saudi Arabia partially prohibits crypto-related activities. These prohibitions may include restricting the marketing of financial products to retail clients and not allowing investment services in cryptoassets. Saudi Arabia does not allow trading of cryptocurrencies. China does not allow any crypto- related activity.

REGULATORY RESPONSES FOR ENABLING TECHNOLOGIES

Fintech provides both opportunities and risks for financial services. These risks may include data privacy, cyber security, third-party risk etc. In addition, there are significant issues of bias, ethics and fairness of models used in machine learning and artificial intelligence applications. Various regulatory regimes have are adjusting existing regulatory requirements to address technology-specific aspects. Some regulators have also developed general principles for the use of fintech.

Due to their increased market acceptance in the provision of financial services, some technologies (such as APIs, cloud computing, and biometrics) have received more attention. The other technologies, such as artificial intelligence and machine learning are subject to risk assessments by the regulators. In most cases, the regulators' approach technology-neutral to develop solid actions to be taken regarding enabling technologies.

Application Programming Interfaces (APIs)

The existing regulatory regimes cover APIs under open banking initiatives. In recent years, APIs are being used to provide a way of sharing customer data between banks and third parties. Various regulatory regimes require banks to create systems that enable third parties to gain permissioned access to customers' data stored in the bank system. In European Union, technical standards on strong customer authentication and common and secure communication poses specific requirements for payment service providers on interfaces. Many countries encourage and facilitate API adoption. In Singapore, regulators issued an API Playbook to provide guidelines for API design and usage. The regulators in Hong Kong implemented an open API framework to facilitate the development and adoption of APIs by banks.

Cloud Computing

In most countries the regulatory regime for cloud computing has been established by either modifying existing regime or by clarifying regulatory expectations regarding use of cloud computing by the financial sector. There also exist specific requirements regarding procedures between banks and cloud service providers. These requirements are intended to ensure sufficient risk management when cloud computing is used in financial institutions. Cross-border nature of cloud services also complicates the effective oversight of these risks. In all regulatory regimes, there are some common requirements for cloud computing use by financial sector. These common requirements include suitable information security, data confidentiality and availability, strong IT and cyber security competences, effective recovery and continuation abilities, suitable audit rights, and on-site inspection.

Biometrics

All regulatory regimes, such as PSD2, GDPR and AML5, aim to promote the use of biometrics data to facilitate customer's remote identification and authentication by financial institutions. In many regulatory regimes, existing regulatory frameworks have been modified to allow the use of biometrics. Most regulatory requirements related to the collection, use and storage of biometric data are focused on risks of data privacy, cyber security, and money laundering.

Distributed Ledger Technology

Currently, few regulatory regimes exist that are specific to distributed ledger technology (DLT). DLT is used for the creation of cryptoassets but may also be used in other applications such as securities settlement and digital identity systems. Due to its extensive early use in the financial industry, the policy responses are still developing. Still, many countries have developed specific regulations for use of DLT by financial institutions. France approved the use of DLT for the record-keeping of issuance and sale of unlisted financial securities. In Luxembourg, regulators allowed securities to be held via distributed electronic registers. In Switzerland, a new Federal Act was introduced to increase legal certainty, remove hurdles, and limit risks of misuse of DLT. Russian regulators enacted a regulatory regime applicable to all economic sectors.

Machine Learning (ML) and Artificial Intelligence (AI)

ML and AI applications in the financial sector are in a nascent stage. As such, the regulatory responses are still developing and there exist no specific regulatory requirements use of ML and AI. Regulators in many countries are developing consultation papers to discuss potential regulation with the industry. Regulators in few countries (such as Singapore, Netherlands, and Hong Kong) have issued non-binding principles. These principles are aimed to foster soundness, fairness, ethics, accountability, skills, and transparency in the use of ML and AI by financial institutions.

POLICY ENABLERS

A digital economy can provide various economic and social opportunities. Therefore, many countries are looking for ways to increase the provision of digital services. Governments are implementing policies to enable the provision of digital services such as digital identification, data protection regimes, cyber security strategies, open banking initiatives, innovation facilitator initiatives etc.

Digital Identification Systems

Digital IDs can facilitate delivery of digital services. This can help increase financial inclusion, increase efficiency, and improve the service. Digital identification can give people access to digital services (such as digital payments). Governments can use digital identification for tangible and non-tangible benefits such as reducing fraud. There exist a wide variety of digital identification systems that uses different technologies. One example is digital identification system based on a permissioned DLT shared by institutions. In many countries, use of digital identification systems is permitted for customers' verification and authentication. In these countries, regulatory provisions exist that govern the use of these systems. Some countries have implemented national digital identity systems. In Sweden citizens can use their BankID to identify themselves during online transactions with banks and government agencies.

Some countries have improved their frameworks to allow digital identification systems that people can use to store their identification data in a secure database. This data can then be shared for multiple purposes with citizens' consent. For example, Australian government has implemented a digital ID ecosystem. This system can be used by government agencies and private businesses to securely verify an individual's identity online. In Singapore, a system called National Digital Identity was implemented. This system allowed citizens and businesses to conduct secure digital transactions with public and private sector organizations.

Data Protection Frameworks

Data bring value to the digital economy. Data protection protocols are not new but increasing digitalization has pushed governments in many countries to issue new regulations or enhance existing ones relating to the collection, use and protection of consumer data. The most common requirement in these regulations is getting consumer consent before collecting, using, or sharing their data. The definition of consumer data is still unclear, and many countries use different definition as to what constitutes a consumer's personal or sensitive data. Irrespective of the definition used, all regulations require explicit specification of the purpose of data collection and use. More comprehensive data protection frameworks, such as GDPR in the EU, also provides new rights for individuals (e.g., data portability). Under such frameworks, citizens can ask the organization to provide their personal data in a generally used format that can be easily shared with others. Citizens can also ask for removal of their personal data if they feel it is no longer necessary for the purpose it was collected. Only few countries require a designated person responsible for the institution's compliance with data protection regulation. In European Union, companies of certain size need to have a data protection officer that works independently and ensures company's compliance with data protection regulations. In Singapore, the Personal Data Protection Act require all organization to designate one or more such individuals.

Cyber Security Frameworks

Cyber risk is a growing global challenge and various regulatory responses are emerging at both national and international level to tackle this risk. The common objective behind these responses is to develop a cyber security framework for risk mitigation, effective response, and recovery from cyber-attacks. Some governments (e.g., France, United Kingdom, USA and Singapore), have set up cyber security centers at national level. In United Kingdom, government conducted sector simulation cyber resilience exercises. In France, G7 cyber-attack simulation exercise was conducted. Its purpose was to simulate cross-border attack on the financial sector. Many countries have already set up national cyber security framework to boost the cyber security of critical sectors (including financial sector) and infrastructure. Financial sector is a critical and highly exposed sector with respect to cyber risk due to their technology-intensive operations and high dependence on information.

Almost all countries have implemented specific regulations for cyber security in the financial sector. Many of these regulations are modified versions of different cyber security frameworks existing at international and national level including the G7 Fundamental Elements of Cybersecurity for the Financial Sector (G7FE) and the G7 Fundamental Elements for Effective Assessment of Cybersecurity in the Financial Sector (G7FEA). Cyber security frameworks for financial institutions vary among countries. However, there exist some commonalities. For examples, all frameworks require a documented cyber security policy, identification of critical information assets to be protected, testing of institutional vulnerability and resilience to cyber risk, clear responsibilities and accountabilities related to cyber security, cyber threat intelligence-sharing, and ensuring the capabilities of third-party providers.

Open Banking Initiatives

Many countries have either adopted or adopting open banking initiatives. These initiatives are aimed at providing permissioned access to customer information from banks to third parties (such as fintech firms). These initiatives are important to build innovative applications and services, increase competition, and encourage innovation in providing digital financial services. Open banking initiatives vary among countries. Some countries follow a prescriptive approach in which banks are mandated to provide permissioned access to customer data to registered third parties. In prescriptive approach, the focus is on data privacy, data security, and third-party risk management. Some countries follow facilitative approach in which regulators issue guidelines to encourage API adoption.

Innovation Facilitators

There are three major types of facilitators: innovation hubs, regulatory sandboxes, and accelerators. Innovation hubs provide support and advice to firms to understand regulatory framework and identify legal issues. A regulatory sandbox is a controlled testing environment. Accelerators are a partnership between fintech companies and government agencies to develop use cases. The innovation facilitators are not mutually exclusive. Many countries have set up both innovation hubs and regulatory sandboxes. Some countries (e.g., Canada, Hong Kong and Singapore) have set up all three facilitators. Out of these three facilitators, innovation hubs are the most common. In some countries, innovation hubs are prerequisite for applying to the regulatory sandbox. Innovation hubs may be established as a supranational collaboration initiative such as one set up by Bank for International Settlements. Regulatory sandboxes follow similar objectives such as reduction of time and cost of providing innovative products or services to consumers. Different operating mechanisms are used for regulatory sandboxes that differ based on various factors (such as targeted participants, testing parameters etc.). In Australia, the regulatory sandboxes are targeted towards only new unregulated entrants. In Abu Dhabi, Japan and the UK, sandbox participants are selected in small groups. In other countries sandbox participants can be accepted when they apply and establish their eligibility.

In general, most sandboxes welcome any innovative idea that could benefit customers. However, some countries narrow their attention to certain topics or technologies. For example, Japan tested a small group of projects based on customer identification. In Abu Dhabi, a group of projects focused on SME finance was tested. Regulatory sandboxes may be established by multiple regulatory bodies. For example, in Hong Kong various regulatory authorities have introduced their respective sandboxes. In some countries, regulatory sandboxes have implemented an express approach for quick adoption of particular fintech innovations. In Singapore, Sandbox Express was created for firms to conduct certain regulated activities. In Hong Kong, the government introduced express track to speed up authorization applications for new insurance companies. Regulatory sandboxes may be established internationally by a group of financial authorities. One example is the Global Financial Innovation Network that is a global sandbox comprises of many financial authorities, central banks, and international organizations. Few countries have also established innovation accelerators where central bank supports the projects that use innovative technologies. In France, the innovation accelerator of Bank of France set up an intrapreneurship program aimed to dedicated supervisory tools.

CHALLENGES FOR AND RESPONSES FROM REGULATORS

Preventing regulatory arbitrage is major challenge for any regulatory approach to fintech activities. Authorities need to ensure that regulations do not establishes unnecessary differences in the requirements. If discrepancies cannot be avoided, there must be strong justification based on different types of risks. Big tech firms have entered in the financial system and present direct competition to traditional financial institutions in the financial system. For regulators, this situation presents new challenges nationally and internationally. Big tech firms have some competitive advantages due to large customer base, high capitalization, and expertise in innovative technologies. This might reduce the strength of financial institutions and therefore authorities need to come up with a policy framework to address risks on fair competition and financial stability. The rise of global cryptoassets (such a Stablecoins) poses new risks (such as risks of monopoly, and financial instability) that will require national and international level collaboration among authorities to ensure a globally consistent response to mitigate these risks. Absence of coherent standards and technology interoperability is another challenge. For example, in the absence of generally accepted standards of API, third parties can suffer from inefficiencies. Similarly, international standards are required for DLT technology.

Ensuring fairness, accountability, and transparency in AI and ML applications is another challenge. Various algorithms operating on similar data may provide diverse results. This situation poses serious concerns about the way data is processed and potential risks of discrimination, financial exclusion, and exploitation. Governance and risk management frameworks need enhancement to address these risks. The number of third-party service providers is increasing as well as reliance of institutions on their services. This dependency, in case of critical services, could disturb the activities of multiple financial market participants. Financial institutions need appropriate management of risks associated with outsourcing. This applies to cloud computing, AI, and ML service providers as well. For developing a digital strategy that leverages digital economy, a digital infrastructure and harmonized policies on digital identification, data privacy, and data security. A prerequisite for this is strong coordination among authorities, industry, and academia. Implementation of digital identification systems can provide economic and social benefits (such as inclusive digital financial services). However, the implementation is faced with many challenges. Authorities need to assess potential risks and misuses of digital ID systems by the public or businesses.

The economic value of consumer data is increasing. Therefore, regulators need to enhance data protection frameworks to give citizens rights to own and control their data. Authorities also need to enhance their coordination at a national and international level. Increasing institutional capacity to respond to cyber threats is a priority for regulators of financial industry. To achieve this goal, authorities would need to implement or strengthen existing cyber security frameworks. Some authorities have introduced assessment for identification of flaws in institutional cyber security framework. Some authorities (e.g., UK) are seeking use of simulations to assess resilience of financial industry against cyber threats. Authorities would also need to address potential risks associated with innovation facilitators. Consumers may consider that that any company in a sandbox or accelerator got quality approval from the regulator. Therefore, regulators need to inform customers that the financial product that they are obtaining is in a testing phase.

CONCLUSION

Fintech has not brought significant changes in the main objective of financial regulators i.e., to ensure safety and soundness of financial system. The regulators must keep a close eye on the threats safety and soundness of the financial system to ensure that all stakeholders trust the financial system. Otherwise, the potential benefits of fintech will not be sustainable. Technological developments have not brought significant financial regulations. The fundamental requirements of consumer protection and system integrity are still the same. For fintech, regulators are trying to develop a regulatory regime that promotes innovation and reduce risks to the financial system. To develop such a regulatory regime, regulators face many policy trade-offs. Fintech activities may represent unidentified risks that could require authorities to enforce stringent requirements. These requirements may be negatively influence competition and innovation. For many fintech activities there exist dedicated regulatory regimes. In absence of dedicated regulatory regime, fintech activities are normally subject to existing regulatory regimes. It is crucial that authorities cooperate and coordinate at the national and international level.

The challenge here is the control of increased coordination within a jurisdiction. Authorities would require adjustments in their supervisory frameworks for fintech activities. These changes may be in the form of a general dedicated fintech unit or a specialized fintech unit. Adequate expertise and resources are key requirements to for the supervision of fintech industry. Another common challenge would be that regulators may need to modify reporting requirements for fintech industry.

REFERENCES

Abraham, F., Schmukler, S. L., & Tessada, J. (2019). Robo-advisors: Investing through machines. *World Bank Research and Policy Briefs,* 134881.

Adrian, T., & Griffoli, T. M. (2019, July). *The Rise of Digital Money*. IMF. https://www.imf.org/en/Publications/fintech-notes/Issues/2019/07/12/The-Rise-of-Digital-Money-47097

Advapay. (2021, November 8). Electronic Money Institution Regulation in the EU – E-Money Directive (EMD2). *Advapay*. https://advapay.eu/electronic-money-institution-regulation-in-the-eu-e-money-directive-emd2/

Alaassar, A., Mention, A.-L., & Aas, T. H. (2022). Facilitating innovation in FinTech: A review and research agenda. *Review of Managerial Science*, 1–34.

Bank of England. (2022). *New Bank Start-Up Unit*. Bank of England. https://www.bankofengland.co.uk/prudential-regulation/new-bank-start-up-unit

Basel Committee on Banking Supervision. (2018). *Sound Practices: Implications of fintech developments for banks and bank supervisors*. BIS. https://www.bis.org/bcbs/publ/d431.htm

Belanche, D., Casaló, L. V., & Flavián, C. (2019). Artificial Intelligence in FinTech: Understanding robo-advisors adoption among customers. *Industrial Management & Data Systems*, *119*(7), 1411–1430. doi:10.1108/IMDS-08-2018-0368

Blandin, A., Cloots, A. S., Hussain, H., Rauchs, M., Saleuddin, R., Allen, J. G., Zhang, B. Z., & Cloud, K. (2019). *Global cryptoasset regulatory landscape study.* University of Cambridge Faculty of Law Research Paper, 23.

Bloomberg. (2022). *WeLend Ltd—Company Profile and News*. Bloomberg Markets. https://www.bloomberg.com/profile/company/1469380D:HK

Buckley, R. P., Arner, D., Veidt, R., & Zetzsche, D. (2020). Building FinTech ecosystems: Regulatory sandboxes, innovation hubs and beyond. *Wash. UJL & Pol'y*, *61*, 55.

Chaves, S. M. (2019). *Industry Study of Electronic Money*. Retrieved From.

Committee on Payment and & Settlement Systems. (2004). *Survey of developments in electronic money and internet and mobile payments*. BIS. https://www.bis.org/cpmi/publ/d62.pdf

Dubey, V. (2019). FinTech innovations in digital banking. [IJERT]. *International Journal of Engineering Research & Technology (Ahmedabad)*, *8*(10), 597–601.

Ehrentraud, J., Ocampo, D. G., Garzoni, L., & Piccolo, M. (2020). *Policy responses to fintech: A cross-country overview* [Basel]. Bank for International Settlements, Financial Stability Institute.

European Banking Authority. (2018). *EBA Report On The Prudential Risks And Opportunities Arising For Institutions From Fintech*. EBA. fundacionmicrofinanzasbbva.org/revistaprogreso/wp-content/up loads/2018/08/pub-Reportonprudentialrisksandopportunitiesari singforinstitutionsfromFinTech.pdf

Financial Stability Board. (2017). *Financial stability implications from FinTech: Supervisory and regulatory issues that merit authorities' attention*. FSB. https://www.fsb.org/wp-content/uploads/R270617.pdf

Financial Stability Board. (2019a, February 14). *FinTech and market structure in financial services: Market developments and potential financial stability implications*. FSB. https://www.fsb.org/2019/02/fintech-and-market-structure-in-financial-services-market-developments-and-potential-financial-stability-implications/

Financial Stability Board. (2019b, June 6). *Decentralised financial technologies: Report on financial stability, regulatory and governance implications*. FSB. https://www.fsb.org/2019/06/decentralised-financial-technologies-report-on-financial-stability-regulatory-and-governance-implications/

FSB. (2017, May 22). *FinTech Credit: Market Structure, Business Models and Financial Stability Implications*. FSB. https://www.fsb.org/2017/05/fintech-credit-market-structure-business-models-and-financial-stability-implications/

Havrylchyk, O. (2018). *Regulatory framework for the loan-based crowdfunding platforms*. Ideas.https://ideas.repec.org/p/oec/ecoaaa/1513-en.html

Hong Kong Monetary Authority. (2019). *Authorization Of Virtual Banks*. HKMA. https://www.hkma.gov.hk/media/eng/doc/key-functions/banking-stability/guide-authorization/Chapter-9.pdf

Horn, M., Oehler, A., & Wendt, S. (2020). FinTech for consumers and retail investors: Opportunities and risks of digital payment and investment services. In Ecological, Societal, and Technological Risks and the Financial Sector (pp. 309–327). Springer.

Huang, R. H., Wang, C. C., & Zhang, O. X. (2022). The development and regulation of robo-advisors in Hong Kong: Empirical and comparative perspectives. *Journal of Corporate Law Studies*, 1–35.

IMF. (2018, September). *The Bali Fintech Agenda*. IMF. https://www.imf.org/en/Publications/Policy-Papers/Issues/2018/10/11/pp101118-bali-fintech-agenda

IMF. (2022). Fast-Moving FinTech Poses Challenge for Regulators. *IMF Blog*. https://blogs.imf.org/2022/04/13/fast-moving-fintech-poses-challenge-for-regulators/

International Organization of Securities Commissions. (2017). *IOSCO Research Report on Financial Technologies (Fintech)*. IOSCO. https://www.iosco.org/library/pubdocs/pdf/IOSCOPD554.pdf

Landerer, L. M. (2022). The Anti-Money-Laundering Directive and the ECJ's Jurisdiction on Data Retention: A Flawed Comparison? *Eucrim-the European Criminal Law Associations'. Forum, 01*, 67–72.

Macheel, T. (2021, June 30). *American Express partners with fintech firms to help customers find mortgages*. CNBC. https://www.cnbc.com/2021/06/30/american-express-is-sending-customers-to-fintech-partners-for-mortgages.html

Madir, J. (2021). *FinTech: Law and Regulation*. Edward Elgar Publishing.

nerdwallet. (2022). Quicken Loans Mortgage Review 2022. *NerdWallet*. https://www.nerdwallet.com/reviews/mortgages/quicken-loans-mortgage

OECD. (2021). *Strengthening Macroprudential Policies in Emerging Asia: Adapting to Green Goals and Fintech*. OECD. doi:10.1787/6f1ed069-

Peterson, I., & Mallesons, W. (2021, September). Banking Regulation in Australia: Overview. *Practical Law*. https://uk.practicallaw.thomsonreuters.com/w-006-9098?transitionType=Default&contextData=(sc.Default)

Raimi, L., Kah, J. M., & Tariq, M. U. (2022). The Discourse of Blue Economy Definitions, Measurements, and Theories: Implications for Strengthening Academic Research and Industry Practice. In Implications for Entrepreneurship and Enterprise Development in the Blue Economy (pp. 1-17). IGI Global.

Reuters. (2017, September 12). Leader of China's $9 billion Ezubao online scam gets life; 26 jailed. *Reuters*. https://www.reuters.com/article/us-china-fraud-idUSKCN1BN0J6

The International Association of Insurance Supervisors. (2017). *FinTech Developments in the Insurance Industry*. IAIS. https://www.iaisweb.org/uploads/2022/01/Report_on_FinTech_Developments_in_the_Insurance_Industry.pdf

He, D., Leckow, R., Haksar, V., Griffoli, T., Jenkinson, N., Kashima, M., Khiaonarong, T., Rochon, C., & Tourpe, H. (2017). *Fintech and Financial Services:Initial Considerations*. IMF. https://www.imf.org/en/Publications/Staff-Discussion-Notes/Issues/2017/06/16/Fintech-and-Financial-Services-Initial-Considerations-44985

World Bank. (2020). *How Regulators Respond To FinTech: Evaluating the Different Approaches – Sandboxes and Beyond*. World Bank. https://openknowledge.worldbank.org/handle/10986/33698

Yan, T. C., Schulte, P., & Chuen, D. L. K. (2018). *InsurTech and FinTech: Banking and insurance enablement. Handbook of Blockchain* (Vol. 1). Digital Finance, and Inclusion.

Section 2
FinTech Challenges

Chapter 3
Why Strong Banks Fail

Peterson K. Ozili
https://orcid.org/0000-0001-6292-1161
Central Bank of Nigeria, Abuja, Nigeria

ABSTRACT

Many bank failures have occurred in history. The lessons learnt from past bank failures remind us that any bank can fail, and they fail for different reasons. The first step to avoid the failure of a strong bank is to identify the factors that cause the failure of a strong bank. This paper focus on strong banks and identifies the reasons why strong banks might fail. The reasons why a strong bank might fail are numerous. The insights offered in the article can help existing banks to avoid a bank failure in the future. The insights also have financial stability implications which need to be taken seriously.

INTRODUCTION

The purpose of this paper is to identify the reasons why strong banks might fail. Banks play an important role in society. As financial intermediaries, they collect funds from savers and depositors and allocate these funds to businesses and entrepreneurs, thereby fulfilling their main intermediary function of channeling funds from surplus units to the deficit units (Hellwig, 1991; Thakor & Boot, 2008; Bord & Santos, 2012). Banks allocate funds to economic agents to carry out investment and production activities towards economic growth.

But for banks to perform their function effectively, regulators want banks to be stable and strong (Einarsson & Marquis, 2001; Gorton & Winton, 2003). A term used to describe this is 'bank stability'. A bank is considered to be stable or strong when the bank has adequate capital, sufficient liquidity, high cost efficiency, high

DOI: 10.4018/978-1-6684-6381-9.ch003

Copyright © 2023, IGI Global. Copying or distributing in print or electronic forms without written permission of IGI Global is prohibited.

profitability, good management quality and low nonperforming loans, which together ensures that the bank is capable of withstanding unexpected losses and external shocks (Brauers et al, 2014; Köhler, 2015; Ozili, 2018). A bank is also considered to be 'strong' if its liquidity ratio, asset quality ratio, efficiency ratio and profitability ratio are within regulatory limits or when the ratios meet and exceed regulatory thresholds, thereby providing additional stability buffers. Banks that meet these criteria are considered to be 'strong,' hence, the term 'strong banks.'

History is replete with many strong and powerful banks that suddenly collapsed. Examples are Northern Rock in the United Kingdom and Bear Stearns in the United States. Many strong banks, that were once reputable and dominated the banking industry, have lost pre-eminence and have either become a shadow of their former selves or have collapsed and disappeared. Bank failure is a major concern for regulators and market participants because of the possible contagion across the banking sector and the subsequent collapse of the financial system (Luu, Doan, & Anh, 2021; Allen & Gale, 2000).

The fact that strong banks can suddenly fail is proof that there is an incomplete understanding of the causes of bank failure. Of course, some would argue that the choices, commitments, and actions of the executive management of strong banks are responsible for the failure of strong banks. While these factors may play a role in the failure of a strong bank, there are deeper causes of bank failure that need to be unmasked. Therefore, this paper identifies some of the reasons why strong banks might fail. An understanding of why strong banks might fail is crucial because it helps in developing prudential regulatory frameworks that enhance the stability and health of the banking sector. The insights gained from such understanding can help existing strong banks to avoid actions that could lead to bank failure in the future. Furthermore, the literature has examined the failure of weak banks (Braun & Deeg, 2020; Tamirisa & Igan, 2008; Tsagkarakis, Doumpos, & Pasiouras, 2021; De Grauwe & Ji, 2013). But there has been very little discussion about the failure of a strong bank. This study focus on strong banks and identifies some factors that could trigger the failure of a strong bank.

This study contributes to the bank stability literature (see, Köhler, 2015; Ozili, 2018; Nier, 2005; Ozili, 2020; Chava & Purnanandam, 2011; Englund, 1999; Cabane & Lodge, 2022; Lskavyan, 2020). It adds to existing studies that examine how certain events have triggered the failure of banks – both weak banks and strong banks. The study extends the literature by turning the focus to strong banks and identifying the factors that could trigger the failure of a strong bank. This paper also contributes to the banking crisis literature. The literature show that strong banks are more likely to survive a banking crisis due to their strong prudential ratios. However, some bank failures may be unrelated to changes in banks' prudential ratios and I identify some factors that could trigger the failure of a strong bank.

The rest of the paper is structured as follows. Section 2 presents a literature review of the general causes of bank failure. Section 3 presents a case study of an erstwhile strong bank that failed. Section 4 presents some reasons why strong banks fail. Section 5 concludes the paper.

RELATED LITERATURE

Some studies define bank failure. For instance, Calomiris (2007) states that bank failures result either from unwarranted depositor withdrawals during a crisis event characterized by contagion or panic, or as the result of fundamental bank insolvency. According to Arena (2005), a bank failure can occur when (i) a financial institution is recapitalized by either the central bank or an agency specifically created to address the crisis or when a financial institution receives a liquidity injection from the monetary authority; (ii) a financial institution's operations are temporarily suspended ("frozen") by the government; (iii) the government closed the financial institution; (iv) the financial institution is absorbed or acquired by another financial institution. Cebula, Koch, and Fenili (2011) show that a bank failure occurs when a bank is forced by regulators either to close or to merge with another banking institution.

Other studies examine the causes and factors that predict bank failure. Estrella, Park and Peristiani (2000) show that a simple leverage ratio and gross revenue ratio perform well in predicting bank failure over longer horizons. Liu and Ngo (2014) examine the effect of elections and political competition on bank failure. They find that bank failure is 45 percent less likely to occur in the year leading up to an election. Amel-Zadeh and Meeks (2013) argue that bank failures might occur despite banks having adequate capital and a solvent balance sheet. They also argue that banks may fail due to sudden shocks to liquidity positions as this was the major cause of the failure of Northern Rock. Antoniades (2021) show that the cause of commercial bank failures during the Great Recession was exposure to the real estate sector. It was argued that the main exposure was credit to non-household real estate borrowers (Antoniades, 2021). Private-label mortgage-backed securities contributed to the failure of large banks (Antoniades, 2021). Also, failed banks skewed their portfolios towards product categories that performed poorly on aggregate which made their downfall unavoidable. Carmona, Climent and Momparler (2019) used extreme gradient boosting methodology to predict bank failure in the U.S. banking sector. They use data from 2001 to 2015 and find that lower values for retained earnings to average equity ratio, pretax return on asset ratio and the total risk-based capital ratio are associated with a higher risk of bank failure. Assaf, Berger, Roman and Tsionas (2019) examine how bank efficiency during normal times affects bank survival, risk, and profitability during financial crises. They used data from five U.S.

financial crises and preceding normal times. They find that cost efficiency during normal times helps to reduce the probability of bank failure during financial crises.

Fungacova, Turk and Weill (2015) show that decaying capital ratios, reduced liquidity, deteriorating loan quality, and depleted earnings are signals of an increased likelihood of bank failure. Chiaramonte, Liu, Poli and Zhou (2016), using data from U.S. commercial banks, find that Z-score can predict 76 percent of bank failure, and the prediction power of Z-score remains stable within the three-year forward window. Daley, Matthews and Whitfield (2008) examine banks in Jamaica, and find that real GDP growth, size and managerial efficiency were the most significant factors contributing to the failure of banks where bank failure was defined to include bailout and regulator-induced or supervised merger. Chennells and Wingfield (2015) show that several governments bailed out failing financial institutions. They proposed a bail-in framework which allows the authorities to make sure that shareholders and creditors of a firm bear the costs of failure without recourse to public funds. Meanwhile, Brown and Dinç (2011) show that a government is less likely to take over or close a failing bank if the banking system is weak.

Cooke, Koch and Murphy (2015) define liquidity mismatch as the risk of a bank being unable to fund increases in assets or meet its obligations as they come due. They show that liquidity mismatch increased in the U.S. banking sector during the run-up to the financial crisis especially among largest institutions. Cooke, Koch, and Murphy (2015) suggest that exposing shareholders to more downside risk can successfully reduce bank failure. Luu, Doan, and Anh (2021) investigate the impact of managerial ability on bank failure, and find that more ably managed banks experienced lower failure probability, and such banks have more adequate capital, better asset quality, greater efficiency in the allocation of resources, higher liquidity and lower risk. Ferreira, Lloyd-Braga and Modesto (2016) revisit the ‘competition-fragility’ and ‘competition-stability’ debate, and argue that more competition always raises the risk of bank default, and a higher intensity of competition in the loan market can result in an increase in deposit rates rather than a decrease of loan rates. Pruitt (2017) shows that a liquidity shortfall in the United States triggered the bankruptcy of several large commercial banks, and bank failures continue to occur with 50 banks failing between 2013 and 2015. Colander et al (2009) argue that economists not only failed to anticipate the 2008 financial crisis; they may have contributed to it by encouraging policy makers and market participants to see more stability and risk-sharing benefits of derivatives before the 2008 financial crisis. Alvarez-Franco and Restrepo-Tobón (2016) show that managerial inefficiency and loan quality are strong predictors of bank failure. Subramanian (2011) shows that the global financial crisis was both a failure of markets and failure of regulation.

Cihak and Poghosyan (2009) analyze the causes of banking distress in Europe and identify a set of indicators and thresholds that can help to distinguish strong banks and weak banks. They found that cost-to-income ratios and basic liquidity indicators do not seem to have a good predictive power. Instead, a liquidity indicator that captures the share of wholesale financing in liabilities have a good predictive power of a banking failure. Also, the probability of distress in a bank is significantly higher if there was a recent distress in a bank of a comparable size in the same country. Andrews (2019) show that weak banks usually have zombie firms as customers, and this explains why weak banks experience distress and are more likely to fail. Zombie firms are firms that would typically exit in a competitive market. Zombie firms are also firms that earn just enough money to continue operating and service their debt. They have no excess capital to spur growth.

Other studies examine weak banks relative to strong banks. For instance, De Grauwe and Ji (2013) show that banks operating in countries with financially strong governments follow business strategies aimed at issuing too much subsidized debt which weaken their balance sheets and make them become more fragile, weak, and less able to withstand future shocks. As a result, there will be weaker banks in countries with financially strong governments. In contrast, banks operating in countries with financially weak governments are forced to strengthen themselves because they are unable to rely on their governments to bail them out if they fail. As a result, there will be more strong banks in countries with financially weak governments. They conclude that financially strong governments breed fragile banks while financially weak governments breed strong banks. Brown and Dinç, (2011) show that a government is less likely to take over or close a failing bank if the banking system is weak because of the too-many-to-fail effect which is stronger for larger banks and when there is a large government budget deficit. Tamirisa and Igan (2008) found that, during credit booms, weaker banks increase lending faster than stronger banks which leads to credit booms. They conclude that supervisors need to carefully monitor the soundness of rapidly expanding banks during credit booms and they should monitor the credit expansion of weak banks.

A CASE STUDY OF A STRONG BANK – NORTHERN ROCK

Background

Northern Rock bank was a strong bank in the United Kingdom. It became a victim of the 2008 financial crisis. Prior to being a bank, Northern Rock was previously a building society. It had demutualized and was listed on the FTSE 100. Soon, it became the fourth biggest bank in the United Kingdom by share of lending. Only 23 percent of its liabilities were in the form of retail deposits by June 2007. The remaining 77 percent of the bank's funding came from a combination of short-term borrowing in the capital markets and securitized notes and other longer-term funding sources (Shin, 2009).

The Cause

When the sub-prime crisis started in America, the short-term funding market and interbank lending froze. What triggered the crisis event was the news that the French bank BNP Paribas had closed the three investment vehicles that invested in U.S. subprime mortgage assets using short-term borrowed money. BNP Paribus took the action because many other investment vehicles and financial institutions that tapped short-term financing had already begun experiencing difficulties in renewing their short-term borrowing (Shin, 2009). Although Northern Rock did not participate significantly in subprime lending, Northern Rock was financing its activities from the same pool of short-term funding (Shin, 2009; Keasey & Veronesi, 2008). Northern Rock bank could not access money from international financial markets or the money market anymore. They became the first casualty in the United Kingdom. The bank requested for liquidity support facility from the Bank of England because it had difficulties in raising funds in the money market to replace its maturing money market borrowings.

Run On the Bank

The BBC broke the news that Northern Rock needed central bank support. The central bank announced that it would provide liquidity support to the bank. The next day after the central bank announcement, there were large queues outside all the branch offices of Northern Rock bank. Depositors had queued up to collect all their deposits at once from Northern Rock. This became the first ever run on a British bank in 150 years.

Consequence

Months after, the bank could not outlive the stigma of the bank run it experienced. Customers did not want to keep money with Northern Rock bank. The bank was later nationalized by the UK government in early 2008. After the collapse of the bank, the bank's assets and operations were split into 'good assets' and 'bad assets' as well as 'good operations' and 'bad operations.' Virgin Money acquired the good part. The government bought the bad part and payed using taxpayers' money. The entire bank was later sold to Virgin money four years later. The demise of Northern Rock bank led to the loss of about 2,500 jobs. The collapse of the erstwhile strong bank 'Northern Rock' also led to the collapse of Northern Rock Foundation, a charitable trust which received 5 percent of Northern Rock bank's profit each year.

Lesson Learned

The most important lesson learnt from the failure of Northern Rock, an erstwhile strong bank, is that the government's agreement to bail out Northern Rock, which triggered a run on the bank, should have been kept secret to prevent panic. The failure to keep the planned intervention secret led to the first run on a British bank since 1866. This demonstrates that a strong bank can fail when there is negative media publicity about its problems. People's reaction to the disclosure of bad information about a bank can lead a large number of depositors to withdraw deposits from the bank. This is one of many cases where a strong bank has failed despite having good prudential regulatory ratios. In the next section, I identify other reasons why a strong bank might fail.

REASONS WHY STRONG BANKS FAIL

Below are some reasons why a strong bank might fail despite having strong prudential ratios and a robust balance sheet.

Engaging in a Bad Acquisition

One quick indicator of whether a strong bank will fail is the type of acquisition the bank wants to close in on, and whether the acquisition will bring doom or bliss to the strong bank. The management of strong banks may focus more on the reward of an acquisition while downplaying the risks of the acquisition as they seek to get the buy-in of shareholders in support of the acquisition. Ideally, both the buyer and seller need to feel that they are getting a good value for the acquisition. The corporate seller has to convince its board and shareholders that the sale price is high enough to ensure that the seller gets good value from selling the business at that price. On the other hand, the corporate buyer wants to avoid paying too much for the acquisition, and convince its board and shareholders that they are getting a good bargain, and that the combination of the two company will bring great value to the buyer such as higher revenue, cost savings and other competitive advantages. Placing more emphasis on reward rather than on the risk of acquisitions has been a reason why large acquisitions by strong banks fail in the banking sector. The executive management of the strong bank and shareholders who gave the approval are to blame for bad acquisitions that lead to the collapse of an erstwhile strong bank. Acquisitions by strong banks go wrong when the management of the buyer bank fails to inform shareholders about the known risks of the acquisition and the full implication of known risks (Howe and Morillon, 2020). A strong bank may fail if the known risks are not properly managed on time, and when unknown risks emerge that affect the bank's market share in the industry. Acquisitions can also go wrong when the seller fails to disclose all its liabilities, especially contingent liabilities and implicit guarantees, to the buyer bank.

Reckless Lending or Pushing Credit Too Far

Risky lending can be pushed too far to a point where borrowers default on loan repayment, and only a small amount of loan recovery can be made from pledged collaterals (Chen, Chou, Chang and Fang, 2015; Nguyen and Boateng, 2013). Strong banks have more freedom to lend money to as many borrowers as possible because they have strong fundamentals and have stable regulatory prudential ratios (Flannery, 1995; Brunnermeier et al, 2009; Tressel and Verdier, 2014; Watanabe, 2007). Banks with strong fundamentals can give too many loans to businesses in a specific sector or too much loans to few companies or individuals, thereby exceeding the regulatory single obligor limit and increasing concentration risk. This creates more credit risk, and may lead to unexpected loan defaults. Unexpected loan defaults can diminish the interest income of strong banks, and decrease their profit. Unexpected loan defaults can also translate credit risk to liquidity risk especially when strong banks need to use the repaid loans to pay depositors that come to collect cash from the bank. This can put strong banks in a difficult position and could lead to bank failure.

Board Squabbles

Board squabbles can create fragilities in the corporate governance of a strong bank. Strong banks may face deep-rooted board squabbles on strategic and tactical issues. Board squabbles may arise from top executive's disagreement about a change of control. Board squabbles may arise from differences in opinions about the strategic direction and decisions of the strong bank. The disgruntled top executives would seek to take sides with major shareholders that share their own perspectives on strategic and tactical issues. This would lead to disagreement among major shareholders, and the disgruntled major shareholders may impose changes on the board that could increase in-fighting within the management ranks of a strong bank. This could lead to bigger problems in the bank as employees may feel divided on the overall positioning of the bank. This could trigger mass resignations, loss of bank customers and loss of market share in the industry. This could lead to the collapse of the strong bank.

Bank Run

A bank run occurs when large number of bank depositors withdraw their money from banks simultaneously based on fears that banks will become insolvent or fears that banks will run out of money to pay all depositors (Brown, Trautmann, & Vlahu, 2017; Ozili, 2018). A strong bank – located in the same neighborhood where a distressed bank is located – may fail when a bank run on a distressed bank triggers a bank run on a strong bank. A bank run on distressed banks can trigger a bank run on strong banks located in the same neighborhood where distressed banks are located. This is because depositors do not have full information about which banks are safe and which banks are about to collapse (Dijk, 2017). They do not know which banks will be the next to fail or go bankrupt. As a result, a large number of depositors would seek safety by taking out all their deposits from all banks both weak banks and strong banks. Consequently, the massive removal of deposits from strong banks would cause strong banks to fail because no bank in the world has all the money to pay its depositors at once.

Major Lawsuits

Lawsuit is one of the risks that banks face (Fiordelisi, Soana, & Schwizer, 2014; Yuan & Zhang, 2015). This is because strong banks take more risks in search for higher profit or increase in market share. As a result, they are more likely to face increasing lawsuits that could potentially cost them millions of dollars in claims. Strong banks increasingly face lawsuits from their customers, competitors, and suppliers and for various reasons such as excess bank charges, wrongful seizure of collateral, contract breaches, fraud, disclosure breaches, etc. Strong banks often respond to lawsuits by hiring the services of some of the best law firms to help with litigation and contract services. They may also have a fully staffed legal services department to help protect the bank against risks arising from lawsuits. However, major lawsuits can damage the reputation of strong banks, and the lawsuit penalty payments can significantly deplete bank profit and capital. If shareholders are unhappy about the reputational damage to the strong bank, they may lose confidence in the strong bank and refuse to recapitalize the bank. This can lead to a collapse of the strong bank.

Withdrawal of Banking License

Bank failure that arises from banking license withdrawal or revocation is not a technical bank failure. Rather, such failure is a statutory bank failure that arise from either a change in bank structure or a change in bank form or operations. A strong bank would face a statutory bank failure when its banking license is withdrawn or revoked by the banking regulator. The withdrawal or revocation of a banking license of a strong bank means that the strong bank can no longer conduct banking business anymore, and would lose its customers and its banking business. Regulators can withdraw a banking license when the strong bank no longer pursues regulated banking or financial activities, or when the strong bank is requesting a license to change to a different institutional category such as changing its business from being a banking institution to being an insurance company. Another scenario is when a strong bank merges with another institution and ceases to be a legal entity in its own right.

Ignoring the Competition and Innovation

Failure to compete and innovate could lead to the downfall of a strong bank. Strong banks may overestimate the strength of their banking business, and turn a blind eye to the competition and innovation occurring in the banking industry. By failing to innovate and ignoring the competition, strong banks would be left behind. By the time the emerging competition and innovation matures, strong banks would realize that they are behind the competition and innovation, and they would be overwhelmed by the competition and innovation in the banking industry. They would struggle to catch up, and might fail. A strong bank that fails to innovate and blatantly ignore competition could face an impending bank failure.

Responding to Competition and Innovation – Too Little, Too Late

When the banking industry changes, the changes are bound to result in losers and winners. The losers are not only those who fail to respond to the changes, the losers will also include those who respond too little or too late. When strong banks face unprecedented changes such as intense competition and innovation in the banking environment, they may not respond effectively to the changes. Strong banks that respond too late or too little to the competition will lose their customers to rival banks, watch their employees leave, and witness a significant decrease in fee income. One of the reasons why a strong bank may act too late or too little could be due to managerial stubbornness, sheer incompetence, inactive inertia, rigid devotion to the status quo, or the strong bank's refusal to change its established patterns of behavior even when the competition in the banking industry requires the strong bank to change its established patterns of behavior.

CONCLUSION

This paper identified the reasons why strong banks might fail. There are multiple reasons why a strong bank might fail, and the reasons offered in this paper are not exhaustive. The study identified the following factors that can lead to the failure of strong banks: engaging in a bad acquisition, reckless lending or pushing credit too far, board squabbles, bank run, major lawsuits, withdrawal of banking license, ignoring competition and innovation, and responding too late to competition and innovation.

The policy implication of this findings is that a strong bank can fail even if it has good micro-prudential regulatory ratios such as capital adequacy and nonperforming loans ratio. Micro-prudential regulatory ratios alone cannot guarantee the safety of banks. Strong banks will require a combination of careful planning, funding, skills, research work, extensive experience, and expert knowledge to navigate the changing banking environment if they do not want to fail. Policy makers also need to focus on entity-based and activity-based regulation to forestall the failure of strong banks. Entity-based and activity-based regulation are justified when the failure of a strong bank is caused by the decisions of its managers and the activities they engage in. Entity-based and activity-based regulation restrict the actions of a strong bank that could increase the risk of failure. Such regulation can impose constraints on one item of bank balance sheets and tighten such constraints for strong banks whose failure will have systemic risk consequences.

Future studies in this area can re-examine the case of strong banks and assess the type of regulation that is appropriate to regulate strong banks. Future studies can also examine other country-specific cases of the failure of strong banks. Future studies can also identify other behavioral factors that increase the risk of failure of strong banks.

REFERENCES

Allen, F., & Gale, D. (2000). Financial contagion. *Journal of Political Economy*, *108*(1), 1–33. doi:10.1086/262109

Alvarez-Franco, P. B., & Restrepo-Tobón, D. A. (2016). Managerial efficiency and failure of US commercial banks during the 2007-2009 financial crisis: Was this time different? *Ecos de Economía*, *20*(43), 4–22. doi:10.17230/ecos.2016.43.1

Amel-Zadeh, A., & Meeks, G. (2013). Bank failure, mark-to-market and the financial crisis. *Abacus*, *49*(3), 308–339. doi:10.1111/abac.12011

Andrews, D. (2019). Breaking the shackles: Zombie firms, weak banks and depressed restructuring in Europe. *ECB Working Paper No. 2240.*

Antoniades, A. (2021). *Commercial bank failures during the Great Recession: The real (estate) story.* SSRN 2325261.

Arena, M. (2005). Bank Failures and Bank Fundamentals: A Comparative Analysis of Latin America and East Asia during the Nineties using Bank-Level Data. *Bank of Canada Working Paper No. 19.*

Assaf, A. G., Berger, A. N., Roman, R. A., & Tsionas, M. G. (2019). Does efficiency help banks survive and thrive during financial crises? *Journal of Banking & Finance, 106*, 445–470. doi:10.1016/j.jbankfin.2019.07.013

Bord, V., & Santos, J. A. (2012). The rise of the originate-to-distribute model and the role of banks in financial intermediation. *Economic Policy Review, 18*(2), 21–34.

Brauers, W. K. M., Ginevičius, R., & Podviezko, A. (2014). Development of a methodology of evaluation of financial stability of commercial banks. *Panoeconomicus, 61*(3), 349–367. doi:10.2298/PAN1403349B

Braun, B., & Deeg, R. (2020). Strong firms, weak banks: The financial consequences of Germany's export-led growth model. *German Politics, 29*(3), 358–381. doi:10.1080/09644008.2019.1701657

Brown, C. O., & Dinç, I. S. (2011). Too many to fail? Evidence of regulatory forbearance when the banking sector is weak. *Review of Financial Studies, 24*(4), 1378–1405. doi:10.1093/rfs/hhp039

Brown, M., Trautmann, S. T., & Vlahu, R. (2017). Understanding bank-run contagion. *Management Science, 63*(7), 2272–2282. doi:10.1287/mnsc.2015.2416

Brunnermeier, M., Crockett, A., Goodhart, C. A., Persaud, A., & Shin, H. S. (2009). *The fundamental principles of financial regulation* (Vol. 11). ICMB, Internat. Center for Monetary and Banking Studies.

Cabane, L., & Lodge, M. (2022). Banking Regulation in and for Crisis. In Oxford Research Encyclopedia of Politics. doi:10.1093/acrefore/9780190228637.013.1599

Calomiris, C. W. (2007). Bank failures in theory and history: the Great Depression and other" contagious" events. *NBER Working Paper No 13597.*

Carmona, P., Climent, F., & Momparler, A. (2019). Predicting failure in the US banking sector: An extreme gradient boosting approach. *International Review of Economics & Finance, 61*, 304–323. doi:10.1016/j.iref.2018.03.008

Cebula, R. J., Koch, J. V., & Fenili, R. N. (2011). The bank failure rate, economic conditions and banking statutes in the US, 1970–2009. *Atlantic Economic Journal, 39*(1), 39–46. doi:10.100711293-010-9258-7

Chava, S., & Purnanandam, A. (2011). The effect of banking crisis on bank-dependent borrowers. *Journal of Financial Economics, 99*(1), 116–135. doi:10.1016/j.jfineco.2010.08.006

Chen, T. H., Chou, H. H., Chang, Y., & Fang, H. (2015). The effect of excess lending on bank liquidity: Evidence from China. *International Review of Economics & Finance, 36*, 54–68. doi:10.1016/j.iref.2014.11.007

Chennells, L., & Wingfield, V. (2015). Bank failure and bail-in: an introduction. *Bank of England Quarterly Bulletin*, Q3.

Chiaramonte, L., Liu, H., Poli, F., & Zhou, M. (2016). How accurately can Z-score predict bank failure? *Financial markets, institutions & instruments, 25*(5), 333-360.

Cihak, M. M., & Poghosyan, M. T. (2009). *Distress in European Banks: An Analysis Basedon a New Dataset*. International Monetary Fund.

Colander, D., Goldberg, M., Haas, A., Juselius, K., Kirman, A., Lux, T., & Sloth, B. (2009). The financial crisis and the systemic failure of the economics profession. *Critical Review, 21*(2-3), 249–267. doi:10.1080/08913810902934109

Cooke, J. B., Koch, C., & Murphy, A. (2015). Liquidity mismatch helps predict bank failure and distress. *Economics Letters, 10*(6), 1–4.

Daley, J., Matthews, K., & Whitfield, K. (2008). Too-big-to-fail: Bank failure and banking policy in Jamaica. *Journal of International Financial Markets, Institutions and Money, 18*(3), 290–303. doi:10.1016/j.intfin.2006.12.002

De Grauwe, P., & Ji, Y. (2013). Strong governments, weak banks. *CEPS Policy Briefs*, (305).

Dijk, O. (2017). Bank run psychology. *Journal of Economic Behavior & Organization, 144*, 87–96. doi:10.1016/j.jebo.2017.08.005

Einarsson, T., & Marquis, M. H. (2001). Bank intermediation over the business cycle. *Journal of Money, Credit and Banking, 33*(4), 876–899. doi:10.2307/2673927

Englund, P. (1999). The Swedish banking crisis: Roots and consequences. *Oxford Review of Economic Policy, 15*(3), 80–97. doi:10.1093/oxrep/15.3.80

Estrella, A., Park, S., & Peristiani, S. (2000). Capital ratios as predictors of bank failure. *Economic Policy Review, 6*(2).

Ferreira, R. D. S., Lloyd-Braga, T., & Modesto, L. (2016). Could competition always raise the risk of bank failure? (No. 27). Bureau d'Economie Théorique et Appliquée, UDS, Strasbourg.

Fiordelisi, F., Soana, M. G., & Schwizer, P. (2014). Reputational losses and operational risk in banking. *European Journal of Finance*, *20*(2), 105–124. doi:10.1080/1351847X.2012.684218

Flannery, M. J. (1995). Prudential regulation for banks. In *Financial Stability in a Changing Environment* (pp. 281–328). Palgrave Macmillan. doi:10.1007/978-1-349-13352-9_8

Fungacova, Z., Turk, R., & Weill, L. (2015). *High Liquidity Creation and Bank Failures: Do They Behave Differently?* International Monetary Fund. doi:10.5089/9781475581805.001

Gorton, G., & Winton, A. (2003). Financial intermediation. In *Handbook of the Economics of Finance* (Vol. 1, pp. 431–552). Elsevier.

Hellwig, M. (1991). Banking, financial intermediation and corporate finance. *European financial integration, 35*, 63.

Howe, J. S., & Morillon, T. G. (2020). Do mergers and acquisitions affect information asymmetry in the banking sector? *Managerial Finance*, *46*(12), 1521–1547. doi:10.1108/MF-03-2020-0127

Keasey, K., & Veronesi, G. (2008). Lessons from the Northern Rock affair. *Journal of Financial Regulation and Compliance*, *16*(1), 8–18. doi:10.1108/13581980810853181

Köhler, M. (2015). Which banks are more risky? The impact of business models on bank stability. *Journal of Financial Stability*, *16*, 195–212. doi:10.1016/j.jfs.2014.02.005

Liu, W. M., & Ngo, P. T. (2014). Elections, political competition and bank failure. *Journal of Financial Economics*, *112*(2), 251–268. doi:10.1016/j.jfineco.2014.02.005

Lskavyan, V. (2020). Banking crisis and bank supervisory accountability. *Journal of Economics and Business*, *107*, 105863. doi:10.1016/j.jeconbus.2019.105863

Luu, H. N., Doan, T. N., & Anh, P. T. H. (2021). Managerial ability and bank failure. *Applied Economics Letters*, *28*(4), 305–309. doi:10.1080/13504851.2020.1752892

Nguyen, V. H. T., & Boateng, A. (2013). The impact of excess reserves beyond precautionary levels on bank lending channels in China. *Journal of International Financial Markets, Institutions and Money*, *26*, 358–377. doi:10.1016/j.intfin.2013.07.002

Nier, E. W. (2005). Bank stability and transparency. *Journal of Financial Stability*, *1*(3), 342–354. doi:10.1016/j.jfs.2005.02.007

Ozili, P. K. (2018). Banking stability determinants in Africa. *International Journal of Managerial Finance*, *14*(4), 462–483. doi:10.1108/IJMF-01-2018-0007

Ozili, P. K. (2020). 100 Quotes from the Global Financial Crisis: Lessons for the future. In *Uncertainty and Challenges in Contemporary Economic Behaviour*. Emerald Publishing Limited. doi:10.1108/978-1-80043-095-220201014

Pruitt, H. (2017). *Predicting bank failure using regulatory accounting data* [Doctoral dissertation, Walden University].

Shin, H. S. (2009). Reflections on Northern Rock: The bank run that heralded the global financial crisis. *The Journal of Economic Perspectives*, *23*(1), 101–119. doi:10.1257/jep.23.1.101

Tamirisa, N. T., & Igan, D. O. (2008). Are weak banks leading credit booms? Evidence from emerging Europe. *Comparative Economic Studies*, *50*(4), 599–619. doi:10.1057/ces.2008.35

Thakor, A. V., & Boot, A. (Eds.). (2008). *Handbook of financial intermediation and banking*. Elsevier.

Tressel, M. T., & Verdier, M. T. (2014). *Optimal prudential regulation of banks and the political economy of supervision*. International Monetary Fund. doi:10.5089/9781498338554.001

Tsagkarakis, M. P., Doumpos, M., & Pasiouras, F. (2021). Capital shortfall: A multicriteria decision support system for the identification of weak banks. *Decision Support Systems*, *145*, 113526. doi:10.1016/j.dss.2021.113526

Watanabe, W. (2007). Prudential regulation and the "credit crunch": Evidence from Japan. *Journal of Money, Credit and Banking*, *39*(2-3), 639–665. doi:10.1111/j.0022-2879.2007.00039.x

Yuan, Q., & Zhang, Y. (2015). Do banks price litigation risk in debt contracting? Evidence from class action lawsuits. *Journal of Business Finance & Accounting*, *42*(9-10), 1310–1340. doi:10.1111/jbfa.12164

Chapter 4
Ratings of Barriers and Challenges of Financial Technology in a Developing Economy

Samuel Narh Dorhetso
https://orcid.org/0000-0001-6070-5633
Accra Institute of Technology, Ghana

ABSTRACT

This study constructed an assessment of the barriers and challenges of financial technology (fintech) and accentuated a critical research area that is relatively new and currently understudied in extant literature. A theoretical framework was developed from a blend of the technology, organization, and environment (TOE) framework and the human, organization, and technology (HOT) fit model. The best-worst method was used to analyze and rank the identified barriers and challenges of fintech according to their weighted averages. The findings of the study point to perceived risk and lack of trust; transaction cost; privacy and security issues; legal and regulatory barriers; and the human element and psychological factors as the highest ranked barriers and challenges of financial technology. This study has significant theoretical and managerial implications for academia, policy makers, and practitioners, as it would stretch their standpoints on the best practices for adoption and implementation of fintech modernisms.

DOI: 10.4018/978-1-6684-6381-9.ch004

Copyright © 2023, IGI Global. Copying or distributing in print or electronic forms without written permission of IGI Global is prohibited.

INTRODUCTION

The delivery of financial services is anticipated to be transformed by financial technology (fintech), which denotes the employment of technology to give access to financial services (Fisher, 2015). Financial technology has also been defined as the deployment of technology to provide financial solutions (Arner, Barberis, & Buckley, 2016). The use of mobile phones to facilitate financial transactions through mobile payments ("momo" payments, as they are termed in Ghana) is a typical application of financial technology. Cryptocurrency exchanges such as Coinbase and Gemini, connecting users to buying or selling cryptocurrencies like bitcoin or litecoin, are also classic examples of applications of fintech. Fintech is a novel financial commerce that deploys technology to improve financial performances (Schueffel, 2017). The Financial Stability Board (2017b) describes fintech as technologically empowered financial innovations that could produce new business models, applications, methods, or yields with an accompanying material effect on financial markets and establishments, and delivery of financial facilities. Fintech can also be conceived as any innovative concept that advance financial service practices by offering technology solutions with regards to dissimilar business circumstances (Leong, 2018). The emphasis on technological innovations and its speed have amplified tremendously, although innovation in finance is not entirely a newfangled concept. Fintech resolutions that utilize big data analytics, artificial intelligence and block-chain technologies are currently presented at an extraordinary speed. These new technologies are transforming the nature of the financial industry, and generating several chances that enhances financial inclusion and improves access to financial services. Developments in e-finance and mobile technology for financial firms, which herded the revolution of fintech, emanated post the global financial crisis in 2008.

The 2008 financial crisis abridged faith in financial establishments, and the supervisory rejoinder to the crunch, including augmented capital demands and compliance costs, and rendered it more tough and costly for banks to give loans (Starnes, Kurdyla & Alexander, 2016). Puzzlingly, this fashioned a chance for less controlled, technology enabled non-bank entities to flourish, as they could give financial facilities more competitively and efficiently than their traditional counterparts who were loaded with heritage arrangements and regulations. The financial crisis coincided with the development of fintech, as consumers switched as a result of hardships faced in using traditional financial services (Mansilla-Fernández, 2017; Nitescu & Murgu, 2019; Knight & Wójcik, 2020). Also, digital revolutions of other businesses made clients more credulous of and contented with fintech solutions. Fintech also raised customer demand for immediacy, and tailored products and facilities. This progress was branded by integration in e-finance modernism, internet technology, social networking facilities, social media, artificial intelligence, and big data analytics (Lee & Shin, 2018). Fintech facilities are present in several transactions such as: mobile payments, e-commerce, portfolio management, risk management, customized consulting, systems integration, et cetera (Nicoletti, 2017). It helps to decentralize access to financial facilities, which is helpful for financial inclusion in emerging markets (Tiron-Tudor et al., 2019). The un-banked categories of the populace, as well as small firms, can access microloans through financial technology, thus enhancing their experience with financial services (Gatto, Polselli & Bloom, 2016; Gatto, 2018). However, the growing impact of fintech, despite its huge opportunities, is constrained with some grave barriers and challenges and it still has a tough path to gait on.

Notwithstanding the opportunities of fintech solutions, it still leaves the door ajar to several barriers and challenges, that may obstruct financial stability and customer protection. Examples of such barriers and challenges are cybersecurity and data privacy issues, low level of financial literacy and lack of consumer trust, problems with keeping up with modern technologies, issues with quality of software, and industry regulation and legal constraints. A few works have studied the barriers and challenges of financial technology (Krishna Priya & Anusha, 2019; Bromberg, Godwin & Ramsay, 2017; Wonglimpiyarat, 2018; Buchak et al., 2018; Tsai & Peng, 2017). Yet studies on the barriers and challenges of financial technology, from the perspective of a developing economy, are still in their infancy. To the best of the researcher's knowledge, no study has examined how these barriers and challenges are relevantly graded with regards to their relative importance to decision making. The relative degree of significance of the barriers and challenges of financial technology are not yet fully clarified in extant literature. Although the fintech zone is growing and has a rising clientele base, there are arguably no studies in extant literature that estimate the relative importance of the barriers and challenges of financial technology. However, knowledge on the relative importance of the barriers and challenges of financial technology may be required for managers and operators in the industry during crucial decisions, especially with regards to the allocation of resources. It is recommended that fintech industry managers should be encouraged to be in tune with the relative importance of its barriers and challenges to reduce their adverse effects on the spread of the innovation. Thus, this study identified a key research gap, and narrowed the knowledge gap by prioritizing the significant barriers and challenges of fintech using the best-worst method.

The best-worst method was chosen over other multi- criteria decision-making models (MCDMs) since it enables a small number of pairwise comparisons and produces high consistency rates. These characteristics of the BWM evince its key advantages over other weighting methods (Rezaei, 2015). Pairwise comparison data was collected from academics and experts in the fintech industry of organizations in

Ghana. The objective of this study was to estimate the relative degree of significance of the barriers and challenges of financial technology, using the technology, organization and environment (TOE) framework (Tornatzky & Fleischer, 1990) and the human, organization, and technology (HOT) fit model (Yusof, Paul & Stergioulas, 2006). A theoretical framework was developed from a mingle of the TOE framework and HOT fit model, and the best-worst method (Rezaei, 2015, 2016; Wang et al., 2019) was used to scrutinize and rank the identified barriers and challenges of financial technology according to their weighted averages. The new model categorized the barriers and challenges of financial technology into technology, organisation, environment and human dimensions. Within each of these dimensions, barriers and challenges were recognized by an amalgamation of literature from previous studies and opinions of fintech industry experts. By analyzing the relative degree of significance of the barriers and challenges of fintech, this paper would make significant contributions to both theory and practice. From a theoretical perspective, the application of the TOE framework and HOT fit model, and the best-worst method, would be extended with new insights from the fintech sector, and the relative significance of the barriers and challenges of the sector would be highlighted. From a managerial viewpoint, guidance for practitioners and policy makers on significant barriers and challenges of financial technology, during strategic decision making and practical implementation, would be provided by the outcome of the research. This inventive research built an estimation of the most significant barriers and challenges of fintech and corroborated some studies on the barriers and challenges of fintech. However, the method and context of this study differ from hitherto published documents on the subject of the study.

LITERATURE REVIEW

Financial facilities accessibility is still a challenge in the developing economies of the world (Demirguc-Kunt et al. 2018; Mohammad 2020). While providing financial facilities through technology is not a novel idea, devotion to fintech from an extensive cluster of stakeholders has been quite new (Arner, Barberis & Buckley, 2016), Consequently, research on the fintech subject in general is still in its initial stage and is increasingly developing. Fintech is developing and expanding in both developed and developing countries (Patil, Dwivedi & Rana, 2018). There have been a few studies on the barriers and challenges of financial technology, but none has been found from extant literature that deals with the relative level of importance of these barriers and challenges. Some of the barriers and challenges of fintech developments identified in extant literature include constraints placed on fintech firms, a less-sophisticated population, regulatory barriers, and information asymmetries (Arner, Barberis, & Buckley,2016; Dhar & Stein, 2017; Moradi, Naderi & Delangizan, 2020; OECD, 2020). Other barriers and challenging factors like consumer expectations concerning performance, perceived benefits, usefulness, usability, and associated risks can also impact a person's intent to embrace fintech facilities (Patil, Dwivedi, & Rana, 2018). The purpose of this study was to determine the relative degree of importance of the barriers and challenges of financial technology. The relevant barriers and challenges were identified from a broad and scrupulous literature review. The decision framework established and used in this research originated from a composite of the technology, organization, and environment (TOE) framework (Tornatzky & Fleischer, 1990), and the human, organisation, and technology (HOT) fit model (Yusof et al., 2006). This idiosyncratic research sought to fill the gap by developing a theoretical framework to study the barriers and challenges of financial technology, with regards to their relative importance. This study focused on the relative prominence of relevant barriers and challenges derived from literature. Nevertheless, it is not really focused on the desk research discovery of another crucial fintech barrier or challenge. The known barriers and challenges of financial technology, from existing literature, were discoursed with respect to technological, organizational, environmental, and human dimensions.

Identification of the Barriers and Challenges of Financial Technology

The decision framework established in this study emanated from a composite of the TOE framework and the HOT fit model. This characteristic framework was used to explore the weights and rankings of the barriers and challenges of financial technology. The model categorized the barriers and challenges of financial technology into technology, organization, environment and human dimensions, as shown in Table 1. Within each of these dimensions, there were driving factors that were recognized by a consolidation of literature from preceding studies and sentiments of fintech industry experts.

Table 1. A theoretical framework on the barriers and challenges of financial technology.

Dimensions	Factors	References
Technological (T)	Privacy and security issues (T1) Rapid developments in technology (T2) Interoperability of technologies (T3) Quality of software system and technology integration (T4)	Abouelmehdi, Beni-Hessane & Khaloufi (2018); Kang (2018), Brownsword (2019), Mittal & Kaur (2013), Jin & Wang (2019); Lee & Shin (2018); Saldinger (2018).
Organizational (O)	Low access to financial services (O1) High consumer expectations/perceived benefits (O2) Funding/cost of adoption (O3) Transaction cost (O4) Perceived risk and lack of trust (O5) Information asymmetry (O6) Institutional constraints on firms (O7)	Demirguc-Kunt et al. (2018); Mohammad (2020), Patil, Dwivedi & Rana (2018), Saldinger (2018); Luther (2016), Shiller (2013); Swiecka et al. (2020), Kim, Ferrin & Rao (2008); Mohammad (2020), Dhar, & Stein (2017); Moradi, Naderi & Delangizan (2020); Błach (2020), Arner, Barberis & Buckley (2016); OECD (2020).
Environmental (E)	Legal and regulatory barriers (E1) Competition (E2) Social norms and values (E3)	Arner, Barberis & Buckley (2016); Baxter (2016), OECD (2020); Carmona et al. (2019), Mohammad (2020).
Human (H)	Knowledge and financial literacy (H1) The human element and psychological factors (H2)	Fraczek & Klimontowicz (2015); Gustman, Steinmeier & Tabatabai (2012): Błach (2020), Saldinger (2018); Vermeulen (2004); Błach (2020).

Source: author's own construct

Technological Dimension

A critical obstacle in implementing fintech is the privacy and security of a person's personal data. Whiles adopting and implementing fintech projects, some effective measures must be taken to protect the sensitive personal information of the users. Privacy is the protection of sensitive information, and it is anchored on how data is used and governed, whilst security focuses on protecting data from theft for profit and destructive attacks (Abouelmehdi, Beni-Hessane, & Khaloufi, 2018). Privacy and security breaches can lead to mistrust of mobile applications and detrimentally affect an individual's intention to use fintech facilities (Kang, 2018). A lack of privacy and security standards can limit the development of fintech schemes that contain personal information such as income levels and medical history. Another fintech barrier and challenge emanates out of rapid developments in technologies such as artificial intelligence (AI), machine learning, and block chain (Brownsword, 2019). To reduce the impact of this constraint, tried and tested technologies must be deployed in fintech as technology tends to get out of date very fast. Governments of developing nations may not be in a good financial standing to procure new servers every year. Consequently, it is better and more secured to use technologies and products which have been tried and tested over longer periods of time, and are interoperable. Interoperability can be defined as the ability of systems and firms of different abilities to work together (Mittal & Kaur, 2013). A lack of interoperability amongst different fintech platforms and firms generates a havoc for the adoption and implementation of fintech applications. The fintech applications must be interoperable so that the newly developed and existing applications can be implemented together. Other critical issues which can become challenges for the adoption and implementation of fintech applications are the need to safeguard the quality of the software system (Jin & Wang, 2019) and the need to select the most suitable mode of technology integration (Lee & Shin, 2018). Selecting the right technology, both for the clients and for the firm, can be delicate for some fintech startups, and will usually develop as the firm improves its product and responds to user needs (Saldinger, 2018).

Organizational Dimension

Limited or in most cases no access to financial services by developing countries is a major barrier to fintech developments. The access to financial facilities remains a challenge in the developing economies of the world (Demirguc-Kunt et al. 2018; Mohammad 2020). Another critical challenge to the adoption of fintech is the very high consumer expectations concerning performance, perceived benefits, usefulness, usability, and associated risks (Patil, Dwivedi & Rana, 2018).

Funding can be particularly challenging for innovative fintech firms that are still evolving their products and ascertaining their markets (Saldinger, 2018). Funding barriers that can affect fintech startups include financial factors such as the cost of adoption. The respective regulatory environment, such as government-initiated measures about cryptocurrencies in some countries, can hypothetically influence the cost of adoption and early adoptions (Luther, 2016). Other pertinent financial barriers and challenges include the cost of transaction (Shiller, 2013; Swiecka et al., 2020), high costs of innovative activity, lack of sources of financing, and the burden of taxation of the industry. Perceived risk is a substantial challenge during the financial consuming course (Kim, Ferrin, & Rao, 2008). Peoples perceived risk and general lack of trust could inhibit their perceived value of fintech platforms. Perceived risk was defined by Kim, Ferrin, & Rao (2008) as people's belief of possible negative consequences when trading online. Building trust of clientele can become a grave barrier and challenge for the adoption and implementation of fintech in firms. Fintech firms usually strive to build trust and loyalty through digital platforms, whiles banking and financial facilities depend on an affiliation with a physical institution which makes it easier to build trust with clients. Although it is not expedient and can constrain access, with microfinance firms, debtors would typically see a loan officer before receiving a loan, which facilitated the establishment of trust. Trust mediates the relationship between perceived risks and fintech application adoption (Mohammad, 2020). Irregularities in data or information asymmetry is another crucial challenge to the adoption and implementation of fintech in firms (Dhar & Stein, 2017; Moradi, Naderi, & Delangizan, 2020). The challenge of information asymmetry emanates as a result of a lack of good sources of information on the market (Błach, 2020). A lack of access to refined financial services data instigates some critical constraints to the adoption of fintech innovations (Cassim, 2020). In general, institutional constraints placed on fintech firms, including unclear institutional tax and accounting regulations, makes the industry unattractive and may slow the progress of adoption and implementation of fintech (Arner, Barberis, & Buckley, 2016; Dhar & Stein 2017; Moradi et al., 2020; OECD, 2020).

Environmental Dimension

Regulatory reactions to innovation have an intense influence on both the new technology based business start-ups and the customary financial facilities firms that are encountering disruption. Typically, disruptive fintech firms will contend for a laissez-faire approach to the regulation of fintech, while traditional financial facilities firms support consistent and technology-neutral regulation (Arner, Barberis, & Buckley, 2016). The important legal and regulatory barriers and challenges in fintech include issues with privacy, data protection, cyber security, digital disclosure, and the deployment of financial facilities and technology to counter money laundering and financial crime. As like as fintech, regtech is a shrinkage of the words 'regulatory' and 'technology'. It has been proposed that regtech will allow regulators to deploy an ever-expanding collection of regulatory skills and tools in order to keep up with the rapid development of markets (Baxter, 2016). The present state of the markets for fintech facilities is largely too dynamic to reach firm suppositions on the actuality of competition barriers and challenges that require the positioning of competition tools on a grand basis (OECD, 2020). Nevertheless, the special role of regulation in the turf of financial facilities directs a note of cautiousness to the suitability of competition policy tools as the desired method to address envisaged challenges (Carmona et al., 2019). Also, Carmona et al. (2019) argues that effects resulting from the use of online-platforms, customer data, algorithms, standardization and interoperability can result in anticompetitive behavior. Social norms and values also have a great propensity to either promote or function as a barrier and challenge that impede fintech adoption and implementation. It has been argued that social norms can have a more significant influence on the adoption of fintech applications than perceived technology risks (Mohammad, 2020).

Human Dimension

The fintech barriers and challenges related to knowledge and financial literacy are very important and they are widely discoursed in extant literature (Fraczek & Klimontowicz, 2015; Gustman, Steinmeier & Tabatabai, 2012). Knowledge barriers include a lack of knowledge on financial innovation, and a lack of qualified employees. A lack of sufficient knowledge of the human elements in firms about the possibilities of applying financial innovations, as well as a dearth of professional staff with satisfactory skills and knowledge of the current market offer of the financial products and facilities available in the financial system create barriers that impede the adoption and implementation of fintech (Błach, 2020). While some firms had initially planned to have an entirely digital client interface, they had to switch plans and integrate more human interfaces. Technology alone is often not sufficient and having a human element, perhaps at the transaction point, or elsewhere in the procedure is critical to client attainment and preservation (Saldinger, 2018). However, the psychological makeup of the human element may either facilitate or create barriers and challenges for the adoption and implementation of fintech. Financial factors, psychological factors, and those related to knowledge could be reduced to some extent through variations in the organizational structure, introduction of new technology, or employee training and progress (Vermeulen, 2004). Psychological factors that serve as barriers and challenges to fintech include a lack of the need or motivation to create innovations and a negative attitude toward innovative processes. This may be as a result of a less-sophisticated population which is averse to change. The psychological barriers of fintech also include reluctance to introduce innovation as a result of: the tradition and convenience of using customary financial solutions; a dearth of trust in both customary and new financial facility providers; and a dread of the risk resulting from the application of financial innovations (Błach, 2020).

RESEARCH METHODOLOGY

The research modelling framework projected in this study entailed the routes to ordering the barriers and challenges of financial technology, using the BWM. The BWM was employed to determine the relative importance of each dimension and barrier or challenge of financial technology. This was done by comparing the best dimension (most important) to the worst (least important) initially and then comparing the other dimensions to the worst afterwards, using a linguistic scale for the pair wise comparison.

Best-Worst Method (BWM)

The BWM is a popular MCDM which evaluates the weights of criteria by using two vectors of pair wise comparisons between the most important and the least important criteria (Mi et al., 2019; Wang et al., 2019). The BWM was selected for this study in lieu of any other MCDM such as the stepwise weight assessment ratio analysis (SWARA), the analytic hierarchy process (AHP), the analytic network process (ANP), the full consistency method (FUCOM) and the level-based weight assessment (LBWA) because it accommodates a small number of pairwise comparisons and yields high consistency rates. These traits of the BWM define its main advantages over other weighting methods. Additionally, since the BWM uses a non-linear model to compute the weights, an optimum range of weights is possible (Rezaei, 2015, 2016, 2020). The application of the BWM by several scholars (Bai, Quayson & Sarkis, 2022; Talib et al., 2020; Orji et al., 2020; Rezaei, 2015) in diverse milieus evinces its value and reliability as an analysis tool. For instance, Bai, Quayson & Sarkis (2022) used it to evaluate the weights of main enablers and sub-enablers by a real case of cocoa supply chain in an emerging African economy and found technical characteristics to be the main enabler whilst blockchain smart contract, blockchain security, and tracking product components were the top three sub-enablers respectively. The following stages are involved in evaluating the weights of criteria using the BWM:

Step 1: Finalization of decision criteria

A set of decision criteria are identified and extracted from an intensive search of literature, and experts' opinions and recorded as $\{C1, C2 \ldots Cn\}$ for n main criteria. In this study, the decision criteria were the barriers and challenges of financial technology.

Step 2: The best (most important) and worst (least important) criteria are selected.

At this stage, the expert selects the most important and least important criteria from the pool of identified decision criteria in Step 1 based on his/ her opinion.

Step 3 A matrix is developed by determining the pair wise comparison between the most important criterion and the other decision criteria. The objective of this step is to determine the preference of the most important criterion to the other decision criteria by using a linguistic scale for the BWM having scores from 1 to 9. The linguistic scale is shown in Table 2. The outcome of the pair wise comparison of the best criterion and other decision criteria is expressed by a 'best-to-others' vector as follows:

$DB = (dB1, dB2, \ldots, dBn)$

Where dBj represents the preference of the most important criterion B over a criterion j amongst the decision criteria, and $dBB = 1$

Step 4: The 'others –to-worst' matrix is developed by conducting a pair- wise comparison of the other decision criteria against the least important criterion using the linguistic scale for BWM shown in Table 2. The outcome of comparison of the other decision criteria to the worst criterion is expressed as follows:

$$DW = \left(dW1, dW2, \ldots, dWn\right)^{q}$$

Where dWj represents the preference of the criterion j amongst the decision criteria in Step 1 above the least important criterion W, and $dWW = 1$.

Step 5: Computing the optimal weights $(p1^*, p2^* \ldots pn^*)$

Weights of criteria are determined such that the maximum absolute differences for all criterion j are minimised over the following set $\{|pB - dBjpj|, |pj - djWpW|\}$. A minimax model can be formulated as:

$$\min \max j\{|pB - dBjwj|, |pj - djWwW|\}$$

Subject to:

$$\sum_j pj = 1 \ldots\ldots\ldots\ldots\ldots\ldots\ldots\ldots \quad (1)$$

$pj \,^3\, 0$, for all criterion j

Model (1) can be solved by converting it into the following linear programming problem model:

$$\text{Min } R^L$$

Subject to:

$|pB - dpj| \text{ £ } R^L$, for all criterion j

$|pj - dpW| \text{ £ } R^L$, for all criterion j

$$\sum_j pj = 1$$

pj^3 0, for all criterion *j*.. (2)

Solving the linear model (2), will result in optimal weights ($p1^*$, $p2^*$ . . . pn^*) and optimal value R^L. Consistency (R^L) of comparisons also needs to be estimated. A value nearer to zero is more desired for consistency (Rezaei, 2016; Wang et al., 2019).

Figure 1. Research modelling framework
Source: author's own construct

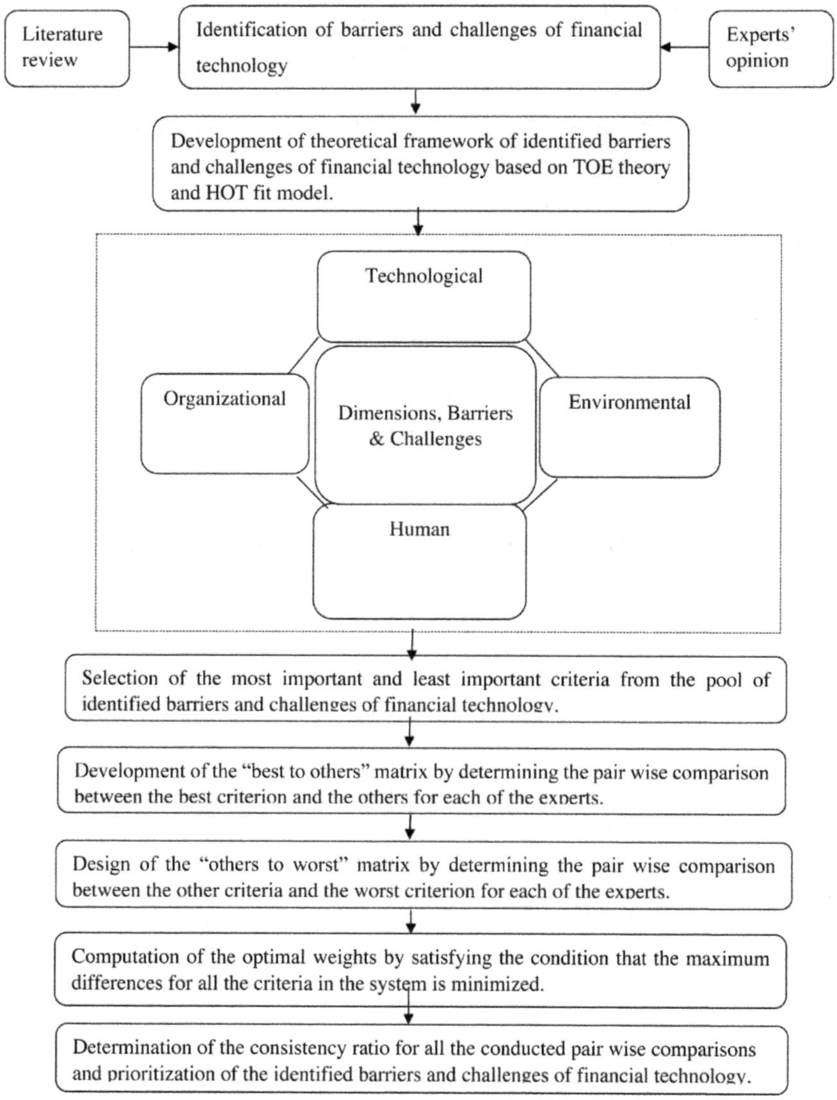

Data Collection

For this inquiry, questionnaires were designed and used to gather data from participants with a minimum of five years of professional management and decision-making experience in the Ghanaian fintech sector. This was done to safeguard the accuracy of data gathered since the experts were reckoned to be reasonably well-informed to efficaciously complete the survey. The experts were purposefully selected from the fields of banking and financial management, telecommunication, small and medium scale enterprise (SME) micro-financing, and mobile money services in the Ghanaian fintech sector. They were assured of the concealment of their reports in order to allow for operative model- building and in- depth observation (Nilashi et al., 2016). Furthermore, the partakers were selected mid-level and above grade executives, hence their answers sufficiently represented the sector under consideration (Fu, Farn, & Chao, 2006).

Table 2. Demographic summary of respondents, and linguistic scale for pair wise comparison in BWM.

Demographic summary of respondents		
Characteristic	**Number of Respondents**	**Percentage of Sample (%)**
Gender		
Male	13	48%
Female	14	52%
Education		
Bachelor/Master degree	13	48%
Doctorate degree	5	19%
Others	9	33%
Years of experience		
1–5	2	7.5%
Above 5	25	92.5%
Roles		
Academic/University lecturer	5	18.52%
Bank Manager	5	18.52%
Telecom Industry Manager	5	18.52%
SME Manager	6	22.22%
Mobile Money Operations Manager	6	22.22%
Linguistic Scale for Pair Wise Comparison in BWM.		

Continued on following page

Table 2. Continued

Demographic summary of respondents		
Characteristic	**Number of Respondents**	**Percentage of Sample (%)**
Linguistic attributes	Scores	
Equally important	1	
Equal to moderately more important	2	
Moderately more important	3	
Moderately to strongly more important	4	
Strongly more important	5	
Strongly to very strongly more important	6	
Very strongly more important	7	
Very strongly to extremely more important	8	
Extremely more important	9	

Source: author's own construct

To conduct the survey, some measures were taken to increase the rate of response and decrease response bias amongst the experts from the selected fintech firms. Originally, a pilot study was done by distributing copies of the google form questionnaire designed for this inquiry to three researchers through emails and interviewing four participants face- to - face to analyze and offer responses. The three researchers that participated in the pilot study were two females and a male who hold PhD degrees and have at least five years of research experience in financial technology, internet and communication technology, and public finance. Also, the specialists who participated in the pilot study have managerial experience of at least five years in the Ghanaian financial technology, public finance and general merchandise industry. Based on the responses from the trial study, the survey questionnaire was improved and copies were emailed to thirty experts. Six experts each were designated to denote the five dissimilar roles of the partakers as shown in Table 2. A follow- up on the experts was done through telephone conversations and personal follow-up visits (Yang et al. 2018). Eventually, twenty-seven completed questionnaires were received out of the thirty that were emailed to the participants, a response rate of 90%. This reaction rate was deemed appropriate for competent analysis and to produce reliable findings, since the BWM employed in this study does not need a large sample size to provide accurate and reliable results (Wang et al., 2019).

RESULTS AND DISCUSSION

Launching with the first stage of the BWM, the dimensions, and barriers and challenges of financial technology that were identified from reviewed literature were evaluated by the expert participants using copies of a questionnaire. The questionnaire was planned to require a 'YES' or 'NO' answer which indicated that a dimension or challenge was 'relevant' or 'not relevant' in the Ghanaian fintech arena. A simple mean method was used to first-rate the variables that were above the arithmetic mean and an analysis of the results at this juncture indicated that all the identified dimensions and barriers were accepted with no supplementary inclusions. Therefore, inclusiveness of pertinent data was safeguarded, and content validity was established.

Calculation of the Weights of Barriers and Challenges (BCs) using BWM

After the finalization of the BCs of fintech adoption, the weights of the BCs were calculated using the BWM. For this research, twenty-seven experts performed the identification of the best and worst criteria for the main dimensions as well as subcategory criteria BCs. Subsequent to obtaining the best and worst criteria, all the participants were requested to give preference ratings of the best criteria to other criteria and other criteria to worst criteria for the main dimension's criteria BCs as well as subcategory criteria BCs. The preference ratings of the first expert, Expert 1, for both the main category criteria BCs, and subcategory criteria BCs are shown in Table 3.

An indistinguishable process of the BWM survey, as described in the preceding paragraph, was completed by all the participants in this study to estimate the performance ratings of the main category and subcategory BCs of fintech innovations. The entire weights of the BCs for both the main category and subcategory were obtained using Equation (1). All the accumulated weights were computed by applying the data sourced from the twenty-seven participants of this study to Equation (2) and estimating the mean using the simple average procedure. The whole results of the evaluation process, expedited by the BWM, is presented in Table 3. The degree of importance of a BCs is revealed by its ranked place in the table. The global ranks of the identified BCs, as depicted in Table 3, were calculated by multiplying the preference weights of the respective BC's dimension with the specific weight of the BC. The rankings of both the main category dimensions and subcategory BCs are discussed in detail in the next section of this article.

Table 3. Pairwise comparison of main category and subcategory BCs by Expert 1, and aggregate weights of main and subcategory BCs for all the experts.

Main Category BCs

Best to Others Technological (T) Organizational (O) Environmental (E) Human (H)
Best criteria: 2 1 3 5
Organizational (O)
Others to Worst Worst criteria: Human (H)
Technological (T) 4
Organizational (O) 4
Environmental (E) 3
Human (H) 1

Technological (T) Subcategory BCs
Best to Others T1 T2 T3 T4
Best criteria: T1 1 5 7 3
Others to Worst Worst criteria: T3
T1 4
T2 5
T3 1
T4 3
Organizational (O) Subcategory BCs
Best to Others O1 O2 O3 O4 O5 O6 O7
Best criteria: O5 6 4 3 2 1 5 7
Others to Worst Worst criteria: O7
O1 3
O2 5
O3 2
O4 3
O5 4
O6 3
O7 1
Environmental (E) Subcategory BCs
Best to Others E1 E2 E3
Best criteria: E1 1 4 3
Others to Worst Worst criteria: E2
E1 4
E2 1
E3 3
Human (H) Subcategory BCs
Best to Others H1 H2
Best criteria: H2 3 1
Others to Worst Worst criteria: H1
H1 1
H2 4
Aggregate Weights of Main and Subcategory BCs for all the Experts.
Main category BCs Weights of main Subcategory Weights of Global weights Ranking
category BCs BCs subcategory BCs
Technological (T) 0.234 T1 0.490 0.115 3
T2 0.161 0.038 11
T3 0.155 0.036 12
T4 0.194 0.045 9
Organizational (O) 0.520 O1 0.059 0.031 13
O2 0.090 0.046 8
O3 0.120 0.062 6
O4 0.232 0.121 2
O5 0.382 0.199 1
O6 0.081 0.042 10
O7 0.036 0.019 14
Environmental (E) 0. 124 E1 0.813 0.101 4
E2 0.088 0.011 16
E3 0.099 0.012 15
Human (H) 0. 122 H1 0.387 0.047 7
H2 0.613 0.075 5

Source: author's own construct

Ranking of the Dimensions of the BCs of Fintech

The results of the computation of the optimal weights, facilitated by the BWM-Solver, are exhibited in Table 3. From the table, it is evident that the organizational dimension erupted as the most significant dimension of the barriers and challenges of financial technology. It is also observed from the table that the technological, environmental and human dimensions followed respectively in order of prominence. From the results, it can be deduced that the barriers and challenges of financial technology that are associated to the organizational context are particularly significant and should be adequately considered to reduce the barriers and challenges of financial technology. The next in level of importance, with regards to the dimensions of the barriers and challenges of financial technology, was the technological dimension. The environmental dimension was ranked in the third position, and the human dimension was the least ranked in this class. It is suggested that financial technology industry managers should be encouraged to be in tune with these barriers and challenges to reduce their adverse effects on the spread of fintech innovation.

Global Ranks of the BCs of Fintech

The global ranks of the BCs of fintech are shown in Table 3. The topmost five BCs under the global ranks, which signify about the top 31% of BCs, belonged to all the four-dimensional contexts measured in this research. These top BCs were perceived risk and lack of trust; transaction cost; privacy and security issues; legal and regulatory barriers; and the human element and psychological factors. As apparent from the results of the study, perceived risk and lack of trust was the topmost ranked BC of fintech. Perceived risk denotes people's belief of possible negative consequences when trading online (Kim, Ferrin & Rao, 2008), and trust mediates the relationship between perceived risks and fintech platform adoption and implementation (Mohammad 2020). The findings of the study prove that peoples perceived risk and general lack of trust could inhibit their perceived value of fintech platforms. The second most important BC in the grading pyramid was transaction cost. Financial constraints such as high transaction costs, high costs of innovative activity, lack of sources of financing, and the burden of taxation of the industry (Shiller, 2013; Swiecka et al., 2020) forms a grave barrier and challenge to fintech adoption and implementation. It is a proven fact that the higher the taxation of the industry, the higher the transaction costs. Privacy and security issues were the third topmost ranked BC in this study. Privacy is fixated on how data is used and governed to protect sensitive information, whilst security focuses on protecting data from theft for profit and destructive attacks (Abouelmehdi, Beni-Hessane & Khaloufi, 2018). Privacy and security gaps can lead to distrust of mobile applications and detrimentally affect a person's intention to use fintech services (Kang, 2018). The findings of this study confirm that a lack of privacy and security standards can limit the development of fintech schemes and hence have a negative effect on its general adoption and implementation. The next amongst the most significant BCs, legal and regulatory barriers, denotes the regulatory responses to innovation that have an intense effect on both the new technology-based business start-ups and the traditional financial services firms that are facing disruption. Disruptive fintech firms will contend for a laissez-faire approach to the regulation of fintech, whereas traditional financial facilities firms support consistent and technology-neutral regulation (Arner, Barberis & Buckley, 2016). The findings of this study corroborate studies on how legal and regulatory barriers can adversely affect the effective deployment of fintech innovation. The human element and psychological factors were the fifth ranked most important BC of fintech, according to this study. Experience has proved that technology alone is often not sufficient and having a human element, perhaps at the transaction point, or elsewhere in the procedure is critical to client attainment and preservation (Saldinger, 2018). Moreover, the psychological temperament of the human element may either facilitate or create barriers and challenges for the adoption and implementation of fintech innovation. Psychological factors that serve as barriers and challenges to fintech include a lack of the need or motivation to create innovations and a negative attitude toward innovative processes. This may be as a result of a less-sophisticated population which is averse to change. The psychological barriers of fintech also include reluctance to introduce innovation as a result of: the tradition and convenience of using customary financial solutions; a dearth of trust in both customary and new financial facility providers; and a dread of the risk resulting from the application of financial innovations (Błach, 2020). Vermeulen (2004) argues that psychological factors, and those related to knowledge could be reduced to some extent through variations in the organizational structure, introduction of new technology, or employee training and development.

Ranking of the BCs within Each Dimension

The subsections in this section ranked the sets of barriers and challenges of fintech within each dimensional context of the investigation conducted. Thus, the barriers and challenges of fintech within the technological, organizational, environmental, and human dimensions were graded.

Technological BCs

The findings of this study projects that privacy and security issues had the highest rank in this dimension. As widely discoursed in the earlier paragraphs of this report, privacy hinges on the protection of sensitive information and security emphasizes on protecting data from theft for profit and destructive attacks. Henceforth, managers and other players in the fintech industry would be more disposed to the patronage of financial technology if the barriers and challenges with regards to privacy and security are sufficiently suppressed to negligible levels. The next ranked BC in this dimensional context was the quality of software system and technology integration, which has also been discussed in earlier sections of this report. The next two ranked BCs in this dimension, in order of prominence, were: rapid developments in technology; and interoperability of technologies.

Organizational BCs

Perceived risk and lack of trust was the utmost ranked BC in the organizational context. As exuded comprehensively in preceding paragraphs, perceived risk signifies people's belief of possible undesirable consequences when trading online, and trust arbitrates the correlation between perceived risks and the adoption of fintech innovations. As per the findings of this study, peoples perceived risk and overall lack of trust could hinder their perceived value of fintech innovations.

Therefore, it is suggested that managers and other players in the fintech industry should focus on the barriers and challenges of fintech with regards to perceived risk and lack of trust, to sufficiently suppress them to insignificant levels. The next six BCs, graded in order of their importance to the adoption of fintech innovations, were: transaction cost; funding/cost of adoption; high consumer expectations/perceived benefits; information asymmetry; low access to financial services; and institutional constraints on firms.

Environmental BCs

From the findings of the study, legal and regulatory barriers ranked as the most significant BC in this dimensional context. The second most significant BC in this context encapsulated issues regarding social norms and values. The third and last placed BC in this dimension was competition.

Human BCs

The fallouts of this study indicate that the human element and psychological factors constituted the highest-ranked BC in this dimension. The second and last ranked BC in this dimension encapsulated issues of knowledge and financial literacy.

Theoretical and Practical Implications

The theory and practice of adopting and utilizing fintech, with regards to its barriers and challenges, is significantly corroborated by this study. Viewing theoretically, the framework of the study based on the TOE and HOT theories helps in understanding the critical zones that, when focused on, can limit the barriers and challenges of the adoption of fintech innovations. From the TOE and HOT theoretical perspectives, the adoption and utilization of fintech is constrained by barriers and challenges classified into technological, organizational, environmental, and human dimensional contexts. This study theoretically enacts an increase in the level of variance elucidated on the barriers and challenges of fintech, characteristically, by using the BWM through the eyes of the TOE and HOT concepts.

The verdicts of this investigation suggest that perceived risk and lack of trust; transaction cost; privacy and security issues; legal and regulatory barriers; and the human element and psychological factors can impede and challenge the adoption of financial technology. These results are consistent with the study by Kim, Ferrin & Rao (2008) with regards to how individuals perceived risk and lack of trust possess a challenge for the adoption of fintech innovation. Perceived risk denotes people's belief of possible undesirable consequences when trading online, and trust is the variable that intervenes between the perceived risks and fintech innovation adoption. These findings are also consistent with studies by Shiller (2013) and Swiecka et al. (2020) with regards to the barriers and challenges of fintech as a result of a high cost of transaction and the burden of taxation of the industry. Additionally, the verdicts of this study are in line with the study by Kang (2018) with regards to how privacy and security breaches can lead to mistrust of mobile applications and detrimentally affect an individual's intention to adopt fintech innovations. However, contrary to studies by Mohammad (2020), the results of this study indicate that perceived risks and lack of trust can have a more significant influence on the adoption of fintech innovations than social norms and values. This may be attributable to the fact that citizens of the country are gradually becoming more used to technological innovations, and traditional and cultural barriers are systematically being sidestepped in favor of technological development. Consequently, the impact of social norms and values on fintech adoption seems to be on a downward spiral.

This research tersely substantiates studies on the barriers and challenges of financial technology. Nevertheless, the method and context used in this work is distinct from other published documents in the subject field. For this unique effort, a theoretical framework based on the TOE and HOT concepts was used to study the barriers and challenges of fintech innovations in Ghana. The established theoretical framework for this study can be applied by any fintech firm to classify its organizational barriers and challenges with respect to their significance ratings.

Managerial Implications

Managers in the fintech industry are offered a comprehensive and in-depth understanding of the barriers and challenges to an efficacious adoption and implementation of fintech innovations by the findings of this study. The study is expressly supportive to managers of fintech firms in developing economies in countries such as Ghana, Kenya, Nigeria, and others where there are very high aspirations for private sector development of fintech innovations, and a concurrent very high appetite of governments towards taxation of the industry with its corresponding threat of proliferations in transaction cost. Managers may adopt the theoretical framework of this study, and lay more emphasis on reducing the hurdles and challenges of fintech to enhance the prospects of its adoption and application. This study would assist managers to underpin the significantly rated barriers and challenges of fintech and pay more attention to them with committed contributions.

CONCLUSION

The level of difference explicated on the barriers and challenges of fintech was heightened by the application of the TOE and HOT theoretical frameworks for this study. With guidance from the TOE and HOT concepts, this study proposed a research framework that is applicable to the setting of financial technology innovation in Ghana. It is envisioned that this study would afford a better understanding of the barriers and challenges to the diffusion of fintech innovations. The fallouts of this investigation demonstrate that the adoption of fintech in the Ghanaian indutry is still in its early stage but characterized by a fast-growing rate of usage. A latitude of four main dimensional context of technology, organization, environment, and human were identified to significantly influence the overall adoption and application of fintech innovations. The value of the developed framework for identifying the barriers and challenges of financial technology has been unveiled by this study. When compared to the customary concepts, this model churns out as a more dependable instrument for the classification of the barriers and challenges of fintech.

The opinions of fintech industry managers in Ghana, which may be branded with prejudiced verdicts and uncertainty, formed part of the basis of this study. In future research, fuzzy logic may be applied to reduce the uncertainty in experts' opinions. Fuzzy logic is an extension of classical logic that includes the uncertainties that factor into human decision-making. It is often used to solve complex problems, where the parameters may be unclear or imprecise. Fuzzy logic may also be used in investment software, where it can be employed to interpret ambiguous or unclear trading signals. In fintech services, fuzzy logic is being used in machine learning and technology systems supporting outputs of investment intelligence (Scott, 2021). Also, in future, other pertinent issues regarding fintech adoption and implementation such as its success factors and drivers may be investigated by using the theoretical framework developed in this study. Similarly, the research modelling framework may be modified to take up other multi-criteria decision methods such as the Analytical Hierarchy Process. A wider perspective of this current effort may be carried out by reaping data from a bigger pool of experts in the fintech industry of other countries. Also, a comparative study may be done by either comparing diverse modelling frameworks on the subject theme or comparing findings of fintech industries of different countries.

REFERENCES

Abouelmehdi, K., Beni-Hessane, A., & Khaloufi, H. (2018). Big healthcare data: Preserving security and privacy. *Journal of Big Data*, *5*(1), 1–18. doi:10.118640537-017-0110-7

Arner, D., Barberis, J., & Buckley, R. P. (2016). The Evolution of Fintech: A New Post-Crisis Paradigm? *Georgetown Journal of International Law*, *47*, 1271.

Bai, C., Quayson, M., & Sarkis, J. (2022). Analysis of Blockchain's enablers for improving sustainable supply chain transparency in Africa cocoa industry. *Journal of Cleaner Production*, *358*, 131896. doi:10.1016/j.jclepro.2022.131896

Baxter, L. G. (2016). 'Adaptive Financial Regulation and Regtech: A Concept Article on Realistic Protection for Victims of Bank Failures'. *Duke Law Journal*, *66*, 567–598.

Błach, J. (2020). Barriers to Financial Innovation—Corporate Finance Perspective. *J. Risk Financial Manag.*, *13*(11), 273. doi:10.3390/jrfm13110273

Bromberg, L., Godwin, A., & Ramsay, I. (2017). Fintech sandboxes: Achieving a balance between regulation and innovation. *Journal of Banking and Finance Law and Practice*, *28*(4), 314–336.

Brownsword, R. (2019). Regulatory fitness: Fintech, funny money, and smart contracts. *European Business Organization Law Review*, *20*(1), 5–27. doi:10.100740804-019-00134-2

Buchak, G., Matvos, G., Piskorski, T., & Seru, A. (2018). Fintech, regulatory arbitrage, and the rise of shadow banks. *Journal of Financial Economics*, *130*(3), 453–483. doi:10.1016/j.jfineco.2018.03.011

Carmona, A. F., Lombardo, A. G., Pastor, R.R., Quirós, C.T., García, J.V., Muñoz, D.R., Martín, L.C. (2019). Competition issues in the Area of Financial Technology (FinTech). *Policy Department for Economic, Scientific and Quality of Life Policies Directorate-General for Internal Policies, European Parliament.*

Cassim, R. (2020). Challenges facing fintechs and opportunities to respond. *South African Reserve Bank, World Fintech Festival.*

Demirguc-Kunt, A., Klapper, L., Singer, D., Ansar, S., & Hess, J. (2018). *The Global Findex Database 2017: Measuring Financial Inclusion and the Fintech Revolution.* World Bank Group. doi:10.1596/978-1-4648-1259-0

Dhar, V., & Stein, R. M. (2017). Economic and Business Dimensions FinTech Platforms and Strategy. *Communications of the ACM, 60*(10), 32–35. doi:10.1145/3132726

Financial Stability Board. (2017b). *Financial Stability Implications for Fintech: Supervisory and Regulatory Issues that Merit Authorities' Attention.* Financial Stability, Board.

Fisher, A. (2015). 'Fintech: The next wave of disruption' *FinanceAsia,* Fraczek, B., & Klimontowicz, M. (2015). Financial literacy and its influence on Young customers' decision factors. *Journal of Innovation Management, 3*(1), 62–84. doi:10.24840/2183-0606_003.001_0007

Fu, J. R., Farn, C. K., & Chao, W. P. (2006). Acceptance of Electronic Tax Filing: A Study of Taxpayer Intentions. *Information & Management, 43*(1), 109–126. doi:10.1016/j.im.2005.04.001

Gatto, A. (2018). Historical Roots of Microcredit and Usury: The Role ofMonti di Pietàin Italy and in the Kingdom of Naples in XV-XX Centuries. *Journal of International Development, 30*(5), 911–914. doi:10.1002/jid.3386

Gatto, A., Polselli, N., & Bloom, G. (2016). Empowering Gender Equality through Rural Development: Rural Markets and Micro-Finance in Kyrgyzstan. In L. Matteo & M. Pace (Eds.), *L'Europa e la Comunità Internazionale Difronte alle Sfide dello Sviluppo.* Giannini Editore.

Gustman, A. L., Steinmeier, T. L., & Tabatabai, N. (2012). Financial knowledge and financial literacy at the household level. *The American Economic Review, 102*(3), 309–313. doi:10.1257/aer.102.3.309

Jin, T., & Wang, Q. (2019). FinExpert: Domain-specific test generation for fintech systems. *In Proceedings of the 27th ACM Joint Meeting on European Software Engineering Conference and Symposium on the Foundations of Software Engineering*, (pp. 853–862). ACM. 10.1145/3338906.3340441

Kang, J. (2018). Mobile Payment in Fintech Environment: Trends, Security Challenges, and Services. *Human-Centric Computing and Information Sciences*, *8*(1), 32. doi:10.118613673-018-0155-4

Kim, D. J., Ferrin, D. L., & Rao, H. R. (2008). A trust-based consumer decision-making model in electronic commerce: The role of trust, perceived risk, and their antecedents. *Decision Support Systems*, *44*(2), 544–564. doi:10.1016/j.dss.2007.07.001

Knight, E., & Wójcik, D. (2020). FinTech, economy and space: Introduction to the special issue. *Environ. Plan. A Econ. Space*, *52*, 1490–1497.

Krishna Priya, P., & Anusha, K. (2019). Fintech Issues and Challenges in India. *International Journal of Recent Technology and Engineering (IJRTE). ISSN*, *8*(3), 2277–3878.

Lee, I., & Shin, Y. J. (2018). Fintech: Ecosystem, business models, investment decisions, and challenges. *Business Horizons*, *61*(1), 35–46. doi:10.1016/j.bushor.2017.09.003

Leong, K. (2018). FinTech (Financial Technology): What is it and how to use technologies to create business value in fintech way? *International Journal of Innovation, Management and Technology*, *9*, 74–78. doi:10.18178/ijimt.2018.9.2.791

Luther, W. J. (2016). Bitcoin and the Future of Digital Payments. *The Independent Review, 20*, 397–440.

Mansilla-Fernández, J. M. (2017). Institutions. *Eur. Econ.*, *3*, 41–50.

Mi, X., Tang, M., Liao, H., Shen, W., & Lev, B. (2019). The state-of-the-art survey on integrations and applications of the best worst method in decision making: Why, what, what for, and what's next? *Omega*, *87*, 205–225. doi:10.1016/j.omega.2019.01.009

Mittal, P., & Kaur, A. (2013). E-Governance - A challenge for India. *International Journal of Advanced Research in Computer Engineering and Technology*, *2*(3).

Mohammad, K. (2020). FinTech in COVID-19 and Beyond: What Factors Are Affecting Customers' Choice of FinTech Applications? *Journal of Open Innovation*, *6*(4), 153. doi:10.3390/joitmc6040153

Moradi, S., Naderi, N., & Delangizan, S. (2020). Analyzing Fintech Startups Development Process in Iran. *Journal of Entrepreneurship Development, 13*, 121–140.

Nicoletti, B. (2017). *The Future of FinTech: Integrating Finance and Technology in Financial Services*. Palgrave Macmillan. doi:10.1007/978-3-319-51415-4

Nilashi, M., Ahmadi, H., Ahani, A., Ravangard, R., & Ibrahim, O. B. (2016). Determining the Importance of Hospital Information System Adoption Factors Using Fuzzy Analytic Network Process (ANP). *Technological Forecasting and Social Change, 111*, 244–264. doi:10.1016/j.techfore.2016.07.008

Nitescu, D. C., & Murgu, V. (2019). The Economic Growth Catalyzers at the European Level, in the Context of the 2008Financial Crisis. *Amfiteatru Economic, 21*(50), 241–257. doi:10.24818/EA/2019/50/241

OECD. (2020). Digital Disruption in Banking and Its Impact on Competition. OECD. http://www.oecd.org/daf/competition/ digital-disruption-in-f inancial-markets.htm

Orji, I. J., Kusi-Sarpong, S., Huang, S., & Vazquez-Brust, D. (2020). Evaluating the factors that influence blockchain adoption in the freight logistics industry. *Transportation Research Part E, Logistics and Transportation Review, 141*, 102025. doi:10.1016/j.tre.2020.102025

Patil, P., Dwivedi, Y., & Rana, N. (2018). Digital Payments Adoption: An Analysis of Literature. ILNCS-10595. Cham: Springer International Publishing, 61.

Rezaei, J. (2015). Best-worst multi-criteria decision-making method. *Omega, 53*, 49–57. doi:10.1016/j.omega.2014.11.009

Rezaei, J. (2016). Best- Worst Multi- Criteria Decision Making Method: Some Properties and a Linear Model. *Omega, 64*, 126–130. doi:10.1016/j.omega.2015.12.001

Rezaei, J. (2020). A concentration ratio for nonlinear best worst method. *International Journal of Information Technology & Decision Making, 19*(03), 891–907. doi:10.1142/S0219622020500170

Saldinger, A. (2018). 5 barriers holding back fintech entrepreneurs. *Dervex.* https://www.devex.com/news

Schueffel, P. (2017). Taming the beast: A scientific definition of fintech. *J. Innov. Manag, 4*(4), 32–54. doi:10.24840/2183-0606_004.004_0004

Scott, G. (2021). *Fuzzy Logic. Fintech, Automated Investing*. Investopedia.

Shiller, R. J. (2013). Capitalism and Financial Innovation. *Financial Analysts Journal, 69*(1), 21–25. doi:10.2469/faj.v69.n1.4

Starnes, S., Kurdyla, M., & Alexander, J. (2016). DeRisking by Banks in Emerging Markets – Effects and Responses for Trade. *IFC EM Compass Note, 24.*

Swiecka, B., Terefenko, P., & Paprotny, D. (2020). Transaction factors' influence on the choice of ´ payment by Polish consumer. *Journal of Retailing and Consumer Services, 58*(102), 264.

Talib, F., Asjad, M., Attri, R., Siddiquee, A.N. (2020). A road map for the implementation of integrated JIT-lean practices in Indian manufacturing industries using the best worst method approach. *J. Ind. Prod. Eng*, 1–17.

Tiron-Tudor, A., Nistor, C. S., êtefĝnescu, C. A., & Zanellato, G. (2019). Encompassing Non-Financial Reporting in A Coercive Framework for Enhancing Social Responsibility: Romanian Listed Companies' Case. *Amfiteatru Economic, 21*(52), 590–606. doi:10.24818/EA/2019/52/590

Tornatzky, L., & Fleischer, M. (1990). *The process of technology innovation.* Lexington Books.

Tsai, C. H., & Peng, K. J. (2017). The FinTech revolution and financial regulation: The case of online supply-chain financing. *Asian J. Law Soc.*, *4*(1), 109–132. doi:10.1017/als.2016.65

Vermeulen, P. (2004). Managing product innovation in financial services firms. *European Management Journal*, *22*(1), 43–50. doi:10.1016/j.emj.2003.11.012

Wang, Z. G., Xu, R., Lin, H., Wang, R. J., & Ren, J. (2019). Energy Performance Contracting, Risk Factors, and Policy Implications: Identification and Analysis of Risks Based on the Best- Worst Network Method. *Energy*, *170*, 1–13. doi:10.1016/j.energy.2018.12.140

Wonglimpiyarat, J. (2018). Challenges and dynamics of FinTech crowd funding: An innovation system approach. *J. High Technol. Manag*, *29*(1), 98–108. doi:10.1016/j.hitech.2018.04.009

Yang, Y., Lau, A. K. W., Lee, P. K. C., Yeung, A. C. L., & Cheng, T. C. E. (2018). Efficacy of China's Strategic Environmental Management in its Institutional Environment. *International Journal of Operations & Production Management*, *39*(1), 138–163. doi:10.1108/IJOPM-11-2017-0695

Yusof, N. M., Paul, R. J., & Stergioulas, L. K. (2006).Towards a Framework for Health Information Systems Evaluation. *The 39th Hawaii International Conference on System Science.* IEEE. 10.1109/HICSS.2006.491

Chapter 5
Determinants of Mobile Money Fraud on C2C E-Commerce:
A Trust Perspective

Eli Fianu
https://orcid.org/0000-0003-2308-6831
Ghana Communication Technology University, Ghana

Zelda Arku
University of Mines and Technology, Ghana

Stephen Boateng
University of Ghana, Ghana

ABSTRACT

The study sought to investigate the determinants of MoMo fraud perception in C2C e-commerce from a trust perspective. The research model comprises a set of relationships between constructs from empirical studies. The constructs are culture (uncertainty avoidance), perceived reputation of mobile service provider, trust in C2C trader, structural assurance, perceived usefulness, and consumer fraud perception. A quantitative research design was used for the study. The sample consisted of three hundred and eighty-seven (387) respondents. Data were analysed using PLS-SEM (partial least squares structural equation modelling) via SmartPLS 3. Culture (uncertainty avoidance) was found to have a significant negative influence on consumer fraud perception. Perceived reputation of the mobile service provider was found to have an insignificant influence on consumer fraud perception. Trust in C2C trader, structural assurance, and perceived usefulness were found to have a significant positive influence on consumer fraud perception.

DOI: 10.4018/978-1-6684-6381-9.ch005

Copyright © 2023, IGI Global. Copying or distributing in print or electronic forms without written permission of IGI Global is prohibited.

INTRODUCTION

Mobile phones have created enormous opportunities for financial growth and are anticipated to be a common instrument for conducting a variety of financial activities (Muganyi et al., 2022; Iman, 2018). Mobile phones are equipped with functionalities that surpass traditional telephony needs and inspire the development of value-added mobile services such as mobile money (Khet & Tha, 2022). Serbeh et al., (2022) defined MoMo as the provision of financial services through a mobile device. MoMo is gradually becoming a major means of payment for the unbanked in less developed economies (Wieser et al., 2019). The rapid growth in MoMo usage is partly on account of the increasing penetration and mobile phones, particularly in emerging economies (Aggarwal et al., 2020). MoMo offers its customers a wide range of services, including quick and dependable financial transactions for things like utility payments, cash withdrawals, and cash deposits.

Mobile money has transformed the lives of millions of people globally. The 2021 industry report by GSMA revealed that there were 1.35 billion registered mobile money accounts globally processing $1 trillion in transactions annually (GSMA, 2022). In developing countries, MoMo is integrating the informal and unbanked population into the financial ecosystem (Ekong & Ekong, 2022). MoMo transactions have grown exponentially in Ghana in the last ten years. The total value of mobile money transactions increased from GHS155.8 billion in 2017 to GHS564.2 billion in 2020 (Bank of Ghana, 2020). The relevance of MoMo transactions to the Ghanaian economy cannot be over-emphasized. However, the success of this service has posed a threat to its providers, since unscrupulous individuals continue to use the mobile money service to defraud others (Akomea-Frimpong et al., 2019). Despite the significance of MoMo, mobile money fraud has become an issue of major concern for all stakeholders (Telecommunication Companies, FinTech Firms, MoMo Merchants, End Users, Banks and Regulators) in recent times. MoMo fraud is orchestrated by cyber-criminals, MoMo merchants, staff of service providers on unsuspecting MoMo subscribers usually through social engineering or hack tools (Kilavo et al., 2022). The Ghana Chamber of Telecommunications reported 278 MoMo–related fraud cases in 2015 and 388 cases in 2016 (Akomea-Frimpong et al., 2019). In April 2021, the chamber mentioned that over 4,000 cases of mobile money fraud were under investigation (Brown, 2021). With the emergence of financial service interoperability, users can link all their MoMo wallets to their bank accounts for seamless cash flow, making the threat of MoMo fraud a menace that is negatively impacting user trust in leveraging MoMo for transactions such as Consumer-to-Consumer (C2C) e-commerce (Gukurume & Mahiya, 2020).

A typical fraud case in the Ghanaian context which remains unresolved was reported in 2019 showing how sophisticated MoMo fraud criminals are becoming. According to the report by Ayettey (2019)

Sometime in July 2019, Stephen said one of his regular customers purchased items valued at GH¢800 and promised to pay for the goods through mobile ... around 2:00 pm the next day, he received a mobile money payment prompt from a vendor of a sum of GH¢800, and this followed a call from his customer confirming payment of the goods she had bought the previous day. ... 15 minutes after ... he received another call from a male caller who introduced himself as the vendor who sent the money. He said the message of the caller was that MTN operators of the mobile network were yet to deduct the money from his account and wanted him (Stephen) to allow cash out for him to rectify the problem. Stephen allowed cash out and within seconds a total of GH¢14,000 in his account vanished. ... "A report was then lodged with the Nima Police Station for investigations to be conducted but the police are yet to get the suspect apprehended," he added (Ayettey, 2019).

The emergence of MoMo services has impacted significantly on the growth of Consumer-to-Consumer (C2C) e-commerce. One consumer selling goods or services to another consumer online is known as "C2C" e-commerce (Purwanto, 2022). C2C e-commerce has a huge potential in Ghana due to the proliferation of mobile devices and social commerce platforms (Entee & Afful-Dadzie, 2020). The popular social media platforms in Ghana are TikTok, Facebook, Twitter, WhatsApp, Instagram, and LinkedIn. These social media platforms are catalysts for the proliferation of C2C e-commerce. With the constant risk of falling victim to MoMo fraud, consumers trust in leverage MoMo for C2C e-commerce is diminishing exponentially (Boßerhof & Decken, 2022). Due of the unpredictability of internet transactions, several studies have emphasized that trust and minimal fraud perceptions are crucial aspects in the successful development of e-commerce (Akomea-Frimpong et al., 2019; Kilavo et al., 2022; Leonard & Jones, 2021). Factors such as uncertainty avoidance, integrity, reputation and structural assurance tend to exacerbate the trust and fraud perception of MoMo C2C e-Commerce stakeholders (Chandra et al., 2010; Xin et al., 2015; Yan & Pan 2015). This study seeks to investigate the determinants of mobile money fraud on C2C e-Commerce from a trust perspective.

While there have been increasing studies on MoMo fraud in recent times, these studies have focused more on the detection, control, and predictive patterns (Akomea-Frimpong et al., 2019; Botchey et al., 2020; El Ayeb et al., 2020). For instance, Akomea-Frimpong et al., (2019) in their empirical paper revealed that fraud in mobile money services is caused by weak internal controls and systems, lack of sophisticated information technology tools to detect the menace, inadequate education and training and the poor remuneration of employees. For fraud prediction, Botchey et al., (2020) sought to provide a solution by looking at "machine learning algorithms based on support vector machines (kernel-based), gradient boosted decision tree (tree-based) and Naïve Bayes (probabilistic based) algorithms." The authors revealed that the use of gradient boosted decision tree holds a great potential in combating the problem of mobile money fraud as it was able to produce near perfect predictive results. Despite the contribution made by extant literature to the discourse of MoMo fraud, there is a dearth of studies exploring the determinants of mobile money fraud from a trust perspective. Also, there is arguably no study that has approached the subject matter focusing on C2C e-commerce within an emerging economy context. In a quest to fill this knowledge gap, this study proposed research model will comprise constructs adapted from the studies of Xin et al., (2015), Chandra et al., (2010), and Yan and Pan (2015). The proposed research model comprises the following, namely, perceived reputation of mobile service providers, structural assurance, uncertainty avoidance, perceived usefulness, trust in c2c traders, consumer fraud perception, and usage intention.

This paper is organized as follows: the next section of the paper outlines a brief review, followed by sections on hypotheses development and methodology, as well as a description of the data source, constructs, variables, and measures. Following that, the PLS-SEM results are presented, followed by the discussion section. The final section of the paper contains the conclusion, conflicts of interest, and funding information.

LITERATURE REVIEW

Mobile Money Fraud

Mobile money fraud is a deliberate act perpetrated by con artists or fraudsters to acquire an unfair advantage against mobile money users, mobile money providers, and mobile money agents (). It is a well-rehearsed scheme by fraudsters to take advantage of the service's stakeholders. These criminals spend a great deal of time planning their schemes and occasionally receive resources and technical aid from gangs that exploit system vulnerabilities to enrich themselves (Maurer, 2012). In this study MoMo fraud has been classified based on the categorisation of Annan (2017). Table 1 outlines the types of MoMo fraud

Table 1. Types of MoMo fraud

	Type of Fraud	Description
1	Mobile network operator fraud	It generally involves a telco employee manipulating a customer's account without authorization.
2	False promotion fraud	Under the pretence of a telecom promotion, the recipient is prompted to enter their PIN as a verification mechanism in order to collect a "prize." The entered PIN grants the fraudster access to the recipient's mobile money account.
3	Scam messages/reversal of erroneous transactions	A bogus SMS indicating a deposit into a customer's account is delivered. The scammer then phones the victim to inform them that the deposit was a mistake and to return the money.
4	Fortuitous scam	Calling clients under the pretence of sending products from relatives living overseas, fraudsters pose as delivery businesses. The customer will then be told to fund a mobile money account in exchange for the delivery of the products.

Source: Annan (2017)

HYPOTHESIS DEVELOPMENT

Uncertainty Avoidance

According to Hofstede, (1980), uncertainty avoidance refers to how threatened people of a culture feel when faced with unclear situations. Previous works on deceptive behaviours and corruption suggest that deception is more likely to occur in collectivist cultures, than in individualist cultures (Triandis et al., 2001; Li et al., 2006). Hence the latter tend to have higher uncertainty avoidance than the former. UA gives distinctions between national cultures and to evaluate emerging technology such as mobile money (Aggarwal et al., 2020; Hassan & Wood, 2020; Rosillo-Díaz et al., 2020). For instance, Rosillo-Díaz et al., (2020) in their study revealed that customers who with lower uncertainty would have a strong intent to use a technology irrespective of the risks associated. Higher uncertainty is hence associated with high fraud perception increasing anxieties about MoMo fraud, hence impacting its application in C2C e-commerce. Several empirical studies have identified avoidance of ambiguity as a significant determinant in terms of MoMo fraud perception (Noreen et al., 20221; Baganzi & Lau, 2017; Al-Adwan et al., 2022). Based on these arguments, it is hypothesized that:

H1: Uncertainty Avoidance has a significant influence on Consumer Fraud Perception in C2C e-commerce.

Perceived Reputation of Mobile Service Provider

Chandra et al., (2010), attributes the "Perceived Reputation of Mobile Service Provider" (PRSMP) as the degree to which consumers trust the mobile service provider's (MSP) competence, honesty, and goodness. A good reputation can be developed over time with the help of many strategies, tools and deliberate effort. According to researchers, "reputation" is difficult to establish yet simple to destroy if not carefully preserved (Chandra et al., 2010). In this paper, reputation of MoMo service provider with regards their capacity and commitment to ensuring end-user protection from fraudsters can impact on Consumer's Fraud Perception. The service providers in this research are the MoMo and the C2C e-commerce providers. Recent studies have emphasized the critical necessity of corporate reputation management and uncertainty reduction, particularly in societies with high fraud tendency and trust deficit (Osakwe & Yusuf, 2021). Chandra et al., (2010) discovered that PRSMP has the capacity to influence consumers' trust in mobile service providers. This assertion is supported by Xin et al., (2013) who found that providers' reputation is negatively correlated to fraud perception in mobile payment services. It is therefore hypothesized that:

H2: Perceived reputation of mobile service provider (PRSMP) has a significant influence on Consumer Fraud Perception in C2C e-commerce.

Trust in C2C Trader

Trust is described as the psychological anticipation of having a reliable companion who won't take advantage of you (Bunduchi, 2005). Trust helps lessen the uncertainty, fear, and anxiety associated with using the service. The authors of this research believe that trust in C2C traders has a significant influence on consumer fraud perception in C2C e-commerce. This construct has received much attention in the literature to study diverse digital platforms including MoMo, e-commerce, and other digital payment systems (Sasongko et al., 2022; Bailey et al., 2022, Yan & Pan, 2015). Furthermore, Chandra et al., (2010) studied how consumers adopt mobile payment systems and discovered that perceived utility and stakeholder trust have a strong impact on adoption intentions. Hence, higher trust in trader implies a lower perceived tendency for deception in a C2C e-commerce transaction. Additionally, fraud perception which impacts trust has a general influence on individuals' inclinations to utilize MoMo payments (Bailey et al., 2022). It is therefore hypothesized that:

H3: Trust in C2C Trader has a significant influence on Consumer Fraud Perception in C2C e-commerce

Structural Assurance

According to Baganzi and Lau, (2017, p 6-7), "perceived structural assurance reflects consumers' beliefs about the availability of legal structures, technological structures and other payment security measures to ensure that mobile money transactions are completed by mobile money services providers". In this study, structural assurance refers to an assessment of the effectiveness of the institutional environment, which comprises the structural and legislative elements for guaranteeing a secure environment for C2C e-commerce transactions. Therefore, consumer's fraud perception with MoMo transactions can be affected by the institutional environment is that all of the assurances, laws and commitments are in place and working to ensure transactions are safe, secure, and dependable. Researchers have employed structural assurance to support consumers' perceptions of the security of mobile money transactions (Osakwe et al., 2020; Chandra et al., 2010; Xin et al., 2015). According to Osakwe et al., (2020) initial trust in mobile money is positively impacted by perceived structural assurance. In addition, a recent study on mobile money has proposed that structural assurance can reduce risk perceptions frequently linked with its use, enhancing trust in mobile money (Rouibah et al., 2016). According to Rouibah et al., (2016), people will tend to have more faith in mobile money if they have access to sufficient transaction safeguards and the chance to file a claim for unsuccessful and/or fraudulent transactions. Based on these arguments, it is hypothesized that:

H4: Structural assurance (SA) has a significant influence on Consumer Fraud Perception in C2C e-commerce.

Perceived Usefulness

Perceived usefulness is defined as "the degree to which an individual believes that using a particular system will enhance user's job performance" (Davis, 1989, p. 12). This construct has received much attention in the literature to study the usefulness of diverse digital platforms (Nel & Boshoff, 2017; 2020; Li et al,.2019; Hing & Vui, 2021; Lwoga & Lwoga, 2017). Lwoga and Lwoga, (2017) conducted a study, the results of which demonstrate that the intention to utilize mobile payments is determined by perceived utility, perceived simplicity of use, social impact, and individual IT innovation. For online shopping platforms, perceived usefulness is related to the perceived benefits such as maximizing timesaving, minimizing cost during a transaction, and making online grocery shopping more convenient (Hing & Vui, 2021). The authors further stated that when evaluating the worth of online customer care products, it is appropriate to take perceived usefulness into account as a predictor. People usually anticipate their own activities' outcomes and base their choices on what they think will be useful. As a result, it affects a customer's desire to embrace and utilize a system. Again, in terms of perceived usefulness and fraud perception, earlier research has revealed empirical support for the notion that the usefulness and usability of mobile technologies are key determinants of trust which impacts consumer perception (Nel & Boshoff, 2017; Li et al., 2019). It is therefore, hypothesized that:

H5: Perceived usefulness (PU) has a significant influence on Consumer Fraud Perception in C2C e-commerce.

Consumer Fraud Perception and Usage Intention in Momo C2C e-Commerce

The mounting awareness, knowledge, and research of Momo C2C e-commerce issues has brought about a growing interest in consumers' perception towards fraud. Customers, retailers, and payment providers continue to incur significant losses due to online fraud every year. There is a relationship between consumer fraud perception and trust for emerging technologies (Sasongko et al., 2022). Consumers with lower fraud perception about a mobile payment service are more inclined to patronize and utilize such services. Fraud perception in C2C e-commerce can be related to consumer trust which according to Cheung and Lee, (2006) requires two essential elements: a willingness to be vulnerable and self-assured expectations. Expectations about the activities that the trusted party might do as well as perceptions of the trustee's prospective dependability, predictability, and competence are the sources of trust (Johansen et al., 2013). This research espouses that consumer fraud perception in MoMo services from a trust perspective has a significant influence on the intention to use MoMo in C2C e-commerce. Consumers may be unsure about the technology and operational environment because the high distrust borne out of high fraud potential or perception (Chandra et al., 2010). Based on these arguments, it is hypothesized that:

H6: Consumer Fraud Perception has a significant influence on intention to use C2C e-commerce

The research model is shown in Figure 1.

Figure 1. The Research Model

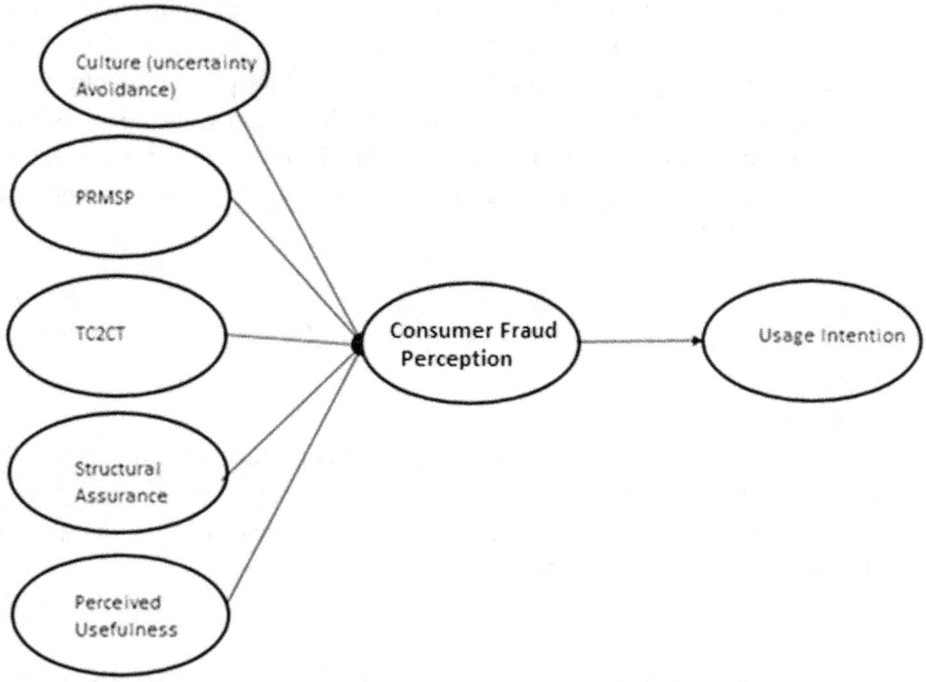

METHODOLOGY

Research Design

The study used a quantitative research design. The quantitative research design was chosen because the researchers wanted to statistically test the influence of independent latent constructs on mediating latent constructs and dependent latent construct via path analysis. The study also adopted a hypothesis-testing design. A claim or hypothesis regarding a parameter in a population is tested using data collected from a sample, a process known as hypothesis testing or significance testing. In this method, we test some hypothesis by determining the likelihood that a sample statistic could have been selected, if the hypothesis regarding the population parameter were true.

Sampling

The population for the study comprised people who use mobile money services and are familiar with social media. A purposive sampling technique was used. Sometimes it may be necessary to get information from particular target groups in place of those that are most easily or conveniently accessible. Here, the sampling is limited to a particular group of persons who are able to supply the needed information, either because they are the only ones with it or because they meet certain criteria established by the researcher. This type of sampling design is called purposive sampling. The sample comprised university students, members of Whatsapp groups, and users of other popular social media platforms. The Cochran (1963) formula for calculating the sample size for an unknown population size (large populations) was used. The formula is shown below:

$$n_0 = Z^2pq/e^2$$

where:

n_0 = sample size

Z = the Z score. A z-score describes the position of a raw score in terms of its distance from the mean, when measured in standard deviation units

p = the estimated proportion of an attribute that is present in the population. This is also known as the prevalence rate

q = 1-p

e = margin of error

A 95% confidence interval is chosen; thus, the margin of error is 0.05. The Z-score at 95% is 1.96. Based on a pilot study, a value of 0.4 was chosen for p.

From equation (1) n_0 = (3.8416 x 0.4 x 0.6)/ 0.0025 = 368.79

The minimum sample size is therefore 369.

Data Collection

An online survey was used for data collection. The link to the online survey was sent to the target population for completion. The link was shared on university students' social media platforms, WhatsApp and Facebook groups, and LinkedIn. C2C e-commerce is conducted on these platforms. Three hundred and thirty-seven (387) responses were received.

Questionnaire Development

Measurement items for uncertainty avoidance were adopted from Yoo et al. (2011). Measurement items for perceived reputation of mobile service provider (PRSMP), trust in C2C trader (TC2CT), structural assurance, perceived usefulness, consumer fraud perception, and usage intention were adopted from Chandra et al., (2010).

DATA ANALYSIS AND RESULTS

PLS-SEM (partial least squares-structural equation modelling) was used to analyse the data with SmartPLS 3. For non-parametric modelling of intricate cause-and-effect interactions between latent variables, PLS-SEM is suitable (Hair et al., 2012). Using SEM, a researcher can simultaneously test and model correlations between numerous independent and dependent variables (Gefen, Straub, & Boudreau, 2000; Hair et al., 2014). SEM differs from first-generation statistical methods like regression and factor analysis in three ways, according to Hair et al., (2014). First, SEM has the capacity to estimate a number of distinct but related correlations simultaneously. In addition, SEM can represent unobserved notions in these interactions and take measurement error into account when making estimates. By assessing the consistency among several manifest variables, or indicators, these latent constructs, or unseen variables, are indirectly measured. Finally, the researcher can define a model using SEM that accounts for the complete set of relationships.

Because of the potential complexity of the research model in the current study, SEM is a suitable technique to analyze the correlations. By using indicators (manifest variables or items) to measure latent factors (unobserved variables), SEM enables researchers to predict measurement error for the observable variables as well. Through confirmatory analysis, this enables researchers to statistically evaluate a priori substantive/theoretical and measurement assumptions against empirical data (Chin, 1998).

The analysis employs the two-step PLS-SEM methodology that Chin (1998) suggested. First, the measurement model (outer model) was evaluated, then the structural model was evaluated (inner model). Prior to PLS-SEM, data cleaning was performed. After the data was cleaned and reviewed for missing values and outliers, 376 responses were kept. Table 2 shows that all the factor loadings are above 0.5.

Table 2. Outer loadings

	Uncertainty Avoidance	Perc_ Reputation Provider	Perceived Usefulness	Structural Assurance	Trust_ C2C Trader	Consumer fraud Perc.	Usage Intention
MSP1		0.8161842					
MSP2		0.9017682					
MSP3		0.9021901					
PU1			0.8257498				
PU2			0.8925285				
PU3			0.8770105				
PU4			0.864572				
PU5			0.857113				
STRC1				0.8281934			
STRC2				0.8830611			
STRC3				0.8684135			
STRC4				0.8288421			
TRAD1					0.8691703		
TRAD2					0.9259573		
TRAD3					0.8673997		
CFP1						0.8606343	
CFP2						0.8760561	
CFP3						0.8896392	
CFP4						0.8372131	
CFP5						0.7217395	
UI1							0.860252
UI2							0.9204758
UI3							0.8871287
UNC1	0.5453452						
UNC2	0.7624356						
UNC3	0.8137596						
UNC4	0.8098678						
UNC5	0.8729837						

Tests for reliability, convergent validity, and discriminant validity were used to evaluate the measurement model. Cronbach's alpha, composite reliability, and Dijkstra-Henseler's rho were used to evaluate reliability. If the values of Cronbach's alpha, composite reliability, and Dijkstra-Henseler's rho are 0.7 or higher, a construct is considered reliable (Hair et al., 2012).

The average variance extracted (AVE) was used to evaluate convergence validity. If a construct has convergent validity, the AVE value must be at least 0.5 (Hair et al., 2012). Table 3 shows that all the constructs display reliability and convergent validity.

Table 3. Construct reliability and validity

Construct	Cronbach's Alpha	rho_A	Composite Reliability	Average Variance Extracted (AVE)
Culture (Uncertainty Avoidance)	0.833	0.912	0.876	0.592
Perc Reputation Provider	0.846	0.867	0.907	0.764
Perceived Usefulness	0.915	0.919	0.936	0.746
Structural Assurance	0.875	0.881	0.914	0.727
Consumer Fraud Perception	0.894	0.904	0.922	0.704
Trust_C2C Trader	0.865	0.868	0.918	0.788
Usage Intention	0.868	0.872	0.919	0.791

Discriminant validity was assessed using the heterotrait-monotrait ratio of correlations ($HTMT^{0.90}$). Discriminant validity between two constructs is confirmed if the HTMT value is less than 0.90. (Hair et al., 2014). Table 4 shows that all the constructs show discriminant validity.

Table 4. Heterotrait-monotrait ratio of correlations (HTMT)

	Culture (Uncertainty Avoidance)	Perc Reputation Provider	Perceived Usefulness	Structural Assurance	Consumer Fraud Perception	Trust_ C2C Trader	Usage Intention
Culture (Uncertainty Avoidance)							
Perc Reputation Provider	0.381						
Perceived Usefulness	0.390	0.434					
Structural Assurance	0.312	0.610	0.590				
Consumer Fraud Perception	0.128	0.474	0.474	0.677			
Trust_C2C Trader	0.348	0.583	0.505	0.640	0.569		
Usage Intention	0.348	0.504	0.710	0.570	0.679	0.543	

The significance of each estimated path was assessed by the structural model using a bootstrapping approach. In order to bootstrap, a large number of replacement samples are taken from the original sample, and each replacement sample's model parameters are estimated. Table 5 shows the outcomes of the bootstrapping technique. Significant paths have p values of 0.05 or less, while non-significant constructs have p values higher than 0.05. Table 5 shows that five of the hypotheses, that is, H1, H3, H4, H5, and H6 were supported whereas one, that is, H1 was not. Thirty-six (36) percent of the variance in usage intention and 43.3 percent of the variance in trust in C2C e-commerce were explained by the suggested model. Table 5 shows the R square values. To evaluate model fit in SmartPLS, the standardized root mean square residual (SRMR) was used. According to Hu and Bentler (1999), models with SRMR values lower than 0.08 have a satisfactory model fit. Table 5 shows an SRMR value of 0.05, indicating that the model fits the data adequately.

Table 5. Hypothesis testing results

Hypothesis	Hypothesized Path	Path Coefficient	t Statistics	P Values	Result
H1	Culture (Uncertainty Avoidance) -> Consumer Fraud Perception	-0.143	3.070	0.002	Supported
H2	Perc_Reputation Provider -> Consumer Fraud Perception	0.098	1.604	0.109	Not supported
H3	Structural Assurance -> Consumer Fraud Perception	0.408	6.882	0.000	Supported
H4	Perceived Usefulness -> Consumer Fraud Perception	0.140	2.690	0.007	Supported
H5	Consumer Fraud Perception -> Usage Intention	0.603	17.760	0.000	Supported
H6	Trust_C2C Trader -> Consumer Fraud Perception	0.210	3.383	0.001	Supported
	R^2 (Consumer Fraud Perception) = 0.433				
	R^2 (Usage Intention) = 0.361				
	SRMR = 0.05				

Table 6 shows indicator data. Figure 2 shows the responses on the mobile service provider. Table 6 shows the outer loadings.

Table 6. Indicator data

Construct	Indicators	Mean	Overall Mean	Median	Standard Deviation	Excess Kurtosis	Skewness
Perceived reputation of MSP	MSP1	3.872	3.742	4.000	0.878	1.641	-0.979
	MSP2	3.684		4.000	0.871	0.650	-0.647
	MSP3	3.670		4.000	0.921	0.734	-0.795
Perceived usefulness	PU1	3.992	3.916	4.000	0.713	1.447	-0.697
	PU2	3.888		4.000	0.764	0.812	-0.635
	PU3	3.830		4.000	0.756	0.688	-0.557
	PU4	3.894		4.000	0.743	1.294	-0.684
	PU5	3.979		4.000	0.714	0.757	-0.540
Structural Assurance	STRC1	3.699	3.699	4.000	0.849	0.701	-0.744
	STRC2	3.588		4.000	0.877	0.422	-0.662
	STRC3	3.777		4.000	0.774	0.909	-0.696
	STRC4	3.734		4.000	0.795	1.015	-0.700
Perceived reputation of C2C Trader	TRAD1	3.569	3.521	4.000	0.741	1.150	-0.456
	TRAD2	3.465		3.000	0.714	0.706	-0.208
	TRAD3	3.529		4.000	0.740	0.619	-0.339
Consumer Fraud Perception	CFP1	3.399	3.380	3.000	0.851	-0.122	-0.189
	CFP2	3.380		3.000	0.897	0.097	-0.359
	CFP3	3.348		3.000	0.859	0.012	-0.307
	CFP4	3.521		4.000	0.792	0.620	-0.635
	CFP5	3.250		3.000	0.963	-0.279	-0.357
Usage Intention	UI1	3.726	3.747	4.000	0.804	1.685	-0.822
	UI2	3.731		4.000	0.822	1.118	-0.737
	UI3	3.785		4.000	0.821	0.912	-0.624
Uncertainty Avoidance	UNC1	4.122	4.236	4.000	0.870	1.683	-1.117
	UNC2	4.338		4.000	0.829	4.049	-1.714
	UNC3	4.362		5.000	0.797	4.373	-1.725
	UNC4	4.093		4.000	0.795	2.704	-1.156
	UNC5	4.266		4.000	0.721	3.457	-1.261

Figure 2. Responses on Mobile Service Provider

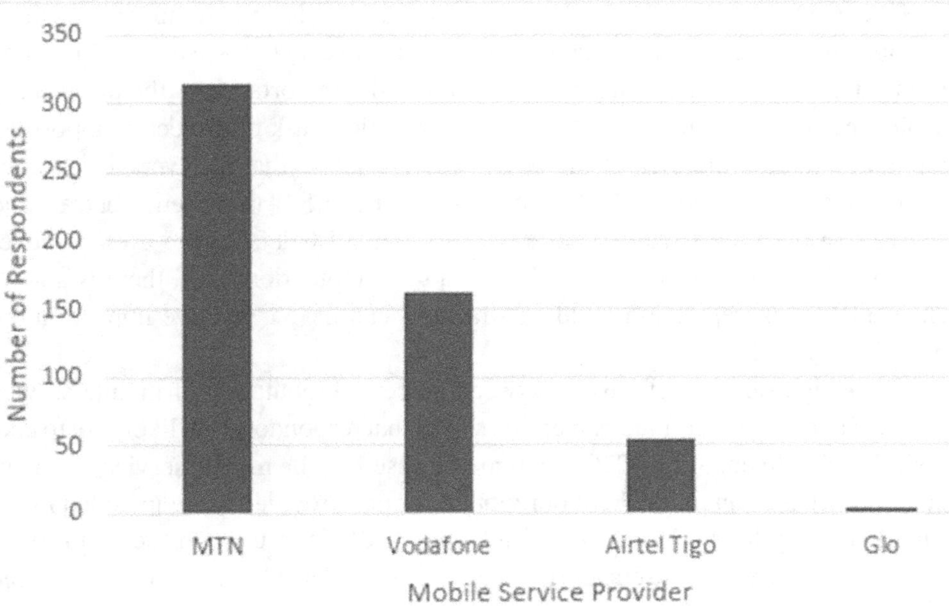

DISCUSSION

The study found culture (uncertainty avoidance) to have a significant negative effect on consumer fraud perception. This finding is consistent with Xin et al., (2015), Seo et al., (2018), and De Meulenaer et al., (2018). The culture construct was measured with items based on reliance on instructions for the performance of tasks, adherence to instructions and procedures, importance of rules and regulations, and adherence to standardised procedures. The negative relationship between uncertainty avoidance and consumer fraud perception suggests that people are less likely to trust C2C e-commerce if they have a higher uncertainty avoidance tendency. The average score of 4.236 for uncertainty avoidance (Table 4) shows that the average respondent has a high uncertainty avoidance (between "agree" and "strongly agree" on the Likert scale). This result also shows that the average respondent is likely to be risk-averse. The C2C trader, therefore, has to put in extra effort to gain the trust of the buyer. The C2C trader has to develop relevant trust-building strategies to get sales from potential buyers. The consumer fraud perception construct had measurement items worded from a fraud perspective; thus, it is imperative that the results be interpreted with "fraud" in mind. The overall mean score of 3.380 for the construct suggests that respondents are somewhat indifferent in their perceptions of fraud in C2C e-commerce.

Perceived reputation of C2C trader was found to have a significant positive relationship with consumer fraud perception (consistent with Xin et al., (2015) and Larasetiati & Ali (2019). This result reinforces the importance of the uncertainty avoidance-trust linkage; the C2C trader has a critical task of projecting a positive reputation to gain the trust of the buyer. Table 4 shows that the average score for the perceived reputation of C2C trader construct is 3.521 (between "neutral" and "agree" on the Likert scale). The score shows that by default, the average buyer does not disagree that the C2C trader has a good reputation; thus, there is a good chance that trust/reputation building strategies can have a positive impact on the buyer's decision.

The insignificant relationship between perceived reputation of mobile service provider and consumer fraud perception shows that respondents are likely not to take their decision to engage in C2C e-commerce based on the mobile service provider, but largely based on the trader. Four mobile service providers were included in the survey, namely MTN, Vodafone, Airtel Tigo, and Glo. Although the majority of respondents were MTN users, the other service providers also enjoyed a reasonable amount of patronage. The responses regarding mobile service provider are shown in Figure 2.

Structural assurance was found to have a positive significant relationship with consumer fraud perception. This result is consistent with Chandra et al., (2010), Osakwe et al., (2020), and Xin et al., (2015). This finding implies that the characteristics of the mobile telephony technology are important determinants of trust (from a fraud perspective) in C2C e-commerce. Mobile service providers should ensure network safeguards such as encryption are implemented to make customers comfortable while using the network for MoMo payments and also ensure there are adequate legal and technological structures to protect customers.

Perceived usefulness had a positive significant influence on consumer fraud perception, which is consistent with studies conducted by Yan and Pan (2015), Nel and Boshoff (2017), and Li et al., (2019). The overall average score of 3.9 (Table 4) shows that generally, the respondents agree that MoMo C2C e-commerce would enable them make purchases quickly, increase their performance in making purchases, and improve their effectiveness in making purchases. MoMo C2C traders should endeavour to provide very good services to enhance the trust customers have in the e-commerce service.

Finally, based on the study, consumer fraud perception has a significant positive influence on the intention to use MoMo C2C e-commerce. Ultimately, fraud or perceptions of fraud will diminish people's intention to use the MoMo platform for C2C e-commerce. MoMo service providers should consistently educate customers on MoMo fraud and secure their networks as well. MoMo fraud is largely dependent on the level of security literacy of the user; thus, education is critical.

CONCLUSION

Generally, the average respondent has a high uncertainty avoidance tendency and is likely to be risk averse. The C2C trader, therefore, has to put in extra effort to gain the trust of the buyer. The C2C trader has to develop relevant trust-building strategies to get sales from potential buyers. The C2C trader has a critical task of projecting a positive reputation to gain the trust of the buyer. There is a good chance that trust/reputation building strategies can have a positive impact on the buyer's decision. Respondents are likely not to take their decision to engage in C2C e-commerce based on the mobile service provider, but largely based on the trader. MoMo C2C traders should endeavour to provide very good services to enhance the trust customers have in the e-commerce service. MoMo service providers should consistently educate customers on MoMo fraud and secure their networks as well.

THEORETICAL IMPLICATIONS

The review of the extant literature shows the lack of a standard theory/model that explains the determinants of consumer fraud perception in the domain of C2C e-commerce as well as the impact of consumer fraud perception on consumer intention to use mobile money for C2C e-commerce. The current research model should be tested in different research settings to establish its robustness for adoption as a reliable model.

PRACTICAL IMPLICATIONS

C2C traders will find the results of this study useful especially in the development of trust-building strategies to increase sales. C2C traders must realise that their revenue growth from the trust/fraud perspective depends largely on them rather than the telcos.

REFERENCES

Abdul-Rahaman, A., & Abdulai, A. (2022). Mobile money adoption, input use, and farm output among smallholder rice farmers in Ghana. *Agribusiness*, *38*(1), 236–255. doi:10.1002/agr.21721

Akomea-Frimpong, I., Andoh, C., Akomea-Frimpong, A., & Dwomoh-Okudzeto, Y. (2019). Control of fraud on mobile money services in Ghana: An exploratory study. *Journal of Money Laundering Control*, *22*(2), 300–317. doi:10.1108/JMLC-03-2018-0023

Al-Adwan, A. S., Alrousan, M. K., Yaseen, H., Alkufahy, A. M., & Alsoud, M. (2022). Boosting Online Purchase Intention in High-Uncertainty-Avoidance Societies: A Signaling Theory Approach. *Journal of Open Innovation*, *8*(3), 136. doi:10.3390/joitmc8030136

Al-Jabari, M. A. R.S (2013). *Factors Influencing Online Shopping Behavior Among Jordanian Academicians*. Mohammed Abdal Razaq Al-Jabari Universiti Utara Malaysia.

Annan, S. (2017). Avoiding Fraud Due to Mobile Money. *Ghana Web*. https://www.ghanaweb.com/GhanaHomePage/features/Avoiding-fra ud-due-to-Mobile-Money-588682

Ayettey, L. T. (2019, October 19), *MOMO Fraud – How Scammers Steal Your Money*. ModernGhana. https://www.modernghana.com/news/962315/momo-fraud-how-scamm ers-steal-your-money.html

Baganzi, R., & Lau, A. K. W. (2017). Examining trust and risk in mobile money acceptance in Uganda. *Sustainability (Switzerland)*, *9*(12), 2233. doi:10.3390u9122233

Bailey, A. A., Bonifield, C. M., Arias, A., & Villegas, J. (2022). Mobile payment adoption in Latin America. *Journal of Services Marketing*, (December). doi:10.1108/JSM-04-2021-0130

Bank of Ghana. (2020). *Payment Systems Oversight Annual Report*. Payment Systems Department Bank of Ghana.

Berraies, S., Ben Yahia, K., & Hannachi, M. (2017). Identifying the effects of perceived values of mobile banking applications on customers: Comparative study between baby boomers, generation X and generation Y. *International Journal of Bank Marketing*, *35*(6), 1018–1038. doi:10.1108/IJBM-09-2016-0137

Boberhoff, T., & con der Decken, J. (2022). *E-Commerce in Nigeria Nigerian E-Commerce landscape and. May*. [Master's thesis, Jönköping International Business School.]

Botchey, F. E., Qin, Z., & Hughes-Lartey, K. (2020). Mobile money fraud prediction—A cross-case analysis on the efficiency of support vector machines, gradient boosted decision trees, and Naïve Bayes algorithms. *Information*, *11*(8), 383. doi:10.3390/info11080383

Brown, N. (2021). Over 4,000 Cyber Fraud Cases Currently Under Investigation. *Joy Online*. https://www.myjoyonline.com/over-4000-cyber-fraud-cases-currently-under-investigation/?param=

Bunduchi, R. (2005). Business relationships in internet-based electronic markets: The role of goodwill trust and transaction costs. *Information Systems Journal*, *15*(4), 321–341. doi:10.1111/j.1365-2575.2005.00199.x

Chandra, S., Lowry, P. B., Rouibah, K., & Shanab, E. A. (2010). *Evaluating the Role of Trust in Consumer Adoption of Mobile Payment Systems*. AIS eLibrary. https://aisel.aisnet.org/cais/vol27/iss1/29

Chin, W. W. (1998). The partial least squares approach to structural equation modeling. *Modern Methods for Business Research*, *295*(2), 295–336.

Cochran, W. G. (1963). *Sampling Techniques* (2nd ed.). John Wiley & Sons.

Davis, F. D. (1989). Perceived usefulness, perceived ease of use, and user acceptance of information technology. *MIS Quarterly: Management Information Systems*, *13*(3), 319–339. doi:10.2307/249008

De Meulenaer, S., De Pelsmacker, P., & Dens, N. (2018). Power Distance, Uncertainty Avoidance, and the Effects of Source Credibility on Health Risk Message Compliance. *Health Communication*, *33*(3), 291–298. doi:10.1080/10410236.2016.1266573 PMID:28094542

Ekong, U. M., & Ekong, C. N. (2022). Digital currency and financial inclusion in Nigeria: Lessons for development. *Journal of Internet and Digital Economics*, *2*(1), 46–67. doi:10.1108/JIDE-11-2021-0018

El Ayeb, S., Hemery, B., Jeanne, F., & Cherrier, E. (2020, December). Community detection for mobile money fraud detection. In *2020 Seventh International Conference on Social Networks Analysis, Management and Security (SNAMS)* (pp. 1-6). IEEE.

Entee, E., & Afful-Dadzie, A. (2020). Coming of Age?: Exploring the Role of Dynamic Capabilities in Social Commerce Firms–Evidence From a Ghanaian Enterprise. In R. Boateng. Handbook of Research on Managing Information Systems in Developing Economies (pp. 281-294). IGI Global.

Gukurume, S., & Mahiya, I. T. (2020). Mobile money and the (un) making of social relations in Chivi, Zimbabwe. *Journal of Southern African Studies*, *46*(6), 1203–1217. doi:10.1080/03057070.2020.1823682

Hair, J. F., Black, W. C., Babin, B. J., & Anderson, R. E. (2014). *Multivariate data analysis* (7th ed.). Pearson Education International.

Hair, J. F., Sarstedt, M., Pieper, T. M., & Ringle, C. M. (2012). The Use of Partial Least Squares Structural Equation Modeling in Strategic Management Research : A Review of Past Practices and Recommendations for Future Applications. *Long Range Planning*, *45*(5–6), 320–340. doi:10.1016/j.lrp.2012.09.008

Hassan, H. E., & Wood, V. R. (2020). Does country culture influence consumers' perceptions toward mobile banking? A comparison between Egypt and the United States. *Telematics and Informatics, 46*(April 2019), 101312. doi:10.1016/j.tele.2019.101312

Hu, L., & Bentler, P. M. (1999). Cutoff criteria for fit indexes in covariance structure analysis: Conventional criteria versus new alternatives. *Structural Equation Modeling*, *6*(1), 1–55. doi:10.1080/10705519909540118

Iman, N. (2018). Is mobile payment still relevant in the fintech era? *Electronic Commerce Research and Applications*, *30*(May), 72–82. doi:10.1016/j.elerap.2018.05.009

Johansen, S. T., Selart, M., & Grønhaug, K. (2013). The effects of risk on initial trust formation. *Journal of Applied Social Psychology*, *43*(6), 1185–1199. doi:10.1111/jasp.12082

Kaabachi, S., Ben Mrad, S., & Petrescu, M. (2017). Consumer initial trust toward internet-only banks in France. *International Journal of Bank Marketing*, *35*(6), 903–924. doi:10.1108/IJBM-09-2016-0140

Khet, K., & Tha, O. (2022). *Mobile money affordances : enabling the way for financial inclusion.* Thirtieth European Conference on Information Systems, Timişoara, Romania.

Kilavo, H. J., Mselle, L. I., Rais, R., & Mrutu, S. I. (2022). Reverse Social Engineering to Counter Social Engineering in Mobile Money Theft: A Tanzanian Context. *Journal of Applied Security Research*, 1–13.

Kim, D. J. (2012). An investigation of the effect of online consumer trust on expectation, satisfaction, and post-expectation. *Information Systems and e-Business Management*, *10*(2), 219–240. doi:10.100710257-010-0136-2

Koomson, I., Bukari, C., & Villano, R. A. (2021). Mobile money adoption and response to idiosyncratic shocks: Empirics from five selected countries in sub-Saharan Africa. *Technological Forecasting and Social Change, 167*(July 2020), 120728. doi:10.1016/j.techfore.2021.120728

Larasetiati, M., & Ali, H. (2019). Model of consumer trust: Analysis of perceived usefulness and toward repurchase intention in online travel agent. *Journal of Economics and Finance*, *3*(8), 350–357. doi:10.21276jef.2019.3.8.5

Leonard, L. N., & Jones, K. (2021). Trust in C2C electronic commerce: Ten years later. *Journal of Computer Information Systems*, *61*(3), 240–246. doi:10.1080/08874417.2019.1598829

Li, J., Wang, J., Wangh, S., & Zhou, Y. (2019). Mobile Payment with Alipay: An Application of Extended Technology Acceptance Model. *IEEE Access: Practical Innovations, Open Solutions*, *7*, 50380–50387. doi:10.1109/ACCESS.2019.2902905

Lwoga, E. T., & Lwoga, N. B. (2017). User acceptance of mobile payment: The effects of user-centric security, system characteristics and gender. *The Electronic Journal on Information Systems in Developing Countries*, *81*(1), 1–24. doi:10.1002/j.1681-4835.2017.tb00595.x

Martin, A. (2019). Mobile money platform surveillance. *Surveillance & Society*, *17*(1/2), 213–222. doi:10.24908s.v17i1/2.12924

Mayer., R, Davis, J., & Schoorman, F. (1995). *An Integrative Model of Organizational Trust. Academy of Management Review, 20*(3), 709–734. http://www.jstor.com/stable/258792 .

Muganyi, T., Yan, L., Yin, Y., Sun, H., Gong, X., & Taghizadeh-Hesary, F. (2022). Fintech, regtech, and financial development: Evidence from China. *Financial Innovation*, *8*(1), 29. doi:10.118640854-021-00313-6

Museba, T. J., Ranganai, E., & Gianfrate, G. (2021). Customer perception of adoption and use of digital financial services and mobile money services in Uganda. *Journal of Enterprising Communities*, *15*(2), 177–203. doi:10.1108/JEC-07-2020-0127

Ndegwa, R. (2014). *Effect of Mobile Money on Non-Performing Loans of Commercial Banks in Kenya*. University of Nairobi.

Nel, J., & Boshoff, C. (2017). Development of application-based mobile-service trust and online trust transfer: An elaboration likelihood model perspective. *Behaviour & Information Technology*, *36*(8), 809–826. doi:10.1080/0144929X.2017.1296493

Noreen, M., Ghazali, Z., & Mia, M. S. (2021). The Impact of Perceived Risk and Trust on Adoption of Mobile Money Services: An Empirical Study in Pakistan. *The Journal of Asian Finance. Economics and Business*, *8*(6), 347–355.

Orlikowski, W., Kim, A., Oborn, E., & Sloan, M. I. T. (2018). Trajectory Dynamics in Innovation : Developing and Transforming a Mobile Money Service Across Time and Place. *Organization Science* .

Osakwe, C. N., Ruiz, B., Amegbe, H., Chinje, N. B., Cheah, J. H., & Ramayah, T. (2020). A multi-country study of bank reputation among customers in Africa: Key antecedents and consequences. *Journal of Retailing and Consumer Services*, *56*(May), 102182. Advance online publication. doi:10.1016/j.jretconser.2020.102182

Osakwe, C. N., & Yusuf, T. O. (2021). CSR: A roadmap towards customer loyalty. *Total Quality Management & Business Excellence*, *32*(13–14), 1424–1440. doi:10.1080/14783363.2020.1730174

Osei-Assibey, E. (2015). What drives behavioral intention of mobile money adoption? The case of ancient susu saving operations in Ghana. *International Journal of Social Economics*, *42*(11), 962–979. doi:10.1108/IJSE-09-2013-0198

Purwanto, A. (2022). What Is the Role of Customer Behavior for Electronic E-Commerce and Modern Market Visit Intention? [JISMA]. *Journal of Information Systems and Management*, *1*(6), 46–57.

Rosillo-Díaz, E., Blanco-Encomienda, F. J., & Crespo-Almendros, E. (2020). A cross-cultural analysis of perceived product quality, perceived risk and purchase intention in e-commerce platforms. *Journal of Enterprise Information Management*, *33*(1), 139–160. doi:10.1108/JEIM-06-2019-0150

Sasongko, D. T., Handayani, P. W., & Satria, R. (2021). Analysis of factors affecting continuance use intention of the electronic money application in Indonesia. *Procedia Computer Science*, *197*, 42–50. doi:10.1016/j.procs.2021.12.116

Seo, S., Kim, K., & Jang, J. (2018). Uncertainty avoidance as a moderator for influences on foreign resident dining out behaviors. *International Journal of Contemporary Hospitality Management*, *30*(2), 900–918. doi:10.1108/IJCHM-03-2016-0152

Serbeh, R., Adjei, P. O. W., & Forkuor, D. (2022). Financial inclusion of rural households in the mobile money era: Insights from Ghana. *Development in Practice*, *32*(1), 16–28. doi:10.1080/09614524.2021.1911940

Srite, M., & Karahanna, E. (2006). The role of espoused national cultural values in technology acceptance. *MIS Quarterly: Management Information Systems*, *30*(3), 679–704. doi:10.2307/25148745

Wieser, C., Bruhn, M., Kinzinger, J., Ruckteschler, C., & Heitmann, S. (2019). *The Impact of Mobile Money on Poor Rural Households: Experimental Evidence from Uganda.* World Bank. doi:10.1596/1813-9450-8913

Xin, H., Techatassanasoontorn, A. A., & Tan, F. B. (2015). Antecedents of consumer trust in mobile payment adoption. *Journal of Computer Information Systems*, *55*(4), 1–10. doi:10.1080/08874417.2015.11645781

Yip Hing, W., & Nyen Vui, C. (2021). Malaysian consumers' purchase intention towards online seafood shopping amid pandemic: The moderating role of the Covid-19 risk perception. *International Journal of Business. Marketing and Communication*, *1*(3), 2785–8413.

Yoo, B., Donthu, N., & Lenartowicz, T. (2011). Measuring hofstede's five dimensions of cultural values at the individual level: Development and validation of CVSCALE. *Journal of International Consumer Marketing*, *23*(3–4), 193–210. doi:10.1080/08961530.2011.578059

Chapter 6
Financing Terrorism With FinTechs in West Africa?

Jean Gondo Tompihe
https://orcid.org/0000-0001-7092-600X
International University of Grand-Bassam, Côte d'Ivoire & Institute for Advanced Study, Princeton University, USA

ABSTRACT

Despite FinTech's considerable financial inclusions in West Africa, its unintended criminogenic features cannot be overlooked. While the region rises as the continental FinTech hub, many countries have collapsed under terrorism. It faces a unique vulnerability to terrorism financing for having a high rate of joblessness among its FinTech-savvy millennials, which overlaps another high rate of joblessness among young terrorist recruits. But by highlighting the difference between the "operational" and "networking" motives of terrorism financing, this chapter demonstrates that the natures of assaults occurring in West Africa are operational financing using rudimentary cash flow carriers across borders. But given the ingenuity with which cybercriminals operate, it conducts a comprehensive analysis of the legislative measures implemented in West Africa to prevent FinTech's terrorism financing risks. It explores futureproofing, cutting-edge, and dynamic technology-based strategy, designed explicitly on cryptocurrencies and virtual assets to anticipate and combat terrorism financing.

DOI: 10.4018/978-1-6684-6381-9.ch006

Copyright © 2023, IGI Global. Copying or distributing in print or electronic forms without written permission of IGI Global is prohibited.

INTRODUCTION

Financial technology (FinTech) applications have seen their global adoption increase in 2020. Compared to 2019, they expanded by 15% and reached the number of 4.6 billion finance apps globally (Liftoff, 2021). In 2020, digital mobile payments like the point of sale (POS) had a worldwide exchange worth $5.204 billion. They are the most significant operational part of FinTech (Statista, 2021). Bitcoin trading alone surpassed $1 trillion for the first time in 2021 (Field, 2021). The story behind these staggering numbers provides insight into how FinTech is revolutionizing the efficiency of the financial sector by overcoming information obstructions and lowering fees for international remittances. What was exclusively revolving around traditional financial market providers (incumbent retail and central banks) providing (1) retail, business, and wholesale customers; (2) insurance and retirement funds; and (3) cash liquidity, capital markets, and foreign exchange is now substantially affected by the innovative intrusion of FinTech that facilitates borrowing, payments and saving, and allocating capital (Sy et al., 2019).

Consequently, FinTech-based technology-driven applications are not only causing disruption to the value chain of traditional financial services but, more importantly, they are transforming customer expectations in the way funds transfer and payment, insurance, and asset management used to be carried out and, by ricochet, they are creating opportunities in the underserved markets. As FinTech is leveraging these financial disruptions with tangible solutions that better address market needs—offering enhanced convenience, accessibility, and personalized products—consumers are familiarizing themselves with the new digital experience. Hence, FinTech's fund transfer companies are focusing on both increased ease and security of remittance practices such as consumer protection, peer-to-peer (P2P) payment solution, contactless technology for digital wallets from generation POS solutions to identity theft that use advanced technologies (e.g., Near Field Communication and QR Codes) for increased customers' involvement in their financial transactions. Moreover, in that dynamic, smartphone mobile operation is changing payment patterns due to its integrated portability, convenience, immediacy, and security. (PricewaterhouseCoopers, 2017).

All over the developing world, Baby Boomers (born roughly between 1946 and 1964) are looking at this precise moment as a massive turning point in their regions' financial market history. From independence to date, they have been eye-witnessing a changing world around them and limitless opportunity, modernization, and prosperity; and this matches their aspirations. The globalized media have been beaming the welfare of the affluent life into their houses daily. And, they want in, not out of this globalization. While they have vividly yearned for enfranchisement in the globalized market economies, their dysfunctional state governance has stood between them and a better life. However, against all odds, FinTech startups and new payment methods are opening the doors to this globalized market. They explicitly provide speedy and easy access to financial services to their underbanked populations (Gross et al., 2012). Indeed, a rebalancing of power on the financial services front is taking place where FinTechs are empowering developing regions' customers to not only suitably initiate but also execute themselves financial transactions, join third-party entities, and access information without constraints on time, location, or the usual heavy banking regulatory burden. In doing so, they are reducing the operational costs of handling financial transactions and improving customer retention. This unforeseen "Financial Inclusion Disruption" is timely. Worldwide, almost 1.4 billion people remain unbanked. In 2014 that number was 2 billion, and the majority live in the underdeveloped world. According to the 2021 Findex survey, 27% of adults without a bank account reported lacking the paperwork needed to open one. In addition, 31% cited distance as an obstacle. Regarding gender variation, 740 million women are unbanked (13% of all adults worldwide and 54% of the unbanked). Age category-wise, "79% of adults worldwide age 25 and older had an account, compared to 66% of those ages 15–24" (World Bank, 2021, p. 26). Fortunately, FinTech-based smartphone innovation is helping to overcome some of these barriers. According to the Gallup World Poll 2019 data, at least 80% of adults worldwide reported ownership of mobile phones (Ibid, p. 4).

Africa has been included in this disruptive financial inclusion process by FinTech. It has improved conventional methods of conducting transactions and given both individuals and companies tremendous options, such as quicker and more effective payment settlements. Mainly, mobile cellular and smartphones have been a handmaiden, with subscriptions growing faster than in the rest of the globe to take advantage of FinTech financial platforms. The continental mobile penetration was 46% in 2021. It is expected to reach 50% in 2025. Smartphone adoption was 64% in 2021. It is expected to reach 75% in 2025 (GSMA Intelligence 2021). The bulk of mobile money transactions is overtaking traditional bank accounts in several African economies (Sy et al., 2019, p. 20). More impressively, with a reported 650 million mobile users on the continent ("81 mobile phones per 100 inhabitants"), this number exceeds that of Europe and North America combined. The rapid adoption of FinTech in Africa is generating unique "triple game changers." It is creating (1) an unprecedented urbanized financial inclusion disruption and (2) a "suitable" FinTech Generation Y consumer profile—known as "Millennials" (born between 1980 and 2000), who possess financial technology literacy by being digitally savvy. And significantly, the trend of these Millennials' digitally savvy demographics will increase exponentially because the African population will surge from 1.2 billion to 2.5 billion by 2050 (UNDESA 2022). Its median age will be under 25 years (African Economic Outlook, 2017). By this logic, the continent is forecasted to be "the FinTech market of tomorrow" (Business Insider Africa, 2022). Lastly, (3) on the aggregate level, FinTech is correcting the longstanding financial market failure in Africa.

But while these three unique game changers unfold, state weakness and fragility prevail or accentuate in many places. Many of the region's countries are either backsliding, teetering on the brink of failure, or have already collapsed under violent extremism or terrorism. The danger for Africa is that despite FinTech's significant socio-financial benefits, its unintended "criminogenic" features cannot be overlooked. Money launderers and terrorism financiers are already misusing many of FinTech's innovative technologies, including the crowdfunding sectors (Soudijn, 2019; Teicher, 2018). Given these contradicting trends brought by FinTech, this chapter analyzes whether its developments could constitute a vulnerability to terrorism financing (TF). West Africa serves as a case study. With 83% penetration of mobile money usage and unprecedented acceleration in adopting Fintech solutions, it is dubbed the "continental Fintech hub" (GIABA, 2020b, p. 2). Yet, terrorism is drawing a new Islamic fundamentalism map in the region.

FINTECH'S SECURITY AND EFFICIENCY PRODUCTION POSSIBILITY FRONTIER

As West Africa is concurrently emerging as a FinTech and Terrorism hub, this chapter examines the potential impact of its high rate of joblessness among the FinTech-savvy Millennials, which overlaps the high rate of joblessness among the young terrorist recruits to highlight some probable vulnerabilities to FinTech-based TF. Importantly, the chapter analyzes how to improve stagnation in security due to weak regulations and legislation, considering FinTech moving up the production possibility frontier in terms of socio-economic efficiency in Africa. Such an analysis of the production possibility frontier between FinTech efficiency and security could be instructive. Indeed, FinTech is undoubtedly improving provisional proficiencies, lowering the expense of delivering monetary services, raising competitiveness, and introducing new services. And even though its emerging cutting-edge technologies improve risk monitoring and lower operational errors, they nonetheless carry emerging vulnerabilities like cyberattacks, money laundering, and terrorist funding, especially in the weak state conditions of West Africa. As such, the chapter explores how legislation could be specifically designed to work and create a balance between FinTech efficiency and security. It thus reviews the legislative initiatives by the Inter-Governmental Action Group against Money Laundering (GIABA) in West Africa to prevent money laundering and terrorism financing. Then, the chapter closes on state-of-the-art anticipatory FinTech capable of lowering levels of vulnerabilities on the production possibility frontier between efficiency and security. This is because Africa's regulatory approaches are rarely proactive. They frequently play catch-up with technological progress. But the ground reality is that change is the one constant in the technological world. Therefore, there needs to be a continual collaboration between regulators and the technology stakeholders for the former to keep on top of disruptive technologies and establish a suitable framework to manage Anti-Money Laundering/ Combating the Financing of Terrorism (AML/CFT) challenges brought by impending or new technological innovation. This anticipatory legislation is based on the tendency of African authorities to ban or impede digital innovation because they are not well-equipped or do not understand it. As such, the chapter looks at ways they must closely cooperate with the legal establishment to ensure that laws are sufficient and not overly restrictive to ensure that developing technologies are AML/ CFT compliant. In essence, the analysis of the production possibility frontier between efficiency and security looks at how regulations should be changed as they become burdensome or overly restrictive and threaten to stifle innovation and investment.

This approach is well-established in the financial industry, where a well-known trade-off between efficiency and security has frequently been considered (Berger, Hancock, & Marquardt 1996). It is well-suited to the analysis of FinTech's disruptive impacts. The trade-off between efficiency and security clearly shows in Figure 1 that as FinTech companies move up the value chain, the choices frontier in terms of efficiency expands. However, as it will be shown, security shrinks, given the lack of human resources, weak legislative framework, and poor enforcement mechanisms to lower vulnerabilities to cyberattacks, money laundering, and terrorist funding. By contrast, as Figure 1 shows, in a strong state context, a market system exhibits a careful balance between efficiency and security at point 1. Subsequently, point 2 would be safer and more effective as technological advancement expands the production possibility frontier between efficiency and security. Point 2 is a provision that facilitates cutting-edge FinTech to reach further an equilibrium where the financial system is *less* vulnerable and much safer. As will be shown, this is not the case in West Africa because its context of weak states exposes inefficient public policies and regulations. Consequently, the provisions move to suboptimal point 3, which shows an increase in efficiency from point 1 but a decrease in security. Thus, to answer how best to reduce the race gap between the skyrocketing FinTech efficiency and the stagnant security in West Africa—moving from Figure 1's points A to B—the chapter starts with FinTech's unfolding triple game changers in the general African and West African contexts of socio-economic efficiency. And because West Africa is dubbed the continental Fintech hub and simultaneously faces a rise in terrorism, the chapter singularly addresses how to fix security stagnation on the production possibility frontier.

Figure 1.

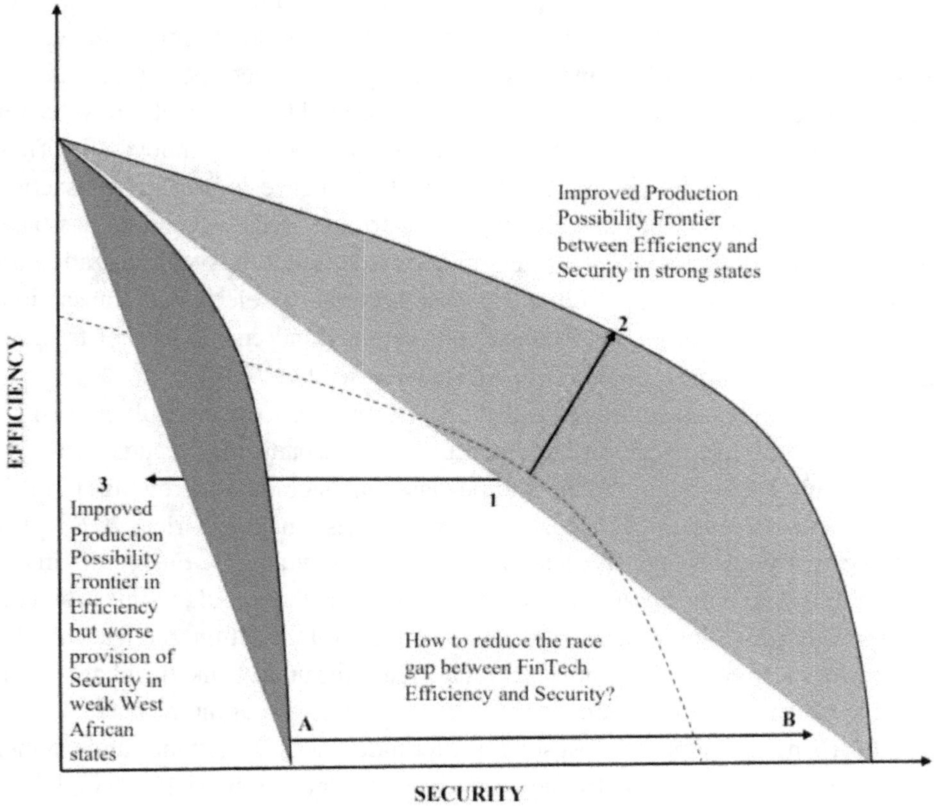

FINTECH DISRUPTIVE GAME CHANGER IN URBANIZED FINANCIAL INCLUSION

Since independence, Africa has been known as the Late Catcher Continent regarding economic development. However, this time, it has caught the boat on the unfolding FinTech evolution. Its rapid urbanization is contributing to the accelerated adoption of FinTech. In 2010, it had seven cities among the 101 global largest (Racki & DeGroot, 2014). It will record the highest surge of most extensive city-urban areas, from 7 in 2010 to almost 20 in 2050, and will closely reach 30 by 2100. Lagos alone will have 88.3 million in 2100 (Hoornweg & Pope, 2016, p. 213). Thus, growing at unparalleled degrees and fashioned through newfangled forces, lots of the continent's cities will be among the biggest ones by 2100 (Bearak et al., 2021). Aided by that huge urbanization push and advanced technological platforms, mobile payment providers are now proficiently offering innovative financial services such as lending rather than just limiting themselves to their initial payment services (Sy et al., 2019). As FinTech is leveraging the movements of disruption with tangible solutions that better address consumers' needs, these unprecedented changes are pressuring the traditional banking industry, which has remained stagnant and failed to facilitate market efficiency and technological reforms. The continent is now turning to FinTech products and services that draw on global technological innovations. These innovations range from Big Data and Artificial Intelligence (AI)-based transactions tailoring financial services and products to distributed ledger technologies based on networking independent computers that share transaction synchronization and Cryptography. While they facilitate robust security of electronic transactions, these innovative technologies increase transparency and enable greater trust and enforcement of business contracts in Africa (see He et al., 2017).

These developments contrasted with the past when Africa had difficulties or limited access to capital to finance businesses. But its fast urbanization trends (with 15% of the population belonging to the middle class that is gradually growing) motivate entrepreneurs to invest in FinTech startups (Business Insider Africa, 2022). And, with the vast pool of underbanked and unbanked populations, FinTech firms are seizing this ideal opportunity to be creative. They use that rapid urbanization to be disruptive in providing financial inclusion solutions. In reaction, the fact that they have historically been ignored by traditional banks, the underbanked, unbanked, and even the banked are now turning to those FinTech startups for their financial needs. Not surprisingly, one of the most sought-after industries is remittance and payment sites, which has led to a +-24% increase in new businesses since 2019 (Ibid).

FINTECH DISRUPTIVE GAME CHANGER WITH A SUITABLE MILLENNIALS CONSUMER PROFILE

Along with its fast urbanization, Africa is forecasted to be the globe's soon-to-be biggest demography. Indeed, between "2022 and 2050, the population of sub-Saharan Africa is expected almost to double, surpassing 2 billion inhabitants by the late 2040s…sub-Saharan Africa will account for more than half of the growth of the world's population between 2022 and 2050. In 2022, the size of the population in this region will grow at an annual rate of 2.5 percent, the highest among all eight regions, or more than three times the global average of 0.8 percent per year" (UNDESA, 2022, p. 5). But the most important story behind these statistics is that the continent's youth, aged between 0 and 24, will grow by 51%, from 628 million in 2017 to 945 million in 2050 (Goalkeepers, 2018, p. 9). Thus, recording the youngest population on earth, coupled with the tendency of young people to adopt FinTech solutions more than older generations, hints that the average FinTech consumer profile matches that of the continent's digitally savvy Generation Y-Millennials. This demographic-comparative advantage is sweepingly modifying the financial consumer's comportment and prospects. The outlooks of this large pool of Millennials represent the next generation of consumers and investors in FinTech. They are best suited for FinTech solutions with the inclination for a state-of-the-art user experience, rapidity, and expediency to accelerate their adoption further. This context constitutes historical collusion: while FinTech is emerging timely as a pain solution-based financial inclusion disruption, at the same time, Africa is also appearing to be the only region undergoing demographic growth embedded with a suitable millennial consumer profile. This historical collusion that some may portray as a "demographic dividend" can produce an opportunity for enhanced economic growth out of FinTech (Sy et al., 2019). Simply put, FinTech expansion of infrastructure and technological innovation can be crucial in making it possible for Africa to use its demographic dividend to generate businesses, expand, and enhance living conditions for everyone.

Indeed, even young people who have never used a computer have developed a rapid skill with which they master new smartphone technology applications. These young people are seizing the drive and amending their societies' rules through interconnecting, sending remittances, buying and selling, and interacting on social media via FinTech applications. Businesswise, the new entrant-young entrepreneurs, are also taking advantage of FinTech, which is reducing the costs of financial entrepreneurship, breaking market barriers, broadening outreach to new sections of the market, and, more importantly, disrupting the monopoly of existing banking incumbents. And given that African cities are joining the levels of humankind's biggest megalopolises, their unprecedented growth rates make smartphones almost omnipresent in African societies. The fact that there is not much onward economic development around this rapid urbanization, and the primary cities remain the only places to get jobs, mobile phone kiosks end up providing various financial services. Close to "20 percent of GDP in transactions are occurring through mobile money, compared with just 7 percent of GDP in Asia and less than 2 percent of GDP in other regions" (Sy et al., 2019, p.7). This high GDP-related mobile money transaction is reflected in the attitude of young Africans. Using FinTech that is overcoming traditional financial barriers, they are optimistic about their ability to become entrepreneurs compared to their peers in other regions (60% of 18 to 34-year-olds in Africa believe that they have the knowledge and skills to create a business, compared to 17% in the European Union and 30% in North America) (World Economic Forum, 2015).

FINTECH DISRUPTIVE GAME CHANGER IN CORRECTING MARKET FAILURE

The skyrocketing young population is correcting "Market Failure" in the financial industry. Market failure results from an inadequate supply of goods and services in the free market. The poor face-to-face user experience in the traditional banking industry is fueling the adoption of FinTech, which instead offers "faceless" onboarding processes and smooth transaction handling with insignificant verification obstructions. Having established themselves as *the* alternative banking agency and mobile money solution, some FinTechs are going as far as procuring micro-credits and micro-savings to serve not only the unbanked but also the banked populations. With such an expansion including corporate businesses as customers, FinTechs are attracting the largest share of assets, almost two-thirds of total funding into technology companies operating across Africa. In 2020, roughly $744 million was invested in Fintech, covering 31% of the continental cash inflows. In 2021, the funding reached $3.03 billion, which counted for 62% of the total investment inflows, according to the latest Africa Investment Report (Briter Bridges, 2021, p. 7). FinTechs are diversifying their investment in capital markets, Real Estate, and agriculture. The crowdfunding firms, like Thrive Agric, that have gained prominence are more obvious. They are solving agricultural financing gaps by gathering funds for individual investors in agri-businesses. Besides agriculture, FinTech-based insurance technology provides consumers with more value-added insurance services. It enables renewal and registration of vehicle documents (e.g., Autogenius), provides competent administration claims infrastructure for insurers (e.g., Curacel), provides agent sales solutions (e.g., Ark Insurance), and provides HMO management software (e.g., Helium Health). Additionally, FinTechs are forming alliances between regional cryptocurrency exchanges like Bitsika, Bitfxt, Buycoins, and Xend in countries like Nigeria and global companies (e.g., Paxful, Cryptofully, Luno). These platforms provide exchanges, wallets, P2P markets, and cryptocurrency payment services. Young people, especially Millennials, are taking full advantage of FinTech's ledgers, such as "gamification," in this significant diversification to attain their own financial goals. They are correcting market failure by specifically adopting cryptocurrency because of the persistent inflation of local currencies, strict and troublesome foreign exchange procedures, and the poor administrative treatment of transfers from the diaspora. This is more noticeable in Nigeria, where the financial literateness of the digitally savvy Millennials is increasingly making traditional banking irrelevant. Given the latent inflation of the Nigerian *Naira*, they are massively using cryptocurrency. This switch is eased by their country's 50% smartphone ownership, which approximates 100 million single subscribers in 2019 (Nigeria Fintech Census, 2020). Africans, in general, are finding blockchain technology—the disseminated digital record-book invention on which cryptocurrencies are grounded—more adaptable than conventional technologies in the clearing, payment, and settlement systems and decreasing transaction mistakes while increasing openness and accountability.

But as mentioned above, even though FinTech can improve allocative efficiencies in Africa by lowering the cost of delivering financial services with cutting-edge technologies helping to improve risk monitoring and reducing operational errors, it is emerging with unintended risks such as cyberattacks, money laundering, and terrorist funding. A 2020 Interpol report points out that "the development of mobile money services in Africa offers criminals a substantial opportunity to utilize these services to target victims in a variety of crimes as well as to enable further other forms of criminality including money laundering" (Interpol, 2020, p. 5). These kinds of reports have raised debates over TF risks. On the one hand, the TF-fearmongering position— "perceived vulnerabilities of new technology as a clear and present danger." African public officials share this point and fear the worst. On the other hand, the TF fear-tempering position appraises new technologies— "as no more or less risky than pre-existing technologies or conventional financial activities" (See Reimer & Redhead, 2022, p. vii). Those working in new technology industries defend this position. Though polarizing, this debate is timely concerning the unparalleled adoption of FinTech in Africa, especially in West Africa. As stated above, that region has a high rate of financial technology penetration. However, simultaneously, a caliphate mapping is being drawn by unhampered Islamic militant groups. Thus, while FinTech is providing an unprecedented urbanized financial inclusion disruption through its suitable Millennial consumer profile, that inclusive disruption is simultaneously greeting a context of heightened terrorism. This unique context could appeal to West African extremist groups to embark on FinTech-related TF at a significant scale. It is thus worth investigating the TF-fearmongering and tampering positions concerning the region.

FINANCING TERRORISM WITH FINTECH IN WEST AFRICA?

Varying frameworks explaining the rise of terrorism in West Africa revolve around outside continental influences. The armed militant and Salafist groups from Northern Africa and the Middle East are credited for the ongoing violent extremism in Sahel West Africa. Having fought with the Mujahidin in Afghanistan and defeated the Soviet Union in 1989, foreign fighters returned to their respective countries. Their wide-ranging brotherhood linkages made them determined to confront their states for political reforms. They often resorted to terrorism when opposed (GIABA, 2020a, p.12). Besides this grand Islamic caliphate ideology argument, poverty is also cited as an explanatory variable (Krueger, 2007). However, this chapter analyzes the journey to violent extremism in West Africa through "a fractured relationship between the state and citizens," where "the belief that government only looks after the interests of a few" (UNDP, 2017, p. 92) becomes the norm of the state administration. Within this exclusionary administrative framework, one can appreciate why young people tend to join terrorist groups. On average, 10 to 12 million incorporate the labor market yearly with limited access to jobs. Two, they constitute 60% of the unemployed. Three, more than 70% survive on less than $2 per day (African Economic Outlook, 2017), which tends to corroborate the poverty argument. But the 2017 UNDP survey reported a slightly different but concise explanation. About 42% of young people who voluntarily join terrorist groups are motivated by joblessness (UNDP, 2017, p. 57). Thus, building on the high rate of joblessness among the FinTech-savvy Millennials, which overlaps the high rate of joblessness among young terrorist recruits, a potential risk of FinTech-related TF exists in West Africa. Despite its considerable socio-economic benefits— "improving financial inclusion and serving as a catalyst for innovation in sectors such as agriculture and other infrastructures in Africa" (Sy et al., 2019, p. vii)—many FinTech developments and their unintended criminogenic features are not adequately regulated. We can evaluate the risk through the 2021 Global Findex survey that shows that "about three in four mobile account owners used their mobile money account to make or receive at least one payment that was not person-to-person…where 15 percent of adults—and 39 percent of mobile money account holders—used one to save…and 7 percent of adults also borrowed using their mobile money account in Africa" (World Bank, 2021, p.3). While this massive adoption of FinTech payment is unfolding in the continent, most of the governments cannot provide the most basic services, and the standard set of administrative privileges and obligations has severed the bond between fellow citizens and the state in many places (See Ghani & Lockhart, 2008; Collier, 2007; Easterly 2006). Subsequently, ruthless webs of criminality, violent extremism, and drugs feed on the populations locked into lives of despair without a stake in their administrative states or any confidence about or charge over their futures. Thus, in places like West Africa, which is carrying a high rate of joblessness among young people who are both technologically savvy Millennials and potential terrorist recruits, the unintended criminogenic features of FinTech could constitute a "ticking time bomb" for TF. That region's 83% penetration of mobile money usage (GIABA, 2020b, p. 2) could ease and accelerate TF.

Nigeria is an excellent West African example to illustrate the dichotomy between the massive adoption of FinTech on the one hand and rising terrorism on the other. Both its economy and population are the largest in all of Africa. The young people in that nation who are proficient in technology are mostly driving demand for FinTech services. Mobile payments increased by roughly 400% between 2019 and 2020, and smartphone adoption increased from 50% in 2019 to 87% in 2020. The usage of Cryptocurrency has augmented meaningfully, with some P2P Bitcoin markets recording up to 140% growth in 2020. According to Paxful, Nigeria had the second biggest Bitcoin transaction bulk globally after the US, reaching 60,214.7 Bitcoins for the last five years (corresponding to $566 million) and above 20,500 coins in 2020 alone, which is approximately $451 million (Gogo, 2020). FinTech incomes were forecasted to reach $ 543 million by the end of 2022. Not surprisingly, the growing operational base of FinTechs is offering instant "unsecured" digital loans, which are gaining popularity. Moreover, by leveraging remittance data through platforms such as Fairmoney and Aella Credit, FinTechs are creating single credit scoring models to foster retail lending. Thus, with a growth in the customer base of 68% (over 10,000 customers, from which 80% comprises retail customers), Nigerian FinTechs are seen as *the* primary driver of financial inclusion. They reduced the rate of unbanked and underbanked from 41.6% in 2016 to 36.8% in 2018 (Nigeria Fintech Census, 2020).

Nevertheless, Nigeria is experiencing vicious and violent extremism from the Islamic sect Boko Haram which is waging a jihadist war against the federal state to supposedly build an "uncorrupt" state run by sharia law. Ahmad Salkida, a news reporter in Nigeria who has had unusual proximity to this terrorist network, says that "although the sect is mainly driven by ideology, pervasive unemployment in northern Nigeria makes for easy recruitment of jobless young people" (Ighobor, 2013). Among the jobless young people, Nigeria's FinTech millennials consumer profile could overlap with the unemployed youth-terrorist recruits. Even in a strong state context, like in Europe, 40% of well-known illicit transactions implicated Bitcoin cryptocurrency in 2015 (EUROPOL, 2015). While emerging as FinTech hubs, Nigeria and the rest of West Africa still carry state weakness characteristics. They are unprepared or ill-equipped to futureproof several emerging and more anonymous FinTech solutions, such as the decentralization of privacy coins. They make de-anonymizing singularly challenging. Even the enforced ID requirements are becoming less effective due to the lack of a principal regulator overriding exchanges on standard prevention measure ledgers. Many e-commerce sites spread vulnerabilities transversely through transaction laundering, using "re-routing of payments for illicit goods/services via seemingly legitimate front businesses" (Akartuna et al., 2022, p.11). A case in point is the buildup of Generative Pre-Trained Transformer 3 (GPT-3) by AI companies such as OpenAI, which produces human text-based, capable of being robotically programmed for machinelike advisory to exchange with users (Floridi & Chiriatti, 2020, p. 3). GPT-3 and other advanced technologies significantly reduce human supervision, specifically in client relationship management, and by ricochet, increasing the paths for unobserved illicit transactions. As these financial tool inventions and technological spreads are growing at an uncontested pace and more stakeholders are entering their markets, criminals could exploit the West African security shortages to launder unlawful funds or finance violent extremism. More worrisome is the deepening bonds in which Boko Haram vowed its allegiance to ISIL in 2015 (renaming itself the Islamic State in West Africa), while AQIM remained an al Qaeda branch since 2007 (CSIS, 2016). These local groups are benefiting substantially from the expertise of both international terror networks in fundraising capacities. As these groups are conglomerating, spurring greater collaboration between global terror networks and their local militant branches, they could successfully misuse digital platforms to transfer cash and amass considerable amounts of money globally than has generally been feasible. Then, Virtual Currencies (VCs) and other platforms of new technologies could tremendously facilitate this process. This is where West Africa, and Africa in general, will pay a heavy price for failing to close their perennial race gap between the speedily changing technological innovations and their slower reform pace of institutional policing. Given this perennial race gap, VCs could appeal to terrorist groups for their global reach, varying degrees of namelessness, and fast transactions.

Many banks are abandoning cross-border remittances because of the acknowledged risks and the high costs of AML/CFT compliance, requiring establishing customer identification programs, screening, and establishing suspicious activity reporting systems. The resulting vacuum is leading many VC businesses to step in. And sometimes, they work unfettered, thereby expanding the risk that VCs can be used without detection (See Buenaventura, 2016). Precisely, the perceived FinTech vulnerability to TF in weak West African states should be noticed simply because the diffusion of service infrastructures involved in executing or transferring remittances in VCs makes it challenging to consign jurisdictional accountability for enforcement and compliance. The bad news for a poorly regulated place like Africa is that the VC industry is embarking on total anonymity by inventing newer technologies to obscure the authentic sources of bitcoin transactions (Redman, 2016). For instance, due to its enhanced anonymity properties, the "drug dealer's cryptocurrency of choice," Monero, is the preferred choice of new cryptocurrencies for cybercriminals (Greenberg, 2017). It is accepted in dark web markets as a Bitcoin alternative, increasing its eminence among users. It ensures customers' privacy by coupling multiple transactions, hiding their amounts, and obscuring the valid ID of fund receivers (Nakamura, 2016). More ingeniously, Dark Wallet, praised by ISIS sympathetic blogs (Greenberg, 2014b), also makes de-anonymizing Bitcoin transactions difficult. It can disrupt the susceptibility of Blockchain identification features by coupling random synchronous transactions and then encrypting receivers' information to enable illicit finance without detection (Greenberg, 2014a). Worse, decentralized applications such as (dApps) and Smart Contracts permit Blockchain users to machinelike trade products and services P2P proficiently compared to traditional economies (Tapscott & Tapscott 2016).

Exaggerated FinTech-TF Risk for Now

But, if one scrutinizes the difference between the "operational" and "networking" motives of TF (Davis, 2021; Ridley, 2012), the above fearmongering argument falls short of convincing. Their idea of FinTech-TF risk is exaggerated for now. Indeed, while operational financing englobes actual or planning assaults, networking financing, by contrast, tends to cover the maintenance, recruitment, and training costs of a terrorist group. This operational/networking divide helps elucidate the different types of TF and, more importantly, whether they are relevant in the West African context. Stated differently, the motive of funds directs the types of financial needs and, to a profound degree, fashions the appropriate financing gear. In Europe and North America, the current and dominant motive of TF is networking. It covers "recruitment and training, the welfare of operatives and sometimes their dependents, the production, and dissemination of propaganda, and–occasionally–support for wider networks of linked or sympathetic operatives" (Reimer & Redhead, 2021, p.5). Among these sympathetic operatives are the so-called "lone wolf" militants. They are engaged in self-activating terrorism, diminishing the weight to fundraise heavily, transfer, or use detectable cash currencies massively. As a result, the current main terrorist risk confronting Europe is self-made terrorism, constituting 74% of assaults and plans (Europol, 2021). Perpetrators tend to embark on low-cost, self-budgeted assaults, funded through unlawful, insignificant drug dealing activities or using their salaries to devise attacks (Reimer & Redhead, 2021). Occasionally, the funds are transferred internationally through established front businesses, banknotes, and remittance companies such as MoneyGram and Western Union. By contrast, operational financing, as in the cases of West Africa, has mainly been dependent on extensive fundraising and physically transferring funds. Boko Haram, ISIS, AQIM, and all their affiliates in the Sahel are active in zones with weak logistical technology and telecommunications infrastructures. Thus, the lack of prerequisite technological amenities significantly limits VCs' use of TF.

By this logic, militant groups did not considerably embark for now on VCs. There is no perceived need to do so. The groups already using or eagerly seeking to use them are criminal networks. They are in places with somewhat developed telecommunication and logistic financial infrastructures (e.g., Nigeria). More importantly, these cybercriminals are well-versed in technical complex lawbreaking operations such as online theft and data sale. By contrast, Boko Haram, ISIS, and AQIM seek to move money to the Sahel zones with poor infrastructures from which they plan and attack through many underground intermediaries to the point that senders and final recipients are not associated digitally. Thus, by circumventing global rules governing terrorist financing, exploiting incomplete implementation of regulatory requirements among West African states, using poorly supervised remittance business companies, or carting hard currencies across borders, there has been no urge from terrorists to invest in new, complicated technologies to transfer funds in the region. Better digital payment systems and prepaid cards are already facilitating quicker and more unidentified transactions with global reach capacity. Accordingly, given the Sahel West African embryonic or little usage of the electronic banking system, terrorist networks resort simply to physically moving cash across the porous borders. The informal, cash-based economies with no financial supervision reinforce the anonymity of transferring money (FATF, October 2015). In sum, given the Sahel West African inhospitable environments with poor technical and less sophisticated systems—making telecommunications networks and Internet services unreliable to support VCs—there has not been any interest in such a value that cannot exchange easily for hard currency needed for operational financing. Essentially, in West Africa, terrorist networks moved funds through traditional exchange-based hawala-like arrangements or criminal activities such as the collection of funds extorted from local communities (Campbell, 2020), cattle rustling (Ntaryike & Lukong, 2016), trade-based terrorist financing through non-profit organizations (FATF, 2014), or proceeds from firearms and drug trafficking (World Bank, 2015).

FUTUREPROOFING FINTECH IN WEST AFRICA

Even though terrorist networks moved funds through rudimentary cash flow carriers across borders, the West African case still calls for caution. After two decades of implementing CFT measures, violent extremism and terrorism continue. While the region has been dubbed the continental FinTech hub, it carries critical ML/TF security shortages. Unfortunately, Africa is experiencing the fastest growth in financial and technological innovation ever. Additionally, as more Africans enter the FinTech industry, criminals are using inadvertent security holes to launder illicit funds. Given this clear, present, and future danger, this chapter builds on a recent study (Akartuna et al., 2022) that uses what is referred to as the "Delphi method." A panel of experts is chosen and invited to respond to a series of questionnaires that explore a particular issue (in our present case, FinTech's impacts on ML/TF) as part of an iterative, multistage process called the Delphi. The first questionnaire asks panel members to review and rate various statements that explore the specified subject of research. In this case, the focus of the study was more on detection-based procedures that implicate upgraded transaction monitoring systems, machine learning, big data, and advanced analytics, which are better suited to clamp down on the latest technology-enhanced illicit transaction trends. Experts from various industries participated in the study's three-round policy Delphi to better understand potential risk-prone technological advances and potential preventative actions. As a result of advancements in dispensed platform innovations, most notably through crypto assets and privacy-enhancing crypto assets, a range of issues regarding ML and TF have been raised. Building on the findings, this chapter mainly focuses on the discoveries that suggest a way to improve the effectiveness of detection-based countermeasures, which are now the world's main preventative measure. However, the nature, usefulness, and degree to which these countermeasures can be implemented depends on particular circumstances and limitations that apply to various stakeholders.

Those circumstances and limitations in West Africa and Africa in general start with solving the perennial race gap between FinTech efficiency and security, which demands, first and foremost, that the continent attracts competent and best-fitted talents in the security and regulatory fields. This tops the list of challenges facing the supervision of FinTech's TF risks. The basic skill sets for AML/CFT are mostly technology capabilities, including Cybersecurity, Software Engineering and Systems Architecture and Development, and Data and Analytics. Falling short of these skill sets, poorly trained law enforcement officials and regulators will make the detection of illicit VC transactions integrally unchallenged. So long as they have access to online set up in the West African jurisdictions with less supervision, terrorists could take advantage of VCs. Such a fertile ground would instantly facilitate money transfers without the banking systems that are obliged to report suspicious transactions. Certainly, the needed basic skill sets for AML/CFT will require re-training to upskill the current workforce while tackling the growing shortage of skill sets for law enforcement actors and regulators in technology capabilities-related cybersecurity, software engineering, systems architecture and development, and data analytics. Considering the current defaulting Regulation Technology (RegTech) of AML/CFT, the weakness in its implementation demands that Africa develops futureproof digital course content and be acquainted with detection-based prevention measures, including higher algorithms and creative value-added training in ID/ Know Your Customer (KYC) requirements. The regional supervisory organizations (the Economic Community of West African States (ECOWAS), the WEST African Monetary Agency, the Central Bank of West African States, and GIABA) will need to be staffed with a competent workforce that adopts CFT compliance standards as applicable. Tackling skill sets shortage will require collaboration with universities to develop relevant, up-to-date digital course content.

Besides these requirements of essential skill sets for AML/CFT, authorities must communicate with relevant technology stakeholders actively to explore how legislation could be specifically designed to work and create a balance between

FinTech efficiency and security. For instance, in reviewing the legislative initiatives by GIABA to prevent money laundering and terrorism financing, ECOWAS leaders expanded the oversight of GIABA to encompass crucial financial intelligence provisions on AML/CFT during the 2007 Niamey meeting. Similarly, the ECOWAS' Counterterrorism Strategy adopted the same measure in 2013 (GIABA, 2020a, p.14). However, two decades after, the scourge of terrorism across the region has persisted. The application of CFT tools has not been appropriate and thoroughly effective. Militant groups are still preserving their organizational operations, expanding in power and number, extending cross-border activities, enrolling additional combatants, sheltering lethal armaments, carrying out further assaults, and withstanding their propaganda in places like Burkina Faso, Cote d'Ivoire, Mali, Niger, and Nigeria. Even though VCs are not in use yet for TF, the fact that militant groups continue to raise funds successfully exposes the failure of the affected West African countries to spot and interrupt TF in their jurisdictions.

Fortunately for Africa, lessons can be learned from cybercriminals who are already making Monero the alternative to Bitcoin in dark web markets. Plus, by introducing advanced technologies such as Dark Wallet, GPT-3, OpenAI, or dApps that significantly reduce human supervision and make de-anonymizing VC transactions difficult, these misuses of FinTech demonstrate that cybercriminals have already "preceded" terrorists in their digital abuses. Their criminal "imprints" in the search for new technics to avoid financial regulatory constraints constitute a *valuable wealth* of information for African regulators. They can learn from these cybercriminal groups' footprints in misusing FinTech solutions to prevent potential TF abuse. Specifically, attention should be paid to detection-based countermeasures, including enhanced technological aptitudes to intervene in *real-time* to match the expedient and speedy context of the new remittance technologies and ultimately alt the misuse of FinTech solutions when occurring (See Akartuna et al., 2022). The foundation of AML monitoring will be real-time identity verification based on AI, robotic learning, and automation processes. And given that circumventing AML/KYC structures is the aggregate objective of cybercriminals, futureproofing-based detection technologies in Africa should be proactively pursued with constant infiltration and examination capacity and state-of-the-art knowledge-based cybersecurity modus operandi. This modus operandi should be crafted based on Due Diligence protocols, explicitly targeting the entrant virtual asset service providers (VASPs) instead of the usual imposition of stringent compliances on clients alone. And although VASPs are obliged to know and understand their customers' behavioral transaction patterns to detect anomalies, these compulsions were set up in the 1990s for the conventional banking systems under the Financial Action Task Force (FATF) (Nance, 2018). Consequently, these outdated AML/CFT measures are ineffective and make disguising identity easy under monitoring obligations such as customer due diligence (CDD) (See Covolo, 2019).

Given the lack of prompt preventative action in Africa, while detection-based countermeasures are proving effective in intervening in real-time to alt the misuse of FinTech solutions when occurring, adopting futureproofing new technologies will be essential to prevent criminals from gaining an advantage against inventors, users, and law enforcement in the continent. Thus, from its baby steps, Africa should use regulatory sandboxes, which are safe harbors where companies can introduce new products in a controlled setting to a small number of clients for a short time while testing their products under lenient regulatory conditions. Thus, from *inception*, the device of crime-resistant services and futureproofing technologies could reduce the repetitive, expensive, and waste of time on patching or modifications of regulations as the continent is used to. These regulatory sandbox contexts could be useful to adopt and customize for various goals, judicial systems, and financial maturity levels because even the much-suspected Bitcoin in TF risk is only semi-anonymous. The cryptographic addresses of senders and receivers are documented with the identity capable of being uncovered (Zarate, 2016). Therefore, Africans can strengthen their RegTech on technologically upgraded transactions or new payment methods and reduce false positive identifications by employing regulatory sandboxes. Through those regulatory sandboxes, Africans can learn how to stop harmful actors from utilizing cutting-edge new technology in a timely and cost-effective manner. Specifically, they can learn how to limit the current staggering rate of false positives at 95-99% (Akartuna et al., 2022, p.2) because the new automated remittance platforms make illicit transactions incredibly difficult to distinguish from licit ones (Wass, 2017).

Burdensome and Overly Restrictive Laws and Regulations

But before embarking on real-time detection-based countermeasures, regulations should first be changed as they are sometimes burdensome or overly restrictive and threaten to stifle innovation and investment. In general, many West African FinTechs find the financial business overregulated. To be sure, national frameworks had been set up by the various West African countries to coordinate supervisory bodies. However, there are still issues with insufficient funding, which results in inadequate oversight and regulation of reporting firms. Additionally, several organizations in the private sector, particularly banks and financial institutions, have carefully designed compliance processes to fulfill their CFT duties. By this logic, there are differences in the conformity rates between banks and other financial structures, particularly the Foreign Exchange Bureaus, which have several sub-agents that are subject to different levels of regulation. And because the regulatory agencies are not carrying out their respective missions quickly and effectively, numerous financial structures are not adhering to their AML/CFT responsibilities and are not penalized correctly. In terms of vulnerabilities, TF is facilitated by some supervisory and reporting entities' institutional inadequacies. This is observed through law enforcement and judicial personnel's limited knowledge of CFT rules and procedures, which is blamed on their inability to investigate, prosecute, and convict defendants about reported suspicious transactions. Therefore, there is a need to increase law enforcement's capacity in the areas of spotting probable terrorist financing schemes as well as looking into and prosecuting suspected terrorist financing instances. But as mentioned above, it is crucial to note that the relevant staff has not received the necessary training on AML/CFT standards and requirements, which could improve their capacity to report findings to the appropriate authorities/Ministries. As a result, they cannot conduct on-site inspections, confirm the veracity of the financial reports, particularly in tracing the sources and consumption of funds, and contrast the figures provided by donors with the actual amounts stated as required by their mandates. In sum, factors preventing stakeholders in West Africa from acting effectively and efficiently include a lack of oversight by the regulatory authority regarding suspicious transaction reporting, the absence of a national list of politically exposed individuals, ignorance of the texts and risks associated with terrorism financing and primarily targeted financial sanctions, a lack of customer information, and the absence of an information system for the financial sector. And even though each West African country has a criminal justice system, we can identify obvious weaknesses in each system's ability to address the dynamics of CFT effectively. The gaps are attributed to a lack of modern technological tools for research, a lack of resources for prosecution, and judges who lack the technical expertise to handle CFT matters in the courts (GIABA 2020a).

But as clearly shown in Figure 1, FinTech companies have moved up the production possibility frontier in terms of efficiency. However, security continues to shrink, given the lack of human resources, weak legislative framework, and poor enforcement mechanisms to lower vulnerabilities to cyberattacks, money laundering, and terrorist funding. From Figure 1, Africa desperately needs to reach a market condition that exhibits a careful balance between efficiency and security at point 1. Subsequently, point 2 would be reached safely and more effectively as technological advancement expands the production possibility frontier between efficiency and security. To reach Point 2 which is a provision that facilitates cutting-edge FinTech to reach further an equilibrium where the financial system is *less* vulnerable and much safer, Africa will need to tackle skill sets shortage, which will require collaboration with universities to develop relevant, up-to-date digital course content. But at present, the context of weak states exposes skill sets shortage and inefficient public policies and regulations. Consequently, the production possibility frontier remains at suboptimal point 3, which shows an increase in efficiency from point 1 but a decrease in security. A case in point is Nigeria. There, regulators started by resorting to outright FinTech banning actions because substitute supervision resources were less available. The supervisory stance on cryptocurrency switched from vigilant to outright hostile as the Central Bank banned local financial businesses from trading in cryptocurrencies. While the Nigerian Cyber Crime Act, 2015 (NCCA) establishes a thorough institutional, regulatory, and legal framework for the ban, deterrence, exposure, and penalty of cybercrimes, the Central Bank prohibited the use of virtual currencies by banks and other financial institutions due to their susceptibility to abuse by criminals, particularly money laundering and activities related to terrorism. These rough decisions harmfully affected Nigerian consumers while accomplishing little in the misuse of FinTech. In reaction, some transactions have switched to P2P dealing, permitting them to circumvent institutional provisions while financial crimes easily relocate to substitute technological ledgers, an exercise known as "displacement" (See Ladegaard, 2019). And, because most pioneering digital innovations are embedded in global capacities reach, displacement is more easily practiced across African countries' borders. These burdensome or overly restrictive regulations are corroborated by 24% of surveyed FinTech firms that find the rigorous regulatory framework to be the most critical challenge they confront as an industry. Specifically, stringent regulation tops the list of policy obstacle areas at 18%, while insufficient capital stands at 14%. In the sectors of KYC and suspicious reporting requirements, more than 50% of respondents express the need for an amendment given the lack of transparency and confidence in regulating FinTech's upgraded segments, such as digital ledger technology and cryptocurrency (Nigeria Fintech Census, 2020).

Subsequently, the Nigerian regulatory agencies started some policy amendments. One notable change has been the 2020 presidential Act on Banks and Other Financial Institutions, which drafts regulatory procedures for financial businesses that are operated digitally. This Presidential Act constituted a turnaround policy and created a path where legislation is specifically designed to work and create a balance between FinTech efficiency and security. This example shows that it is necessary that AML/CFT authorities communicate with relevant technology stakeholders to enhance the quality and implementation of regulations and make FinTech an economic differentiator in Africa. Falling short of that cooperation, coupled with the increasing cost of global AML/CFT compliance ($213.9 billion in 2020 compared to $180.9 billion in 2019), these costs may tempt FinTech startups to cut corners in the continent, where supervision is traditionally poorly enforced (See LexisNexis, 2020). If new VCs become less detectable, their usage on a scale by terror networks will make future measures to track and prevent TF risks much more difficult in Africa. This is because, in the dark web markets, reputation is paramount. They have numerous ranks of admission, and the highest tend to impose multiple screenings before accessing them or to be known because "participants are highly vetted…often well-structured and policed, with their own constitution-like rules and guidelines to follow" (Ablon, Libicki, & Golay, 2014, p.23). Thus, to effectively futureproof new technologies in Africa, particularly West Africa, regulation and policy should not continue to stand out as *the* primary barrier for FinTechs. And this is doable. For example, by improving skill sets shortage and inefficient public policies and regulations, the National Bank of Rwanda employs an electronic data warehouse to simplify and streamline the reporting processes for the supervision of more than 600 financial institutions, including banks, microfinance institutions, and cooperative savings and credit organizations (Sy et al., 2019).

But, above all, no society facing terrorism, as in West Africa, can successfully combat TF with a fractured relationship between states and citizens, where 78% of surveyed respondents among terrorist recruits are expressing "low rating levels of trust in the police, politicians, military, the intelligence services, penitentiary authorities, national and local government" (UNDP 2017, p. 82). Societal trust in governance should be restored alongside the adoption of futureproofing FinTech. Otherwise, given that (a) the embarkation on the terrorism journey is meaningfully driven by "a fractured relationship between the state and citizens," where "the belief that government only looks after the interests of a few" (Ibid, p. 92), (b) the youth population aged 15 to 24 is on the verge of doubling by 2050, and (c) that youth constitutes 60% of the unemployed, while joblessness facilitates terrorism recruitment, then, rather than constituting a demographic dividend for exponential growth out of FinTech, its massive adoption among the digitally savvy Millennials could constitute a clear and future danger.

REFERENCES

Ablon, L., Libicki, M. C., & Golay, A. A. (2014). *Markets for Cybercrime Tools and Stolen Data: Hackers' Bazaar*. RAND. https://www.rand.org/content/dam/rand/pubs/research_reports/RR600/RR610/RAND_RR610.pdf

African Economic Outlook. (2017). *Entrepreneurship and Industrialization*. OECD. https://read.oecd-ilibrary.org/development/african-economic-outlook-2017_aeo-2017-en#page112

Akartuna, E. A., Johnson, S. D., & Thornton, A. (2022). Preventing the money laundering and terrorist financing risks of emerging technologies: An international policy Delphi study. *Technological Forecasting and Social Change*, *179*, 121632. doi:10.1016/j.techfore.2022.121632

Bearak, M., Moriarty, D., & Ledger, J. (2021, November 19). Africa's Rising Cities: How Africa will become the center of the world's urban future. *The Washington Post*. https://www.washingtonpost.com/world/interactive/2021/africa-cities/

Berger, A. N., Diana, H., & Jeffrey, M. (1996). A Framework for Analyzing Efficiency, Risks, Costs, and Innovations in the Payments System. *Journal of Money, Credit and Banking*, *28*(4), 696–732. doi:10.2307/2077917

Bridges, B. (2021). Africa Investment Report 2021. file:///C:/Users/HP/Downloads/03012022_AfricaInvestmentReport.pdf, p. 7

Buenaventura, L. (2016, September 11). There's a $500 Billion Remittance Market, and Bitcoin Startups Want In on It. *Quartz*. https://qz.com/775159/theres-a-500-billion-remittance-market-and-bitcoin-startupswant-in-on-it/

Business Insider Africa. (2022). Why Africa is the fintech market of tomorrow. *Business Insider Africa*. https://africa.businessinsider.com/local/markets/why-africa-is-the-fintech-market-of-tomorrow/4v98418

Campbell, J. (2020, November 18). Financing Boko Haram. *Council On Foreign Relations. Blog*. https://www.cfr.org/blog/financing-boko-haram

Collier, P. (2007). *The Bottom Billion: Why the Poorest Countries Are Failing and What Can Be Done About It*. Oxford University Press.

Covolo, V. (2019). *The EU Response to Criminal Misuse of Cryptocurrencies: The Young, Already Outdated 5th Anti-Money Laundering Directive*. Social Science Research Network. doi:. doi:10.2139/ssrn.3503535

CSIS. (2016). *Militancy and the Arc of Instability: Violent Extremism in the Sahel*. CSIS. http://csis-website-prod.s3.amazonaws.com/s3fs-public/publication/160922_Sanderson_MilitancyArcInstabilitySahel_Web.pdf

Davis, J. (2021). Illicit Money: Financing Terrorism in the 21st Century. London: Lynne Rienner.

Easterly, W. (2006). The White Man's Burden: Why the West's Efforts to Aid the Rest Have Done So Much Ill and so Little Good. Penguin Book, NY, NY.

Europol. (2021). *European Union Terrorism Situation and Trend*. Europol. https://www.europol.europa.eu/activities-services/main-reports/internet-organised-crime-threat-assessment-iocta-2015.

FATF. (2014). *Risk of Terrorist Abuse in Non-Profit Organisations.* FATF. https://www.fatf-gafi.org/media/fatf/documents/reports/Risk-of-terrorist-abuse-in-non-profit-organisations.pdf

FATF. (2015). *Money Laundering Through the Physical Transportation of Cash.* FATF. https://www.fatf-gafi.org/media/fatf/documents/reports/money-laundering-through-transportation-cash.pdf

Field, M. (2021, February 9). Bitcoin value overtakes Russian ruble at $860bn. *The Telegraph.* https://www.telegraph.co.uk/technology/2021/02/09/bitcoin-value-overtakes-russian-ruble-at860bn/

FinTechNGR. (2020). *Nigeria Fintech Census 2020.* FinTech.https://assets.ey.com/content/dam/ey-sites/ey-com/en_ng/ey-fintech-nigeria-census-final.pdf

Floridi, L., & Chiriatti, M. (2020). GPT-3: Its Nature, Scope, Limits, and Consequences. *Minds and Machines, 30*(4), 681–694. doi:10.100711023-020-09548-1

Ghani, A., & Lockhart, C. (2008) *Fixing Failed States.* Oxford University Press.

GIABA. (2020a). *Assessment of Counter Terrorist Financing Capacities in West Africa.* GIABA. https://www.giaba.org/media/f/1132_ENG-Assessment%20of%20the%20CFT%20Capacities%20in%20GIABA%20MS.pdf

GIABA. (2020b). *Money Laundering/Terrorist Financing Risks and Opportunities of FinTech Transformation in West Africa.* GIABA. https://www.giaba.org/media/f/1125_ENG%20-%20ML-TF%20RISKS%20AND%20OPPORTUNITIES%20OF%20FINTECH-3.pdf

Goalkeepers. (2018). *The Stories Behind the Data 2018. Bill & Melinda Gates Foundation.* file:///C:/Users/HP/Downloads/report_en.pdf

Gogo, J. (2020, December 17). *Nigeria is Paxful's Second Biggest P2P Bitcoin Market, Trades Top $566 million in Five Years.* Bitcoin.com. https://news.bitcoin.com/nigeria-is-worlds-second-biggest-p2p-bitcoin-market-trades-top-566-million-in-five-years/

Goldman, Z. K., Maruyama, E., Rosenberg, E., Saravalle, E., & Solomon-Strauss, J. (2017 May). Terrorist Use of Virtual Currencies; Containing the Potential Threat. *CNAS.* https://s3.amazonaws.com/files.cnas.org/documents/CNASReport-TerroristFinancing-Final.pdf?mtime=20170502033819

Greenberg, A. (2014a, April 29). Dark Wallet' Is About to Make Bitcoin Money Laundering Easier Than Ever. *Wired.* https://www.wired.com/2014/04/dark-wallet/

Greenberg, A. (2014b, July 11). Waiting for Dark: Inside Two Anarchists' Quest for Untraceable Money. *Wired*. https://www.wired.com/2014/07/inside-dark-wallet/

Greenberg, A. (2017, January 25). Monero, the Drug Dealer's Cryptocurrency of Choice, Is on Fire, *Wired*. https://www.wired.com/2017/01/monero-drug-dealers-cryptocurrency-choice-fire/

Gross, M.B., Hogarth, J.M., & Schmeiser, M.D. (2012). Use of Financial Services by the Unbanked and Underbanked and the Potential for Mobile Financial Services Adoption. *Federal Reserve Bulletin 98*(4). doi:, 0–0. doi:10.17016/bulletin.2012.98-4

GSMA. (2021). *The Mobile Economy 2022*. GSM. https://www.gsma.com/mobileeconomy/wp-content/uploads/2022/02/280222-The-Mobile-Economy-2022.pdf

He, D., Leckow, R., Haksar, V., Mancini-Griffoli, T., Jenkinson, N., Kashima, M., Khiaonarong, T., Rochon, C., & Tourpe, H. (2017). *Fintech and Financial Services: Initial Considerations*. International Monetary Fund.

Hoornweg, D., & Pope, K. (2016). Population predictions for the world's largest cities in the 21st century Environment and Urbanization. *Sage Journals, 29*(1), 195–216. doi: www.sagepublications.com doi:10.1177/0956247816663557

Ighobor, K. (2013, May). *Africa's Youth: a "ticking time bomb" or an opportunity?* Africa Renewal. https://www.un.org/africarenewal/magazine/may-2013/africa%E2%80%99s-youth-%E2%80%9Cticking-time-bomb%E2%80%9D-or-opportunity

Interpol. (2020). *Mobile money and organized crime in Africa*. Interpol. https://enactafrica.org/research/interpol-reports/mobile-money-and-organised-crime-in-africa

Krueger, A. (2007). *What Makes a Terrorist: Economics and the Roots of Terrorism*. Princeton University Press.

Ladegaard, I. (2019). Crime displacement in digital drug markets. *The International Journal on Drug Policy, 63*, 113–121. doi:10.1016/j.drugpo.2018.09.013 PMID:30572247

LexisNexis. (2020). *True Cost of Financial Crime Compliance Study: Global Report*. Lexis Nexis. https://risk.lexisnexis.com/insights-resources/research/true-cost-of-financial-crime-compliance-study-global-report#:~:text=This%20is%20not%20without%20cost,%24180.9%20billion%20the%20previous%20year

Liftoff. (2021). *Mobile Finance Apps Report: Banking on the Future of Fintech.* https://content.liftoff.io/hubfs/aaa_Reports/2021/2021%20Finance%20Report/Finance%20Report%202021%20-%20EN.pdf?_ga=2.110491333.1392937753.1618499511-196886098.1618499511

Nakamura, Y. (2016, August 29). New Digital Currency Spikes As Drug Dealers Get More Secrecy. *Bloomberg*. https://www.bloomberg.com/news/articles/2016-08-29/new-digital-currency-spikes-after-giving-criminals-more-secrecy

Nance, M. T. (2018). The regime that FATF built: An introduction to the Financial Action Task Force. *Crime, Law, and Social Change*, *69*(2), 109–129. doi:10.100710611-017-9747-6

Ntaryike, D., & Lukong, P. (2016, August 29). Cattle rustling. *Bloomberg*. www.bloomberg.com/news/articles/2016-08-29/cameroon-closes-down-cattle-market-as-militants-turn-to-rustling

PricewaterhouseCoopers. (2017). *Nigeria FinTech Survey 2017*. PWC. https://www.pwc.com/ng/en/pdf/nigeria-fintech-report-2017.pdf

Racki, J., Patel, P., & DeGroot, D. (2014). Africa 2050: Urbanization. *Global Journal of Emerging Market Economies*, *61*(1), 15–34. doi:10.1177/0974910113511191

Redman, J. (2016, July 21). Tumbling Bitcoins: A Guide Through the Rinse Cycle. *Bitcoin.com*. https://news.bitcoin.com/tumbling-bitcoins-guide-rinse-cycle/

Reimer, S., & Redhead, M. (2021, May). A New Normal: Countering the Financing of Self-Activating Terrorism in Europe. *RUSI Occasional Chapters*.

Reimer, S., & Redhead, M. (2022, April). Bit by Bit: Impacts of New Technologies on Terrorism Financing Risks. *RUSI Occasional Chapter*.

Ridley, N. (2012). *Terrorist Financing: The Failure of Counter Measures*. Edward Elgar.

Soudijn, M. R. J. (2019). Using Police Reports to Monitor Money Laundering Developments. Continuity and Change in 12 Years of Dutch Money Laundering Crime Pattern Analyses. [ProQuest Central; Social Science Premium Collection.]. *European Journal on Criminal Policy and Research*, *25*(1), 83–97. doi:10.100710610-018-9379-0

Statista. (2021). *Digital Payments report 2021.* Statista. https://www.statista.com/study/41122/fintech-report-digital-payments/

Sy, A., Maino, R., Massara, A., Perez-Saiz, H., & Sharma, P. (2019). *FinTech in Sub-Saharan African Countries A Game Changer?* IMF. https://www.imf.org/en/Publications/Departmental-Chapters-Policy-Chapters/Issues/2019/02/13/FinTech-in-Sub-Saharan-African-Countries-A-Game-Changer-46376

Tapscott, D., & Tapscott, A. (2016). *Blockchain Revolution.* Penguin.

Teicher, R. (2018, March 18). *How Uber ghost rides are linked to online money laundering.* The Next Web. https://thenextweb.com/news/uber-ghost-rides-linked-online-money-laundering#:~:text=Laundering%20large%20amounts%20of%20money,operator%20of%20the%20laundering%20scheme

UNDESA. (2022). *World Population Prospects 2022.* UN. https://www.un.org/development/desa/pd/sites/www.un.org.development.desa.pd/files/wpp2022_summary_of_results.pdf

UNDP. (2017). *Journey to extremism in Africa: drivers, incentives and the tipping point for recruitment.* UN. https://digitallibrary.un.org/record/3841751?ln=en

Wass, S. (2017, May 10). Regtech could save banks £2.7bn on AML compliance. *Global Trade Review.* https://www.gtreview.com/news/global/regtech-could-save-banks-2-7bn-yearly-on-aml-compliance/

World Bank. (2015). *Trafficking and Fragility in West Africa.* World Bank. https://documents1.worldbank.org/curated/en/401851468184741492/pdf/98903-WP-AFR-P148420-Box-393185B-PUBLIC-Trafficking-FINAL.pdf

World Bank. (2021). *The Global Findex Database 2021.* World Bank. https://www.worldbank.org/en/publication/globalfindex/Report

World Economic Forum. (2015). *Why Africa's Young People Should Turn to Entrepreneurship.* WEF. https://www.weforum.org/agenda/2015/06/africas-young-people-entrepreneurship/

Zarate, J. C. (2016, June 23). The Next Terrorist Financiers: Stopping Them Before They Start. *Statement to the Financial Services Committee, Task Force to Investigate Terrorism Financing, U.S. House of Representatives.* https://www.govinfo.gov/content/pkg/CHRG-114hhrg25849/html/CHRG-114hhrg25849.htm

Chapter 7
Mobile Payment Systems and Impulsive Buying:
A Conceptual Paper

Aidatu Abubakari
Lakeside University College, Ghana

Rita Boateng
Lakeside University College, Ghana

Abdul Karim Mutawakil
Lakeside University College, Ghana

ABSTRACT

Mobile payment systems have created a lot of opportunities for both businesses and consumers to easily transact business. Due to the portable and interactive nature of mobile devices, mobile payment systems have aided most consumers in their daily business activities. In spite of their numerous benefits, mobile payment systems can create problems for consumers, and one such problem is impulse buying. Consumers usually make unplanned purchases spontaneously and intuitively after being exposed to exciting cues like price promotions, limited offers, and attractive product appearances; mobile payment systems facilitate these purchases. In the light of this, the current study synthesizes some scholarly works on mobile payment systems and impulse buying. The paper contributes to the growing body of literature on the dark side of financial technologies.

DOI: 10.4018/978-1-6684-6381-9.ch007

Copyright © 2023, IGI Global. Copying or distributing in print or electronic forms without written permission of IGI Global is prohibited.

INTRODUCTION

Consumers' buying behavior has been significantly transformed by modern developments in financial technology. One such development is the use of mobile payment systems. Thus, studies in psychology and consumer behavior have accordingly given increased scholarly consideration to the psychological (cognitive, affective, and conative) influences of various payment methods like credit/debit cards, cash and mobile payment methods (Xu et al., 2022). Also, the development of the World Wide Web has led to tremendous changes in the financial technology landscape which has facilitated payment for consumers of diverse products and services (Xu et al., 2022). Despite the numerous benefits of mobile payment systems, there are massive dark sides that pose certain dangers to consumers. For instance, impulsive buying is a major unintended consequence of the growth of mobile payment systems and it is of growing concern for scholars and practitioners (Halim, 2021; Um et al., 2022; Yang et al., 2021).

Impulsive buying is viewed as an unplanned purchase or making purchase decisions on the spot (Zheng et al., 2019). Impulse purchases are usually done in a sudden, robust and sustained manner. These behaviors offer a fun boost and make buyers more emotional rather than rational in their purchase decisions (Halim, 2021). Impulse purchases are often done without regard to their consequences. Since mobile payment systems perform the role of physical wallets and permit consumers to reload electronic cash with mobile devices, they have become major promoters of impulse buying. Other major drivers of impulse buying include factors such as age, gender, emotions, product attributes, social factors and media promotions (Um et al., 2022; Yang et al., 2021; Zheng et al., 2019).

Impulse purchases are prevalent in both brick-and-mortar contexts as well as online settings. Particularly, with the advancements in financial technology, prior studies have found about 30 to 50% of all retail sales to come from impulse purchases (Liu et al., 2013). Also, about 90% of consumers buy on impulse occasionally (Hausman, 2000). Other studies have also revealed that almost 40% of all money spent on e-commerce sites are from impulse purchases (Verhagen & van Dolen, 2011).

Impulse buying is problematic for consumers for diverse reasons. First, individuals mostly involve in impulse buying for mood-repair and mood-enhancement (Spiteri Cornish, 2020). Yet this enhanced mood is fleeting and they do not end up being happier beyond the temporary emotional states linked with the purchase experience. Also, the positive feelings linked to impulse buying is normally partly deflated if consumers assess the functional and economic benefits of the item purchased when they get home. This is an indication that there is a shift of focus from the product itself to the consumption of the product (Spiteri Cornish, 2020). Furthermore, past research suggests that consumers experience regret concerning the items purchased, especially, if they are of a low quality, bad value for money or unsuited. They also experience regret as a result of self-recrimination when the buying decision is unreasonable and indefensible (Banning, 2015; Um et al., 2022). Impulse purchases can also cause buyers to experience post-purchase regret arising from owning a product that is not needed and remain unused.

Despite the wide prevalence of impulse buying both in the online and offline contexts, rather limited reviews have been done on the link between mobile payment systems and impulse buying. Prior studies on consumer buying behavior suggest that consumers' form decisions consciously and deliberately. Thus, theories of conscious behavior like theory of reasoned action and the theory of planned behavior have widely been applied as vital theoretical lenses. Inspired by current advances in financial technology and recent advances in consumer psychology on automatic and impulse purchases, this conceptual study examines impulse buying and its linkages with mobile payment systems. The study intends to contribute to the growing body of literature on the dark side of financial technologies and its implications for consumers and practitioners.

Mobile Payment Systems

Mobile payment refers to payments made using a mobile device to initiate, authorize, and confirm exchanges (Moghavvemi et al., 2021). It is also described as a kind of payment transaction processing where the payer utilizes mobile communication techniques and mobile devices to initiate, authorize or complete payments (Goeke & Pousttchi, 2010). It is a form of value transfer analogous to other payment instruments used by consumers, but it heavily depends on advanced features of mobile phones and the tokenization of consumers' financial credentials (Moghavvemi et al., 2021).

There are two broad types of mobile payments: remote and proximity. Remote payment systems involve remote transactions where there is no direct contact between the consumer and the merchant's point of sale system, which is through contactless payment (Shen & Yazdanifard, 2015). Remote payment systems require customers to register and download an application (e.g. PayPal and GoPago) before using these systems. Conversely, proximity payment systems require customers to present their mobile phones, tablets or credit cards at the payment terminals, also, payment processes are facilitated by near field communication (NFC).

Mobile payment methods use high-performance mobile-operating systems and wireless networks to facilitate financial transactions. Aside the two broad classifications, mobile payments can be categorized into four according to Gobry (2012) (carrier billing, near field communication (NFC), apps, and card readers). Each category has its own benefits and downsides. In carrier billing, transactions are directly charged to users' phone bills and they are mostly used for buying digital contents (Moghavvemi et al., 2021). Carrier billing is useful for penetrating developing economies with limited access to credit and debit cards as well as market segments involving kids. NFC, also known as mobile point of sale or mobile contactless payment is a type of proximity payment. Almost, one third of the world's cell phones are equipped with NFCs. It has transformed payment processes and minimized the transaction times for consumers and merchants. With NFCs, consumers NFC-enabled phones come into close contact with merchants' contactless payment terminal. An app is the commonest type of mobile payment and has the largest group of users. Numerous banks and merchants provide mobile banking services through mobile applications. The last category is payments through a card reader. This is a fairly new approach of mobile payment and it is supported by large mobile payment companies. It involves the use of a portable credit card reader installed on mobile devices to accept magnetic stripes, contactless payment and chip cards.

The pervasiveness of advanced mobile devices have created numerous avenues for using them in conducting numerous personal and professional activities. One major area where mobile devices perform a significant function is the domain of mobile payments (Verkijika, 2020). Payment systems have evolved in recent years from just cash or credit card transactions to several kinds of mobile payment systems. The transition has occurred because of advances in technology, changes in the global economy, the proliferation of social media and high mobile phone penetration rates. Mobile phones have become a pervasive commodity these days, as a result, individuals are benefiting from the expediency and ease of making payments for products and services using mobile devices (Ramos et al., 2019). Mobile payment systems have adapted to a new business climate which facilitates business transactions regardless of time (Yong et al., 2022).

The decrease in technical challenges for mobile payments, the advent of financial services apps and the rise in access to mobile devices are indicative of the fact that gradually, these means of payment will become more ubiquitous and easier to use in the future (Verkijika, 2020). Global adoption of Mobile payment systems is increasing, however, its patronage relies on access to new technologies, lifestyle choices as well as economic factors (Hsiao, 2021). Scholars are increasingly convinced that mobile payments are a suitable means of payment, with several merits over conventional payment systems (Cao et al., 2018; Hsiao, 2021). This follows from the numerous benefits of mobile payments like convenience, speed of transaction, bulk payments, security, and the elimination of the need for cash (Yong et al., 2022).

In spite of the potential advantages of mobile payment systems, their adoption around the globe has witnessed a slow growth (Koenig-Lewis et al., 2015). Indeed, numerous consumers still have preference for cash payment systems (Ramos et al., 2019). For instance, there is evidence suggesting that there is an upsurge in the use of cash in over 40 nations across the globe, with a forecasted 83% of all worldwide payments being made in cash (Gillespie, 2017). The situation is more alarming in the developing world where cash payments account for more than 90% of all payments (Moeng 2017, as cited in Verkijika, 2020). Regardless of the fact that cash is still predominant, there are optimistic predictions that mobile payment systems will witness unprecedented growth in the near future. Even so, businesses have a huge challenge in convincing consumers to use mobile payment systems as an alternative to other forms of popular payment systems, this has been a bane to the uptake of the technology (Verkijika, 2020).

Impulsive Buying Behavior

Consumers normally make unintended purchases spontaneously and intuitively after exposure to exciting signals like price promotion, advertisements of limited offers and attractive product appearances (Liu et al., 2013). This sort of purchase is referred to as impulse buying. Piron, (1991) described impulse buying as a purchase that is unplanned, the result of an exposure to a stimulus, and decided on the spot. This type of purchase has three major features (it is not planned, it occurs as a result of an exposure to a stimulus, and it is decided on the spot).

Impulse buying occurs both in physical as well as virtual stores. From the perspective of diverse stimulus, four different kinds of impulse buying have been identified; pure impulse buying, reminder impulse buying, suggestive impulse buying and planned impulse buying (Zheng et al., 2019). Pure impulse buying is usually a novelty and an escape purchase that breaks a normal buying pattern. Reminder impulse buying occurs when a person recollects a past experience with products when he or she saw it. Suggestive impulse buying takes place when a person sees a product for the first time and visualizes a need for it. Planned impulse buying happens when buyers buy a product they did not plan to buy but take advantage of promotions (Zheng et al., 2019). These kinds of impulse buying share one thing in common, that is, they are all unintended purchases. The stimulus factors in an impulse buying situation could be actual products, the shopping environment or the individuals who escort people for shopping. Consumer buying behavior is considered as impulse as long as it does not involve an extended period of research. In the marketing research context, impulse buying behavior was initially described as a purchase behavior that is not planned (Piron, 1991), however, this perspective has been criticised by some scholars who perceive impulse buying not only as an unplanned behavior but also as an experience of an urge to buy (Yang et al., 2021). Thus, some scholars describe it as involving a sudden and most often powerful and persistent urge to buy something instantaneously (Yang et al., 2021).

Impulse buying has been examined both in the offline and online context, and results suggest that consumer characteristics, situational stimuli, store features and product characteristics influenced impulse buying (Chan et al., 2017). In the online context, scholars opine that consumers in e-commerce have a higher likelihood to engage in impulse buying due to the fact that the e-commerce environment allows consumers to search and make comparisons between manufacturers and products more efficiently within a limited period of time and limited social pressure from other consumers and sales staff. In the online context, environmental factors contained in shopping websites and the effect of consumer characteristics were found to influence impulse buying (Chen & Yao, 2018).

Impulse Buying in Mobile Commerce

The swift development of wireless technology and the surge in the penetration of mobile devices have increased the popularity of mobile commerce among shoppers (Zheng et al., 2019). As of 2017, 82% of people living in the USA used mobile devices for shopping and sales amounted to almost 42 billion dollars in 2013 (Zheng et al., 2019). In the light of the fast and extensive development of mobile technologies and applications, the use of mobile payment systems and mobile commerce has also witnessed a tremendous growth. Both scholars and practitioners are making attempts to further understand factors contributing to the surge in the use of mobile payment systems and mobile commerce.

Mobile commerce is defined as any transaction with a monetary value either direct or indirect that is conducted over a wireless telecommunication network. In contrast with conventional shopping, mobile commerce could offer a totally novel service capability, like location awareness, context sensing and push delivery which is supported by the characteristic of portability of mobile device. Prior research has explored certain aspects of mobile commerce like its adoption, consumers' trust, and post purchase experience (Liébana-cabanillas et al., 2019; Lin et al., 2014; Revels et al., 2010). Though these studies have contributed to the literature on mobile commerce, impulse buying has not received significant research attention. The results of Lee et al. (2014) suggests that mobile commerce increased impulsivity in buying because of its features like high interactivity and convenience. Mobile payment systems have been found to induce consumers to make impulse purchases. Furthermore, the results of Chen and Yao (2018) indicate that the features of mobile transactions are strong precursors for consumers' impulse purchases compared to transactions on other buying channels.

Past research on impulse buying in the online context also suggests that environmental factors significantly influence impulse buying in mobile commerce. For instance, Parboteeah et al. (2009) assert that perceived visual appeal and information fit-to-task were key factors that encouraged consumers to engage in impulse buying. Their results suggest that consumers are more likely to engage in impulse buying if their interaction with the shopping environment is pleasant. Similarly, the results of Verhagen and van Dolen (2011) revealed that a website's functional convenience and representational delight have an effect on positive and negative shopping emotions, which in turn affect impulse buying in mobile commerce. The results further suggest that emotions of positive affect are key drivers of impulse buying in mobile commerce. Thus, the literature generally suggests that impulse buying can be assessed from two major perspectives, the state of mind created by the environment and personality traits of the consumer.

Mobile Payment Systems and Impulse Buying

Mobile payment systems offer consumers a form of e-wallet which acts as a physical wallet and permits them to reload electronic money with their mobile devices (Yong et al., 2022). Mobile payment systems save time because users do not need to constantly log on to mobile banking systems. They also allow users to make payment transactions once topped up, hence, it has become a major driver of impulse buying (Um et al., 2022). Mobile payment methods have become very popular with consumers because they do not rely on cash or credit cards. Hence, customers could easily purchase several products using their digital wallets (Srivastava et al., 2010). Unlike credit and debit cards, mobile payment systems have lower security threats and transactions do not go through a third party directly, these features have made it convenient for consumers to use them for spontaneous purchases (Chan et al., 2017).

Factors that Influence Impulse Buying on Mobile Payment Systems

Impulse buying can be triggered by diverse factors including the store environment, life satisfaction, self-esteem, and the emotional condition of the individual at the time of purchase (Gogoi & Shillong, 2020). It can also be stimulated by an unexpected need, visual stimulus, and promotional campaigns and by a decline of an individual's cognitive capacity to assess the benefits and problems linked to the purchase. Some of these factors are discussed below:

Visual Appeal

Visual appeal refers to the extent to which consumers find products attractive due to the way these products are displayed. In the online context, it has to do with the display of web pages and website product information (Chen et al., 2020). It is a major factor that significantly influences consumers' purchase of products online. Visual appeal can trigger impulse buying in the online context if consumers positively evaluate the online store atmosphere and the visual presentation of items (Chen et al., 2020). Consumers in online shops give more attention to visual perceptions of website information and it influences their decisions to make a purchase or not (Spiteri Cornish, 2020). The more positive their evaluation of visual perceptions of a particular platform, the greater the likelihood that they will regard it as a useful shopping platform as it triggers their perceived visual enjoyment and emotional excitement.

Portability

A striking feature of mobile payment systems is the portability and mobility of the devices used to make payments for transactions made. This feature comes with a lot of benefits, but can also be a trigger for impulse purchases (Zheng et al., 2019). Consumers can easily search for products online and can make payments for these products easily with their e-wallets as such, barriers to making purchases are limited, this could facilitate impulse buying. Furthermore, even in offline contexts consumers could still make payments for products using their e-wallets, and they can also withdraw cash from their e-wallets to make purchases if they feel a sudden urge to purchase an item (Chen & Yao, 2018). Thus, the portability of devices used for making payments could be a major trigger for impulse purchases. Consumers feel more valued and satisfied about purchasing if it requires less time and effort. Mobile payment systems aid consumers to make purchase decisions by giving them real time information on their e-wallets, hence, they are able to quickly make a purchase without a critical evaluation, this feature of mobile payment systems is a major trigger for impulse buying.

Ease of Use

Impulse purchases are influenced by the ease with which mobile payment systems can be used and purchase made. Mobile payment system operators who offer consumers with well-designed interfaces which require less effort to learn or use allow consumers to easily find information and make purchases (Lin & Lo, 2016). Also, ease of use of shopping environments have been found to significantly influence a consumer's positive affect. This could also trigger impulse purchases. Hence, the more user-friendly the interface of mobile payment systems and the shopping environments, the greater the likelihood that consumers will feel pleased.

Promotional Campaigns

The consumption impulse formation and enhancement (CIFE) model proposed by Dholakia (2000) posits that the marketing stimuli in consumption settings maximizes the probability that individuals will demonstrate impulse buying behaviors. The higher the discounts offered on products or the more convincing and persuasive the salespersons and experts sound, the greater the likelihood that consumers will buy on impulse (Kim & Johnson, 2016; Park & Noh, 2012). Surprising promotions and limitations on the purchase of some items are two major factors that can make consumer unable to resist the urge to shop, which can eventually result in a purchase which is impulsive in nature (Aggarwal et al., 2011; Nusair et al., 2010).

Promotional incentives used to trigger impulse purchases include price promotions and non-price promotions. These two promotional strategies are regarded as marketing stimuli in consumption settings to assess whether promotions influence impulse purchase behaviors. For consumers who buy on impulse, minimizing the spending budget is one of the most important factors, hence, price and non-price promotions could be major facilitators of impulse buying (Chen & Yao, 2018). Discounted prices create shifts in consumers' emotions, as such, consumers who think they could gain feel pleased and this increases their positive affect and pushes them to actually spend more (Song et al., 2015). Instant economic stimulants influence consumers to change their standards of reference for the prices of products and this shift influences their readiness to buy (Nusair et al., 2010). Hence, consumers respond positively and give in to impulse purchases when they are offered discounted prices on products.

Additionally, businesses sometimes limit the supply of products or their promotion periods to pressurize consumers to make purchases or to minimize the time spent on hesitation. This strategy influences impulse buying as it heightens the sense of urgency and encourages the mindset of purchasing products that have been discounted (Vaidyanathan & Aggarwal, 2003). Scarcity is used as a strategic limitation of the supply, time, or other purchase conditions of product to convey a signal to consumers that the chance of buying that product is low (Aggarwal et al., 2011). This limited supply of resources is a comparatively strong factor because the signals sent puts pressure on consumers to speed their decision-making process, eventually leading them to make a purchase (Chen & Yao, 2018). Lin and Lin (2013) argue that promotional messages on digital platforms that the supply of products is limited or only available within particular periods can trigger an intense urge to make impulse purchases. The results of Song et al. (2015) suggests that promotional messages regarding scarcity and product discounts influences consumers. These promotional strategies influence the attractiveness of products. If demand is higher than supply, consumers tend to believe that the product is popular, this thinking changes their normative assessment and leads to immediate purchases (Parker & Lehmann, 2011).

PROBLEMS OF IMPULSE BUYING

Though impulse purchases offer several advantages for businesses, at the consumer level it could create a number of challenges. Impulse purchases are made in the moment without much thought, they are more likely to be returned once the buyer has had more time to consider their purchase. Buyer's remorse can occur when the purchaser regrets the item they have purchased, leading to its return to the store. There are numerous costs associated with returned items, including the cost of return shipping, the time required to inspect the returned item, and any stock write-offs for items that cannot be easily repackaged and resold.

Cognitive dissonance is one of the possible negative effects of impulse purchases. It is a situation of uneasiness related to a customer's uncertainty about the product selection (Chen et al., 2020). Cognitive dissonance can occur in situations where the marketer typically offers incentives for customer engagement and the customer actually makes a purchase because of the incentives offered not because they have need for the product. An impulsive online shopper is more likely to experience post-purchase dissonance due to post-purchase anxiety regarding possible unintended outcomes (Telci et al., 2011).

Other consequences include budgetary infringement, disappointment, and a sense of guilt. Consumers experience poor service when evaluating the shopping experience of unplanned purchases. Impulse purchases can be psychologically uncomfortable state associated with regret and anxiety. People who buy on impulse experience an emotional lack of control caused by the conflict between the immediate reward and the negative consequences that can result from the purchase. It can also precipitate chronic and pathological compulsive behavior (Pandya & Pandya, 2020).

Using Self-regulation to Reduce Impulse Purchases on Mobile Payment Systems

Self-regulation refers to the ability of humans to control their thoughts, emotions, and behaviour in pursuit of a higher goal (Čerešník, 2013) when presented with an appetitive stimulus. This ability relates to how well we are able to function in society, with research indicating that individuals with low self-regulation frequently encounter difficulties in their daily lives and are subjected to greater pressure from their environment (Nováková & Vávrová, 2015).

Self-regulation allows individuals to control their behaviour in order to achieve important goals. It is also a process that maintains control over an individual's cognition and emotions, which are considered influential factors in the achievement of goals. This concept is comprised of three elements: goal setting, productive behaviour that leads to goal attainment, and monitoring actions to achieve goals (Ceresnik, 2013).

Self-regulation grants a person control over their own psychological and physiological state, as such, it can aid individuals to overcome their tendencies to purchase on impulse. Thus, the primary cause of the problems would be that people with poor self-regulation are more likely to act on their immediate desires, a behaviour that could be problematic depending on the nature of the desires.

Baumeister and Vohs (2007) have identified four distinct self-regulation components: standards of desirable behaviour, motivation to meet standards, monitoring of situations and thoughts preceding violations of standards, and willpower or inner strength to control urges. When a person lacks one or more of these components, self-regulation does not advance, which may result in an increase in impulsive or thoughtless behaviour. Self-regulation is impulse control in the face of short-term desires, as our ability to self-regulate has been linked to a higher psychological well-being due to the fact that consumers are able to regulate themselves. Consumers who are also able to regulate their emotions and possess the motivation and willpower to maintain the regulation that they have imposed on themselves will be better able to avoid impulse purchases.

The table below summarizes some past studies on mobile payment systems and impulse buying and their key findings.

Table 1. Summary of past studies on mobile payment systems and impulsive buying

Authors /Year	Research Focus	Findings
Zheng et al. (2019)	The study draws on the stimulus-organism-response (S-O-R) paradigm to analyze the situational factors and reaction factors in mobile commerce and their relationship with impulse buying	Portability, visual appeal and interpersonal influence) affected hedonic browsing and utilitarian browsing. Hedonic browsing directly and positively influences consumers' urge to buy impulsively, whereas utilitarian browsing indirectly influences consumers' urge to buy impulsively through hedonic browsing.
Um et al. (2022)	The study assesses buyers' motivations to purchase tourism products through mobile commerce and how these motives impact consumers' impulse buying behavior.	Convenience and ubiquity influence perceived value. Also, perceived value, notice of special promotion, and impulsiveness have a direct effect on impulse buying behavior.
Chen and Yao (2018)	The study examines how situational factors affect impulsive buying behavior by integrating the stimulus organism response model, impulsivity traits and other external variables.	Personality factors of an impulsive buying tendency, normative evaluation, and positive affect are key determinants of impulse buying, while ubiquity, ease of use, information exchange, discounted price, and scarcity are important precursors.
Yong et al. (2022)	The study assesses the link between perceived enjoyment and satisfaction with using E-wallet on impulsive buying behavior.	Perceived enjoyment of using an E-wallet positively affected impulse buying while satisfaction with E-wallet had no significant relationship with impulse buying.
Yang et al. (2021)	The study assesses how consumers' perceived value affect impulse buying behavior (IBB) in mobile commerce.	The results show that perception of hedonic value significantly and directly

Continued on following page

Table 1. Continued

		influenced impulse buying behavior.
Chen et al., (2020)	The study integrates visual appeal, emotional responses, and consumers' impulse buying tendencies to explore their effects on impulse buying and post-purchase behavior.	The results show that pleasure directly influences consumers' impulse buying, whereas arousal indirectly influences consumers' impulse buying through pleasure. Impulse buying directly influences consumers' product dissonance but indirectly influences consumers' emotional dissonance through product dissonance. Emotional dissonance directly influences consumers' return intention and indirectly influences consumers' return intention through emotional dissonance.
Spiteri Cornish (2020)	The study used an experimental design to demonstrate that post-purchase experience reinforces or curtails future impulse buying.	A negative post-purchase experience results in post-purchase regret, which in turn curtails future impulse buying. In contrast, a positive post-purchase experience reinforces impulse buying. Consumers utilize three types of coping mechanisms to mitigate post-purchase regret, i.e. planful problem solving, positive reinterpretation and mental disengagement.
Zhang et al. (2020)	The study explored the generation process of consumers' impulsive purchase intention during the COVID-19 outbreak from the perspective of system users.	The "stimulation-reaction-intention" impulsive purchase model of consumers' mobile shopping was confirmed.
Zhou and Gu (2015)	The study framed a price reduction in the amount of money versus percentage on products to investigate how the underlying mechanism	Compared with percentage-off presentation, the findings

Continued on following page

Table 1. Continued

	(anticipated regret) influences likelihood to impulse buying.	indicate that presentation shown at the amount of money leads to higher anticipated regret and consumer impulse buying intention. Price level of product is the boundary condition, which plays a moderating role

THE FUTURE OF MOBILE PAYMENT SYSTEMS

Reports from MEF's third annual Global Mobile Money report 2015 suggests that e-commerce and mobile banking are continuously growing with about 69% of users of mobile devices conducting their banking activities through mobile devices (Bezhovski, 2016). The increasing use of mobile payment systems has urged developed markets to install device penetration systems and infrastructure that support mobile transactions in-store. Furthermore, contactless payment methods have gained increased popularity with the introduction of wearable technology that provide fast, easy and secured means to pay at various places. Mobile money outlets are outnumbering traditional banking outlets in a lot of markets worldwide (Bezhovski, 2016). The rate of mobile payment transactions is rising worldwide, this clearly indicates that there is a cashless future ahead with more secured and convenient options for making payments through mobile devices. In some places mobile payment systems have created new opportunities for merchants and consumers. Mobile payment systems have also exposed consumers to new forms of risks with regard to privacy and security issues. Thus, careful planning is needed to make security an intrinsic element of mobile payment methods in the future. To ensure a prosperous future of the mobile payment industry, mobile phone manufacturers, telecommunication companies and the payment industries ought to collaborate in order to create a platform that ensures the most secure environment for mobile payment.

CONCLUSION

Implications and Recommendations for Future Research

Mobile payment systems have several benefits for consumers and firms, as such, firms in the industry are constantly looking for innovative ways to provide convenience and ease for customers. Features of mobile devices like portability, interactivity and ease of use make them a preferred payment channel. Though mobile payment systems offer several advantages to consumers, they can also trigger impulse buying. The ease with which payments are made with mobile payment systems can significantly contribute to impulse buying which has detrimental effects on consumers like financial hardships, guilt, regrets, and emotional trauma. Though the aim of mobile payment systems is not to create impulse purchases, it is clearly an unintended negative consequence of mobile payment systems which scholars and practitioners need to pay attention to.

This has some implications for consumers. First, the existence of mobile payment systems makes them more impulsive because mobile payment systems have advantages that makes it easier for people to make safe and stress-free payments. Second, perceived enjoyment, promotions, visual display, and emotional factors have been found to significantly influence impulse buying, consumers must be aware of these factors and use self-regulation to control impulse purchases. Third, perceived enjoyment of e-commerce and mobile payment systems could also trigger impulse buying, it therefore behooves on consumers to enhance awareness and understanding of impulse purchase intents so they can control it. They should make mindful purchases to avoid unnecessary expenses.

The study, though, important has some limitations that could offer avenues for further research. First the study was conceptual in nature, thus, no empirical data was tested to assess the effects of mobile payment systems on impulse buying. As a result, future research could employ an experimental research design or other research designs to empirically assess the effects of mobile payment systems on impulse buying. Additionally, future studies could also use more rigorous approaches like meta-analytic reviews, systematic reviews, or a bibliometric analysis to assess the current state of the literature on impulse purchases.

REFERENCES

Aggarwal, P., Jun, S., & Huh, J. (2011). Scarcity messages. *Journal of Advertising*, *40*(3), 19–30. doi:10.2753/JOA0091-3367400302

Banning, M. E. (2015). Shared entanglements – Web 2.0, info-liberalism & digital sharing. *Information Communication and Society*, *19*(4), 489–503. doi:10.1080/1369118X.2015.1061573

Baumeister, R., & Vohs, K. (2007). Self-regulation, ego depletion, and motivation. *Social and Personality Psychology Compass*, *1*(10), 1–14.

Bezhovski, Z. (2016). The Future of the Mobile Payment as Electronic Payment System. *European Journal of Business and Management*, *8*(8), 127–132.

Cao, X., Yu, L., Liu, Z., Gong, M., & Adeel, L. (2018). Understanding mobile payment users' continuance intention: A trust transfer perspective. *Internet Research*, *28*(2), 456–476. doi:10.1108/IntR-11-2016-0359

Čerešník, M. (2013). Self-regulation of adolescents: Gender specifications. *Procedia: Social and Behavioral Sciences*, *106*, 2365–2374. doi:10.1016/j.sbspro.2013.12.271

Chan, T. K., Cheung, C. M., & Lee, Z. W. (2017). The state of online impulse-buying research: A literature analysis. *Information & Management*, *54*(2), 204–217. doi:10.1016/j.im.2016.06.001

Chen, C., & Yao, J. (2018). What drives impulse buying behaviors in a mobile auction? The perspective of the Stimulus-Organism-Response model. *Telematics and Informatics*, *35*(5), 1249–1262. doi:10.1016/j.tele.2018.02.007

Chen, W. K., Chen, C. W., & Lin, Y. C. (2020). Understanding the influence of impulse buying toward consumers' post-purchase dissonance and return intention: An empirical investigation of apparel websites. *Journal of Ambient Intelligence and Humanized Computing*, (March). doi:10.100712652-020-02333-z

Dholakia, U. (2000). Temptation and resistance: An integrated model of consumption impulse formation and enactment. *Psychology and Marketing*, *17*(11), 955–982. https://doi.org/10.1002/1520-6793(200011)17:11<955::AID-MAR3>3.0.CO;2-J doi:10.1002/1520-6793(200011)17:11<955::AID-MAR3>3.0.CO;2-J

Gillespie, B. J. (2017). Characteristics of the mobile population. In *Household Mobility in America* (pp. 49–87). Palgrave Macmillan. doi:10.1057/978-1-349-68271-3_3

Gobry, P. E. (2012). Mobile payments: what's taking so long, and who's going to win. *Business Insider*. https://www.businessinsider.com/mobile-payments-whats-taking-so-long-and-whosgoing-to-win-201

Goeke, L., & Pousttchi, K. (2010). A scenario-based analysis of mobile payment acceptance. *Proceedings of the Ninth International Conference on Mobile Business and Ninth Global Mobility Roundtable*. IEEE. 10.1109/ICMB-GMR.2010.81

Gogoi, B., & Shillong, I. (2020). Do impulsive buying influence compulsive buying? *Academy of Marketing Studies Journal*, *24*, 1–15.

Halim, E. (2021). The Impacts of E-Payment System and Impulsive Buying to Purchase Intention in E-commerce. *2020 International Conference on Information Management and Technology(ICIMTech), May*, 847–852. IEEE. 10.1109/ICIMTech50083.2020.9211154

Hausman, A. (2000). A multi-method investigation of consumer motivations in impulse buying behavior. *Journal of Consumer Marketing*, *17*(5), 403–426. doi:10.1108/07363760010341045

Hsiao, M. (2021). Post-purchase behaviour from customer perceived value of mobile payment services. *Journal of Modelling in Management*. doi:10.1108/JM2-11-2020-0293

Kim, A., & Johnson, K. (2016). Power of consumers using social media: Examining the influences of brand-related user-generated content on Facebook. *Computers in Human Behavior*, *58*, 98–108. doi:10.1016/j.chb.2015.12.047

Koenig-Lewis, N., Marquet, M., Palmer, A., & Zhao, A. (2015). Enjoyment and social influence: Predicting mobile payment adoption. *Service Industries Journal*, *35*(10), 537–554. doi:10.1080/02642069.2015.1043278

Lee, T., Park, C., & Jun, J. (2014). Two faces of mobile shopping: Self-efficacy and im_pulsivity. *International Journal of E-Business Research*, *10*(1), 15–32. doi:10.4018/ijebr.2014010102

Liébana-Cabanillas, F., Molinillo, S., & Ruiz-Montañez, M. (2019). To use or not to use, that is the question : Analysis of the determining factors for using NFC mobile payment systems in public transportation. *Technological Forecasting and Social Change*, *139*, 266–276. doi:10.1016/j.techfore.2018.11.012

Lin, J., Wang, B., Wang, N., & Lu, Y. (2014). Understanding the evolution of consumer trust in mobile commerce: A longitudinal study. *Information Technology Management*, *15*(1), 37–49. doi:10.100710799-013-0172-y

Lin, P., & Lin, Z. (2013). Buying impulse triggered by digital media. *Service Industries Journal*, *33*(9–10), 892–908. doi:10.1080/02642069.2013.719887

Lin, S., & Lo, L. Y. (2016). Evoking online consumer impulse buying through virtual layout schemes. *Behaviour & Information Technology*, *35*(1), 38–56. doi:10.1080/0144929X.2015.1056546

Liu, Y., Li, H., & Hu, F. (2013). Website attributes in urging online impulse purchase: An empirical investigation on consumer perceptions. *Decision Support Systems*, *55*(3), 829–837. doi:10.1016/j.dss.2013.04.001

Moghavvemi, S., Xin, T., Wai, S., & Yen, S. (2021). Drivers and barriers of mobile payment adoption: Malaysian merchants ' perspective. *Journal of Retailing and Consumer Services*, *59*, 102364. doi:10.1016/j.jretconser.2020.102364

Nováková, R. K., & Vávrová, S. (2015). Self-regulation of behaviour in the context of peer pressure and risk behaviour. *Procedia: Social and Behavioral Sciences*, *171*, 158–165. doi:10.1016/j.sbspro.2015.01.102

Nusair, K., Jin Yoon, H., Naipaul, S., & Parsa, H. (2010). Effect of price discount frames and levels on consumers' perceptions in low-end service industries. *International Journal of Contemporary Hospitality Management*, *22*(6), 814–835. doi:10.1108/09596111011063106

Pandya, P., & Pandya, K. (2020). An empirical study of compulsive buying behaviour of consumers. *Alochana Chakra Journal*, *9*(6), 4102–4114.

Parboteeah, D., Valacich, J., & Wells, J. D. (2009). The influence of website characteristics on a consumer's urge to buy impulsively. *Information Systems Research*, *20*(1), 60–78. doi:10.1287/isre.1070.0157

Park, H., & Noh, M. (2012). The influence of innovativeness and price sensitivity on purchase intention of smart wear. *Journal of the Korean Society of Clothing and Textiles*, *36*(2), 218–230. doi:10.5850/JKSCT.2012.36.2.218

Parker, J., & Lehmann, D. (2011). When shelf-based scarcity impacts consumer preferences. *Journal of Retailing*, *87*(2), 142–155. doi:10.1016/j.jretai.2011.02.001

Piron, F. (1991). Defining impulse purchasing. *Advances in Consumer Research. Association for Consumer Research (U. S.)*, *18*(1), 509–514.

Ramos, I., Luna, D., Liébana-cabanillas, F., Sánchez-fernández, J., & Muñoz-leiva, F. (2019). Mobile payment is not all the same : The adoption of mobile payment systems depending on the technology applied. *Technological Forecasting and Social Change*, *146*, 931–944. doi:10.1016/j.techfore.2018.09.018

Revels, J., Dewi, T., & Yelena, T. (2010). Understanding consumer intention to use mobile services. [AMJ]. *Australasian Marketing Journal*, *18*(2), 74–80. doi:10.1016/j.ausmj.2010.02.002

Shen, O., & Yazdanifard, R. (2015). Has mobile payment finally live up to its expectation in replacing cash and credit? *International Journal of Management. Accounting and Economics*, *2*(5), 489–498.

Song, H. G., Chung, N., & Koo, C. (2015). *Impulsive Buying Behavior of Restaurant Products in Social Commerce: A Role of Serendipity and Scarcity Message.* Pacis. https://pacis2015.comp.nus.edu.sg/_proceedings/PACIS_2015_submission_400.pdf

Spiteri Cornish, L. (2020). Why did I buy this? Consumers' post-impulse-consumption experience and its impact on the propensity for future impulse buying behaviour. *Journal of Consumer Behaviour, 19*(1), 36–46. doi:10.1002/cb.1792

Srivastava, S. C., Chandra, S., & Theng, Y. (2010). Evaluating the role of trust in consumer adoption of mobile payment systems: An empirical analysis. *Communications of the Association for Information Systems, 27*(1), 561–568.

Telci, E. E., Maden, C., & Kantur, D. (2011). The theory of cognitive dissonance: A marketing and management perspective. *Procedia: Social and Behavioral Sciences, 24*, 378–386. doi:10.1016/j.sbspro.2011.09.120

Um, T., Chung, N., & Stienmetz, J. (2022). Factors affecting consumers' impulsive buying behavior in tourism Mobile commerce using SEM and fsQCA. *Journal of Vacation Marketing*, 1–9. doi:10.1177/13567667221090991

Vaidyanathan, R., & Aggarwal, P. (2003). Who is the fairest of them all? An attributional approach to price fairness perceptions. *Journal of Business Research, 56*(6), 453–463. doi:10.1016/S0148-2963(01)00231-4

Verhagen, T., & van Dolen, W. (2011). The influence of online store beliefs on consumer on line impulse buying: A model and empirical application. *Information & Management, 48*(8), 320–327. doi:10.1016/j.im.2011.08.001

Verkijika, S. F. (2020). An affective response model for understanding the acceptance of mobile payment systems. *Electronic Commerce Research and Applications, 39*, 100905. doi:10.1016/j.elerap.2019.100905

Xu, C., Unger, A., Papastamatelou, J., & Raab, G. (2022). The influence of Internet shopping and use of credit cards on gender differences in compulsive buying. *Journal of Internet and Digital Economics, 2*(1), 27–45. doi:10.1108/JIDE-11-2021-0017

Yang, F., Tang, J., Men, J., & Zheng, X. (2021). Consumer perceived value and impulse buying behavior on mobile commerce : The moderating effect of social influence. *Journal of Retailing and Consumer Services, 63*, 102683. doi:10.1016/j.jretconser.2021.102683

Yong, Y., Chin, L., Gan, L., & Wei, T. (2022). Do E - wallets trigger impulse purchases ? An analysis of Malaysian Gen-Y and Gen-Z consumers. *Journal of Marketing Analytics*. doi:10.1057/s41270-022-00164-9

Zhang, W., Leng, X., & Liu, S. (2020). Research on mobile impulse purchase intention in the perspective of system users during COVID-19. *Personal and Ubiquitous Computing*.

Zheng, X., Men, J., Yang, F., & Gong, X. (2019). Understanding impulse buying in mobile commerce: An investigation into hedonic and utilitarian browsing. *International Journal of Information Management*, *48*, 151–160. doi:10.1016/j.ijinfomgt.2019.02.010

Zhou, H., & Gu, Z. (2015). The Effect of Different Price Presentations on Consumer Impulse Buying Behavior: The Role of Anticipated Regret. *American Journal of Industrial and Business Management*, *05*(01), 27–36. doi:10.4236/ajibm.2015.51004

Section 3
Central Bank Digital Currency

Chapter 8
Learnings From Discontinued Central Bank Digital Currencies (CBDC):
A Multiple Case Study Analysis

John Agyekum Addae
https://orcid.org/0000-0002-6374-5195
LUT University, Finland & Ghana Communication Technology University, Ghana

Kwame Simpe Ofori
https://orcid.org/0000-0001-7725-9756
International University of Grand-Bassam, Côte d'Ivoire & University of Electronic Science and Technology of China, China

Sheraz Ahmed
https://orcid.org/0000-0001-6836-2030
LUT University, Finland

ABSTRACT

The financial and monetary system is transitioning into contactless payment options and digital currencies. About 90 percent of the world's central banks are engaged in CBDC research, proof of concept, pilot, development, and launch, while the remaining are overlooking CBDC offerings. Notwithstanding, many central banks have cancelled their CBDC following their launch. While learning from the past failure is extoled as a virtue, learning from failed CBDC is seldom in the CBDC ecosystem, contrary to dominant literature on CBDC development and scalability. This study explores reasons why central banks discontinued already launched CBDC's. The authors adopted criterion sampling to select failed CBDC. This multiple case content analysis shows that low levels of trust, cybersecurity concerns, inadequate digital identification infrastructure, and obsolete and uncompetitive technology are the leading triggers of failed CBDC. Through the lens of actor-network theory (ANT), actors contributing to CBDC failure was identified

DOI: 10.4018/978-1-6684-6381-9.ch008

Copyright © 2023, IGI Global. Copying or distributing in print or electronic forms without written permission of IGI Global is prohibited.

INTRODUCTION

CBDC stands for central bank digital currency. It is a digital version of a country's fiat currency, issued and backed by the central bank of that country. CBDCs can be used for digital transactions in the same way that physical cash is used for transactions in the real world. They are typically designed to be used by consumers and businesses for everyday transactions and can be stored and exchanged electronically. There are several advantages of CBDCs that are considered important for the development and use of digital currencies in future. CBDCs can make it easier for people who are currently unbanked or underbanked, such as those living in rural areas or those without access to traditional banking services, to participate in the digital economy. CBDCs can improve the speed and efficiency of digital payments, as they can be exchanged and processed quickly and securely. CBDCs can increase the stability of the financial system by reducing the risk of bank runs. CBDCs can give central banks more control over monetary policy by allowing them to conduct transactions directly with commercial banks and other market participants. CBDCs can reduce the risk of fraud and money laundering by providing secure and traceable digital transactions. CBDCs can improve cross-border payments by providing a digital currency that is widely accepted and easily transferable. CBDCs can provide a secure and efficient means of digital transactions that is under the control of the central bank and the government rather than the private sector, strengthening the country's digital sovereignty.

It's worth noting that the benefits of CBDCs will depend on their design and how they are implemented. Despite of many advantages, developing and implementing a CBDC can be a complex and technically challenging process. Legal and regulatory issues also raise pertinent questions by privacy and anti-money laundering programs about the transparency and oversight. Mass adoption of CBDCs will require a robust infrastructure, user-friendly interfaces, and a reliable network of merchants and service providers that accept CBDCs. If not designed properly, CBDCs could also lead to financial exclusion for certain groups of people, particularly those who are not able or willing to use digital platforms for transactions. According to CBDC Tracker[1], ten of the global central banks have launched pilot versions of digital currencies during 2020-22, for example, People's Bank of China launched a pilot program for its digital Yuan in four cities in 2020 and expanded the program to include more cities in 2021. The Banque de France has been one of the most active central banks in terms of piloting the digital currencies for wholesale and retail customers in cooperation with Tunisian and Singaporean central banks. Other notable central banks are Reserve Bank of India, Central bank of Nigeria, The Bank of Ghana, and The Monetary Authority of Singapore. In 2022, The Central of Bahamas, and The Bank of Jamaica have officially launched their digital currencies.

The financial and monetary system is transitioning into contactless payment options and digital currencies. The Euro zone has witnessed a 25% drop in cash transaction whereas contactless payment options has also significantly increased in China (Tronnier et al., 2022). CBDC is considered to herald a new monetary era (Wang et al., 2022a). CBDC seeks to limit physical currency to accelerate a secure and efficient fast payment system (Bian et al., 2021).

These developments has engendered central banks to refocus on CBDCs. About 60-90% of central bank are engaged in various stages of CBDC research, pilot or development (Allen et al., 2022; Boar & Wehrli, 2021; Ferrari et al., 2022; Huang & Mayer, 2022; Laboure et al., 2021; Ozturkcan et al., 2022; Pelagidis & Kostika, 2022; Xu, 2022; Yang & Zhou, 2022). The Bank for International Settlement estimates that within three years, fifty percent of the world's population will be using CBDC (Laboure et al., 2021; Tronnier et al., 2022).

Discussions on the benefit and dark side of CBDC is fearless. Scholars, market actors, and policymakers have explored the pros and cons of a CBDC (Cunha et al., 2021). Most strand of CBDC studies, are "explorative studies without empirical test" (Ozili, 2022, p. 7). Another strand of CBDC studies focus on CBDC development and adoptions (e.g. Liu et al., 2022; Solberg Söilen & Benhayoun, 2022; Tronnier et al., 2022). In addition, the fierce debate between proponents and opponents of CBDC also calls for additional research in order to bring closure to the debate. Accordingly, Ozili, (2022) orate that future research are need to ascertain CBDC actual benefits and consequences.

Whiles the proponents of CBDC are enjoying all the support, conversely, voice about the potential risk of CBDC are equally loud. Proponents of CBDC have espouse benefits associated with CBDC offering. CBDC will expand e-commerce (Lee et al., 2021). The implementation of the CBDC has the potential to result in an increase in consumption of 15% in Canada and 34% in the United States (Davoodalhosseini, 2022). In the same light, the issuing of CBDCs has the potential to boost GDP by as much as 3% (Barrdear & Kumhof, 2016). Evidence from Ozili, (2022) suggests that a CBDC could expand access to financial services and promote more financial inclusion. Besides, CBDC promote cost saving including low printing cost of physical currency (Allen et al., 2022)

On the contrary, concerns have been raised about the negative side of CBDC. Production and distribution of CBDCs will cause environmental harm, including higher energy use and carbon emissions (Laboure et al., 2021). Moreover, CBDC possess unprecedented threat to monetary sovereignty (Huang & Mayer, 2022) especially CBDC hold geopolitical trigger especially between US and China (Huang & Mayer, 2022). Privacy invasion occasioned by CBDC is pronounced (Cunha et al., 2021). CBDCs have the potential to exacerbate financial uncertainty (Wang et al., 2022a). The use of CBDCs could have adverse effects on financial intermediation, destabilize the banking sector and induce bank run (Bian et al., 2021; Lee et al., 2021; Meaning et al., 2021). Notwithstanding CBDC negative outlook, Wang et al., (2022) contends that the potential adverse effects of CBDCs would be minimal at most.

It is popular to report a success, but we have a tendency not probe into failed project. Success is usually more interesting to talk about than failure. Recently, failed FinTech offering have attracted scholar interest (Bernards, 2019; Jinasena et al., 2020) including Stablecoin's failure (Briola et al., 2022); bitcoin failure (Malik et al., 2022; Zook & Blankenship, 2018); P2P lending and its platform failure (Deng, 2022; Klein et al., 2021); crowdfunding failure (Mazzocchini & Lucarelli, 2022; Schwienbacher, 2019) and cryptocurrencies failures (Gandal et al., 2021). To the best of our knowledge, no studies have documented learning from failed CBDC. Danneels & Vestal, (2020) and Cooper et al. (2004) orate that firms must extol failure virtues and make effort to learn from past failures. It is rare for the lessons that can be learnt from failed project to be formally disseminated and most of the time they are not even documented (Perros et al., 2022, p. 8).

This study contributes to CBDC intellectual structure in several aspects. First, since about 98% of global CBDC are in the development stage, lesson from cancelled CBDC around the global will guide CDBC developer and stakeholders. Second, our study offer new insight and document reasons accounting for failed CBDC project distinct from dominant literature on CBDC brighter side. Moreover, we provide a significant contribution to the body of empirical knowledge by shedding light on CBDC failures, a research strand which were previously unexplored. In order to bridge the gap between literature and practice, this paper comes in handy to deepens our understanding on CBDC.

The next section of the study proceeds as follows. Section 2 survey literature follow by description of the study methodology in section 3. The results are presented in section 4. Whereas section 5 concludes the study with policy implication and direction for future research.

CBDC RELATED LITERATURE

Theoretical Foundation for Discontinued CBDC

Actor-network Theory (ANT) offer theoretical lens to explain failed CBDC offering. Essentially, ANT postulated by Latour, (1987) place premium on human and non-human actors interactions in the CBDC ecosystem. Latour, (2005) advance that non-human factors, such as technology, ought to be considered "symmetrical" with humans and, hence, ought to also be recognized as actors. Similarly, Shin (2016) opines that technology is not a passive creature, but rather an actor that possesses a certain degree of autonomy and activity in its own right.

By apply ANT to explained failed CBDC project, the theory can explain how inappropriate and inadequate CBDC technologies (e.g. DLT and DLT technologies) and inaction of CBDC ecosystem actors (e.g. Central banks, technology providers, customers) will leads to failed CBDC offering. Thus, actors in CBDC ecosystem formal and informal networks must collaborate and create strategic system to foster CBDC growth and sustainability.

The contribution of ANT on knowledge production and technology development in multiple and cross discipline is prevalent (P.-C. Chen & Hung, 2016). Despite ANT widespread scholarship, few studies have applied ANT to explain project-offering failure. For example, P.-C. Chen & Hung, (2016) use ANT to identify inefficiencies in R&D innovation system. Neyland & Simakova, (2012) report ANT evidence for e-waste market failure whereas Dery et al., (2013) document that by using ANT, we can gain a deeper understand of information system implementation pitfalls. Shim & Shin, (2016), ANT inspired study also reveal how FinTech ecosystem actors including social and state actors are collaborating to foster FinTech growth in China and expanding its global presence.

Failed Fintech Offering

When a newly announced Fintech offering to provide financial services does not produce the expected results, it is considered a failed offering. This might occur for many different reasons, including lack of customer interest, or poor execution. There have been many failed Fintech offerings in the past (Bernards, 2019; Jinasena et al., 2020).

On the digital asset front, Gandal et al., (2021) report that around 44% of publicly traded coins are abandoned. Providing support for Stablecoins failures, Briola et al., (2022) in their research demonstrate that Terra, a fiat-based stable coin lost its peg to the U.S. dollar (USD) and ultimately failed. Experts also predicted that 95% of new crypto firms entering the crypto market would fail (Briola et al., 2022). While document evidence for cryptocurrencies failures (Gandal et al., 2021), evidence of bitcoin failure equally abounds bitcoin failure (Malik et al., 2022; Zook & Blankenship, 2018);

FinTech platforms, in the same spirit, have seen their fair share of failures. For example, most crowd funders end up withdrawing their contributions, which constrain crowdfunding campaigns' backers to invest only 18% of the total project value leading to crowdfunding failure (Mazzocchini & Lucarelli, 2022; Schwienbacher, 2019). Deng, (2022) also offered an explanation for why China's peer-to-peer lending industry was such a failure. Similarly, Klein et al., (2021), shed light on why peer-to-peer (P2P) lending platforms fail. According to them, age riskier borrowers are the leading cause of P2P lending platform failures.

Merit and Demerits of Issuing CBDC

Many benefits have been advanced in support of CBDC. Particularly for the unbanked and underbanked, CBDC can facilitate simpler access to financial services. By cutting out multiple financial intermediaries and speeding up settlements, CBDC further streamlines the payment process. As a result of CBDC, central banks may have access to additional instruments for implementing monetary policy, which may have a positive impact on the economy. Besides, because CBDC are built on distributed ledger technology (DLT), which is more secure than traditional systems, CBDC have the potential to be more resistant to cyber attacks. Table 1 summarizes the merits CBDC offering.

Table 1. Merits of issuing CBDC

Main reason	Dimension	References
Monetary Policy consolidation	Support unconventional monetary policy	(Cunha et al., 2021; Laboure et al., 2021; Ozili, 2022; Wang et al., 2022b; Yang & Zhou, 2022)
	Promote Financial stability	(Cunha et al., 2021; Laboure et al., 2021; Meaning et al., 2021; Oh & Zhang, 2022; Ozili, 2022; Wang et al., 2022b; Yang & Zhou, 2022)
	Protect monetary sovereignty	(Ozturkcan et al., 2022)
	Reduce cost of printing notes and coins	(Cunha et al., 2021; Ozili, 2022; Zhang & Huang, 2022)
	promoting cashless economy	(Cunha et al., 2021; Oh & Zhang, 2022)
Promote Financial Inclusion	Upscale Financial inclusion	(Allen et al., 2022; Cunha et al., 2021; Laboure et al., 2021; Ozili, 2022)
Mitigate against financial crime	Overcome illicit payment and limiting financial crime	(Cunha et al., 2021; Oh & Zhang, 2022; Ozili, 2022; Wang et al., 2022b)
	Limiting tax invasion	(Cunha et al., 2021; Oh & Zhang, 2022; Wang et al., 2022b)
	Promote payment security	(Laboure et al., 2021)
Efficient and safer Domestic and Cross-border Payment system	Facilitate payment efficiency	(Cunha et al., 2021; Laboure et al., 2021; Zhang & Huang, 2022)
	Expand e-commerce	(Lee et al., 2021)
	Lower transaction cost	(Oh & Zhang, 2022; Yang & Zhou, 2022)
	Increase transaction convenience	(Zhang & Huang, 2022)

Conversely, despite CBDC numerous benefits, it is also not without drawbacks. Privacy concerns are raised since CBDC systems frequently gather and store significant amounts of sensitive information, such as personal and financial details. This can also put customers' personal and financial information at risk, rendering them exposed to cyberattacks. Likewise, CBDCs rely on digital infrastructure and technology, which can be vulnerable to cyberattacks. This can put customers' personal and financial information at risk. Furthermore, CBDCs may face technical challenges such as scalability and interoperability with existing systems. Introduction of CBDC may disrupt the existing banking system and risk of facilitation systemic bank runs. Finally, negative impact of CBDC on the environment is also pronounce. CBDCs rely on digital infrastructure, which requires energy to power servers and data centers. This could lead to increased carbon emissions from the energy used to power these facilities. The increased use of digital currencies could lead to an increase in the number of data centers needed to support the infrastructure, which could have a negative impact on the environment. CBDCs may require increased energy consumption, particularly if the underlying technology is based on proof of work (PoW) algorithms, which are energy intensive. Critical issues hampering CBDC are presented in table 2

Table 2. Demerits hampering CBDC offering

Legal and Regulation	sovereign regulatory interoperability	(H. Chen & Siklos, 2022; Cheng, 2022; Cunha et al., 2021; Lee et al., 2021)
Geopolitical issue	CBDC hold geopolitical trigger for currency dominance conflicts and trade war	(H. Chen & Siklos, 2022; Ozili, 2022; Wang et al., 2022a)
	Possess a challenge to monetary sovereignty	(Huang & Mayer, 2022)
Risk Factors	structural disintermediation of banks	(Yang & Zhou, 2022)
	risk of facilitation systemic bank runs	(Briola et al., 2022; Wang et al., 2022a; Yang & Zhou, 2022)
	Security concerns and Cyberattacks	(Bhaskar et al., 2022; Ozili, 2022)
	Privacy concerns	(Cheng, 2022; Ozili, 2022)
Environmental Issue	High Energy consumption and Emissions	(Laboure et al., 2021; Wang et al., 2022a)

CBDC Development Stages

The vast majority of central banks are currently playing an active role in CBDC research, proof of concept, pilot, or have already launched. Most central banks follow four steps in CBDC development namely (1) research, (2) proof of concept (PoC), (3) pilot, and (4) launch (Morgan, 2022). According to a 2021 Bank for International Settlements (BIS) survey on CBDC, around 60 central banks are exploring its prospects since 2014, with 86% actively involved in CBDC research, 60% doing proofs of concepts, and 14% pushing forward with CBDC piloting (Boar & Wehrli, 2021).

CBDC research phase of central bank digital currency (CBDC) is the initial stage of development where central banks explore the feasibility and potential benefits and drawbacks of issuing a CBDC. This phase typically involves conducting research, studying existing systems, and engaging with stakeholders to gather information and feedback. In the research stage, central banks engage in conceptualization and testing, all with the goal of testing the fundamental assumptions and determining whether its digitalized currency would be successful or otherwise. Usually, Most of the central banks started their CBDC research on their own (or in-house) without any external collaboration. At some point, central banks reach out to external experts including IT expert both in academia and in industry to drive CBDC research.

Most central banks begin the journey to issue CBDC with a extensive research (Cunha et al., 2021; Pocher & Veneris, 2022). CBDC ecosystem began CBDC research in 2014 (Boar & Wehrli, 2021; Cheng, 2022; Cunha et al., 2021; Pocher & Veneris, 2022). UK, EU, China, Germany, Singapore, Japan and Brazil launched research into CBDC between 2014 to 2016 (Pocher & Veneris, 2022). Most central banks are researching into wholesale CBDC (Barotini & Holden, 2019; Boar & Wehrli, 2021; Pocher & Veneris, 2022).

PoC denote experimentation of conceptualized CBDC including testing of CBDC technology. Many central banks, as shown by Barontini and Holden (2019), have moved beyond CBDCs research into experimentation and proof-of-concept, including testing to technologies (Barotini & Holden, 2019, p. 7). About 80% of central banks engage in CBDC are at the proof-of-concept stage (Boar & Wehrli, 2021; Cheng, 2022; Ferrari et al., 2022; Pocher & Veneris, 2022). Further, most CBDC PoC are based on blockchain and distributed ledger technology (Auer et al., 2020, p. 5). As such, (Zhang & Huang, (2022) demonstrate that the central banks of Canada, South Africa, Thailand, and Hong Kong all built their CBDC Proof of Concepts on Blockchain technology. Currently, PoC experiments are being conducted with the digital euro as well (Allen et al., 2022; Auer et al., 2020; Cunha et al., 2021; Ferrari et al., 2022).

During the CBDC piloting phase, a central bank will test and evaluate the efficacy of a digital version of its currency. Such assessments include checking the CBDC's security and resilience, and conducting technical evaluations of the infrastructure and systems needed to support the CBDC. The pilot phase involves making CBDC accessible to a small group of participants in a controlled environment to test its functionality and usability. The objective of the piloting phase's is to detect and address any technical, legal, or operational concerns before making the CBDC extensively available to the public. A great number of nations are now developing CBDCs using pilot projects. At least about 20 central banks are at the CBDC piloting stage (Cunha et al., 2021). Take China as an example. Following the successful implementation of e-CNY in 10 cities across China, including Shenzhen, Suzhou, Xiong'an, Chengdu, Shanghai, Hainan, Changsha, Xi'an, Qingdao, and Dalian, Beijing is the next city on the agenda for widespread use of the digital currency (Cheng, 2022; Cunha et al., 2021; Ferrari et al., 2022; Huang & Mayer, 2022; Ozturkcan et al., 2022). There is a reported 261 million new e-CYN users by the end of 2021, resulting in transactions of about $13.78 billion USD (Huang & Mayer, 2022, p. 331). Besides, e-Peso pilot phase managed by Central Bank of Uruguay was deem successful (Barotini & Holden, 2019)

Finally, CBDC is launched after the central banks is confident of market acceptance. The majority of central banks are making rapid progress toward the launch of their CBDC, with China taking the lead (Ozturkcan et al., 2022; Xu, 2022). In October of 2020, the Central Bank of The Bahamas became the first bank to formally launch a CBDC under the name Sand Dollar (Auer et al., 2020; Boar & Wehrli, 2021; Cunha et al., 2021; Laboure et al., 2021; Pocher & Veneris, 2022; Xu, 2022). Table 3 and Figure 1 both provide statistical information on the different stages of CBDC development.

Table 3. Statistics of CBDC development stages

CBDC development stages	Boston Group and EY CBDC Tracker[2]	Atlantic Council CBDC Tracker[3]
Research stage	86	39
Pilot stage	15	17
Proof of concept stage	20	-
Development stage	-	33
Launched stage	2	11
Cancelled CBDC	6	2
Inactive CBDC	-	15

Figure 1. Statistics of CBDC development stages

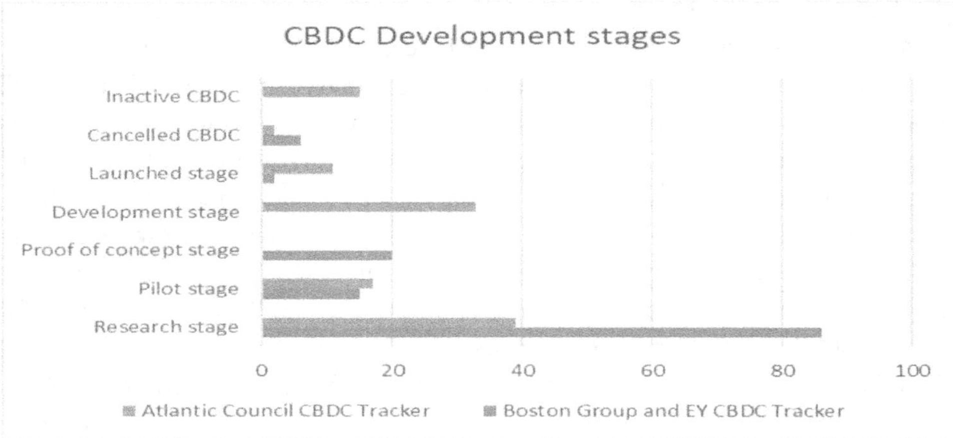

METHODOLOGY

Research Design

Case study approach was employed for this study. The choice of case study enables the research to answer "why" and "how" question (Franceschelli et al., 2018). Case studies also serve as the starting point for inferential empirical analysis (Ferrigno et al., 2022). In this paper, we follow prior studies to conducted multiple case study (Sternberg et al., 2021). Scholars have espoused the advantages of multiple case study. The use of multiple case studies enable the researcher to analyze each cash distinctively in detailed and synthesize pattens across cases (Ranta et al., 2021, p. 5).

Data Collection

Our case study data were drawn from the Boston Consulting Group's, Ernst & Young's, and the Atlantic Council's comprehensive CBDC tracker[4] database (Morgan, 2022). More than ninety-five percent of the world's GDP is represented in these databases, which cover well over 105 Countries exploring CBDC. Currently, 110 CBDCs are actively being explored. Twenty-six are still in the development stage, while 15 are already in pilot. CBDC in research account for Forty-six and eleven have been successfully launched. Sadly, after launching, about 12 have had to be canceled. This study perform case study analysis of cancelled CBDC. The selection of the cases are based on the following four factors: 1- We adopted criterion sampling to select our cancelled CBDC cases for the study (Patton, 1990, p. 176). 2- We selected cases based on data accessibility (Ferrigno et al., 2022). 3- the cases would advance and shed light on ongoing CBDC research and discourse (Siggelkow, 2007). and 4- To be included, the database above must classify the said CBDC as discontinued. The eligible cases are presented in table 4. We proceeded to collect secondary data. We relied on multiple data sources to improve trustworthiness (Ferrigno et al., 2022) and data triangulation (Jick, 1979). Employing data triangulation increases both data completeness (Eisenhardt, 1989) and findings reliability (Jick, 1979). We followed the works of Ferrigno et al., (2022) and Franceschelli et al., (2018) to extract data about our selected cases from central banks publications, specialist websites and YouTube videos. Using these secondary data sources enrich the depth of information about the selected cases (Franceschelli et al., 2018).

Table 4. Sample cases and data sources.

Data Sources	Project Orchid	Philippines CBDC	Haiti CBDC	E-kroner	Dinero electronico	Avant	Total
Central bank announcement and publications	5	3	2	7	2	5	24
Specialist Websites, and Articles consulted	30	18	8	45	12	35	148
YouTube Video	17	12	2	8	2	15	56

Data Analysis

In the analysis phase, we conducted content analysis of the selected case through manual coding similar to prior studies (Creamer & Ghoston, 2012; Ferrigno et al., 2022; Ranta et al., 2021). Inductive approach to coding and multiple rounds of coding characterizes our coding process (Linneberg & Korsgaard, 2019). We coded for both implicit and explicit case content (Creamer & Ghoston, 2012, p. 114). At the start of the coding, three authors independently coded a sample case to establish "clarity assessment". Following that, the three writers met to compare and review the sample code in order to analyze the accuracy and reliability of the chosen codes. At this point, all the ambiguous codes were clarified, and a unanimous consensus was reached on how they should be defined and coded for the entire data. Finally, the Independent scholar validated the coding results and the data analysis. Besides, our coding process satisfied inter-coding reliability (Landis & Koch, 1977). Table 5, 6, and 7 summarize our results.

RESULTS

Overview of Failed CBDC

CBDC was first developed in Finland in 1993, but today most Asian countries are at the forefront of its development and launch. The usual lifespan of a failed CBDC is anywhere from three months to three years, with the exception of Finland's CBDC, which travel for ten years. All of the failed CBDCs are retail CBDCs, and most of them are account based. Our findings indicate that the CBDC using DLT as well as those using non-DLT were unsuccessful. Both Table 5 and Table 6 provide a description of the characteristics of CBDCs that were unsuccessful.

Table 5. Summary of cancelled CBDC

Failed CBDC	Host Country	Responsible central bank	Continent	Launch data	Cancelled date
Project Orchid	Singapore	Monetary Authority of Singapore	Asia	Nov 2021	March 2022
Philippines CBDC	Philippines	Central Bank of the Philippines	Asia	Nov 2021	Feb. 2022
Haiti CBDC	Haiti	The Bank of the Republic of Haiti	North America	June 2019	July 2020
E-kroner	Denmark	Danmarks Nationalbank	EU/Nordic	Dec 2017	April 2021
Dinero electronico	Ecuador	Central Bank of Ecuador	South American	Sept 2014	Dec 2017
Avant	Finland	Bank of Finland	EU/Nordic	1993	2003

Table 6. Nature of failed CBDC

Failed CBDC	CBDC Type	Technology Provider	Structure	DLT / non-DLT
Project Orchid	Retail	Accenture	Account/Token	DLT
Philippines CBDC	Retail	Soramitsu	Account	DLT
Haiti CBDC	Retail	Bitt Inc.	Account	Non-DLT
E-kroner	Retail	Accenture	Account/Token	DLT
Dinero electronico	Retail	Mobile Money channels	Account	Non-DLT
Avant	Retail	Toimiraha	Account	Non-DLT

Learnings from Discontinued CBDC

There are several learnings gleaned from the discontinued CBDC. Inadequate infrastructure to support the CBDC ecosystem is the primary factor that contributes to the failure of CBDC, followed closely by a lack of interest on the part of customers in CBDC offerings. Also, it is seen that the concentration of data in the hands of central banks could lead to increased privacy risks for citizens, as it would create incentives for cyberattacks and a high systemic risk of individual or general surveillance in case of data breaches or unauthorized access. Additionally, wrong design choices in the underlying technological infrastructure of digital payments could exacerbate existing privacy and data protection issues, such as the unlawful use of transactional data for credit evaluation and cross-selling initiatives. A lack of security in the CBDC infrastructure could also lead to a significant loss of trust from users. The remaining contributing factors are identified in Table 7.

Table 7. Failed CBDC motivation, reason(s) for cancelation and ANT actors

Failed CBDC	Motivation(s) for CBDC launch	Reason(s) for Cancelation	ANT Actors
Project Orchid	To deepen resilience of the payment system To improve the efficiency and resilience of the existing electronic payment system To maintain inclusive access to money and payments To give greater access to digital payments To protecting public interests in retail payments To protect the public's interest in digital payments and reinforce trust in the Singapore monetary system To keep pace with advances in payment technology	Irrelevant Retail CBDC	Central Bank and Technology providers
		Singapore banking system unreadiness	Banks
		Inadequate infrastructure for cross-border payment	Government
		Global CBDC Challenge	Central Banks
		risks and uncertainties associated with CBDC	Central Bank, Government, technology providers, customers

Continued on following page

Table 7. Continued

Failed CBDC	Motivation(s) for CBDC launch	Reason(s) for Cancelation	ANT Actors
Philippines CBDC	To foster robust, competitive and reliable payment systems To improve the efficiency, safety and robustness of domestic and cross-border payments	Discontinued existing CBDC to refocus wholesale CBDC adoption the in future	Central Bank
		Higher exposure to cyberattacks on its CBDC system	Central Bank and Technology providers
		Inadequate digital Identify system and Fintech Infrastructure	Government
		Significant CBDC inherent risk and challenges	Central Bank, Government, technology providers, customers
Haiti CBDC	boost financial inclusion Foster interoperability and promote dynamic payment system Promote Cashless Society	Inadequate digital Infrastructure to support Fintech ecosystem	Central Bank and Government
E-kroner	Deepen cashless economy	Low Adoption	Customers
Dinero electronico	promote anti-dollarisation	Low level of trust leading to low Adoption	Central Bank
Avant	To promote payment system interoperability To establish a single national electronic payment system	Obsolete and uncompetitive Technology	Central Bank and technology provider

DISCUSSION AND IMPLICATION

We present evidence that demonstrates how a low degree of trust might result in CBDC cancellations. These findings are consistent with those of Blumen, (2016) who found that around 80 percent of projects fail owing to a lack of support from stakeholders.

There are a lot of positive outcomes to reporting on failed projects. Reporting on failed project foster discovering, examining, rectifying, and lessons sharing. However, scholars orate that failure occurs but infrequently reported (Catalano et al.,

2019). Vicarious learning and the promotion of a culture of 'safe fail' both benefit greatly from the practice of sharing failure experiences through the documentation and dissemination of failure reports. Thus, our results document lessons from failed CBDC to deepen scanty literature on failed projects. Contrary to dominant literature on CBDC development, our studies to the best of our knowledge represent pioneered research into discontinued CBDC which is seldom in the literature. Our study also contributes to growing literature on learning from past failure as a best practice (Cooper et al., 2004; Danneels & Vestal, 2020). Likewise, our study draws right lessons for organization learning to promote CBDC.

From the managerial implication standpoint, our studies draw lessons for CBDC ecosystem stakeholder to learn from failure experiences to guide future development of CBDC offerings. This study further encourages managers to be tolerance to failed CBDC and to make efforts to learn from these discontinued CBDC's. Institutions that have a negative view on failure run the risk of missing out on excellent opportunities for advancement. Failures should be viewed as great learning opportunities and should be treated as such by organizations, which should then encourage open exchange of knowledge about those failures. Largely, failed CBDC possess financial stability risk. Thus, learning from this study will shape before, during and after failed CBDC mitigation strategies (Briola et al., 2022).

Scholar must foster further research collaboration with CBDC developers, technology providers and central banks to strengthen CBDC interoperability, scalability, and security concerns to forestall CBDC cancellation after launch.

Limitation and Direction for Future Research

As is the case with all research, ours is not free of its share of limitations. Despite this, we have high hopes that the limitations of the study may stimulate new avenues of research for the future. First, our study performed content analysis, thus the use of fuzzy-set qualitative comparative analysis is desirable for future studies. Second, we conduct an analysis of secondary data about unsuccessful CBDC. Therefore, future research may consider employing primary data sources, such as conducting in-depth interviews with the governor of the central bank and as well as monetary authorities, such as in-depth interviews with the central bank governor and monetary authorities, to determine why their CBDC were discontinued after their implementation. We further recommend process study to explore the processes as it unfold that culminated into failed CBDC. Through the lenses of stakeholder and contingency theory, future research could examine the cultural, political, regulatory, and technological factors that hamper CBDC development. We analyzed failed CBDC; future research might look at alternative failed digital currencies especially failed cryptocurrencies and Stablecoins.

CONCLUSION

This paper engenders discussions of learning from Failed CBDC. Multiple discontinued CBDC's were analyzed. Our results demonstrated that the low level of trust, cybersecurity concerns, Inadequate digital Identify infrastructure, Obsolete and Uncompetitive Technology are the leading triggers of failed CBDC. Failed CBDC has a wider implication for financial stability. Overall, CBDCs are still a new and developing concept and there are still many questions that need to be answered about how they will work in practice. Central banks will likely continue to experiment with and refine different models for CBDCs in order to achieve the best possible outcomes while minimizing the disadvantages.

REFERENCES

Allen, F., Gu, X., & Jagtiani, J. (2022). Fintech, Cryptocurrencies, and CBDC : Financial Structural Transformation in China. *Journal of International Money and Finance*, *124*, 102625. doi:10.1016/j.jimonfin.2022.102625

Auer, R., Cornelli, G., & Frost, J. (2020). Rise of the Central Bank Digital Currencies: Drivers, Approaches and Technologies. *Bank for International Settlements*, *880*. doi:10.2139srn.3724070

Barotini, C., & Holden, H. (2019). Proceeding with caution - a survey on central bank digital currency. *Bank for International Settlements*, *101*(101), 1–15.

Barrdear, J., & Kumhof, M. (2016). The Macroeconomics of Central Bank Issued Digital Currencies. In *Bank of England Working Paper,* (Issue 605). https://www.bankofengland.co.uk/-/media/boe/files/working-paper/2016/the-macroeconomics-of-central-bank-issued-digital-currencies.pdf?la=en&hash=341B602838707E5D6FC26884588C912A721B1DC1

Bernards, N. (2019). Tracing mutations of neoliberal development governance: 'Fintech', failure and the politics of marketization. *Environment & Planning A*, *51*(7), 1442–1459. doi:10.1177/0308518X19862576

Bhaskar, R., Imran, A., Bansal, S., & Pandey, K. (2022). Research in International Business and Finance Central Bank Digital Currencies : Agendas for future research. *Research in International Business and Finance*, *62*(July), 101737. doi:10.1016/j.ribaf.2022.101737

Bian, W., Ji, Y., & Wang, P. (2021). The crowding-out effect of central bank digital currencies : A simple and generalizable payment portfolio model. *Finance Research Letters*, *43*(February), 102010. doi:10.1016/j.frl.2021.102010

Blumen, R. (2016). Jürgen laartz and alexander budzier on why large IT projects fail. *IEEE Software*, *33*(4), 117–120. doi:10.1109/MS.2016.102

Boar, C., & Wehrli, A. (2021). Ready, steady, go? – Results of the third BIS survey on central bank digital currency. *BIS Papers*, *114*, 77–82.

Briola, A., Vidal-tomás, D., Wang, Y., & Aste, T. (2022). Anatomy of a Stablecoin ' s failure : The Terra-Luna case. *Finance Research Letters*, *103358*(September). doi:10.1016/j.frl.2022.103358

Catalano, A. S., Lyons-White, J., Mills, M. M., & Knight, A. T. (2019). Learning from published project failures in conservation. *Biological Conservation*, *238*(September), 108223. doi:10.1016/j.biocon.2019.108223

Chen, H., & Siklos, P. L. (2022). Central bank digital currency : A review and some. *Journal of Financial Stability*, *60*(February), 100985. doi:10.1016/j.jfs.2022.100985

Chen, P.-C., & Hung, S.-W. (2016). An actor-network perspective on evaluating the R&D linking efficiency of innovation ecosystems. *Technological Forecasting and Social Change*, *112*, 303–312. doi:10.1016/j.techfore.2016.09.016

Cheng, P. (2022). Decoding the rise of Central Bank Digital Currency in China: Designs, problems, and prospects. *Journal of Banking Regulation*, *13*(7). doi:10.105741261-022-00193-5

Cooper, R. G., Edgett, S. J., & Kleinschmidt, E. J. (2004). Benchmarking NPD Best Practices. *Research Technology Management*, *47*(1), 31–43. doi:10.1080/08956308.2004.11671606

Creamer, E. G., & Ghoston, M. (2012). *Using a Mixed Methods Content Analysis to Analyze Mission Statements From Colleges of Engineering*. Sage. doi:10.1177/1558689812458976

Cunha, P. R., Melo, P., & Sebastião, H. (2021). From Bitcoin to Central Bank Digital Currencies : Making Sense of the Digital Money Revolution. *Future Internet*, *13*(165), 1–19. doi:10.3390/fi13070165

Danneels, E., & Vestal, A. (2020). Normalizing vs. analyzing: Drawing the lessons from failure to enhance firm innovativeness. *Journal of Business Venturing*, *35*(1), 105903. doi:10.1016/j.jbusvent.2018.10.001

Davoodalhosseini, S. M. (2022). Journal of Economic Dynamics & Control Central bank digital currency and monetary policy. *Journal of Economic Dynamics & Control*, *142*, 104150. doi:10.1016/j.jedc.2021.104150

Deng, J. (2022). The crowding-out effect of formal finance on the P2P lending market: An explanation for the failure of China's P2P lending industry. *Finance Research Letters*, *45*(May 2021), 102167. https://doi.org/10.1016/j.frl.2021.102167

Dery, K., Hall, R., Wailes, N., & Wiblen, S. (2013). Lost in translation? An actor-network approach to HRIS implementation. *The Journal of Strategic Information Systems*, *22*(3), 225–237. doi:10.1016/j.jsis.2013.03.002

Eisenhardt, K. M. (1989). Building: Constructing identities. *Building Theories from Case Study Research*, *14*(4), 532–550. doi:10.4324/9781351106573-2

Ferrari, M., Mehl, A., & Stracca, L. (2022). Central bank digital currency in an open economy. *Journal of Monetary Economics*, *127*, 54–68. doi:10.1016/j.jmoneco.2022.02.001

Ferrigno, G., Del Sarto, N., Cucino, V., & Piccaluga, A. (2022). Connecting organizational learning and open innovation research: An integrative framework and insights from case studies of strategic alliances. *The Learning Organization*, *29*(6), 615–634. doi:10.1108/TLO-03-2021-0030

Franceschelli, M. V., Santoro, G., & Candelo, E. (2018). Business model innovation for sustainability: A food start-up case study. *British Food Journal*, *120*(10), 2483–2494. doi:10.1108/BFJ-01-2018-0049

Gandal, N., Hamrick, J. T., Moore, T., & Vasek, M. (2021). The rise and fall of cryptocurrency coins and tokens. In Decisions in Economics and Finance, 44(2). Springer International Publishing. doi:10.100710203-021-00329-8

Huang, Y., & Mayer, M. (2022). Digital currencies, monetary sovereignty, and U.S.–China power competition. *Policy and Internet*, *14*(March), 324–347. doi:10.1002/poi3.302

Jick, T. D. (1979). Mixing Qualitative and Quantitative Methods : Triangulation in Action. *Administrative Science Quarterly*, *24*(4), 602–611. doi:10.2307/2392366

Jinasena, D. N., Spanaki, K., Papadopoulos, T., & Balta, M. E. (2020). Success and Failure Retrospectives of FinTech Projects: A Case Study Approach. *Information Systems Frontiers*. doi:10.100710796-020-10079-4

Klein, G., Shtudiner, Z., & Zwilling, M. (2021). Why do peer-to-peer (P2P) lending platforms fail? The gap between P2P lenders' preferences and the platforms' intentions. *Electronic Commerce Research, 0123456789*. doi:10.100710660-021-09489-6

Laboure, M., Heinz, G., Singh, S., Stefan, K., Markus, H., & Bank, D. (2021). Cryptocurrencies and CBDC. *The Route Ahead.*, *12*(5), 663–676. doi:10.1111/1758-5899.13017

Landis, J. R., & Koch, G. G. (1977). The Measurement of Observer Agreement for Categorical Data. *Biometrics*, *33*(1), 159–174. doi:10.2307/2529310 PMID:843571

Latour, B. (1987). Science In Action. In Harvard Univerty Press.

Latour, B. (2005). Reassembling the Social: An Introduction to Actor-Network Theory. In Oxford University Press.

Lee, Y., Son, B., Jang, H., Byun, J., Yoon, T., & Lee, J. (2021). Atomic cross-chain settlement model for central banks digital currency. *Information Sciences*, *580*, 838–856. doi:10.1016/j.ins.2021.09.040

Linneberg, M. S., & Korsgaard, S. (2019). Coding qualitative data : A synthesis guiding the novice data. *Qualitative Research Journal*, *19*(3), 259–270. doi:10.1108/QRJ-12-2018-0012

Liu, X., Wang, Q., Wu, G., & Zhang, C. (2022). Determinants of individuals' intentions to use central bank digital currency: Evidence from China. *Technology Analysis and Strategic Management*, 1–15. doi:10.1080/09537325.2022.2131517

Malik, N., Aseri, M., Singh, P. V., & Srinivasan, K. (2022). Why Bitcoin Will Fail to Scale? *Management Science*, *68*(10), 7323–7349. doi:10.1287/mnsc.2021.4271

Mazzocchini, F. J., & Lucarelli, C. (2022). Success or failure in equity crowdfunding? A systematic literature review and research perspectives. *Management Research Review*. doi:10.1108/MRR-09-2021-0672

Meaning, J., Dyson, B., Barker, J., & Clayton, E. (2021). Broadening narrow money: Monetary policy with a central bank digital currency. *International Journal of Central Banking*, *17*(2), 1–42. doi:10.2139srn.3180720

Morgan, J. (2022). Research in International Business and Finance Systemic stablecoin and the defensive case for Central Bank Digital Currency : A critique of the Bank of England ' s framing. *Research in International Business and Finance*, *62*, 101716. doi:10.1016/j.ribaf.2022.101716

Neyland, D., & Simakova, E. (2012). Managing electronic waste: A study of market failure. *New Technology, Work and Employment, 27*(1), 36–51. doi:10.1111/j.1468-005X.2012.00276.x

Oh, E. Y., & Zhang, S. (2022). *Informal economy and central bank digital currency.* doi:10.1111/ecin.13105

Ozili, P. K. (2022). Central bank digital currency research around the world: a review of literature. *Journal of Money Laundering Control.* doi:10.1108/JMLC-11-2021-0126

Ozturkcan, S., Senel, K., & Ozdinc, M. (2022). Framing the Central Bank Digital Currency (CBDC) revolution. *Technology Analysis and Strategic Management, 0*(0), 1–18. doi:10.1080/09537325.2022.2099261

Patton, M. (1990). Qualitative Evaluation and Research method. In *Qualitative Research Practice*. Sage. doi:10.4135/9781848608191.d38

Pelagidis, T., & Kostika, E. (2022). Investigating the role of central banks and cryptoassets. *Economia e Politica Industriale, 49*(3), 481–507. doi:10.100740812-022-00227-z

Perros, T., Bisaga, I., Broad, O., Macon, L., Fennell, P. J., & Tomei, J. (2022). Lost learnings: Breaking the silence of failure in the energy and development sector. *Energy Research and Social Science, 92*(December 2021), 102804. doi:10.1016/j.erss.2022.102804

Pocher, N., & Veneris, A. (2022). Privacy and Transparency in CBDCs: A Regulation-by-Design AML/CFT Scheme. *IEEE eTransactions on Network and Service Management, 19*(2), 1776–1788. doi:10.1109/TNSM.2021.3136984

Ranta, V., Aarikka-Stenroos, L., & Väisänen, J. M. (2021). Digital technologies catalyzing business model innovation for circular economy—Multiple case study. *Resources, Conservation and Recycling, 164*(September 2020), 105155. doi:10.1016/j.resconrec.2020.105155

Schwienbacher, A. (2019). Equity crowdfunding: Anything to celebrate? *Venture Capital, 21*(1), 65–74. doi:10.1080/13691066.2018.1559010

Shim, Y., & Shin, D. H. (2016). Analyzing China's Fintech Industry from the Perspective of Actor-Network Theory. *Telecommunications Policy, 40*(2–3), 168–181. doi:10.1016/j.telpol.2015.11.005

Shin, D. H. (2016). Application of actor-network theory to network neutrality in Korea: Socio-ecological understanding of network dynamics. *Telematics and Informatics*, *33*(2), 436–451. doi:10.1016/j.tele.2015.10.002

Siggelkow, N. (2007). Persuasion with case studies. *Academy Of Management Journal*, *50*(1), 20–24. doi:10.5465/amj.2007.24160882

Solberg Söilen, K., & Benhayoun, L. (2022). Household acceptance of central bank digital currency: The role of institutional trust. *International Journal of Bank Marketing*, *40*(1), 172–196. doi:10.1108/IJBM-04-2021-0156

Sternberg, H., Linan, I., Prockl, G., & Norrman, A. (2021). Tragedy of the facilitated commons: A multiple-case study of failure in systematic horizontal logistics collaboration. *Journal of Supply Chain Management, February 2020*, 30–57. doi:10.1111/jscm.12278

Tronnier, F., Harborth, D., & Hamm, P. (2022). Investigating privacy concerns and trust in the digital Euro in Germany. *Electronic Commerce Research and Applications, 53*(October 2021). doi:10.1016/j.elerap.2022.101158

Wang, Y., Lucey, B. M., Vigne, S. A., & Yarovaya, L. (2022a). Technological Forecasting & Social Change The Effects of Central Bank Digital Currencies News on Financial Markets. *Technological Forecasting and Social Change*, *180*(May), 121715. doi:10.1016/j.techfore.2022.121715

Wang, Y., Lucey, B. M., Vigne, S. A., & Yarovaya, L. (2022b). The Effects of Central Bank Digital Currencies News on Financial Markets. *Technological Forecasting and Social Change*, *180*(May), 121715. doi:10.1016/j.techfore.2022.121715

Xu, J. (2022). Developments and Implications of Central Bank Digital Currency: The Case of China e-CNY. *Asian Economic Policy Review*, *17*(2), 235–250. doi:10.1111/aepr.12396

Yang, J., & Zhou, G. (2022). A study on the influence mechanism of CBDC on monetary policy: An analysis based on e- CNY. *PLoS One*, *17*(7), 1–27. doi:10.1371/journal.pone.0268471 PMID:35802595

Zhang, T., & Huang, Z. (2022). Blockchain and central bank digital currency. *ICT Express*, *8*(2), 264–270. doi:10.1016/j.icte.2021.09.014

Zook, M. A., & Blankenship, J. (2018). New spaces of disruption? The failures of Bitcoin and the rhetorical power of algorithmic governance. *Geoforum*, *96*(September), 248–255. doi:10.1016/j.geoforum.2018.08.023

ENDNOTES

1 https://cbdctracker.org
2 https://cbdctracker.org
3 https://www.atlanticcouncil.org/cbdctracker/
4 https://cbdctracker.org

Chapter 9
Digital, Programmable Euro:
From Paper to Programmable Money

Guneet Kaur
Cointelegraph, UK

Devesh Kumar Vishwakarma
Deloitte, India

ABSTRACT

The financial system has been changing rapidly with the recent advancements in technologies underlying the money and payment systems. With the increase in the involvement of technology in the financial world and the emergence of new technologies like distributed ledger technologies (DLT), there has been a rising trend of creating private cryptocurrencies and stablecoins to replace existing currencies and assets. The increasing influence of big-tech companies in the financial systems and the usage of unregulated cryptocurrencies and stablecoins pose many challenges for financial authorities worldwide, generating the need for government intervention. As a result, numerous central banks worldwide are looking for possibilities to change their monetary systems by including central bank digital currencies (CBDCs) like the digital euro in their offerings. However, it is uncertain how these CBDCs and other digital money initiatives will impact the existing systems and provide solutions to existing problems and benefit the citizens and other stakeholders.

DOI: 10.4018/978-1-6684-6381-9.ch009

Copyright © 2023, IGI Global. Copying or distributing in print or electronic forms without written permission of IGI Global is prohibited.

INTRODUCTION

In recent years, there has been exponential growth in the awareness and implementation of blockchain technology in the last four years. Starting from 2015, blockchain technology has gained widespread usage, compared to the awareness and trust that blockchain technology had at the time of its introduction in 2008 (Yli-Huumo et al., 2016). There has been significant research and innovation going on blockchain technology around the world, along with finding the possible applications of the immutable, trustless, decentralized, and consensus characteristics to find its applications in the field of finance, industrial and social sectors. Due to this hype about blockchain technology and the exaggeration of its benefits, there have been misplaced expectations and also unknown misunderstandings of this technology. The existing financial industry is based on a centralized trust-based infrastructure. Blockchain promises a secure distributed framework to facilitate sharing, exchanging and integrating digital information across all users and third parties (Yaga et al., 2019). Adopting blockchain in the finance industry and its databases and smart contracts in automated transaction systems can increase the dependability and provenance of financial systems. Blockchain is immutable and trustless, giving a new opportunity for people to send money to people in a peer-to-peer mechanism across the world in an insignificant time (Zheng et al., 2017).

Blockchain technology led to the development of cryptocurrencies that aim to disrupt fiat money. These are digital currencies with different monetary supply systems and transaction networks, much like Bitcoin. Cryptocurrencies are community-based digital currencies developed and widely adopted as instruments for incentive and governance programs, internal rewards, and customer loyalty programs in closed-form environments. To protect the customers' interests in the traditional banking system and compete with digital currencies, central banks worldwide have also started exploring distributed ledger technology to develop central bank digital currencies (CBDCs) (Barrdear & Kumhof, 2021). A critical difference between CBDCs and cryptocurrencies is that the rules governing CBDC networks are set by a central bank. In crypto networks, the user base, which makes decisions by consensus, is given authority. In this context, this research discusses using distributed ledger technologies and smart contracts in creating CBDCs using digital euro as a case study of existing experiments around this concept.

LITERATURE REVIEW

The Existing Monetary System

Early transaction systems had people trading goods with each other based on the value of things exchanged. This system of trading goods was called the barter system. People began shifting to exchanging goods with precious metals like gold coins as time passed. As governments and banks formed, gold coins were shifted to banknotes and coins, which were called physical cash. The value of this cash was based on the gold standard. The gold standard was discontinued in the 1970s, and the central banks generated cash through lending activities and purchasing assets (Sahr, 2022).

Earlier, most of the payments happened via physical cash. As things moved digital, only a tiny fraction of physical cash is used in the current monetary system. According to the Statistical Data Warehouse of the European Central Bank, around 87% of the Euro money supply is commercial bank money recorded in the accounts of the citizens in their banks. There are three types of Central Bank-issued money -

1. **Physical Cash:** Physical cash is the only legal tender that the Central Bank issues. It can be used anonymously, without any intermediary, and is accessible to the general public. There is no interest rate in holding cash.
2. **Bank Money:** Bank money is issued by commercial banks to their account holders. Although the cash component of bank money is significantly less, it can be claimed by its owners anytime. Therefore, holding bank money is risky due to liquidity, market, and creditor risks. Bank money has an interest rate set by the individual banks and depends on the central bank's refinancing rates (Kitamura, 2022).
3. **Central Bank Reserves:** Central Bank Reserves are issued by the central banks to commercial banks and other larger entities like governments. These reserves are not accessible to the general public. Central Bank reserves are risk-free as they are generated by the only institutions that can generate legal tender and are not exposed to liquidity or creditor risks like bank money (Auer et al. 2022). Central Bank reserves have interest rates remunerated at the Central Bank deposit rate.

The issue with the current monetary system is that with the increase in the advancement of technology, there have been numerous ways in which it can be exploited. In the case of physical cash, there have been no or minimal advancements to how cash is generated, making it easy for criminals to make counterfeit cash and release it in the market. Apart from physical cash, there have been various instances of how bank accounts have been hacked, not only for citizens but also for large institutions making them lose billions of dollars. Also, with the increase in the involvement of big technology firms in the finance sector, there has been an undue power shift in their hands, putting the existence of central banks under threat. All these issues led to making structural changes in the current financial system.

Programmable Money and Programmable Payments

Before the digital revolution, money and payments used to take place in the form of physical currencies like coins and notes; for more significant transactions, people used cheques and demand drafts that the banks issued. These methods of payment had their limitations and technical challenges. As technology advanced, money and transactions moved on to digital systems solving some of the issues associated with the physical method of payments.

Even though digitalization solved some issues, it also had its issues. The financial systems run on centralized servers, making them have a single point of failure, making it possible for hackers to gain access to these servers and perform financial frauds. The other main issue with digitizing the payments is that the internet was made to share information and not payments. Implementing payments online has created a lot of security risks.

Using the blockchain's capabilities, we can implement smart contracts and digital assets to automate conditional payment systems. The existing financial systems work on manual conditional approvals for completing transactions. Individuals or financial institutions using these systems can define the conditions required to complete the transactions and, therefore, can be made automatic on the blockchain. Using programmable money, i.e., cryptocurrencies, the transaction policies, and conditions are not attached to the account but to the money itself.

Blockchain-Based Assets

Blockchain-based assets are assets that are technologically embedded in distributed ledgers that run on a vast network of nodes that are present worldwide. These assets are issued and owned digitally and are defined in the blockchain systems. Assets are stored in the ledger as a sequence of records which are stored as transactions in the blocks of the blockchain (Dawson, 2022). These assets can be transferred to other accounts and are then recorded in the ledger as transactions.

Blockchain-based assets work in the following way:

- Party A requests a transaction with party B, such as a money transfer, a contract, or the sharing of records; This transaction is broadcast to a distributed network of "nodes" or computers, who will authenticate it following a consensus mechanism that is an agreed-upon set of rules;

- When the transaction is approved, a new "block" will be added to the Blockchain, timestamped, with the transaction data inserted and a pointer to the previous block in the chain;
- A hash is calculated on the prior block's hash and the data contents of the new block to process the new block using the cryptographic hashing technique (Feng et al., 2022). The new block's hash is then calculated from the outcome.

An example from the insurance industry will help understand how blockchain-based assets, in particular cryptocurrencies, can be used to settle claims, pay premiums, etc. In some jurisdictions, crypto assets can be used to pay insurance premiums or compensate claimants. Cryptocurrency assets may potentially be used as the underlying investment in some unit-linked life insurance policies. Initial Coin Offerings (ICOs) may also be used by insurance ventures to raise funding. In addition, the growing tokenization of assets, such as in real estate transactions, may have implications for the insurance industry.

Stablecoin Tokens

Stablecoins are cryptocurrencies that tokenize fiat money and are backed and stabilized by them. Stablecoins were initially made to be used in the crypto markets to trade other crypto assets. There are many stablecoins like Tether, USDCoin, etc. Stablecoins are electronic token-based digital currencies that are exchanged peer-to-peer (Arslanian, 2022). These tokens are not issued by the banks and are validated by the token rather than identified by the holder of the tokens.

Stablecoins, as mentioned before, are cryptocurrencies whose values are stabilized by tieing them to fiat currencies and other stable assets. Bitcoin was created by a person or a group of anonymous individuals called Satoshi Nakamoto in the year 2009, revealing the potential of Blockchain and Distributed Ledger Technologies to the world. Subsequently, there was a rise in the number of cryptocurrencies and "stablecoin" projects like Ethereum, Tether, USDCoin, etc., from 2014. With the current technological issues in monetary systems, Bitcoin and other cryptocurrencies gained much popularity because of their features. Even though these cryptocurrencies are not seen as alternatives to the existing sovereign currencies because of their price volatility and early implementation issues, stablecoins are seen as something that can be used as an alternative to fiat money and reduce the regulation and control of the central banks in the monetary systems (d'Avernas et al., 2022).

Stablecoins are majorly aimed at being used in specific use cases like being used in online payments in the e-commerce industry, gaming industry, and other places involving online trade of goods or services. Stablecoins are also expected to be involved in a lot of future applications involving Web3 technologies, also making them one of the large-scale payment alternatives to sovereign currencies, by being embedded in these applications and being used in smart contracts as digital money. The total market value of stablecoins is predicted to be around 170 Billion USD in May 2022, which is expected to increase with time. At the level at which the stablecoin market and overall cryptocurrency market are growing, it will need much stronger regulation to protect the users and the economy from the financial risks associated with them.

Central Bank Digital Currencies (CBDCs)

Central Bank Digital Currencies or CBDCs are digital versions of state-issued currencies, which are equivalent to cash, but commercial banks hold these reserves at the central banks. When we talk about CBDCs, the question that arises is how they differ from the existing digital money that everyone holds in their banks. The difference between CBDCs and digital money lies in how they are transacted. The existing system of digital money transactions is based on account-based credit and debit, which involves intermediaries like commercial banks to complete the transactions. Digital Money transactions happen between accounts maintained by Commercial banks. In contrast, if we transact using CBDCs, the transactions will happen directly between accounts held by Central Banks as CBDCs are issued by them, removing any third-party involvement in the transactions.

CBDCs are token-based currencies that work on the Blockchain, established and maintained by the Central Banks and other stakeholders if any. These blockchains can be private or permissioned based on the requirements, making it possible for only the Central Banks and other parties involved to access the transaction history and other information. There are two types of CBDCs, Wholesale CBDCs, and Retail CBDCs. The Wholesale CBDCs are used for facilitating payments between commercial and central banks or between entities that hold their accounts in the central banks.

Retail CBDCs are something people can use, which makes financial inclusion easier as there are no restrictions for people to use them apart from having a mobile phone. The Central Banks can directly control CBDCs, making it easier for them to include people in the economy and also allowing them to influence monetary policy and spur spending to kickstart the economy during a recession or add an expiry date to the money transferred to individuals to compel users to use the money and prevent holdings, increasing the velocity of money in the economy.

Digital Currencies and Tech-Payment Giants have put the working of banks under threat by revolutionizing the way people use money. The increased power and control in the hands of tech giants have consequences that will affect not only banks but also consumer privacy, government power, and the stability of the entire financial system.

Design Choice for CBDCs

The foundational choice for CBDCs is their architecture for the CBDC. Architecture for the CBDC is the operational structure of the CBDC by the Central Banks and the private intermediaries involved in the process. Auer et al. (2020) classified CBDCs into four different architectures, which are direct, hybrid, intermediated, and synthetic. These architectures are explained below:

1. Direct CBDCs: In this architecture, the complete payment and retail systems are maintained by the Central Bank. The CBDCs provided in the Direct CBDC architecture are a direct claim on the Central Bank, and all the transactions and ledger management are done by the Central Banks.
2. Hybrid CBDCs: In this architecture, the Central Banks, as well as private intermediaries work together to provide a single system. The retail payments are handled by the intermediaries, and the central ledger is maintained by the Central Banks. Just like direct CBDCs, the CBDCs provided in the hybrid architecture are also direct claims on the Central Banks. Central banks are a backup system and can take full control when the intermediaries fail to provide their services.
3. Intermediated CBDCs: The architecture of intermediated CBDCs is similar to the Hybrid Architecture, but here the Central Banks only maintain the wholesale ledgers and the private intermediaries take care of the retail payments.
4. Synthetic CBDCs: Indirect or synthetic CBDC refers to a payment system run by agents that resemble restricted payment banks. These intermediaries, who handle all retail payments, are liable to consumers. These intermediaries must completely indemnify the central bank for any obligations owed to retail clients.

The second most important design choice is the infrastructure of the CBDC, as it must be secure from outages. The infrastructure can be based on centralized databases or DLT. The choice of infrastructure must be based on the efficiency and the degree of protection required for the system. Using DLT makes the system removes the trust from the intermediaries in the technology and makes it secure from external attacks. Central Banks use permissioned blockchains, which enables them to add only the parties required to be involved in the system.

The third choice considers access to the system. It is important for authorities to link the payment system with the identities of the individuals to perform law enforcement and to make the system well-functioning and away from fringe elements. It is very hard for the central authorities to provide access to these technological advancements to the lower economic strata, ie. the unbanked people who only rely on cash.

The e-Krona Project

The e-Krona Project is one of the most advanced CBDC projects by the Sveriges Riksbank, which is the world's oldest central bank. Sweden is one of the most digitized economies of the world, and in recent times, people there have stopped using cash and have moved on to digital payment mechanisms. The Riksbank has been working on different ways and approaches to implement the CBDCs as a complement to the cash payment system and is currently working on the proof-of-concept to implement the e-Krona Project.

The e-krona project aims to implement a hybrid CBDC architecture, where the Central Bank will implement the central ledger, and the retail services will be provided by the private intermediaries. The CBDC provided by the e-krona project will be a direct claim on the Central Bank, i.e., the Riksbank. The infrastructure used in the e-krona project is a DLT-based implementation using R3 Corda's permissioned blockchain.

The current implementation of the e-krona project provides account-based access to the CBDCs, along with an option of low-key token-based prepaid cards. The CBDCs are issued by the Riksbank and are held in the accounts managed by the intermediaries. This account-based implementation is done in a way that the information of the account holder is anonymous, but the intermediaries are responsible for the KYC of all the users, whereas the Riksbank only records the transactions done by those users. Regarding the interlinkages, the e-krona project focuses only on domestic usage. For using CBDCs, non-residents will be provided with prepaid cards for small purchases.

DIGITAL EURO: OBJECTIVES AND ADVANTAGES OF PROGRAMMABLE EURO

With the increase in the usage of digital payment methods, there has been an increase in the control that tech companies have on the monetary system of any country. Moreover, with disruptive technologies like Distributed Ledger Technologies coming into existence, there was a sudden increase in cryptocurrencies made to create global currencies and remove the dependency on state-issued money. This increased involvement of big tech companies and their increased influence on the financial system required central banks to take some steps. If we talk the European Central Bank (ECB), they started a project to implement a blockchain-based Euro, a CBDC, called Digital Euro. However, the ECB has clarified that the new central bank currency, called Digital Euro, would supplement cash, not substitute for it. This is unavoidable because an estimated 30 million persons in the EU do not have bank accounts (Passacantando, 2021). In addition, the ECB has emphasized that the new currency would stimulate competition rather than stifle it by establishing a governmental monopoly. For example, private solutions for adequate digital retail payments in the euro area should neither be discouraged nor displaced by the prospect of central bank measures to issue a digital euro," according to the ECB (Passacantando, 2021). The ECB has gone so far as to say that if alternate solutions become available, a digital euro may not be launched.

Main Features of a DLT-based Euro

The CBDC would be a central bank obligation available to all individuals and businesses across Europe, not just banks. In contrast to cash, it would serve as a means of exchange as well as a kind of compensation. Regarding the two main concerns, no technical information has yet been provided. First, consider whether a bearer instrument akin to cash or an account-based system akin to electronically accessible bank deposits should be used (or both). The second is whether or not banks and other financial institutions should act as intermediaries between this access and its users (Bechtel et al., 2022). The bearer payment tool may function via a device, or "token," that is utilized offline. It would serve as the apparent replacement for banknotes and might call for storing a specific quantity of euros in a digital wallet that could be topped off using an online account. Online access is required to add money to an offline device, such as a digital wallet. As an alternative, the bearer instrument might function online using the ECB accounts offered at the points of sale. It would be a "simple, risk-free and reliable digital means of payment, accepted throughout the euro area," and it would be free for basic use. Depending on its technical capabilities, the device may also be usable by those who do not currently have bank accounts (Klein et al., 2020).

In theory, any user of the digital euro might have a direct account with the ECB. However, given the risks involved, it would be challenging, technically, and undesirable. The ECB, like most central banks, is exploring a two-tier system in which banks have direct access to central bank accounts and control the interface with clients' accounts with the central bank for the account-based digital euro. In this manner, banks might continue to work with their clients to provide value-added services. Furthermore, European laws and regulations governing money laundering would have to be complied with by a web-based central bank's digital euro. The regulation explicitly makes user identification for high-value transactions mandatory. Additionally, the ECB plans to limit some users, including non-residents of the eurozone, and on particular operations. It must be able to recognize users to accomplish this. The bearer instrument could be anonymous when used offline.

Key Advantages of a Digital Euro

One of the main goals of a digital euro issued by the Eurosystem would be to serve as a monetary anchor and a public good in the digital era. It might promote financial innovation and boost the payments system's general effectiveness. Therefore, the design of the digital euro is crucial and must improve the functionality of current payment methods. While final decisions on the digital euro's design are not finalized yet, some essential factors are already becoming clear: A digital euro must benefit users to be approved as a future currency. According to research, customers emphasize accessibility, low cost, fast speed, security, and consumer protection, while retailers prioritize these factors (Ignatescu & Onufreiciuc, 2021). In addition, users should have the highest level of privacy protection, be able to decide how much information they wish to provide, and always conform to the law. Moreover, in order to improve financial inclusion, widespread distribution should also help those segments of the population who had little or no access to financial services in the past.

The advantages of issuing a Digital Euro based on DLT include the following:

I. **Increased Efficiency:** With the implementation of DLT, the flow of cash will be peer-to-peer, meaning the money will be sent from accounts directly, without intermediaries, saving time and effort used in completing transactions and making them faster. Also, with the peer-to-peer transfer of funds, there will be a reduction in the costs of payments as well.

II. **Increased Automation:** We can use distributed ledger technologies to use smart contracts and perform peer-to-peer (P2P) transactions between accounts and devices. This can make a pathway to increase the machine economy by making it possible to perform transactions between the machines automatically. It is believed that in the future, there will be more than 20 billion devices, which is around three times the world population.

III. **Increased Security:** As the banks moved digital, all the systems run on central servers maintained by the banks or by any third-party provider. By implementing Digital Euro on DLTs, the transaction data can be stored on a decentralized group of computers worldwide. This decentralization makes the system very secure and resistant to external attacks.

IV. **Integrating factor at the European level:** In the eurozone area, the digital euro will operate as an integrating force for the payment system and other technological advancements like electronic identity. In this sense, it would also be a driving force behind digitization, opening up hitherto unimaginable business opportunities.

V. **Encourage competition and act as a check on certain trends brought on by the digitization of financial services:** The availability of new private digital currencies encourages the decentralization of the established value chain and has the potential to uncontrollably speed up the issuance of new money and credit to the economy. Additionally, they could encourage market monopolies or excessive fragmentation, harming users and financial stability. Therefore, creating a Digital Euro would enable the preservation of consumer protection mechanisms, the protection of privacy, the fight against money laundering, and the encouragement of competition, to name a few.

VI. **Reduction in Manipulation:** As the digital euro will be implemented by using distributed ledger technologies, the complete process of making the transactions run on a large set of computers around the world makes it nearly impossible for anyone to manipulate the transactions on their own. This type of resistance to manipulation will allow the people to trust the system and transact with unknown people without having to trust them. Blockchain is one of the most used distributed ledgers. Blockchains can be public, private, or consortium. The ECB will use private or permissioned blockchain, as per its requirements, where it can add other stakeholders to the blockchain.

Main Challenges Concerned with the Implementation of a Digital Euro or CBDCs

As indicated before, adopting a CBDC would significantly affect both commercial banks and central banks conducting business and pursuing policy goals. In addition, the various payment practices and banking systems of member nations would add to the difficulties for the digital currency of a monetary union. For instance, because the public would replace bank deposits with CBDCs, there is a severe risk that CBDCs could result in bank disintermediation. As a result, banks would have to charge higher interest rates to maintain their funding capability, forcing them to raise the cost of loans or cut back on lending (Passacantando, 2021). However, this result could not be very quantifiably significant and, to some extent, might even be preferred. The traditional intermediation model, which relies on a maturity mismatch between assets and liabilities and requires banks to finance long-term investments while meeting investors' short-term liquidity demands, would also need to be gradually abandoned by banks. They may, for instance, provide or act as an intermediary for a greater choice of financial and savings tools for the general population. On the other hand, they might provide improved access to corporate clients' capital markets or combine their products with those in the capital markets. This process might be aided by a review of the laws governing some particular industries, such as securitization.

Another issue is that the digital euro may make bank runs more likely. For example, bank customers wouldn't have to wait in line at ATMs or bank branches during a crisis of confidence since they could withdraw money online from the comfort of their homes (Passacantando, 2021). This possibility already exists de facto for extensive value deposits, which can be converted at any time into Treasury bills or other low-risk assets. When made available to the general public, this might be used for low-value deposits that could be quickly turned into risk-free CBDC. People may start using cash instead of bank deposits. It occurred in 2008 when withdrawals from bank deposits soared following the failure of Lehman Brothers and persisted at a high level throughout the sovereign debt crisis of 2010–13 (Arnaboldi, 2019). This risk could be reduced by placing quantitative restrictions on the CBDC's use or compensation. To lessen the number of bank deposits that are converted into CBDC during times of crisis, the ECB thinks that a variable compensation scheme may be implemented. But given that it would convey to the markets the central bank's worries based on the specific information at its disposal, which is not always made public, a rate change of this kind would be a susceptible device to use during financial crises (Gross et al., 2021).

However, it is improbable that a bank run would spread throughout the entire Eurozone. Most of the time, it would impact either specific institutions or the whole banking system of some member countries. In the former scenario, more substantial conventional lending of last resort mechanisms may be sufficient. In the latter scenario, it would undoubtedly be highly challenging to lower the compensation of the digital currency throughout the entire Eurozone in response to financial turmoil in a few member countries. It is a well-known issue that the eurozone is vulnerable to the possibility of fragmented financial crises. Policy solutions are also prominent, but there is no agreement on implementing them. Among them include:

- Completing the banking union.
- Introducing cross-border deposit insurance in particular.
- Creating a viable bank crisis resolution mechanism.
- Strengthening the public safety net in the event of a systemic collapse.

Further advancement on these fronts is necessary to create a digital euro because of the potential influence on financial instability. In addition, the failure of the new currency to gain widespread acceptance may be a significant risk for the ECB. However, countries that already employ digital instruments would continue to do so because of the value-added services they provide concerning the CBDC and the laxer quantitative restrictions. In contrast, countries that are more cash-oriented would continue to use cash. Moreover, since the first mover, whether a private firm or a foreign central bank, could obtain a stable dominant position in the current dynamic economy, this danger will increase the longer it takes to implement the project. The potential failure or dysfunction of the IT infrastructure on which the CBDC is based, represents another significant risk. Unfortunately, incidents of this do happen even in the best clearing or settlement networks, stock exchanges, and regulated and controlled market infrastructures. The ECB would suffer significant reputational damage due to the unexpected inability to use the euro, even for a brief period. Another concern is whether the central bank will be held accountable for financial losses incurred by some consumers. For example, if the CBDC were to be used for illicit operations like tax evasion, drug trafficking, money laundering, and financing terrorism, at least for the portion covered by anonymity, that would be a different issue.

The development of the new platform will necessitate significant technological investments in order to reduce these risks. It would be crucial to be transparent about whether the social benefits and returns on these investments balance each other out.

DIGITAL EURO: A MONETARY POLICY INSTRUMENT

With the growing popularization of digital payment methods like credit and debit cards, net banking and, more recently, mobile payment systems, there has been a considerable decline in the use of physical cash in people's daily lives (Nuño, 2018). On the other side, the development of digital ledger technologies and cryptocurrencies has made the demand for central banks to issue their digital currencies. It is believed that central bank digital currencies or CBDCs will improve the monetary policies and the functioning of the existing payment system. These benefits are also accompanied by technological risks associated with these changes in the monetary system. Implementing CBDCs will help the government to have implemented something similar to banknotes in a digital form. CBDCs will increase the productivity of the current system. If CBDCs are remunerated, their interest rates will become available to the public, even the unbanked people, who cannot open their bank accounts due to bank policies. With CBDCs, the interest rate will benefit the general people and their savings and investment decisions directly or indirectly, making the monetary policies decoupled from the bank's financial situations (Zellweger-Gutknecht et al., 2021).

Also, commercial banks have a policy of zero lower bound, where people holding accounts in those banks will have to keep a certain minimum amount of money to keep the bank account active (Gross & Schiller, 2021). This lower bound of account balance depends on the banks and sometimes removes a section of people who cannot maintain these account balances. If a centralized virtual currency like Digital Euro is implemented, there would be a specific interest rate, making the holders gain interest in holding the CBDC. In addition, the Digital Euro will also help governments fight money laundering and tax fraud (Gross & Schiller, 2021). As mentioned before, holding and transacting in physical cash is anonymous, and governments cannot check where and how the transactions are happening. With the virtual currencies under the control of central repositories of administrators, the money will be provided digitally to the account holders by the central banks. Therefore, central banks can keep track of all transactions, making the use of digital money in illegal activities challenging.

In addition, a digital euro, or more specifically, digital euro transactions, could provide the central bank with new data, depending on how they are created. As a result, it might contribute to preserving or perhaps improving the Eurosystem's capacity to gather monetary data in real-time. However, this might only serve as a supplemental justification for adopting a digital euro. Additionally, the substantial dangers associated with such a design may outweigh any potential benefits. A digital euro may theoretically serve as a channel for the dissemination of its own monetary policy impulses. It should be created with variable features in order to achieve this. For example, the capability of paying or receiving interest on holdings of digital euros would be the most significant changeable feature. The imposition of limitations on such holdings, whether per person, per transaction, or overall, and as an alternative to or in conjunction with interest, would be another obvious possibility. As a result, the central bank could affect consumer demand, for instance, by charging or paying interest. A digital euro created in this fashion would be welcomed by many economists and legal experts since it might greatly expand the central bank's policy options from policy rate and the monetary aggregate perspectives. These arguments are made by those who support the viewpoint: The better pass-through of policy rate changes caused by an interest-bearing digital euro could increase the effectiveness of monetary policy by affecting the circumstances in which liquidity is available. This is because banks would be compelled to boost interest rates if they wanted to stop their customers from converting deposits into digital euros if the central bank increased both its policy rate and interest rates on a digital euro (Zellweger-Gutknecht et al., 2021). The effective lower bound (ELB) limitation may also be eased by a negative interest-bearing digital euro, but only if cash were also eliminated or made expensive. Furthermore, it is anticipated that if a digital euro were interest-free, monetary policy counterparties may choose to retain digital euros rather than reserves, which would cause the ELB to drop almost to zero. As a result, the Eurosystem could not continue using negative interest rates in its monetary policy.

Additionally, a digital euro would make it possible for the public sector to quickly and directly pay members of the general public, increasing available liquidity without using an interest rate policy. Such payments might either be given out for free by the Eurosystem members or made by the government and paid for with tax money and other public funding sources (Wagner et al., 2021). They may serve various purposes, such as stimulating aggregate demand, providing frantic people and businesses with emergency funds to ease hardship brought on by unusual events, or even having an expiration date built in to encourage expenditure. However, in terms of economics, negative interest rates are equivalent to taxes. Negative rates were only directly applied to monetary policy counterparties based on contractual agreements made on the open market or within the framework of facilities that the banks use voluntarily. Hence, the rule that any tax must have a solid legal foundation was not applicable until this point. However, when digital euros are issued to carry out a public obligation, it is unlikely that such an exception will be possible.

Meanwhile, independent researchers have failed to offer convincing proof of the overall beneficial consequences of low-interest rates. For example, the proportionality rule might be broken by an adverse interest digital euro. By forbidding counterparties from owning digital euros (whether as legal or beneficial owners) or applying the reserve rate to their holdings of digital euros, the intended goal is to prevent monetary policy counterparties from evading the central bank's interest rate policy. This rule would be enforceable because all counterparties are institutions that must abide by regulations. Finally, introducing a digital euro with a negative interest rate could cause public unrest, making it politically inefficient to introduce it.

REGULATORY CONSIDERATIONS

If the CBDC agreements can be categorized as a payment system, it must be evaluated whether they are systemically important. If the arrangement includes a set of tools, processes, and guidelines for the transfer of money between or among participants, including the participants and the body managing the arrangement, it could be referred to as a payment system (Liao & Caramichael, 2022). Given its anticipated involvement in the financial system, determining systemic importance would also be crucial. The main criteria could be similar to those for private payment systems, such as the volume and value of completed transactions, participants' numbers and types, markets served, interconnection, and any alternatives that may be accessible (Johnstone, 2020). Regardless of its current and projected scale, the CBDC arrangement is extremely likely to be considered systematically essential, given the public's high expectations of CBDC. As a result, the CBDC arrangement should be subject to stricter regulation, monitoring, and inspection as a central bank-administered Financial Market Infrastructure (FMI) as soon as it is recognized as a systemically important payment system. Retail payment systems may have systemic importance, despite the fact that attention on this topic is typically directed at large-value payment systems. This would apply to CBDC agreements as well.

Regardless of all the benefits that cryptocurrencies and stablecoins bring to the financial system, some of their features like anonymous peer-to-peer transactions, borderless payments and stability risks raise many regulatory concerns (Bechtel et al., 2022). Stablecoins have and are potential to create an international payment system and therefore to address these concerns, it is required to create a robust framework and regulatory system at an international level. There have been discussions on these regulatory considerations on international forums like G7, G20, FATF, FSB and others. To start with, all the stablecoins have a basic registration, making the regulatory authorities have all the required information about the stablecoin and keep a close monitoring on its operations. The monitoring of stablecoins will make the authorities keep an eye on the potential financial risks and prevent people from indulging in such stablecoins. Additionally, countries need to create internal cooperation by signing Memorandums of Understandings (MoUs) to share information between different relevant authorities.

Creating international standards will help regulatory authorities to create an embedded supervision mechanism. The embedded supervision mechanism is a framework to automate the monitoring of compliance terms by directly accessing the ledgers in DLT-based systems, as the data in the ledgers of the DLT-based systems contain a lot of information that can be very useful for monitoring. The embedded supervision method is a low-cost, high-value compliance method that can help small and large institutions in the system to have equal access to compliance methodologies. Additionally, the authorities must learn more about the advantages and hazards of CBDC by gradually developing it through pilot projects or regulatory sandboxes, which would also help them improve internal capacity. For example, experts in appropriate fields, such as operational, cyber, payment, and settlement risks, may need to be hired and retained. Keeping abreast of emerging technology and hazards is advised for the central bank and financial sector authorities (Morgan, 2022). Indirect operating models will benefit the most from using pilots and sandboxes to ensure that laws, rules, and oversight cover new institutions and activities.

DISCUSSION AND FUTURE WORK

Technology has been advancing at a high rate recently, and so is its influence in all the other sectors, one of them being finance. Finance has been evolving continuously with technology, whether by making the banks digital, to including ATMs for making cash collection easier and available on-demand. Technology has not only influenced the financial systems but also the monetary systems through the introduction of distributed ledger technologies like blockchain, stablecoins, and cryptocurrencies.

These modern digital assets are unregulated and therefore pose financial as well as monetary stability risks. As the payment habits of people have changed with the modern technological offerings provided by the big-tech companies, it becomes very important for authorities like central banks and governments to create proper regulations and supervisory frameworks to keep track of these unregulated markets and also to provide people with other government-backed alternatives like CBDCs to reduce the excessive control and dependency on the big-tech firms and unregulated financial systems like Bitcoin.

In order to evolve the financial systems with the advancements in technology, central banks plan to create their own digital money, called central bank digital currencies (CBDCs). These new technologies provide us with a lot of new features and also provide solutions to the problems in the existing systems. Along with the benefits, these new technologies also create regulatory and supervisory challenges that need to be taken care of to reduce the risks. Although the current offered a broad perspective around the CBDCs, in particular, the digital euro, future scientific studies could include textual analyses of data about CBDCs to evaluate the effects of their acceptance among retail customers.

CONCLUSION

In this paper, the authors have discussed the possibilities of implementing a digital euro, which will be a central bank digital currency issued by the European Central Bank (ECB). The need to create a digital euro arises due to the decline in the usage of physical cash in the payment practices of people and the increased involvement of big-tech companies in the finance industry. The evolution of distributed ledger technologies and private digital currencies has also put the functioning of central banks under threat. People have started using these commercial and private currencies, and if widely used, they can threaten the implementation of monetary policies.

With the introduction of the new digital currency, the European payment system, which has been very inventive in its retail component but is still somewhat fragmented along national lines, will have the chance to become much more efficient.

Additionally, it might enhance the euro's function as a global reserve currency and the transmission mechanism for monetary policy. The project is necessary because, if nothing were done, the risk that only international corporate entities or foreign central banks would offer digital payment systems across Europe would increase. Therefore, implementing a CBDC will help central banks to create a mechanism to control the monetary systems, solve issues that arise in the existing monetary systems, and provide added benefits to the people like improved efficiency, reduced transaction costs, and faster transactions.

Nonetheless, keeping bank disintermediation minimum will be one of the biggest challenges. Despite the fact that the CBDC discussion undoubtedly overestimated this risk, it is a crucial issue for Europe due to the substantial reliance on bank intermediation of European firms, particularly the SMEs that make up the majority of the industrial sector in many member nations. Furthermore, instability concerns should not be undervalued because, as recent events have demonstrated, they can force banking markets to divide along national borders. Further research is necessary to determine whether the CBDC could increase these dangers. Still, it would also be challenging to develop mitigation strategies, such as changing interest rates on the CBDC, whose effects would be highly variable among nations. For example, digital money might be created to help the banking system gradually adjust to the new setting. However, to meet their financial demands, the banking industry and the business sector will eventually have to rely more heavily on the capital markets. To diversify the investments of the additional funds at its disposal, the ECB will also need to depend more on capital market instruments.

Therefore, the introduction of the digital euro should not be seen in isolation from the initiatives to remove barriers to the Capital Markets Union. To reduce the dangers of financial market volatility and increase the function of the euro as an international currency, the launch of the currency must be accompanied by the completion of the banking union. In the future, scientific research can be undertaken, such as textual analysis of CBDCs-related data to assess the impact of its adoption among retail customers.

REFERENCES

Arnaboldi, F. (2019). The Euro Area Banking System: Where Do We Stand? In Risk and Regulation in Euro Area Banks (pp. 1-19). Palgrave Macmillan.

Arslanian, H. (2022). Stablecoins. In *The Book of Crypto* (pp. 149–170). Palgrave Macmillan. doi:10.1007/978-3-030-97951-5_7

Auer, R., Cornelli, G., & Frost, J. (2020). *Rise of the central bank digital currencies: drivers, approaches and technologies*. Academic Press.

Auer, R., Frost, J., Gambacorta, L., Monnet, C., Rice, T., & Shin, H. S. (2022). Central bank digital currencies: Motives, economic implications, and the research frontier. *Annual Review of Economics, 14*(1), 697–721. doi:10.1146/annurev-economics-051420-020324

Barrdear, J., & Kumhof, M. (2021). The macroeconomics of central bank digital currencies. *Journal of Economic Dynamics & Control*, 104148.

Bechtel, A., Ferreira, A., Gross, J., & Sandner, P. (2022). The Future of Payments in a DLT-based European Economy: A Roadmap. In *The Future of Financial Systems in the Digital Age* (pp. 89–116). Springer. doi:10.1007/978-981-16-7830-1_6

d'Avernas, A., Maurin, V., & Vandeweyer, Q. (2022). *Can Stablecoins be Stable?* University of Chicago, Becker Friedman Institute for Economics Working Paper, (2022-131).

Dawson, A. (2022). Data-driven Consumer Engagement, Virtual Immersive Shopping Experiences, and Blockchain-based Digital Assets in the Retail Metaverse. *Journal of Self-Governance & Management Economics, 10*(2).

Feng, Z., Da, H., Xiao, M., Zhao, C., Zuo, Z., & Qi, J. (2022, March). Supply Chain Finance in Blockchain-based Digital Asset Platform. In *The 2022 4th International Conference on Blockchain Technology* (pp. 74-80). 10.1145/3532640.3532650

Gross, J., & Schiller, J. (2021). A model for central bank digital currencies: Implications for bank funding and monetary policy. *Available at SSRN 3721965*.

Gross, J., Sedlmeir, J., Babel, M., Bechtel, A., & Schellinger, B. (2021). Designing a central bank digital currency with support for cash-like privacy. *Available at SSRN 3891121*.

Ignatescu, C., & Onufreiciuc, R. (2021). Digital Euro: A (Digital) Symbol of Progress and Integration in Europe. *Logos Universality Mentality Educ. Novelty Sect.: L., 9*(1), 74–82. doi:10.18662/lumenlaw/9.1/58

Johnstone, S. (2020). Secondary markets in digital assets: Rethinking regulatory policy in centralized and decentralized environments. *Stan. J. Blockchain L. & Pol'y, 3*, 146.

Kitamura, Y. (2022). Can we stabilize the price of a cryptocurrency? Understanding the design of Bitcoin and its potential to compete with Central Bank money. In *Quest for Good Money* (pp. 103–123). Springer. doi:10.1007/978-981-19-5591-4_6

Klein, M., Gross, J., & Sandner, P. (2020). *The digital euro and the role of DLT for central bank digital currencies.* Frankfurt School of Finance & Management GmbH, FSBC Working Paper.

Liao, G. Y., & Caramichael, J. (2022). *Stablecoins: Growth Potential and Impact on Banking*. Academic Press.

Morgan, J. (2022). Systemic stablecoin and the defensive case for Central Bank Digital Currency: A critique of the Bank of England's framing. *Research in International Business and Finance*, *62*, 101716. doi:10.1016/j.ribaf.2022.101716

Nuño, G. (2018). Monetary policy implications of central bank-issued digital currency. *Banco de Espana Article*, *15*, 18.

Passacantando, F. (2021). The Digital Euro: Challenges and Opportunities. *The (Near) Future of Central Bank Digital Currencies*, 113.

Passacantando, F. (2021). *Could a digital currency strengthen the euro?* Luiss School of European Political Economy *Policy Brief* 9.

Sahr, A. (2022). Claims to Sovereignty: MMT as a challenge to money's technical imaginary. In Capital Claims: Power and Global Finance (pp. 88-103). Routledge.

Wagner, E., Bruggink, D., & Benevelli, A. (2021). Preparing euro payments for the future: A blueprint for a digital euro. *Journal of Payments Strategy & Systems*, *15*(2), 165–187.

Yaga, D., Mell, P., Roby, N., & Scarfone, K. (2019). *Blockchain technology overview.* arXiv preprint arXiv:1906.11078.

Yli-Huumo, J., Ko, D., Choi, S., Park, S., & Smolander, K. (2016). Where is current research on blockchain technology? A systematic review. *PLoS One*, *11*(10), e0163477. doi:10.1371/journal.pone.0163477 PMID:27695049

Zellweger-Gutknecht, C., Geva, B., & Grünewald, S. N. (2021). Digital Euro, Monetary Objects, and Price Stability: A Legal Analysis. *Journal of Financial Regulation*, *7*(2), 284s–318. doi:10.1093/jfr/fjab009

Zheng, Z., Xie, S., Dai, H., Chen, X., & Wang, H. (2017, June). *An overview of blockchain technology: Architecture, consensus, and future trends. In 2017 IEEE international congress on big data (BigData congress).* IEEE.

Chapter 10
Unpacking Central Bank Digital Currency (CBDC) Implementation Challenges and Risks

Kwami Ahiabenu
https://orcid.org/0000-0002-8254-3214
Global Centre for FinTech Innovations, Canada

ABSTRACT

This chapter outlines the risks and challenges involved in implementing central bank digital currency (CBDC). Interest in CBDC is currently growing, with a number of central banks paying it serious consideration, and a number of countries are implementing or piloting CBDC. Although CBDC holds a great deal of promise, its implementation is not without difficulty. This chapter highlights the major implementation issues, such as CBDC contributing to financial exclusion, technology risks, CBDC's inability to work in an offline environment, lack of privacy, and confidential consideration, since anonymity is difficult to achieve. The chapter concludes by highlighting the need to deploy CBDC with greater attention paid to societal, economic, and political factors instead of a purely technocratic approach.

INTRODUCTION

The rapid development of digital finance and financial technology has inspired a number of innovations, including cryptocurrency. Due to these innovations, the monopoly to issue currency, previously the sole prerogative of the central bank, has

DOI: 10.4018/978-1-6684-6381-9.ch010

Copyright © 2023, IGI Global. Copying or distributing in print or electronic forms without written permission of IGI Global is prohibited.

been broken, and the private sector can now issue digital currency (Engert & Fung, 2017; Kilponen et al., 2017). Since then, the exceptional growth of cryptocurrency and the acceleration of digital payments has led central banks to aggressively consider issuing their own digital currencies, known as central bank digital currency (CBDC; Alonso et al., 2021; Engert & Fung, 2017). According to Opare and Kim, (2020), since the birth of the first private digital currency, Bitcoin, in 2009, there have been over 5,000 privately issued digital currencies, and it is predicted that these digital currencies, including Bitcoin, Ethereum, and many others, will threaten financial system stability and the maintenance of monetary policy. For this reason, numerous central banks are investigating CBDC as a strategy to mitigate this risk. Furthermore, global events such as the COVID-19 pandemic and the emergence of global stablecoins put forward by Meta (formerly Facebook) known as Libra have accelerated central banks' interest in CBDC (Morales-Resendiz et al., 2021; Ponce et al., 2020). In assessing how Libra and Euro CBDC influences European banks, Sandner et al., (2020) argued that this may lead to large-scale disintermediation of the financial sector, and digital bank runs could be a possibility. However, private digital currency and CBDC should be seen as opportunities rather than threats.

There are numerous reasons for the launch of CBDC, including the central banks' need to maintain monetary control, ensure central bank relevance in a rapidly evolving digital financial system, provide an alternative to cryptocurrency, and enable financial inclusion as a response to the declining use of cash and advancement in digital payments as a tool in the digitalisation of economies (Alonso et al., 2020). However, CBDC represents a highly debatable issue, possessing an equal share of proponents as well as antagonists. Persons expressing opposition to CBDC state the following reasons to justify their position:

1. CBDC can accelerate financial exclusion;
2. CBDC is expensive, but offers no immediate tangible benefits;
3. CBDC can distort the financial system, especially the disintermediation of commercial banks;
4. CBDC can lead to loss of monetary policy control by central banks;
5. CBDC can increase the financial system's exposure to digital and cyber-security vulnerabilities;
6. There are no guarantees of public demand for CBDC;
7. There remains insufficient evidence proving the CBDC concept;
8. There have been failed attempts to implement CBDC; and
9. CBDC cannot effectively replace cash.

According to BIS (2021a) and Kiff et al. (2020b), the introduction of CBDC represents a complex issue possessing multidimensional perspectives expanding beyond a central bank's typical application of information technology, as it requires extensive political, social, and detailed design choices. Furthermore, launching a CBDC could trigger major disruptions to the central bank's monetary policy role, negatively influencing financial sector stability, currency exchange rate, and efficient operations of a country's payment system.

As noted by Wang et al., (2022) CBDC is now quite popular and receiving a great deal of attention and discussion by researchers and practitioners alike, with the majority of available studies focussing on CBDC's analysis, technological innovations, characteristics, potential advantages, risks, security, privacy, design, impact on monetary policy, and commercial bank intermediation. Some CBDC studies focus on CBDC design (Agur et al., 2022; Maniff, 2020) or on central bank digital currency and its impact on monetary policy (Bossu et al., 2020; Chen & Siklos, 2022; Davoodalhosseini, 2021; Mohammad et al., 2020; Nelson, 2021; Schiller & Gross, 2021). Meanwhile, there are also some studies on CBDC implementation risks, such as by Bofinger, Haas (2021), and Ozili (2021). A few authors, such as Didenko and Buckley (2021), describes CBDC implementation challenges, while others, such as Tronnier et al. (2022), investigate specific implementation challenges related to privacy concerns and trust in digital euros. None of these studies pursue CBDC implementation challenges or risks linked to financial exclusion, primary reasons for discontinuing CBDC implementation, or documentation of lessons learned from attempts at CBDC pilots and implementation.

To fill this research gap, this chapter seeks to clarify CBDC implementation challenges and risks through the lens of the following questions: What are the main challenges confronting CBDC implementation; how does CBDC enable financial exclusion; and what are the main lessons learned from CBDC implementation? To answer these questions, the author relied on an extensive literature review premised on literature search and evaluation. To this end, inclusion criteria were anchored on specific key words drawn from the research questions. The author undertook literature identification by combing through Google Scholar; academic journal databases; reports by central banks; international bodies such as World Bank, IMF, and Bank for International Settlements (BIS); and general online searches focussing on authoritative news and industry websites. All the content obtained through the search process was further evaluated for its relevance and currency in relation to the research questions. Lastly, using a descriptive review, the author examined each of the acquired studies in order to establish the current state of the literature on each specific research question. A key limitation of this study is that it is based on secondary data coupled with inferences while excluding the collection of primary data, which could have provided additional context and insights to further enrich its findings.

The primary motivation for this work is to contribute to the literature regarding CBDC's negative effects on existing payment systems. In so doing, this paper adds to the CBDC literature by highlighting often overlooked areas, such as CBDC's possible negative impact on financial inclusion. At the same time, this paper synthesises key challenges confronting CBDC implementation from different jurisdictions. The remainder of this chapter is organised into five main thematic areas in response to the research questions. To begin, section 2 provides a brief overview of CBDC and describes the status of CBDC implementation around the world. Following this, section 3 outlines the main challenges confronting CBDC implementation, the impact of CBDC on financial inclusion, and main lessons learned from CBDC implementation. The discussion of this chapter is found in section 4 and section 5 concludes this chapter by highlighting the main elements of this chapter's findings and their implications.

BRIEF OVERVIEW AND IMPLICATIONS OF CBDC DEPLOYMENT

Although CBDC is a popular term, it is not well defined, since there remains no universal definition, and it can refer to several concepts. The underlying characteristic is that it represents a new form of central bank money, denominated on the existing unit of account, thus serving as a store of value and medium of exchange. It is imperative to point out that some central banks are already offering a type of digital money in terms of reserves or settlement account balances in their dealings with commercial banks and other financial entities holding accounts at the central bank. Due to the difficulties involved in arriving at a universal definition of CBDC, it might to easier to highlight its differences: '*A CBDC is a digital form of central bank money that is different from balances in traditional reserve or settlement accounts*' (Löber & Houben, 2018 p.4). In this way, CBDC can be described as a digital form of central-bank-issued money that is available for use by the general public, and it is similar to physical currency that comes in the form of notes and coins. Instead of holding money as paper notes or coins, however, the currency is now digitally represented, linked to one's identity and held in a digital wallet or account. When a country issues a CBDC, its total issued legal tender will be cash, bank accounts, and digital currency. The key defining characteristic of CBDC is that the legal authority of a country issues it through its central bank, and it remains distinct from other digital currencies, such as cryptocurrency, which lacks a centralised issuing authority of a state, and thus is not pegged to the value of any country's fiat currency.

In terms of classification, CBDC can be broadly categorised as wholesale CBDC, which forms the basis of exchange and trading between private and central banks, mirroring the traditional wholesale financial system. Retail CBDC, or general purpose CBDC, connotes digital money in the hands of end-users for day-to-day transactions, which requires a mechanism for distribution to end users. To ensure retail CBDC functions properly, a new ecosystem is constantly evolving, comprising central banks, commercial banks, payment providers, technology operators responsible for maintaining the CBDC application, and front-line service providers, who process CBDC payments and transactions.

It is projected that over 60 central banks have been exploring CBDCs since 2014, with over 88% of these implementations using blockchain as the technology of choice. Additionally, far more CBDC projects have been entering implementation phases, and retail CBDCs have grown popular in emerging economies where financial inclusion is a key motivation for CBDC. Meanwhile, wholesale CBDCs are generally linked to countries with developed interbank systems and capital markets (PwC, 2021).

Continuing, CBDC can also be classified based on three design choices: who issues the CBDC, its distribution, and where it is held (Geroni, 2021). First, in terms of CBDC issuance, the central banks can select a direct model, indirect model, and hybrid model. For the direct model, the central bank issues CBDC directly to customers; the downside is that this is disruptive and places an additional cost burden on the central bank in terms of customer management, including KYC (know your customer) and anti-money laundering (AML) checks. However, the indirect model mimics the traditional system wherein commercial banks re-issue central bank money by integrating the digital currency functions in the onboarding process, thereby reducing costs. The downside includes a risk to customers who cannot claim 100% of their CBDC funds, since it is part and parcel of the bank's balance sheet.

Meanwhile, the hybrid model combines the indirect and direct model features, which could mean the central bank is making CBDC 100% claimable as a legal tender while the commercial banks deals with onboarding issues. Second, when it comes to how the CBDC is distributed, there is the option of a single-tier setup linked to a direct model, with the central bank issuing digital currencies to customers. Another option includes the two-tier structure, which functions as a distribution hierarchy, with central banks issuing the digital currencies and the commercial banks being responsible for last-mile distribution. The third design consideration relates to the form in which the CBDC is held, either as a token or an account.

Central banks typically issue two types of money while providing infrastructure support to a third type of money. The first type includes physical cash available to all users, while the second concerns electronic bank deposits referred to as reserves or interbank settlement, available to licensed financial institutions. The third type of money is private money linked to a central bank's infrastructure-supporting role, made available through electronic commercial bank deposits. Additionally, the central banks serve as a lender of last resort through contingent liquidity provision.

The current architecture makes cash and reserves a liability for the central bank, whereas commercial banks deposits are not; therefore, it is envisaged that CBDC will serve as a new type of central bank money with its reserves as a liability of the central bank (Cœuré et al., 2020). Given that price stability represents one of the core mandates of central banks, it becomes imperative to understand how CBDC will influence central banks' roles in the control of inflation. In one such study of CBDC's possible impact on inflation, Chen and Siklos (2022) determined that, within the framework of McCallum's rule, which describes the stance of monetary policy linked to money growth, the evolution of financial sophistication such as CBDC does not contribute to the loss of inflation control. However, CBDC can also potentially influence inflation in a manner that cannot be anticipated.

THE IMPLEMENTATION OF CBDC IN REAL WORLD SETTINGS

In terms of CBDC implementation, most central banks follow four steps in their CBDC consideration and implementation strategies—namely, research, proof of concept, pilot, and the decision of whether to implement or cancel CBDC implementation. The first step involves undertaking detailed research and experimentation from policy, regulatory, technical, cultural, operational, and implementation angles. The CBDC research scope and focus is linked to the motivation for the rollout of the CBDC, therefore research perspective varies from country to country. However, two key issues come into play—namely, the need to understand CBDC as a means of payments as well as how it can enhance monetary policy tools. Furthermore, the CBDC research phase also focusses on understanding the broader issues of digital currencies within the evolution of financial technologies (Fintech), risks, legal implications, governance, regulatory issues, implication for financial inclusion, overall impact and implication of CBDC, and CBDC's influence on the use and demand for cash (Kiff et al., 2020b; Sarmiento, 2022).

Over 105 countries, which represent 95% of the World's GDP and nine out of 10 central banks globally, are actively exploring a CBDC; as of August 2022, 69 countries are researching options for rolling out CBDC, 18 countries have reached proof of concept stage, seven countries (Singapore, Philippines, Haiti CBDC, Denmark, Ecuador, Finland, and Japan) have cancelled CBDC implementation, 15 countries are undergoing a CBDC pilot, and 11 countries have fully implemented CBDC. The 11 countries who have fully implemented CBDC in one form or the other include the Bahamas, Nigeria, Jamaica, Antigua and Barbuda, Dominica, Grenada, Montserrat, St. Kitts and Nevis, Saint Lucia, and St. Vincent and the Grenadines (Atlantic Council, 2022; Kosse & Mattei, 2022; Mikhalev et al., 2022).

In October 2020, the Bahamas became the first country to implement CBDC, known as the Sand Dollar, working with NZIA ltd as its technical partner. The goal of Sand Dollar was to improve financial services to multiple islands, which are difficult to reach due to physical geography, thereby making it not profitable for commercial banks. Beyond the financial inclusion agenda, the Sand Dollar was intended to strengthen security against illicit economic activities and money laundering (Wenker, 2022).

The Eastern Caribbean Currency Union (ECCU) comprises seven countries—namely, Antigua and Barbuda, Dominica, Grenada, Montserrat, St. Kitts and Nevis, Saint Lucia, and St. Vincent and the Grenadines—launched the digital currency DCash on 31 March 2021. This currency was designed to increase the speed of financial transaction and financial inclusion with technical support from Bitt Inc. However, DCash suffered a major disruption From January to March 2022. After resumption of services, the ECCU, the first currency union in the world to issue a digital currency, explained that the disruption was due not to any external intervention, but rather to internal technical issues. How to deal with CBDC downtime thus represents an important learning experience for the ECCU and for central banks considering CDBC (ECCB, 2022).

The National Bank of Cambodia officially launched its CBDC in October 2020, known as Bakong. Today, this is recognised as one of the world's first CBDCs based on a blockchain nationwide payment system with an inclusive financial system as its goal. The central bank of Cambodia developed Bakong, named after an ancient temple in Cambodia, in conjunction with the Japanese blockchain technology company Soramitsu. The Bakong is offered in partnership with local banks based on interoperability schema, thereby ensuring Bakong's widespread acceptance reaching nearly 7.9 million users, which is almost half the country's population of 16.7 million, with a recorded 6.8 million transactions worth approximately $2.9 billion. Currently, Bakong users are able to undertake cross-border remittance between Malaysia and Cambodia (Iwamoto, 2022). It must be noted that Bakong is not a CBDC per se, depending on which definition is in use; this is because it is not a liability on the central bank balance sheet, but is instead more of a digital conventional payment system based on the existing Cambodia faster payments system 'FAST', which is itself based on commercial banks holding bank settlement accounts with the central bank.

On October 2021, Nigeria became the first African country and major world economy to fully launch CBDC, known as eNaira, in association with Bitt Inc. as a technical partner. The goal of eNaira was to improve monetary policy transmission, ensure efficient payments, and accelerate financial inclusion. However, digital illiteracy and cyber-attacks were identified as some of the risks involved in implementing eNaira (Ozili, 2021). eNaira processed over 4 billion nairas ($9.3

million) based on 840,000 downloads and approximately 270,000 active wallets. Nigeria's population stands at over 200 million, making it currently the largest economy in Africa with over $430 billion in gross domestic product (GDP). The Central Bank of Nigeria noted that the commercial banks are not aggressively pushing the eNaira, since they do not see immediate revenue from participation in the eNaira rollout (Ahiabenu, 2022).

On Monday, August 9, the Bank of Jamaica (BOJ) minted Jamaica's first batch of CBDC (JAM-DEX) at a total of J$230 million with NZIA ltd as its technical partner. The primary motivation for this launch was to increase financial inclusion and commitment to Jamaica's transition to a digital economy (Bank of Jamaica, 2022).

CBDC IMPLEMENTATION CHALLENGES

Although CBDC holds a great deal of promise and potential, it is not without its risks. According to Bindseil (2022), CBDC can lead to risks of structural and cyclical bank disintermediation, increased reliance on central bank credit, bank runs, and decreased efficacy of central bank's monetary policy tools, such as its ability to implement negative interest rate policies (NIRP). Another author, Nelson (2021), suggested that CBDC can lead to instability in central banks' reserve balances, create the need for an ever-larger central bank's balance sheet, and may negatively influence central banks' profits and potential anger over negative interest rates on CBDC. One key function of a central bank is to ensure stability of a financial system through the use of monetary policy by setting benchmark interest rates. However, if the CBDC interest rate is at the rates closer to safe assets, the volatility of public demand for CBDC can be significant, leading to significant outflows of reserves.

Lee et al. (2021) suggested other potential negative effects of CBDC, including the ability to heavily monitor individual's transactions using CBDC, loss of anonymity compared to the use of cash, restrictions or limits on savings using CBDC, negative interest rates, and real-time monetary policy effects of inflation. From the user's perspective, CBDC could also mean automatic collection of taxes, government fines, child support, tickets, and student loans. Furthermore, commercial bank disintermediation can occur where there be no need for commercial banks, since CBDC is serving customers directly. As such, the role of commercial banks as middlemen will be removed. Lastly, governments could potentially shut customers off from CBDC, with far reaching implications, especially when cashless society becomes a reality due to the eventual elimination of physical cash.

Reasons for Countries Discontinuing CBDC Implementation

A number of reasons have been suggested for why some central banks are not going ahead with implementing CBDC. In the case of Malaysia, its central bank, Bank Negara Malaysia (BNM), continues to assess CBDC potential; however, it has elected not to go ahead with CBDC implementation at this stage due to the fact that it does not possess the universal characteristics of money, the risks associated with its usage as a store of value and medium of exchange, lack of scalability, and vulnerability to cyber threats (Hafez, 2021). Banco Central del Ecuador, the central bank of Ecuador, also discontinued its CBDC, known as Dinero Electrónico, which was intended to increase financial inclusion and reduce the need to hold and distribute large quantities of USD notes. However, the CBDC process was truncated due to opposition from private banks (Arauz et al., 2021). Additionally, Tunisia's e-Dinar and Senegal's eCFA were cancelled due to lack of traction.

Today, CBDCs are entering a competitive marketplace comprised of a plethora of payment instruments. As such, the goals of CBDC deployment cannot be successful unless it captures shares from existing payment instruments; inability to do so will result in CBDCs struggling to compete. Accordingly, Meyers (2022) noted that CBDC runs a high risk of becoming a costly waste of resources and time, since the benefits and privacy provisions are not sufficient to entice consumers to use it. In turn, this means that CBDC may not achieve widespread adoption while simultaneously failing to achieve central bank motivation for launching it. On the face of it, CBDC appears promising and exciting; however, CBDC cannot provide additional benefits over and above what consumers are already enjoying. An investment in using regulation as a tool to make the existing payment systems cheaper and more competitive can serve consumers better than issuing a CBDC.

One of the reasons assigned by central banks for not pushing CBDC deployment is linked to their inability to solve the offline conundrum, since widespread adoption of CBDC includes a function of how to ensure CBDC works in an offline environment. This challenge was critically exposed when the Eastern Caribbean's CBDC DCash experienced an outage for six weeks in early 2022 due to a technical issue linked to the need for the Internet connection to work effectively (Benton, 2022). Nigeria's CBDC eNaria also went offline on 15 September due to technical issues (CBN, 2022). This situation of CBDC unavailability will be particularly dire when, in the future, there is an increased reliance on CBDC, with CBDC even potentially replacing physical cash.

Systemic Risk, Destabilisation, and Changes to Financial-sector Market Structure

Regarding CBDC's impact on the financial system, it must be noted that CBDC, especially interest-bearing CBDC, can drastically change the structure of the financial system, as increased CBDC usage can lead to a decrease in the use of commercial banks. In turn, this could result in a reduced volume of bank deposits, which serve as a source for lending. As a result, the cost of borrowing may reduce, and the availability of credits may be constricted. Furthermore, an interest-bearing CBDC could result in customers shifting from other sources of investment, such as money market mutual funds, treasury bills, and other investment instruments, subsequently reducing the funding available for governments and the private sector. The solution lies in designing CBDC as a non-interest-bearing form, which will make it less attractive than commercial bank deposits, or else designing a CBDC type that imposes a limit on the amount a user can hold (Boucher et al., 2022). In terms of CBDC's impact on private payments actors offering credit, debit, and mobile money wallets, Bansal and Singh, (2021) suggested that CBDC could significantly change and disrupt current domestic and international payment systems, since it offers benefits of faster transactions, lower costs, and offline capabilities, meaning some customers may select CBDC over these existing channels. In turn, the business models of payment providers could be affected.

One of the major implications of CBDC concerns its impact on financial intermediation. As such, it is a critical issue to manage financial intermediation risks through CBDC design with inbuilt safeguarding mechanisms and implementation plans. The primary risk occurs when there is a significant shift of funds from bank deposits into CBDC. However, building in sufficient time and flexibility can allow the system to adjust. Therefore, the level of financial intermediation risks becomes a function of the future structure of the financial size and scope of CBDC adoption, as well as the type of CBDC design. Given the rapid evolution and dynamic nature of the financial system, it is likely that private sector developments may create similar deposit substitution risks irrespective of CBDC. As a result, CBDC may rather generate additional innovative opportunities for the banks to ring-fence their financial intermediation function. Furthermore, if CBDC is introduced abruptly, these risks can be exacerbated while, at the same time, new forms of digital money and CBDC can increase latent risks of systemic bank runs (BIS, 2021b).

Authors Allen et al. (2020), Bindseil (2022), and Schilling et al. (2020) discuss how, in case of systemic uncertainty regarding banks, CBDC can provide a risk-free and relatively easy alternative to traditional bank deposits held in a commercial bank. In so doing, it can contribute significantly to systemic runs on banks in financial crisis situations, thereby threatening the safety and stability of the financial system.

To deal with possible systemic runs, Popescu (2022) argues that, provided the central bank acts as a lender of last resort and offers emergency liquidity support to banks in times of a crisis, plus CBDC resolution frameworks, domestic deposit insurance, and effective banking regulation, the risk of domestic bank runs can be reduced, and generally, this strategy can improve an economy's financial stability. Author Bindseil (2022) further proposed a two-tier CBDC design as a solution to the risk of domestic runs, since it would effectively disincentivise CBDC through a less attractive remuneration rate.

Privacy, Consumer Protection, and the Prevention of Financial Crimes

Given the digital nature of a CBDC, achieving full anonymity in CBDC transactions is unrealistic. By design, it is expected to generate detailed information concerning each user's transactions. As such, the protection of CBDC users personal information is key, and modalities for accessing this information, as well as the conditions under which its usage can occur, remain critical. Therefore, privacy and consumer protection must be central to the design of CBDC, especially in an era of big data and dataveillance, a portmanteau of 'data' and 'surveillance' that describes the practice of collecting online data, metadata and monitoring end users' activities. Although CBDC is championed as a tool to promote financial inclusion, lack of adequate laws safeguarding the potential risks of individual privacy undermine the goal of financial inclusion. A retail CBDC may facilitate regulatory compliance and monetary oversight, but it places a great deal of data and information in the hands of government entities, especially the central bank. As such, CBDC design must integrate a solid privacy framework to deal with privacy risks while stimulating trust in the CBDC (Atako, 2021; and Bijlsma et al., 2021). Furthermore, a CBDC design must necessarily incorporate the compliance with anti-money laundering (AML) and countering the financing of terrorism (CFT) laws and regulations in order to prevent crimes and illicit use of CBDC (Esoimeme, 2021). One key policy challenge facing central banks regarding the consideration of issuing CBDC concerns how to balance privacy and reduce illegal activity. Didenko and Buckley (2021) argue that, in addition to ensuring CBDC design conforms to regulatory expectations and disclosure laws, there is also a need for strong coordination between various government actors operating in the payment's ecosystem.

Technology Risks

Technology risks remain a major issue on the minds of central banks as they consider implementing CBDC. Depending on CBDC's technical characteristics, these risks may take different forms. Cyber threats, risk of counterfeiting, single points of failure, vendor risks, and technology capture represent some of the substantial technology risks to be considered when CBDC implementation considerations are being made. According to the World Economic Forum (2021), issuing CBDC also comes with other technology risks, such as credential theft and loss, where users may lose access to their CBDC wallet due to theft. Another risk concerns abuse by authorities with privileged roles. This includes central banks or government agencies, law enforcement may have the ability to initiate privileged actions such as freezing the withdrawal of funds in a CBDC wallet without a user's consent. The solution to the abuse of such privilege lies in ensuring the limitation of third-party abilities to perform validated or invalidated transactions rather than these authorities. For instance, the central bank's roles must be limited to functional responsibilities required to make the CBDC function. Furthermore, CBDC can suffer from 'double spending' issues, which describe a form of counterfeiting wherein a CBDC user can spend funds on their CBDC wallets multiple times illegitimately.

Another technology risk facing CBDC concerns the advancement of quantum computing, which may compromise major data-encryption methodologies and cryptographic mechanisms employed in data access, protection, and integrity. In turn, this means that attackers can use advanced quantum computing to compromise CBDC, rendering it insecure. Consequently, when designing CBDC, steps must be taken to address how advancement in quantum computing can influence CBDC security. It is important to point out that most CBDCs are built on blockchain, which invariably remains a technology undergoing evolution, with the attendant risks. Furthermore, CBDC may necessitate centralisation, which creates a number of cyber-risk vulnerabilities and single points of failure. An attack on CBDC could possess far-reaching implications for the financial system, in terms of contributing to long lasting mistrust in CBDC, and by extension, the financial system.

Another technology challenge confronting CBDC rollout concerns vendor risks and technology capture. There is now a growing list of CBDC vendors making a number of claims for their technology. However, such technology lacks a track record, as CBDC represents an emerging area with no precedents. The risk of technology capture is thus not far-fetched, which may lead to a monopoly reinforcing a single point of failure challenge (de Bonis & Ferrero, 2022).

Given the widespread use of CBDC and its role in the financial system, there could be multiple points of entry compared to the existing payment system in terms of the security perspective. It is inevitable that this will be a subject of possible attacks and hacks. Therefore, it is imperative that CBDC design provides paramount consideration to its technical infrastructure in order to ensure it remains resilient to operational disruptions. One key consideration is to enable offline capability, which ensures CBDC can work for users who lack access to the Internet, and this will also ensure it works when there are online disruptions (Choi et al., 2021).

Reasons for Not Considering CBDC Implementation

The Bank of Japan (BOJ) has expressed caution in implementing the CBDC project due to a lack of interest from the public, a strong preference for cash by citizens, and a high ratio of bank accounts in Japan. As the BOJ noted, it '*currently has no plan to issue CBDC, the BOJ considers it important to prepare thoroughly to respond to changes in circumstances in an appropriate manner*' (BOJ, 2022, p. 1). The BOJ recognises that the future of payment systems are changing to make them suitable for the digital age, and CBDC is expected to play a role in this future. Therefore, CBDC is viewed as a public good that will complement and coexist with other private payment services. However, like other developed countries, the BOJ also believes that, at this time, there is no urgency to issue CBDC. Additionally, there are a few countries that have made a clear, strong case for CBDC; as such, it remains part of future payments and settlement use cases.

In the case of Canada, although the Central Bank of Canada is building its institutional capacity and studying options to issue CBDC when the need arises, it currently has no immediate plans to launch a CBDC. The Bank of Canada has set the following conditions to warrant its issuance of CBDC—namely, when there is a drastic decline in the use of physical notes or when more alternative private-sector-issued digital currencies become widely used as an alternative to the Canadian dollar. The Central Bank of Canada further expects that, when CBDC is introduced, it will be characterised by resilience, universal accessibility, secured medium of exchange, competition with other payment instruments, and an acceptable level of privacy (Bank of Canada, 2020).

HOW DOES CBDC ENABLE FINANCIAL EXCLUSION?

Financial inclusion remains a major motivation for CBDC rollout. In fact, Elliot (2019) maintains that, if the CBDC design is not configured properly, this could increase contextual inequalities along existing fault lines of digital, financial, and economic disparities present in the society. For instance, if mobile phones, especially smartphones, become a key channel for accessing CBDC, this will mean that only persons with a phone, Internet access, or network access can utilise CBDC. In another study concerning the relationship between financial inclusion and CBDC, Ozili (2022) further highlighted several reasons why CBDC can negatively influence financial inclusion. For instance, digital illiteracy may pose a barrier to the use of CBDC, there may be high levels of digital exclusion, digital devices needed to access CBDC may be costly for the poor, CBDCs may not prioritises financial inclusion as a main objective, people may retain strong preference for cash over digital currency, and non-interest bearing CBDCs may hinder financial inclusion. Financial exclusion can occur when some persons in society, who may have access only to cash, for example, the elderly and members of vulnerable groups who typically need a simple and more user-friendly means of accessing a CBDC and will be financially excluded if CBDC is not designed with these group of users in mind (Barotini & Holden, 2019).

The fact remains that CBDC is essentially a technologically driven solution, since users will, in one form or another, need technological tools to access it. Therefore, CBDC does not come with a solution that solves some of the underlying causes of financial inclusion; rather, it may led to financial exclusion unless steps are taken to tackle the root cause of financial exclusion, such as the need to make CBDC a national right for citizens and increase efforts to promote financial inclusion.In dealing with the impact of CBDC as a tool for financial exclusion, authors (Nadir et al., 2022) suggested that it will be prudent for a country to consider alternative approaches to CBDC, for example, implementing a fast payments system while expanding access to a country's payment system for financially excluded persons in the interim to enable a gradual introduction of CBDCs at a future date. Using this approach can expand financial inclusion, thereby ameliorating the effects of CBDC as a tool for financial exclusion.

Invariably, inclusion represents a function of access to resources and positive externalities emitting from the benefits of an inclusive financial system. Consequently, CBDC cannot act on their own as a mechanism for financial inclusion; if CBDC is applied as an exclusive tool for financial inclusion, it will instead increase financial exclusion. The solutions to this issue lie in leveraging CBDC as a tool to promote access to financing for the unbanked and underbanked. Central Bank of Kenya (2022) noted that CBDC can led to financial exclusion if the design of the CBDC, especially its technological infrastructure plus technical literacy design is not framed in a manner which will make it accessible to all members of the society. Therefore, to ensure all sections of the public access CBDC, there is a need to guarantee all the underlying technology and users' know-how do not become a constraint for some individuals consuming CBDC. In this direction, CBDC is a "double-edged sword" when it comes to financial inclusion since a retail CBDC may be used as a tool to provide access to persons in the financially excluded bracket, at the same time, lack of technological infrastructure and technical know-how can become a constraint for marginalized persons thereby exacerbating financial exclusion.

The arguments for justifying CBDC as a tool for financial inclusion include its ability to improve access to digital financial services, enable efficiency in the payments system, and decrease costs. In unpacking the justification of CBDC as a tool for financial inclusion, when it comes to its promise to improve access to digital financial services, it must be noted that the persons in the financially excluded bracket usually operate in a cash economy. Therefore, reaching out to them requires investment in last-mile distribution networks and efficient liquidity management as a bridge between cash and digital economy. As such, CBDC can be useful in offering channels to financial access, but it is not sufficient to tackle the peculiar needs of this target audience. Additionally, CBDC's promise to offer a more efficient and cheaper means of payment may be problematic based on comparison with existing means of payments, such as mobile money wallets, which bring payments to the doorstep of the financially excluded. The current configuration of payment service delivery requires boots on the ground in the form of agents capable of servicing the clients' needs. The notion that CBDC can replace this last-mile mechanism in a cheaper and more efficient manner may not be possible (Bull et al., 2021).

One of the reasons presented for introducing CBDC is to provide an alternative to cryptocurrencies and other forms of innovation, such as issuance of private digital currency. However, Coulter (2022) argues that CBDC, which is designed without a clear path for connecting with the existing digital public and private currencies on the market, will mean confusion in its relationship and interdepency with other payment instruments. As such, the goal of an open, competitive, and innovative free digital currency market and ecosystem cannot be achieved. Furthermore, the fact that CBDC does not provide a path for interoperability with other digital innovative digital payments, including blockchain, will risk making CBDC an economic and institutional relic that is not fully linked to the overall fintech economy. This exclusion will subsequently mean consumers cannot take full advantage of a host of benefits a retail CBDC can offer, since it is designed as an island.

Another element of exclusion could be fees. The use of cash by users does not come with any fees; therefore, retail CBDC, which is designed to serve as a digital version of existing fiat, must be free of charge to use. Unfortunately, CBDC comes with costs. Some authors (Chiu et al., 2019; Kiff et al., 2020b) suggest that, if CBDC fees are prohibitive, especially the fees charged by the CBDC private sector payment interface provider—namely, third-party intermediaries needed to deliver CBDC to the last mile—then this will create a fertile ground for financial exclusion.

WHAT ARE THE MAIN LESSONS LEARNED FROM CBDC IMPLEMENTATION?

An overriding lesson to guide the implementation of CBDC concerns the need to use a flexible and adaptable approach, since CBDC deployment remains linked to numerous unanswered questions. Furthermore, evidence is lacking concerning best practices or proven solutions, and more so, there is no universal CBDC solution, since each individual country's context matters. To date, CBDC deployment lessons mostly concern pilots and proof of concept rather than actual implementation, since only a few countries have implemented CBDC. The few countries who have actually implemented CBDC have done so for only a few years. As such, the CBDC implementation landscape essentially remains a work in progress.

The suggested best practice sequence for rollout of the CBDC decision-making process includes four steps: research, proof of concept (PoC), pilot launch, or cancelled. The key distinction between pilot and PoC is that a pilot involves live users, whereas PoC does not. The critical lesson in terms of a sequence is that most central banks may not necessarily go through this sequence, but there is always PoC, even if the results are not published. However, some central banks may skip the pilot and instead prefer a soft launch. Therefore, one can consider some of the so-called 'pilots' as soft launches.

Nigeria's implementation of CBDC, eNaira, paints a picture of CBDC implementation challenges, though the CBDC is still less than one year old, making it relatively new. Even still, one key lesson learned from its implementation concerns the lack of co-operation from banks as key partners in its implementation. This lack of significant push from the banks could be conjectured as one of the reasons for eNaira's low uptake. In the case of the Eastern Caribbean Currency Union (ECCU)'s CBDC, known as Dcash, the main lesson learned from its implementation concerns the need to build a robust infrastructure to ensure uptime of CBDC, a lesson informed by Dcash malfunctioning over a period of three months. Here, it is important to emphasise that the ECCU, which is the first currency union in the world to issue CBDC, explained that the disruption was not caused by external intervention, but rather was due to internal technical issues. Therefore, this establishes the need for central banks considering operationalisation of CBDCs to take steps to strengthen the internal mechanisms needed for CBDCs to work all the time. Furthermore, they should establish a backup measure, which could be an offline option that enables CBDC to operate seamlessly when there is major downtime (ECCB, 2022).

The National Bank of Cambodia's nationwide digital payments platform, Bakong, which is based on blockchain, is not CBDC per se, since it is not a liability on the central bank's balance sheet. That said, it still offers an important lesson for developing a digital payment system that can provide a pathway for financial inclusion without issuing central bank currency. The lesson in question is that fast payments are now in considerable demand around the world, and central banks can promote the effective uptake of fast payments without needing to create fiat-backed digital cash. This approach is attested by the widespread use of Bakong in Cambodia, which serves 7.9 million users, comprising nearly half the country's population of

16.7 million, with a recorded 6.8 million transactions worth approximately $2.9 billion (Iwamoto, 2022).

Beyond the few countries that have implemented CBDC, a considerable number of CBDC pilots have been implemented to date. While these do not offer data and insights from a full-fledged implemented CBDC perspective, they still provide valuable lessons to help guide CBDC rollout. For instance, the outcome from most CBDC pilot projects underscores the need for CBDC to be carefully designed while simultaneously working to tackle the 'CBDC trilemma', which concerns how to strike a balance between the three objectives of payment efficiency, financial stability, and price stability, since all of them cannot be achieved at the same time.

An effective starting point for lessons in CBDC deployment is to highlight a cautionary tale. The introduction of new payment instruments is not a negligible task. Many digital financial system deployments are struggling, and only a few of such implementations will succeed. Therefore, the introduction of CBDC, which represents a major and drastic endeavour with a number of moving parts and far-reaching implications for the financial, monetary, and overall economy, should be approached from the standpoint of a clear strategy backed by evidence of options to ensure its success. Furthermore, another key lesson drawn from pilots of retail CBDC is to select the proper environment with the presence of significant payment service providers capable of providing access points for end users to make payments using retail CBDC. The main message here is that the pilot environment and conditions should be as similar as possible to real-life situations in which CBDC will ultimately be implemented. This is because some retail CBDC pilot environments have been dissimilar from what occurs in CBDC usage context. Furthermore, another condition to promote the effective usage of CBDC is to use it as the mechanism for large and recurrent government payments. This strategy can go a long way to stimulating CBDC demand and usage (Ponce et al., 2020).

The motivation for CBDC deployment differs; however, financial inclusion and cultural factors always remain at the centre of decision-making. Lessons drawn from implementation of Mexico's CBDC, e-Peso, emphasise cultural dimensions in the same manner as technical consideration in CBDC design choices. The cultural implication of a change brought about by CBDC may be incremental, but this can be irreversible in the long term. Therefore, investment in idiosyncratic elements of CBDC deployment, such as historical consideration, economy organisation, and social implication of money must be made a key component of a CBDC project. Another lesson learned from the deployment of e-Peso is that CBDC should be promoted for either small cash or large cash payments. The e-Peso pilot selected the goal of limiting CBDC for small payments as an important consideration, since this speaks to the need to facilitate small cash payments via CBDC, and the promotion of CBDC for small cash payments is less disruptive in terms of its negative impact on other monetary instruments, especially private digital means of payments (Sarmiento, 2022).

Morales-Resendiz et al. (2021) listed three key lessons on CBDC design options, operations, and implementation issues that can be drawn from retail CBDC pilots. In terms of CBDC design lessons, framing the scope of CBDC, reviewing the legal framework needed to implement CBDC, establishing CBDC transactions limit, illustrating use case, and features represent important considerations. In terms of lessons learned regarding the operational side of CBDC deployment, there is a need for clearly defined layers of processing between central banks, technology entities, and financial sector actors. Here, the division of work should focus on availability and scalability. Furthermore, the proposed CBDC architecture must be assessed in terms of potential risks using a number of tools, such as principles for financial market infrastructure (PFMI), in order to ensure operational risks are mitigated. In terms of implementation, the major relevant lessons from retail CBDC pilots concern the need for CBDC as a payment-driven policy characterised by clearly defining the central bank's dual role as an operator and overseer, working hand in hand with other stakeholders. Another lesson learned from implementation perspectives is to enable an inclusive ecosystem, which is key for adoption and usage, coupled with CBDC education.

CONCLUSION

This chapter focusses on CBDC implementation in terms of key challenges, risks, and implementation issues. To tackle this chapter's objective, the following questions were posed: What are the main challenges confronting CBDC implementation; how does CBDC enable financial exclusion; and what are the main lessons learned from CBDC implementation?

First, it came to light that, although a number of central banks, especially in emerging economies, are racing to consider implementing CBDC, there remains no agreement concerning a universal benefit of CBDC; rather, country-specific context becomes a key deciding factor. For instance, a number of advanced economies are not rushing to implement CBDC because, in their perspective, the advanced nature of their payment system does not warrant introducing a digital currency backed by a central bank. Continuing, financial inclusion is often stated as one of the key reasons for introducing CBDC. However, evidence from this chapter demonstrates that, depending on the CBDC's design, it may led to financial exclusion, especially due to a lack of digital financial literacy on the part of unsophisticated users, the need for Internet or access to devices needed to utilise CBDC, and the fact that CBDC may cannibalise existing digital payments tools driving financial inclusion, such as mobile money. Therefore, CBDCs must be designed to work in both online and offline environments with apparent interoperability features at the core of their design.

Second, the negative side of CBDC represents a major issue of concern. Privacy and confidential issues are worrying if not addressed properly. For example, by design, CBDC means creating a centralised database of all users' spending behaviour coupled with detailed information on users' financial transactions. When cash is no longer in use, authorities could simply prevent a user from spending funds on their CBDC wallets. This situation calls for a CBDC design that delinks such privileges from the functional roles of central banks as CBDC custodians. There is no easy solution to this issue, but having multiple distributed decision points may help resolve this problem (BIS, 2021a).

To conclude, CBDC is here to stay. With the adoption rate expected to increase by the day, CBDC prospects appear exciting and promising. However, several shortcomings remain that require careful attention and strategy. The solution lies in focussing not only on technological consideration in the CBDC's design, but also on societal, economic, and political factors to address these challenges.

REFERENCES

Agur, I., Ari, A., & Dell'Ariccia, G. (2022). Designing central bank digital currencies. *Journal of Monetary Economics*, *125*, 62–79. Advance online publication. doi:10.1016/j.jmoneco.2021.05.002

Ahiabenu, K. (2022). *Nigerian Central Bank Digital Currency (CBDC) eNaira struggles with uptake*. https://www.knowledgeinnovations.com/2022/08/22/nigerian-central-bank-digital-currency-cbdc-enaira-struggles-with-uptake
/

Allen, J. G., Kumhof, M., Bateman, W., Lastra, R. M., Gleeson, S., & Omarova, S. T. (2020). *Central Bank Money: Liability, Asset, or Equity of the Nation?* Cornell Law School Research Paper No. 20-46. doi:10.2139/ssrn.3730608

Alonso, S. L. N., Fernández, M. Á. E., Bas, D. S., & Kaczmarek, J. (2020). Reasons fostering or discouraging the implementation of central bank-backed digital currency. *A review. Economies*, *8*(2), 41. Advance online publication. doi:10.3390/economies8020041

Alonso, S. L. N., Jorge-Vazquez, J., & Forradellas, R. F. R. (2021). Central banks digital currency: Detection of optimal countries for the implementation of a CBDC and the implication for payment industry open innovation. *Journal of Open Innovation*, *7*(1), 72. Advance online publication. doi:10.3390/joitmc7010072

Arauz, A., Garratt, R., & Ramos, F. D. F. (2021). Dinero Electrónico: The rise and fall of Ecuador's central bank digital currency. *Latin American Journal of Central Banking*, *2*(2), 100030. Advance online publication. doi:10.1016/j.latcb.2021.100030

Atako, N. (2021). Privacy Beyond Possession: Solving the Access Conundrum in Digital Dollars. In Vanderbilt Journal of Entertainment & Technology Law.

Atlantic Council. (2022). *Central Bank Digital Currency Tracker*. https://www.atlanticcouncil.org/cbdctracker/

Bank of Canada. (2020). *Contingency Planning for a Central Bank Digital Currency*. https://www.bankofcanada.ca/2020/02/contingency-planning-central-bank-digital-currency/

Bank of Jamaica. (2022, August 9). *Ceremonial First Minting of BOJ CBDC*. https://boj.org.jm/core-functions/currency/cbdc/ceremonial-first-minting-of-boj-cbdc/

Bansal, R., & Singh, S. (2021, April 13). *How Will Digital Currencies Change Wallets?* https://carnegieindia.org/2021/04/13/how-will-digital-currencies-change-wallets-pub-84310

Barotini, C., & Holden, H. (2019). Proceeding with caution - a survey on central bank digital currency. Bank for International Settlements.

Benton, P. R. (2022). *Market Landscape: Central Bank Digital Currencies*. Academic Press.

Bijlsma, M., van der Cruijsen, C., Jonker, N., & Reijerink, J. (2021). *What triggers consumer adoption of CBDC?* DNB Working Paper. doi:10.2139/ssrn.3836440

Bindseil, U. (2022). Central Bank Digital Currencies in a World with Negative Nominal Interest Rates. *Perspectives in Law*, Business and Innovation. doi:10.1007/978-981-16-7830-1_5

BIS. (2021a). *Central bank digital currencies: system design and interoperability*. www.bis.org

BIS. (2021b). *Central bank digital currencies: financial stability implications*. BIS.

Bofinger, P., & Haas, T. (2021). *Central bank digital currencies risk becoming a gigantic flop*. Academic Press.

BOJ. (2022, July 5). *Central Bank of Japan (BOJ) Liaison and Coordination Committee on Central Bank Digital Currency.* https://www.boj.or.jp/en/announcements/release_2022/rel220705b.pdf

Bossu, W., Itatani, M., Margulis, C., Rossi, A. D. P., Weenink, H., & Yoshinaga, A. (2020). Legal Aspects of Central Bank Digital Currency. *IMF Working Papers, 20*(254). doi:10.5089/9781513561622.001

Boucher, J., Fisch, E., Levi, S., Nguyen, B., Maalouf, K., & Perry, J. (2022, February 4). *The Federal Reserve Weighs Risks and Benefits of a US Central Bank Digital Currency.* https://www.skadden.com/insights/publications/2022/02/the-federal-reserve-weighs-risks

Bull, G., Cook, W., Kerse, M., & Staschen, S. (2021, May 13). *Is Financial Inclusion a Reason to Push Central Bank Digital Currencies?* https://www.cgap.org/blog/financial-inclusion-reason-push-central-bank-digital-currencies

CBN. (2022). *Unavailability of eNaira services- Central Bank of Nigeria(CBN).* Twitter. https://twitter.com/cenbank/status/1570316506562437120

Central Bank of Kenya. (2022). *Discussion Paper on Central Bank Digital Currency.* https://www.centralbank.go.ke/uploads/discussion_papers/CentralBankDigitalCurrency.pdf

Chen, H., & Siklos, P. L. (2022). Central bank digital currency: A review and some macro-financial implications. *Journal of Financial Stability, 60*, 100985. Advance online publication. doi:10.1016/j.jfs.2022.100985

Chiu, J., Davoodalhosseini, M., Jiang, J., & Yu, Z. (2019). *Bank Market Power and Central Bank Digital Currency: Theory and Quantitative Assessment.* Bank of Canada Staff Working Paper 2019-20.

Choi, K. J., Henry, R., Lehar, A., Reardon, J., & Safavi-Naini, R. (2021). A Proposal for a Canadian CBDC. SSRN *Electronic Journal.* doi:10.2139/ssrn.3786426

Cœuré, B., & Cunliffe, J.. (2020). *Central bank digital currencies: Foundational principles and core features.* https://www.bis.org/publ/othp33.pdf

Coulter, K.-A. (2022). 'Stop Creating Private Money!': Should the Bank of England Introduce a Central Bank Digital Currency to Compete with Cryptocurrency? A Review of the UK Bank of England's Proposed Retail CBDC. SSRN *Electronic Journal.* doi:10.2139/ssrn.4078059

Davoodalhosseini, S. M. (2021). Central bank digital currency and monetary policy. *Journal of Economic Dynamics & Control*. Advance online publication. doi:10.1016/j.jedc.2021.104150

de Bonis, R., & Ferrero, G. (2022). *Technological progress and institutional adaptations: the case of the Central Bank Digital Currency (CBDC)*. Bank of Italy Occasional Paper No. 690. doi:10.2139/ssrn.4109510

Didenko, A. N., & Buckley, R. P. (2021). *Central Bank Digital Currencies: A Potential Response to the Financial Inclusion Challenges of the Pacific*. UNSW Law Research Paper No. 21-63. Asian Development Bank Economics Working Paper Series. doi:10.2139/ssrn.3937698

ECCB. (2022). *DCash Service to Resume Next Week*. https://www.eccb-centralbank.org/news/view/dcash-service-to-resume-next-week

Elliot, O. (2019, June 12). *Central bank digital currency: friend or foe of mobile money in sub-Saharan Africa?* https://www.fsdafrica.org/news/central-bank-digital-currency-friend-or-foe-of-mobile-money-in-sub-saharan-africa/

Engert, W., & Fung, B. S. C. (2017). *Central Bank Digital Currency: Motivations and Implications*. Bank of Canada Staff Discussion Paper 16.

Esoimeme, E. (2021). A Critical Analysis of the Effects of the Central Bank of Nigeria's Digital Currency Named ENaira on Financial Inclusion and AML/CFT Measures. SSRN *Electronic Journal*. doi:10.2139/ssrn.3921396

Geroni, D. (2021, September 16). *Understanding The Types Of Central Bank Digital Currencies (CBDC)*. https://101blockchains.com/types-of-central-bank-digital-currencies/

Hafez, Y. (2021). *BNM has no immediate plan to issue Central Bank Digital Currency*. https://www.mof.gov.my/portal/en/news/press-citations/bnm-has-no-immediate-plan-to-issue-central-bank-digital-currency-yamani-hafez

Iwamoto, K. (2022, January 2). *Cambodia's digital currency reaches nearly half the population*. https://asia.nikkei.com/Business/Finance/Cambodia-s-digital-currency-reaches-nearly-half-the-population

Kiff, J., Alwazir, J., Davidovic, S., Farias, A., Khan, A., Khiaonarong, T., Malaika, M., Monroe, H., Sugimoto, N., Tourpe, H., & Zhou, P. (2020). A Survey of Research on Retail Central Bank Digital Currency. *IMF Working Papers, 20*(104). doi:10.5089/9781513547787.001

Kilponen, J., Jokivuolle, E., Kauko, K., Miettinen, P., & Vanhala, J. (2017). *Central bank digital currency*. www.suomenpankki.fi

Kosse, A., & Mattei, I. (2022). *Bank for International Settlements (BIS) Papers No 125 Gaining momentum-Results of the 2021 BIS survey on central bank digital currencies*. https://www.bis.org/publ/bppdf/bispap125.pdf

Lee, D. K. C., Yan, L., & Wang, Y. (2021). A global perspective on central bank digital currency. *China Economic Journal, 14*(1), 52–66. Advance online publication. doi:10.1080/17538963.2020.1870279

Löber, K., & Houben, A. (2018). *Committee on Payments and Market Infrastructures Markets Committee Central bank digital currencies*. https://www.bis.org/cpmi/publ/d174.pdf

Maniff, J. L. (2020). *Motives Matter : Examining Potential Tension in Central Bank Digital Currency Designs*. Federal Reserve Bank of Kansas City.

Meyers, Z. (2022, July 7). *Why would anyone use a central bank digital currency?* https://www.cer.eu/sites/default/files/insight_ZM_digcurrency_7.6.22.pdf

Mikhalev, I., Struchkov, I., Kiff, J., Burchardi, K., Gross, J., Song, B., Gourav, R., Song, B., & Roy, G. (2022). *CBDC tracker*. https://cbdctracker.org

Mohammad, D., Francisco, R., & Yu, Z. (2020). *CBDC and Monetary Policy*. https://www.banqueducanada.ca/2020/02/note-analytique-personnel-2020-4/

Morales-Resendiz, R., Ponce, J., Picardo, P., Velasco, A., Chen, B., Sanz, L., Guiborg, G., Segendorff, B., Vasquez, J. L., Arroyo, J., Aguirre, I., Haynes, N., Panton, N., Griffiths, M., Pieterz, C., & Hodge, A. (2021). Implementing a retail CBDC: Lessons learned and key insights. *Latin American Journal of Central Banking, 2*(1), 100022. doi:10.1016/j.latcb.2021.100022

Nadir, M., Pesme, J., & Popovic, A. (2022, December 1). *Is Central Bank Digital Currency the right tool to expand financial inclusion?* https://blogs.worldbank.org/allaboutfinance/central-bank-digital-currency-right-tool-expand-financial-inclusion

Nelson, B. (2021, April 15). *The Benefits and Costs of a Central Bank Digital Currency for Monetary Policy*. https://bpi.com/the-benefits-and-costs-of-a-central-bank-digital-currency-for-monetary-policy/

Opare, E. A., & Kim, K. (2020). A Compendium of Practices for Central Bank Digital Currencies for Multinational Financial Infrastructures. *IEEE Access: Practical Innovations, Open Solutions*, *8*, 110810–110847. doi:10.1109/ACCESS.2020.3001970

Ozili, P. K. (2021). Central Bank Digital Currency in Nigeria: Opportunities and Risks. SSRN *Electronic Journal*. doi:10.2139/ssrn.3917936

Ozili, P. K. (2022). Can Central Bank Digital Currency Increase Financial Inclusion? Arguments for and Against. In Big Data Analytics in the Insurance Market (pp. 241–249). Emerald Publishing Limited. doi:10.1108/978-1-80262-637-720221013

Ponce, J., Martínez-Jaramillo, S., & Sanz, L. (2020). *Implementing a CBDC: Lessons Learnt and Key Insights Policy Report*. https://www.cemla.org/fintech/docs/2020-Implementing-CBDC.pd
f

Popescu, A. (2022). *Cross-Border Central Bank Digital Currencies, Bank Runs and Capital Flows Volatility*. WP/22/83.

PwC. (2021). *PwC CBDC global index*. https://www.pwc.com/gx/en/industries/financial-services/assets/pwc-cbdc-global-index-1st-edition-april-2021.pdf

Sandner, P., Gross, J., Grale, L., & Schulden, P. (2020). The Digital Programmable Euro, Libra and CBDC: Implications for European Banks. SSRN *Electronic Journal*. doi:10.2139/ssrn.3663142

Sarmiento, A. (2022). Seven lessons from the e-Peso pilot plan: The possibility of a Central Bank Digital Currency. *Latin American Journal of Central Banking*, *3*(2), 100062. doi:10.1016/j.latcb.2022.100062

Schiller, J., & Gross, J. (2021). A model for central bank digital currencies: implications for bank funding and monetary policy. *Beiträge Zur Jahrestagung Des Vereins Für Socialpolitik 2021: Climate Economics*.

Schilling, L., Fernández-Villaverde, J., & Uhlig, H. (2020). *Central Bank Digital Currency: When Price and Bank Stability Collide*. doi:10.3386/w28237

Shirai, S. (2022, July 12). *Central Bank Digital Currency cast aside as cash reigns king in Japan*. Academic Press.

Tronnier, F., Harborth, D., & Hamm, P. (2022). Investigating privacy concerns and trust in the digital Euro in Germany. *Electronic Commerce Research and Applications*, *53*, 101158. doi:10.1016/j.elerap.2022.101158

Wang, Y., Lucey, B. M., Vigne, S. A., & Yarovaya, L. (2022). The Effects of Central Bank Digital Currencies News on Financial Markets. *Technological Forecasting and Social Change*, *180*, 121715. doi:10.1016/j.techfore.2022.121715

Wenker, K. (2022). *Retail Central Bank Digital Currencies (CBDC), Disintermediation and Financial Privacy: The Case of the Bahamian Sand Dollar*. Academic Press.

World Economic Forum. (2021, November 20). *4 key cybersecurity threats to new central bank digital currencies*. https://www.weforum.org/agenda/2021/11/4-key-threats-central-bank-digital-currencies/

Compilation of References

Abbasi, K., Alam, A., Du, M., & Huynh, T. L. D. (2020, May). FinTech, SME efficiency and national culture: Evidence from OECD countries. *Technological Forecasting and Social Change*, *163*, 120454. doi:10.1016/j.techfore.2020.120454

Abdul-Rahaman, A., & Abdulai, A. (2022). Mobile money adoption, input use, and farm output among smallholder rice farmers in Ghana. *Agribusiness*, *38*(1), 236–255. doi:10.1002/agr.21721

Ablon, L., Libicki, M. C., & Golay, A. A. (2014). *Markets for Cybercrime Tools and Stolen Data: Hackers' Bazaar*. RAND. https://www.rand.org/content/dam/rand/pubs/research_reports/RR600/RR610/RAND_RR610.pdf

Abouelmehdi, K., Beni-Hessane, A., & Khaloufi, H. (2018). Big healthcare data: Preserving security and privacy. *Journal of Big Data*, *5*(1), 1–18. doi:10.118640537-017-0110-7

Abraham, F., Schmukler, S. L., & Tessada, J. (2019). Robo-advisors: Investing through machines. *World Bank Research and Policy Briefs,* 134881.

Abubakar, L., & Handayani, T. (2018) Financial Technology: Legal Challenges for Indonesia Financial Sector. In *IOP Conf. Ser.: Earth Environ. Sci. 175 IOP Conf. Series: Earth and Environmental Science*, (p. 12204). IOP. 10.1088/1755-1315/175/1/012204

Adrian, T., & Griffoli, T. M. (2019, July). *The Rise of Digital Money*. IMF. https://www.imf.org/en/Publications/fintech-notes/Issues/2019/07/12/The-Rise-of-Digital-Money-47097

Advapay. (2021, November 8). Electronic Money Institution Regulation in the EU – E-Money Directive (EMD2). *Advapay*. https://advapay.eu/electronic-money-institution-regulation-in-the-eu-e-money-directive-emd2/

African Economic Outlook. (2017). *Entrepreneurship and Industrialization*. OECD. https://read.oecd-ilibrary.org/development/african-economic-outlook-2017_aeo-2017-en#page112

Aggarwal, P., Jun, S., & Huh, J. (2011). Scarcity messages. *Journal of Advertising*, *40*(3), 19–30. doi:10.2753/JOA0091-3367400302

Agoba, A. M., Sare, Y. A., & Bugri-Anarfo, E. (2017). Financial Inclusion and Monetary Policy: A Review of Recent Studies. *Ghana Journal of Development Studies*, *14*(1), 231. doi:10.4314/gjds.v14i1.12

Agur, I., Ari, A., & Dell'Ariccia, G. (2022). Designing central bank digital currencies. *Journal of Monetary Economics*, *125*, 62–79. Advance online publication. doi:10.1016/j.jmoneco.2021.05.002

Ahiabenu, K. (2022). *Nigerian Central Bank Digital Currency (CBDC) eNaira struggles with uptake.* https://www.knowledgeinnovations.com/2022/08/22/nigerian-central-bank-digital-currency-cbdc-enaira-struggles-with-uptake
/

Akartuna, E. A., Johnson, S. D., & Thornton, A. (2022). Preventing the money laundering and terrorist financing risks of emerging technologies: An international policy Delphi study. *Technological Forecasting and Social Change*, *179*, 121632. doi:10.1016/j.techfore.2022.121632

Akomea-Frimpong, I., Andoh, C., Akomea-Frimpong, A., & Dwomoh-Okudzeto, Y. (2019). Control of fraud on mobile money services in Ghana: An exploratory study. *Journal of Money Laundering Control*, *22*(2), 300–317. doi:10.1108/JMLC-03-2018-0023

Alaassar, A., Mention, A.-L., & Aas, T. H. (2022). Facilitating innovation in FinTech: A review and research agenda. *Review of Managerial Science*, 1–34.

Al-Adwan, A. S., Alrousan, M. K., Yaseen, H., Alkufahy, A. M., & Alsoud, M. (2022). Boosting Online Purchase Intention in High-Uncertainty-Avoidance Societies: A Signaling Theory Approach. *Journal of Open Innovation*, *8*(3), 136. doi:10.3390/joitmc8030136

Al-Jabari, M. A. R.S (2013). *Factors Influencing Online Shopping Behavior Among Jordanian Academicians.* Mohammed Abdal Razaq Al-Jabari Universiti Utara Malaysia.

Allen, J. G., Kumhof, M., Bateman, W., Lastra, R. M., Gleeson, S., & Omarova, S. T. (2020). *Central Bank Money: Liability, Asset, or Equity of the Nation?* Cornell Law School Research Paper No. 20-46. doi:10.2139/ssrn.3730608

Allen, F., & Gale, D. (2000). Financial contagion. *Journal of Political Economy*, *108*(1), 1–33. doi:10.1086/262109

Allen, F., Gu, X., & Jagtiani, J. (2022). Fintech, Cryptocurrencies, and CBDC : Financial Structural Transformation in China. *Journal of International Money and Finance*, *124*, 102625. doi:10.1016/j.jimonfin.2022.102625

Alonso, S. L. N., Fernández, M. Á. E., Bas, D. S., & Kaczmarek, J. (2020). Reasons fostering or discouraging the implementation of central bank-backed digital currency. *A review. Economies*, *8*(2), 41. Advance online publication. doi:10.3390/economies8020041

Alonso, S. L. N., Jorge-Vazquez, J., & Forradellas, R. F. R. (2021). Central banks digital currency: Detection of optimal countries for the implementation of a CBDC and the implication for payment industry open innovation. *Journal of Open Innovation*, *7*(1), 72. Advance online publication. doi:10.3390/joitmc7010072

Alvarez-Franco, P. B., & Restrepo-Tobón, D. A. (2016). Managerial efficiency and failure of US commercial banks during the 2007-2009 financial crisis: Was this time different? *Ecos de Economía*, *20*(43), 4–22. doi:10.17230/ecos.2016.43.1

Amel-Zadeh, A., & Meeks, G. (2013). Bank failure, mark-to-market and the financial crisis. *Abacus*, *49*(3), 308–339. doi:10.1111/abac.12011

Andrews, D. (2019). Breaking the shackles: Zombie firms, weak banks and depressed restructuring in Europe. *ECB Working Paper No. 2240.*

Andrianaivo, M., & Kpodar, K. (2012). Mobile phones, financial inclusion, and growth. *Revista de Economia Institucional*, *3*(2), 1–30.

Annan, S. (2017). Avoiding Fraud Due to Mobile Money. *Ghana Web*. https://www.ghanaweb.com/GhanaHomePage/features/Avoiding-fra ud-due-to-Mobile-Money-588682

Anshari, M., Almunawar, M. N., Masri, M., & Hrdy, M. (2021). Financial Technology with AI-Enabled and Ethical Challenges. *Society*, *58*(3), 189–195. doi:10.100712115-021-00592-w

Antoniades, A. (2021). *Commercial bank failures during the Great Recession: The real (estate) story.* SSRN 2325261.

Apeti, A. E., & Edoh, E. D. (2023). Tax revenue and mobile money in developing countries. Journal of Development Economics, 161(April 2022), 103014. https://doi.org/ doi:10.1016/j.jdeveco.2022.103014

Arauz, A., Garratt, R., & Ramos, F. D. F. (2021). Dinero Electrónico: The rise and fall of Ecuador's central bank digital currency. *Latin American Journal of Central Banking*, *2*(2), 100030. Advance online publication. doi:10.1016/j.latcb.2021.100030

Arena, M. (2005). Bank Failures and Bank Fundamentals: A Comparative Analysis of Latin America and East Asia during the Nineties using Bank-Level Data. *Bank of Canada Working Paper No. 19.*

Arnaboldi, F. (2019). The Euro Area Banking System: Where Do We Stand? In Risk and Regulation in Euro Area Banks (pp. 1-19). Palgrave Macmillan.

Arner, D., Barberis, J., & Buckley, R. P. (2016). The Evolution of Fintech: A New Post-Crisis Paradigm? *Georgetown Journal of International Law*, *47*, 1271.

Arslanian, H. (2022). Stablecoins. In *The Book of Crypto* (pp. 149–170). Palgrave Macmillan. doi:10.1007/978-3-030-97951-5_7

Asamoah, D., Takieddine, S., & Amedofu, M. (2020). Examining the effect of mobile money transfer (MMT) capabilities on business growth and development impact. *Information Technology for Development*, *26*(1), 146–161. doi:10.1080/02681102.2019.1599798

Assaf, A. G., Berger, A. N., Roman, R. A., & Tsionas, M. G. (2019). Does efficiency help banks survive and thrive during financial crises? *Journal of Banking & Finance*, *106*, 445–470. doi:10.1016/j.jbankfin.2019.07.013

Atako, N. (2021). Privacy Beyond Possession: Solving the Access Conundrum in Digital Dollars. In Vanderbilt Journal of Entertainment & Technology Law.

Atlantic Council. (2022). *Central Bank Digital Currency Tracker*. https://www.atlanticcouncil.org/cbdctracker/

Auer, R., Banka, H., Yaa Boakye-Adjei, N., Faragallah, A (2022) J. Frost, H. Natarajan, & J. Prenio. (eds) *Central bank digital currencies: a new tool in the financial inclusion toolkit?* FSI Insights 41

Auer, R., Cornelli, G., & Frost, J. (2020). *Rise of the central bank digital currencies: drivers, approaches and technologies*. Academic Press.

Auer, R., Cornelli, G., & Frost, J. (2020). Rise of the Central Bank Digital Currencies: Drivers, Approaches and Technologies. *Bank for International Settlements, 880*. doi:10.2139srn.3724070

Auer, R., Frost, J., Gambacorta, L., Monnet, C., Rice, T., & Shin, H. S. (2022). Central bank digital currencies: Motives, economic implications, and the research frontier. *Annual Review of Economics, 14*(1), 697–721. doi:10.1146/annurev-economics-051420-020324

Ayettey, L. T. (2019, October 19), *MOMO Fraud – How Scammers Steal Your Money*. ModernGhana. https://www.modernghana.com/news/962315/momo-fraud-how-scammers-steal-your-money.html

Ayyagari, M., Demirgüç-Kunt, A., & Maksimovic, V. (2011). ' Firm Innovation in Emerging Markets: The Role of Finance, Governance, and Competition'. *Journal of Financial and Quantitative Analysis, 46*(6), 1545–1580. https://www.jstor.org/stable/41409661. doi:10.1017/S0022109011000378

Aziz, A., & Naima, U. (2021). Rethinking digital financial inclusion: Evidence from Bangladesh. *Technology in Society, 64*, 101509. doi:10.1016/j.techsoc.2020.101509

Baganzi, R., & Lau, A. K. W. (2017). Examining trust and risk in mobile money acceptance in Uganda. *Sustainability (Switzerland), 9*(12), 2233. doi:10.3390u9122233

Bai, C., Quayson, M., & Sarkis, J. (2021). COVID-19 pandemic digitization lessons for sustainable development of micro-and small- enterprises. *Sustainable Production and Consumption, 27*, 1989–2001. doi:10.1016/j.spc.2021.04.035

Bai, C., Quayson, M., & Sarkis, J. (2022). Analysis of Blockchain's enablers for improving sustainable supply chain transparency in Africa cocoa industry. *Journal of Cleaner Production, 358*, 131896. doi:10.1016/j.jclepro.2022.131896

Bailey, A. A., Bonifield, C. M., Arias, A., & Villegas, J. (2022). Mobile payment adoption in Latin America. *Journal of Services Marketing*, (December). doi:10.1108/JSM-04-2021-0130

Baltagi, B. H. (2012). *Econometric Analysis of Panel Data* (4th ed.). Wiley.

Bank of Canada. (2020). *Contingency Planning for a Central Bank Digital Currency.* https://www.bankofcanada.ca/2020/02/contingency-planning-central-bank-digital-currency/

Bank of England. (2022). *New Bank Start-Up Unit.* Bank of England. https://www.bankofengland.co.uk/prudential-regulation/new-bank-start-up-unit

Bank of Ghana. (2020). *Payment Systems Oversight Annual Report.* Payment Systems Department Bank of Ghana.

Bank of Jamaica. (2022, August 9). *Ceremonial First Minting of BOJ CBDC.* https://boj.org.jm/core-functions/currency/cbdc/ceremonial-first-minting-of-boj-cbdc/

Banning, M. E. (2015). Shared entanglements – Web 2.0, info-liberalism & digital sharing. *Information Communication and Society, 19*(4), 489–503. doi:10.1080/1369118X.2015.1061573

Bansal, R., & Singh, S. (2021, April 13). *How Will Digital Currencies Change Wallets?* https://carnegieindia.org/2021/04/13/how-will-digital-currencies-change-wallets-pub-84310

Barefoot, J. A. (2020) *Digital Technology Risks for Finance: Dangers Embedded in Fintech and Regtech.* 151. Harvard Kennedy School. https://www.hks.harvard.edu/centers/mrcbg/publications/awp/awp151

Barotini, C., & Holden, H. (2019). Proceeding with caution - a survey on central bank digital currency. Bank for International Settlements.

Barotini, C., & Holden, H. (2019). Proceeding with caution - a survey on central bank digital currency. *Bank for International Settlements, 101*(101), 1–15.

Barrdear, J., & Kumhof, M. (2016). The Macroeconomics of Central Bank Issued Digital Currencies. In *Bank of England Working Paper,* (Issue 605). https://www.bankofengland.co.uk/-/media/boe/files/working-paper/2016/the-macroeconomics-of-central-bank-issued-digital-currencies.pdf?la=en&hash=341B602838707E5D6FC26884588C912A721B1DC1

Barrdear, J., & Kumhof, M. (2021). The macroeconomics of central bank digital currencies. *Journal of Economic Dynamics & Control*, 104148.

Basel Committee on Banking Supervision. (2018). *Sound Practices: Implications of fintech developments for banks and bank supervisors.* BIS. https://www.bis.org/bcbs/publ/d431.htm

Baumeister, R., & Vohs, K. (2007). Self-regulation, ego depletion, and motivation. *Social and Personality Psychology Compass, 1*(10), 1–14.

Baxter, L. G. (2016). 'Adaptive Financial Regulation and Regtech: A Concept Article on Realistic Protection for Victims of Bank Failures'. *Duke Law Journal, 66*, 567–598.

Bearak, M., Moriarty, D., & Ledger, J. (2021, November 19). Africa's Rising Cities: How Africa will become the center of the world's urban future. *The Washington Post*. https://www.washingtonpost.com/world/interactive/2021/africa-cities/

Bechtel, A., Ferreira, A., Gross, J., & Sandner, P. (2022). The Future of Payments in a DLT-based European Economy: A Roadmap. In *The Future of Financial Systems in the Digital Age* (pp. 89–116). Springer. doi:10.1007/978-981-16-7830-1_6

Beck, T., Senbet, L. and Simbanegavi, W. (2015) 'Financial Inclusion and Innovation in Africa: An Overview', *Journal of African Economies*, *24*(suppl_1), pp. i3–i11. doi: . doi:10.1093/jae/eju031

Beck, T., & Levine, R. (2002). Industry growth and capital allocation: Dose having a market- or bank-based system matter? *Journal of Financial Economics*, *64*(2), 147–180. doi:10.1016/S0304-405X(02)00074-0

Belanche, D., Casaló, L. V., & Flavián, C. (2019). Artificial Intelligence in FinTech: Understanding robo-advisors adoption among customers. *Industrial Management & Data Systems*, *119*(7), 1411–1430. doi:10.1108/IMDS-08-2018-0368

Benton, P. R. (2022). *Market Landscape: Central Bank Digital Currencies*. Academic Press.

Berger, A. N., Diana, H., & Jeffrey, M. (1996). A Framework for Analyzing Efficiency, Risks, Costs, and Innovations in the Payments System. *Journal of Money, Credit and Banking*, *28*(4), 696–732. doi:10.2307/2077917

Bernards, N. (2019). Tracing mutations of neoliberal development governance: 'Fintech', failure and the politics of marketization. *Environment & Planning A*, *51*(7), 1442–1459. doi:10.1177/0308518X19862576

Berraies, S., Ben Yahia, K., & Hannachi, M. (2017). Identifying the effects of perceived values of mobile banking applications on customers: Comparative study between baby boomers, generation X and generation Y. *International Journal of Bank Marketing*, *35*(6), 1018–1038. doi:10.1108/IJBM-09-2016-0137

Bezhovski, Z. (2016). The Future of the Mobile Payment as Electronic Payment System. *European Journal of Business and Management*, *8*(8), 127–132.

Bhaskar, R., Imran, A., Bansal, S., & Pandey, K. (2022). Research in International Business and Finance Central Bank Digital Currencies : Agendas for future research. *Research in International Business and Finance*, *62*(July), 101737. doi:10.1016/j.ribaf.2022.101737

Bian, W., Ji, Y., & Wang, P. (2021). The crowding-out effect of central bank digital currencies : A simple and generalizable payment portfolio model. *Finance Research Letters*, *43*(February), 102010. doi:10.1016/j.frl.2021.102010

Bijlsma, M., van der Cruijsen, C., Jonker, N., & Reijerink, J. (2021). *What triggers consumer adoption of CBDC?* DNB Working Paper. doi:10.2139/ssrn.3836440

Bindseil, U. (2022). Central Bank Digital Currencies in a World with Negative Nominal Interest Rates. *Perspectives in Law*, Business and Innovation. doi:10.1007/978-981-16-7830-1_5

Birch, D., & Young, M. A. (1997). Financial services and the Internet - what does cyberspace mean for the financial services industry? *Internet Research*, *7*(2), 120–128. doi:10.1108/10662249710165262

BIS. (2021a). *Central bank digital currencies: system design and interoperability.* www.bis.org

BIS. (2021b). *Central bank digital currencies: financial stability implications.* BIS.

Błach, J. (2020). Barriers to Financial Innovation—Corporate Finance Perspective. *J. Risk Financial Manag.*, *13*(11), 273. doi:10.3390/jrfm13110273

Blandin, A., Cloots, A. S., Hussain, H., Rauchs, M., Saleuddin, R., Allen, J. G., Zhang, B. Z., & Cloud, K. (2019). *Global cryptoasset regulatory landscape study.* University of Cambridge Faculty of Law Research Paper, 23.

Bloomberg. (2022). *WeLend Ltd—Company Profile and News.* Bloomberg Markets. https://www.bloomberg.com/profile/company/1469380D:HK

Blumen, R. (2016). Jürgen laartz and alexander budzier on why large IT projects fail. *IEEE Software*, *33*(4), 117–120. doi:10.1109/MS.2016.102

Boar, C., & Wehrli, A. (2021). Ready, steady, go? – Results of the third BIS survey on central bank digital currency. *BIS Papers*, *114*, 77–82.

Boberhoff, T., & con der Decken, J. (2022). *E-Commerce in Nigeria Nigerian E-Commerce landscape and. May.* [Master's thesis, Jönköping International Business School.]

Bofinger, P., & Haas, T. (2021). *Central bank digital currencies risk becoming a gigantic flop.* Academic Press.

BOJ. (2022, July 5). *Central Bank of Japan (BOJ) Liaison and Coordination Committee on Central Bank Digital Currency.* https://www.boj.or.jp/en/announcements/release_2022/rel220705b.pdf

Bollaert, H., Lopez-de-Silanes, F., & Schwienbacher, A. (2021). Fintech and access to finance. *Journal of Corporate Finance*, *68*(March), 101941. doi:10.1016/j.jcorpfin.2021.101941

Bord, V., & Santos, J. A. (2012). The rise of the originate-to-distribute model and the role of banks in financial intermediation. *Economic Policy Review*, *18*(2), 21–34.

Boshkov, T. (2016) Growing the Global Economy through SMEs International Aspirations. LAP LAMBERT Academic Publishing.

Boskov, T., & Drakulevski, L. (2017). Addressing the Role of Risk Management and Digital Finance Technology on Financial Inclusion. *Quality - Access to Success*, *18*(161), 113–115. http://eprints.ugd.edu.mk/18591/

Bossu, W., Itatani, M., Margulis, C., Rossi, A. D. P., Weenink, H., & Yoshinaga, A. (2020). Legal Aspects of Central Bank Digital Currency. *IMF Working Papers, 20*(254). doi:10.5089/9781513561622.001

Botchey, F. E., Qin, Z., & Hughes-Lartey, K. (2020). Mobile money fraud prediction—A cross-case analysis on the efficiency of support vector machines, gradient boosted decision trees, and Naïve Bayes algorithms. *Information, 11*(8), 383. doi:10.3390/info11080383

Boucher, J., Fisch, E., Levi, S., Nguyen, B., Maalouf, K., & Perry, J. (2022, February 4). *The Federal Reserve Weighs Risks and Benefits of a US Central Bank Digital Currency.* https://www.skadden.com/insights/publications/2022/02/the-federal-reserve-weighs-risks

Brauers, W. K. M., Ginevičius, R., & Podviezko, A. (2014). Development of a methodology of evaluation of financial stability of commercial banks. *Panoeconomicus, 61*(3), 349–367. doi:10.2298/PAN1403349B

Braun, B., & Deeg, R. (2020). Strong firms, weak banks: The financial consequences of Germany's export-led growth model. *German Politics, 29*(3), 358–381. doi:10.1080/09644008.2019.1701657

Bridges, B. (2021). Africa Investment Report 2021. file:///C:/Users/HP/Downloads/03012022_AfricaInvestmentReport.pdf, p. 7

Briola, A., Vidal-tomás, D., Wang, Y., & Aste, T. (2022). Anatomy of a Stablecoin ' s failure : The Terra-Luna case. *Finance Research Letters, 103358*(September). doi:10.1016/j.frl.2022.103358

Bromberg, L., Godwin, A., & Ramsay, I. (2017). Fintech sandboxes: Achieving a balance between regulation and innovation. *Journal of Banking and Finance Law and Practice, 28*(4), 314–336.

Brown, N. (2021). Over 4,000 Cyber Fraud Cases Currently Under Investigation. *Joy Online.* https://www.myjoyonline.com/over-4000-cyber-fraud-cases-currently-under-investigation/?param=

Brown, C. O., & Dinç, I. S. (2011). Too many to fail? Evidence of regulatory forbearance when the banking sector is weak. *Review of Financial Studies, 24*(4), 1378–1405. doi:10.1093/rfs/hhp039

Brown, M., Trautmann, S. T., & Vlahu, R. (2017). Understanding bank-run contagion. *Management Science, 63*(7), 2272–2282. doi:10.1287/mnsc.2015.2416

Brownsword, R. (2019). Regulatory fitness: Fintech, funny money, and smart contracts. *European Business Organization Law Review, 20*(1), 5–27. doi:10.100740804-019-00134-2

Brunnermeier, M., Crockett, A., Goodhart, C. A., Persaud, A., & Shin, H. S. (2009). *The fundamental principles of financial regulation* (Vol. 11). ICMB, Internat. Center for Monetary and Banking Studies.

Buchak, G., Matvos, G., Piskorski, T., & Seru, A. (2018). Fintech, regulatory arbitrage, and the rise of shadow banks. *Journal of Financial Economics, 130*(3), 453–483. doi:10.1016/j.jfineco.2018.03.011

Buckley, R. P., Arner, D., Veidt, R., & Zetzsche, D. (2020). Building FinTech ecosystems: Regulatory sandboxes, innovation hubs and beyond. *Wash. UJL & Pol'y*, *61*, 55.

Buenaventura, L. (2016, September 11). There's a $500 Billion Remittance Market, and Bitcoin Startups Want In on It. *Quartz*. https://qz.com/775159/theres-a-500-billion-remittance-market-and-bitcoin-startupswant-in-on-it/

Bull, G., Cook, W., Kerse, M., & Staschen, S. (2021, May 13). *Is Financial Inclusion a Reason to Push Central Bank Digital Currencies?* https://www.cgap.org/blog/financial-inclusion-reason-push-central-bank-digital-currencies

Bunduchi, R. (2005). Business relationships in internet-based electronic markets: The role of goodwill trust and transaction costs. *Information Systems Journal*, *15*(4), 321–341. doi:10.1111/j.1365-2575.2005.00199.x

Burjorjee, D. M., & Scola, B. (2015) *A Market Systems Approach to Financial Inclusion Guidelines for Funders*. CGAP. www.cgap.org

Business Insider Africa. (2022). Why Africa is the fintech market of tomorrow. *Business Insider Africa*. https://africa.businessinsider.com/local/markets/why-africa-is-the-fintech-market-of-tomorrow/4v98418

Cabane, L., & Lodge, M. (2022). Banking Regulation in and for Crisis. In Oxford Research Encyclopedia of Politics. doi:10.1093/acrefore/9780190228637.013.1599

Calomiris, C. W. (2007). Bank failures in theory and history: the Great Depression and other" contagious" events. *NBER Working Paper No 13597.*

Campbell, J. (2020, November 18). Financing Boko Haram. *Council On Foreign Relations. Blog*. https://www.cfr.org/blog/financing-boko-haram

Cao, X., Yu, L., Liu, Z., Gong, M., & Adeel, L. (2018). Understanding mobile payment users' continuance intention: A trust transfer perspective. *Internet Research*, *28*(2), 456–476. doi:10.1108/IntR-11-2016-0359

Carayon, P. (1993). *'Effect of electronic performance monitoring on job design and worker stress: Review of the literature and conceptual model', Human Factors*. SAGE PublicationsSage CA. doi:10.1177/001872089303500301

Carmona, A. F., Lombardo, A. G., Pastor, R.R., Quirós, C.T., García, J.V., Muñoz, D.R., Martín, L.C. (2019). Competition issues in the Area of Financial Technology (FinTech). *Policy Department for Economic, Scientific and Quality of Life Policies Directorate-General for Internal Policies, European Parliament.*

Carmona, P., Climent, F., & Momparler, A. (2019). Predicting failure in the US banking sector: An extreme gradient boosting approach. *International Review of Economics & Finance*, *61*, 304–323. doi:10.1016/j.iref.2018.03.008

Caruana, J. (2016) 'Financial inclusion and the fintech revolution: implications for supervision and oversight', in M. Gamser (eds) *Third GPFI-FSI Conference on Standard-Setting Bodies and Innovative Financial Inclusion: New Frontiers in the Supervision and Oversight of Digital Financial Services.*

Cassim, R. (2020). Challenges facing fintechs and opportunities to respond. *South African Reserve Bank, World Fintech Festival.*

Catalano, A. S., Lyons-White, J., Mills, M. M., & Knight, A. T. (2019). Learning from published project failures in conservation. *Biological Conservation, 238*(September), 108223. doi:10.1016/j.biocon.2019.108223

CBN. (2022). *Unavailability of eNaira services- Central Bank of Nigeria(CBN).* Twitter. https://twitter.com/cenbank/status/1570316506562437120

Cebula, R. J., Koch, J. V., & Fenili, R. N. (2011). The bank failure rate, economic conditions and banking statutes in the US, 1970–2009. *Atlantic Economic Journal, 39*(1), 39–46. doi:10.100711293-010-9258-7

Central Bank of Kenya. (2022). *Discussion Paper on Central Bank Digital Currency.* https://www.centralbank.go.ke/uploads/discussion_papers/CentralBankDigitalCurrency.pdf

Čerešník, M. (2013). Self-regulation of adolescents: Gender specifications. *Procedia: Social and Behavioral Sciences, 106*, 2365–2374. doi:10.1016/j.sbspro.2013.12.271

Chandra, S., Lowry, P. B., Rouibah, K., & Shanab, E. A. (2010). *Evaluating the Role of Trust in Consumer Adoption of Mobile Payment Systems.* AIS eLibrary. https://aisel.aisnet.org/cais/vol27/iss1/29

Chan, T. K., Cheung, C. M., & Lee, Z. W. (2017). The state of online impulse-buying research: A literature analysis. *Information & Management, 54*(2), 204–217. doi:10.1016/j.im.2016.06.001

Charaia, V., Chochia, A., & Lashkhi, M. (2021). Promoting fintech financing for SME in S. Caucasian and baltic states, during the COVID-19 global pandemic. *Business, Management, and Economics Engineering, 19*(2), 358–372. doi:10.3846/bmee.2021.14755

Chava, S., & Purnanandam, A. (2011). The effect of banking crisis on bank-dependent borrowers. *Journal of Financial Economics, 99*(1), 116–135. doi:10.1016/j.jfineco.2010.08.006

Chaves, S. M. (2019). *Industry Study of Electronic Money.* Retrieved From.

Chen, C., & Yao, J. (2018). What drives impulse buying behaviors in a mobile auction? The perspective of the Stimulus-Organism-Response model. *Telematics and Informatics, 35*(5), 1249–1262. doi:10.1016/j.tele.2018.02.007

Cheng, P. (2022). Decoding the rise of Central Bank Digital Currency in China: Designs, problems, and prospects. *Journal of Banking Regulation, 13*(7). doi:10.105741261-022-00193-5

Chen, H., & Siklos, P. L. (2022). Central bank digital currency : A review and some. *Journal of Financial Stability*, *60*(February), 100985. doi:10.1016/j.jfs.2022.100985

Chennells, L., & Wingfield, V. (2015). Bank failure and bail-in: an introduction. *Bank of England Quarterly Bulletin*, Q3.

Chen, P.-C., & Hung, S.-W. (2016). An actor-network perspective on evaluating the R&D linking efficiency of innovation ecosystems. *Technological Forecasting and Social Change*, *112*, 303–312. doi:10.1016/j.techfore.2016.09.016

Chen, T. H., Chou, H. H., Chang, Y., & Fang, H. (2015). The effect of excess lending on bank liquidity: Evidence from China. *International Review of Economics & Finance*, *36*, 54–68. doi:10.1016/j.iref.2014.11.007

Chen, W. K., Chen, C. W., & Lin, Y. C. (2020). Understanding the influence of impulse buying toward consumers' post-purchase dissonance and return intention: An empirical investigation of apparel websites. *Journal of Ambient Intelligence and Humanized Computing*, (March). doi:10.100712652-020-02333-z

Chiaramonte, L., Liu, H., Poli, F., & Zhou, M. (2016). How accurately can Z-score predict bank failure? *Financial markets, institutions & instruments, 25*(5), 333-360.

Chin, W. W. (1998). The partial least squares approach to structural equation modeling. *Modern Methods for Business Research*, *295*(2), 295–336.

Chiu, J., Davoodalhosseini, M., Jiang, J., & Yu, Z. (2019). *Bank Market Power and Central Bank Digital Currency: Theory and Quantitative Assessment.* Bank of Canada Staff Working Paper 2019-20.

Choi, K. J., Henry, R., Lehar, A., Reardon, J., & Safavi-Naini, R. (2021). A Proposal for a Canadian CBDC. SSRN *Electronic Journal*. doi:10.2139/ssrn.3786426

Cihak, M. M., & Poghosyan, M. T. (2009). *Distress in European Banks: An Analysis Basedon a New Dataset*. International Monetary Fund.

Cochran, W. G. (1963). *Sampling Techniques* (2nd ed.). John Wiley & Sons.

Cœuré, B., & Cunliffe, J.. (2020). *Central bank digital currencies: Foundational principles and core features*. https://www.bis.org/publ/othp33.pdf

Colander, D., Goldberg, M., Haas, A., Juselius, K., Kirman, A., Lux, T., & Sloth, B. (2009). The financial crisis and the systemic failure of the economics profession. *Critical Review*, *21*(2-3), 249–267. doi:10.1080/08913810902934109

Collier, P. (2007). *The Bottom Billion: Why the Poorest Countries Are Failing and What Can Be Done About It*. Oxford University Press.

Committee on Payment and & Settlement Systems. (2004). *Survey of developments in electronic money and internet and mobile payments*. BIS. https://www.bis.org/cpmi/publ/d62.pdf

Cooke, J. B., Koch, C., & Murphy, A. (2015). Liquidity mismatch helps predict bank failure and distress. *Economics Letters, 10*(6), 1–4.

Cooper, R. G., Edgett, S. J., & Kleinschmidt, E. J. (2004). Benchmarking NPD Best Practices. *Research Technology Management, 47*(1), 31–43. doi:10.1080/08956308.2004.11671606

Corbett, J. M. (1987). A psychological study of advanced manufacturing technology: The concept of coupling. *Behaviour & Information Technology, 6*(4), 441–453. doi:10.1080/01449298708901855

Coulter, K.-A. (2022). 'Stop Creating Private Money!': Should the Bank of England Introduce a Central Bank Digital Currency to Compete with Cryptocurrency? A Review of the UK Bank of England's Proposed Retail CBDC. SSRN *Electronic Journal*. doi:10.2139/ssrn.4078059

Covolo, V. (2019). *The EU Response to Criminal Misuse of Cryptocurrencies: The Young, Already Outdated 5th Anti-Money Laundering Directive*. Social Science Research Network. doi:. doi:10.2139/ssrn.3503535

Creamer, E. G., & Ghoston, M. (2012). *Using a Mixed Methods Content Analysis to Analyze Mission Statements From Colleges of Engineering*. Sage. doi:10.1177/1558689812458976

CSIS. (2016). *Militancy and the Arc of Instability: Violent Extremism in the Sahel*. CSIS. http://csis-website-prod.s3.amazonaws.com/s3fs-public/publication/160922_Sanderson_MilitancyArcInstabilitySahel_Web.pdf

Cunha, P. R., Melo, P., & Sebastião, H. (2021). From Bitcoin to Central Bank Digital Currencies : Making Sense of the Digital Money Revolution. *Future Internet, 13*(165), 1–19. doi:10.3390/fi13070165

d'Avernas, A., Maurin, V., & Vandeweyer, Q. (2022). *Can Stablecoins be Stable?* University of Chicago, Becker Friedman Institute for Economics Working Paper, (2022-131).

Daley, J., Matthews, K., & Whitfield, K. (2008). Too-big-to-fail: Bank failure and banking policy in Jamaica. *Journal of International Financial Markets, Institutions and Money, 18*(3), 290–303. doi:10.1016/j.intfin.2006.12.002

Danneels, E., & Vestal, A. (2020). Normalizing vs. analyzing: Drawing the lessons from failure to enhance firm innovativeness. *Journal of Business Venturing, 35*(1), 105903. doi:10.1016/j.jbusvent.2018.10.001

Davis, J. (2021). Illicit Money: Financing Terrorism in the 21st Century. London: Lynne Rienner.

Davis, F. D. (1989). Perceived usefulness, perceived ease of use, and user acceptance of information technology. *MIS Quarterly: Management Information Systems, 13*(3), 319–339. doi:10.2307/249008

Davoodalhosseini, S. M. (2022). Journal of Economic Dynamics & Control Central bank digital currency and monetary policy. *Journal of Economic Dynamics & Control, 142*, 104150. doi:10.1016/j.jedc.2021.104150

Dawson, A. (2022). Data-driven Consumer Engagement, Virtual Immersive Shopping Experiences, and Blockchain-based Digital Assets in the Retail Metaverse. *Journal of Self-Governance & Management Economics*, *10*(2).

de Bonis, R., & Ferrero, G. (2022). *Technological progress and institutional adaptations: the case of the Central Bank Digital Currency (CBDC)*. Bank of Italy Occasional Paper No. 690. doi:10.2139/ssrn.4109510

De Grauwe, P., & Ji, Y. (2013). Strong governments, weak banks. *CEPS Policy Briefs*, (305).

De Hoyos, R. E., & Sarafidis, V. (2006). Testing for cross-sectional dependence in panel-data models. *The Stata Journal*, *6*(4), 482–496. doi:10.1177/1536867X0600600403

De Meulenaer, S., De Pelsmacker, P., & Dens, N. (2018). Power Distance, Uncertainty Avoidance, and the Effects of Source Credibility on Health Risk Message Compliance. *Health Communication*, *33*(3), 291–298. doi:10.1080/10410236.2016.1266573 PMID:28094542

Demirguc-Kunt, A., & Klapper, L. (2012). Measuring Financial Inclusion: The Global Findex Database. *Policy Research Working Paper 6025*. World Bank: Washington, D.C

Demirguc-Kunt, A., Klapper, L., Singer, D., & Ansar, S. (2022). *The Global Findex Database 2021: Financial Inclusion, Digital Payments, and Resilience in the Age of COVID-19*. World Bank Publications. doi:10.1596/978-1-4648-1897-4

Demirguc-Kunt, A., Klapper, L., Singer, D., Ansar, S., & Hess, J. (2018). *The Global Findex Database 2017: Measuring Financial Inclusion and the Fintech Revolution*. World Bank Group. doi:10.1596/978-1-4648-1259-0

Demirguc-Kunt, A., & Maksimovic, V. (2002). Funding growth in bank-based and market-based financial system: Evidence from firm-level data. *Journal of Financial Economics*, *65*(3), 337–363. doi:10.1016/S0304-405X(02)00145-9

Deng, J. (2022). The crowding-out effect of formal finance on the P2P lending market: An explanation for the failure of China's P2P lending industry. *Finance Research Letters, 45*(May 2021), 102167. https://doi.org/10.1016/j.frl.2021.102167

Dery, K., Hall, R., Wailes, N., & Wiblen, S. (2013). Lost in translation? An actor-network approach to HRIS implementation. *The Journal of Strategic Information Systems*, *22*(3), 225–237. doi:10.1016/j.jsis.2013.03.002

Dhar, V., & Stein, R. M. (2017). Economic and Business Dimensions FinTech Platforms and Strategy. *Communications of the ACM*, *60*(10), 32–35. doi:10.1145/3132726

Dholakia, U. (2000). Temptation and resistance: An integrated model of consumption impulse formation and enactment. *Psychology and Marketing*, *17*(11), 955–982. https://doi.org/10.1002/1520-6793(200011)17:11<955::AID-MAR3>3.0.CO;2-J doi:10.1002/1520-6793(200011)17:11<955::AID-MAR3>3.0.CO;2-J

Didenko, A. N., & Buckley, R. P. (2021). *Central Bank Digital Currencies: A Potential Response to the Financial Inclusion Challenges of the Pacific.* UNSW Law Research Paper No. 21-63. Asian Development Bank Economics Working Paper Series. doi:10.2139/ssrn.3937698

Dijk, O. (2017). Bank run psychology. *Journal of Economic Behavior & Organization, 144*, 87–96. doi:10.1016/j.jebo.2017.08.005

Diniz, E., Birochi, R., & Pozzebon, M. (2012). Triggers and barriers to financial inclusion: The use of ICT-based branchless banking in an Amazon county. *Electronic Commerce Research and Applications, 11*(5), 484–494. doi:10.1016/j.elerap.2011.07.006

Dubey, V. (2019). FinTech innovations in digital banking. [IJERT]. *International Journal of Engineering Research & Technology (Ahmedabad), 8*(10), 597–601.

Easterly, W. (2006). The White Man's Burden: Why the West's Efforts to Aid the Rest Have Done So Much Ill and so Little Good. Penguin Book, NY, NY.

ECCB. (2022). *DCash Service to Resume Next Week.* https://www.eccb-centralbank.org/news/view/dcash-service-to-resume-next-week

Ehrentraud, J., Ocampo, D. G., Garzoni, L., & Piccolo, M. (2020). *Policy responses to fintech: A cross-country overview* [Basel]. Bank for International Settlements, Financial Stability Institute.

Einarsson, T., & Marquis, M. H. (2001). Bank intermediation over the business cycle. *Journal of Money, Credit and Banking, 33*(4), 876–899. doi:10.2307/2673927

Eisenhardt, K. M. (1989). Building: Constructing identities. *Building Theories from Case Study Research, 14*(4), 532–550. doi:10.4324/9781351106573-2

Ekong, U. M., & Ekong, C. N. (2022). Digital currency and financial inclusion in Nigeria: Lessons for development. *Journal of Internet and Digital Economics, 2*(1), 46–67. doi:10.1108/JIDE-11-2021-0018

El Ayeb, S., Hemery, B., Jeanne, F., & Cherrier, E. (2020, December). Community detection for mobile money fraud detection. In *2020 Seventh International Conference on Social Networks Analysis, Management and Security (SNAMS)* (pp. 1-6). IEEE.

Elliot, O. (2019, June 12). *Central bank digital currency:friend or foe of mobile moneyin sub-Saharan Africa?* https://www.fsdafrica.org/news/central-bank-digital-currency-friend-or-foe-of-mobile-money-in-sub-saharan-africa/

Emara, N., & Moheildin, M. (2021). Beyond the digital dividends: Fintech and extreme poverty in the Middle East and Africa. *Proceedings of Middle East Economic Association, 23*(2), 41–73.

Engert, W., & Fung, B. S. C. (2017). *Central Bank Digital Currency: Motivations and Implications.* Bank of Canada Staff Discussion Paper 16.

Englund, P. (1999). The Swedish banking crisis: Roots and consequences. *Oxford Review of Economic Policy*, *15*(3), 80–97. doi:10.1093/oxrep/15.3.80

Entee, E., & Afful-Dadzie, A. (2020). Coming of Age?: Exploring the Role of Dynamic Capabilities in Social Commerce Firms–Evidence From a Ghanaian Enterprise. In R. Boateng. Handbook of Research on Managing Information Systems in Developing Economies (pp. 281-294). IGI Global.

Esoimeme, E. (2021). A Critical Analysis of the Effects of the Central Bank of Nigeria's Digital Currency Named ENaira on Financial Inclusion and AML/CFT Measures. SSRN *Electronic Journal*. doi:10.2139/ssrn.3921396

Estrella, A., Park, S., & Peristiani, S. (2000). Capital ratios as predictors of bank failure. *Economic Policy Review*, *6*(2).

European Banking Authority. (2018). *EBA Report On The Prudential Risks And Opportunities Arising For Institutions From Fintech*. EBA. fundacionmicrofinanzasbbva.org/revistaprogreso/wp-content/up loads/2018/08/pub-Reportonprudentialrisksandopportunitiesari singforinstitutionsfromFinTech.pdf

Europol. (2021). *European Union Terrorism Situation and Trend*. Europol. https://www.europol.europa.eu/activities-services/main-reports/inte rnet-organised-crime-threat-assessment-iocta-2015.

Evans, R. H. (1996). An analysis of criterion variable reliability in conjoint analysis. *Perceptual and Motor Skills*, *84*(3), 988–990. doi:10.2466/pms.1996.82.3.988

Fanta, A., & Makina, D. (2019). The Relationship Between Technology and Financial Inclusion: Cross-Sectional Evidence. In *Extending Financial Inclusion in Africa* (pp. 211–230). Elsevier. doi:10.1016/B978-0-12-814164-9.00010-4

FATF. (2014). *Risk of Terrorist Abuse in Non-Profit Organisations*. FATF. https://www.fatf-gafi.org/media/fatf/documents/reports/Risk-of-terrorist-abuse-in-non-profit-organisations.pdf

FATF. (2015). *Money Laundering Through the Physical Transportation of Cash*. FATF. https://www.fatf-gafi.org/media/fatf/documents/reports/money-laundering-through-transportation-cash.pdf

Feng, Z., Da, H., Xiao, M., Zhao, C., Zuo, Z., & Qi, J. (2022, March). Supply Chain Finance in Blockchain-based Digital Asset Platform. In *The 2022 4th International Conference on Blockchain Technology* (pp. 74-80). 10.1145/3532640.3532650

Ferrari, M., Mehl, A., & Stracca, L. (2022). Central bank digital currency in an open economy. *Journal of Monetary Economics*, *127*, 54–68. doi:10.1016/j.jmoneco.2022.02.001

Ferreira, R. D. S., Lloyd-Braga, T., & Modesto, L. (2016). Could competition always raise the risk of bank failure? (No. 27). Bureau d'Economie Théorique et Appliquée, UDS, Strasbourg.

Ferrigno, G., Del Sarto, N., Cucino, V., & Piccaluga, A. (2022). Connecting organizational learning and open innovation research: An integrative framework and insights from case studies of strategic alliances. *The Learning Organization*, *29*(6), 615–634. doi:10.1108/TLO-03-2021-0030

Field, M. (2021, February 9). Bitcoin value overtakes Russian ruble at $860bn. *The Telegraph*. https://www.telegraph.co.uk/technology/2021/02/09/bitcoin-value-overtakes-russian-ruble-at860bn/

Financial Stability Board. (2017). *Financial stability implications from FinTech: Supervisory and regulatory issues that merit authorities' attention*. FSB. https://www.fsb.org/wp-content/uploads/R270617.pdf

Financial Stability Board. (2017b). *Financial Stability Implications for Fintech: Supervisory and Regulatory Issues that Merit Authorities' Attention*. Financial Stability, Board.

Financial Stability Board. (2019a, February 14). *FinTech and market structure in financial services: Market developments and potential financial stability implications*. FSB. https://www.fsb.org/2019/02/fintech-and-market-structure-in-financial-services-market-developments-and-potential-financial-stability-implications/

Financial Stability Board. (2019b, June 6). *Decentralised financial technologies: Report on financial stability, regulatory and governance implications*. FSB. https://www.fsb.org/2019/06/decentralised-financial-technologies-report-on-financial-stability-regulatory-and-governance-implications/

FinTechNGR. (2020). *Nigeria Fintech Census 2020*. FinTech.https://assets.ey.com/content/dam/ey-sites/ey-com/en_ng/ey-fintech-nigeria-census-final.pdf

Fiordelisi, F., Soana, M. G., & Schwizer, P. (2014). Reputational losses and operational risk in banking. *European Journal of Finance*, *20*(2), 105–124. doi:10.1080/1351847X.2012.684218

Fisher, A. (2015). 'Fintech: The next wave of disruption' *FinanceAsia*, Fraczek, B., & Klimontowicz, M. (2015). Financial literacy and its influence on Young customers' decision factors. *Journal of Innovation Management*, *3*(1), 62–84. doi:10.24840/2183-0606_003.001_0007

Flannery, M. J. (1995). Prudential regulation for banks. In *Financial Stability in a Changing Environment* (pp. 281–328). Palgrave Macmillan. doi:10.1007/978-1-349-13352-9_8

Floridi, L., & Chiriatti, M. (2020). GPT-3: Its Nature, Scope, Limits, and Consequences. *Minds and Machines*, *30*(4), 681–694. doi:10.100711023-020-09548-1

Franceschelli, M. V., Santoro, G., & Candelo, E. (2018). Business model innovation for sustainability: A food start-up case study. *British Food Journal*, *120*(10), 2483–2494. doi:10.1108/BFJ-01-2018-0049

FSB. (2017, May 22). *FinTech Credit: Market Structure, Business Models and Financial Stability Implications*. FSB. https://www.fsb.org/2017/05/fintech-credit-market-structure-business-models-and-financial-stability-implications/

Fu, J. R., Farn, C. K., & Chao, W. P. (2006). Acceptance of Electronic Tax Filing: A Study of Taxpayer Intentions. *Information & Management*, *43*(1), 109–126. doi:10.1016/j.im.2005.04.001

Fungacova, Z., Turk, R., & Weill, L. (2015). *High Liquidity Creation and Bank Failures: Do They Behave Differently?* International Monetary Fund. doi:10.5089/9781475581805.001

Gandal, N., Hamrick, J. T., Moore, T., & Vasek, M. (2021). The rise and fall of cryptocurrency coins and tokens. In Decisions in Economics and Finance, 44(2). Springer International Publishing. doi:10.100710203-021-00329-8

Gatto, A. (2018). Historical Roots of Microcredit and Usury: The Role ofMonti di Pietàin Italy and in the Kingdom of Naples in XV-XX Centuries. *Journal of International Development*, *30*(5), 911–914. doi:10.1002/jid.3386

Gatto, A., Polselli, N., & Bloom, G. (2016). Empowering Gender Equality through Rural Development: Rural Markets and Micro-Finance in Kyrgyzstan. In L. Matteo & M. Pace (Eds.), *L'Europa e la Comunità Internazionale Difronte alle Sfide dello Sviluppo*. Giannini Editore.

Geroni, D. (2021, September 16). *Understanding The Types Of Central Bank Digital Currencies (CBDC)*. https://101blockchains.com/types-of-central-bank-digital-currencies/

Ghani, A., & Lockhart, C. (2008) *Fixing Failed States*. Oxford University Press.

GIABA. (2020a). *Assessment of Counter Terrorist Financing Capacities in West Africa*. GIABA. https://www.giaba.org/media/f/1132_ENG-Assessment%20of%20the%20CFT%20Capacities%20in%20GIABA%20MS.pdf

GIABA. (2020b). *Money Laundering/Terrorist Financing Risks and Opportunities of FinTech Transformation in West Africa*. GIABA. https://www.giaba.org/media/f/1125_ENG%20-%20ML-TF%20RISKS%20AND%20OPPORTUNITIES%20OF%20FINTECH-3.pdf

Gillespie, B. J. (2017). Characteristics of the mobile population. In *Household Mobility in America* (pp. 49–87). Palgrave Macmillan. doi:10.1057/978-1-349-68271-3_3

Goalkeepers. (2018). *The Stories Behind the Data 2018. Bill & Melinda Gates Foundation.* file:///C:/Users/HP/Downloads/report_en.pdf

Gobry, P. E. (2012). Mobile payments: what's taking so long, and who's going to win. *Business Insider*. https://www.businessinsider.com/mobile-payments-whats-ta king-so-long-and-whosgoing-to-win-201

Goeke, L., & Pousttchi, K. (2010). A scenario-based analysis of mobile payment acceptance. *Proceedings of the Ninth International Conference on Mobile Business and Ninth Global Mobility Roundtable*. IEEE. 10.1109/ICMB-GMR.2010.81

Gogo, J. (2020, December 17). *Nigeria is Paxful's Second Biggest P2P Bitcoin Market, Trades Top $566 million in Five Years.* Bitcoin.com. https://news.bitcoin.com/nigeria-is-worlds-second-biggest-p2p-bitcoin-market-trades-top-566-million-in-five-years/

Gogoi, B., & Shillong, I. (2020). Do impulsive buying influence compulsive buying? *Academy of Marketing Studies Journal, 24*, 1–15.

Goldman, Z. K., Maruyama, E., Rosenberg, E., Saravalle, E., & Solomon-Strauss, J. (2017 May). Terrorist Use of Virtual Currencies; Containing the Potential Threat. *CNAS*. https://s3.amazonaws.com/files.cnas.org/documents/CNASReport-TerroristFinancing-Final.pdf?mtime=20170502033819

Gollapudi, S. P. V., Choppella, V., Sanagavarapu, L. M., Chimalakonda, S., & Reddy, Y. R. (2019). Promoting better financial inclusion through web page transformation—A systematic literature review. *Journal of Banking and Financial Technology, 3*(2), 131–147. doi:10.100742786-019-00010-0

Gonzalez, A. (2014). *Exporting Financial Services in Latin America and the Caribbean, Economic Modelling*. Elsevier. doi:10.1016/j.econmod.2014.04.013

Gorton, G., & Winton, A. (2003). Financial intermediation. In *Handbook of the Economics of Finance* (Vol. 1, pp. 431–552). Elsevier.

Greenberg, A. (2014a, April 29). Dark Wallet' Is About to Make Bitcoin Money Laundering Easier Than Ever. *Wired.* https://www.wired.com/2014/04/dark-wallet/

Greenberg, A. (2014b, July 11). Waiting for Dark: Inside Two Anarchists' Quest for Untraceable Money. *Wired.* https://www.wired.com/2014/07/inside-dark-wallet/

Greenberg, A. (2017, January 25). Monero, the Drug Dealer's Cryptocurrency of Choice, Is on Fire, *Wired.* https://www.wired.com/2017/01/monero-drug-dealers-cryptocurrency-choice-fire/

Gross, J., & Schiller, J. (2021). A model for central bank digital currencies: Implications for bank funding and monetary policy. *Available at SSRN 3721965.*

Gross, J., Sedlmeir, J., Babel, M., Bechtel, A., & Schellinger, B. (2021). Designing a central bank digital currency with support for cash-like privacy. *Available at SSRN 3891121.*

Gross, M.B., Hogarth, J.M., & Schmeiser, M.D. (2012). Use of Financial Services by the Unbanked and Underbanked and the Potential for Mobile Financial Services Adoption. *Federal Reserve Bulletin 98*(4). doi:, 0–0. doi:10.17016/bulletin.2012.98-4

GSMA. (2021). *The Mobile Economy 2022.* GSM. https://www.gsma.com/mobileeconomy/wp-content/uploads/2022/02/280222-The-Mobile-Economy-2022.pdf

Gukurume, S., & Mahiya, I. T. (2020). Mobile money and the (un) making of social relations in Chivi, Zimbabwe. *Journal of Southern African Studies, 46*(6), 1203–1217. doi:10.1080/03057070.2020.1823682

Gupta, A., Li, H., & Sharda, R. (2013). Should I send this message? Understanding the impact of interruptions, social hierarchy and perceived task complexity on user performance and perceived workload. *Decision Support Systems*, *55*(1), 135–145. doi:10.1016/j.dss.2012.12.035

Gustman, A. L., Steinmeier, T. L., & Tabatabai, N. (2012). Financial knowledge and financial literacy at the household level. *The American Economic Review*, *102*(3), 309–313. doi:10.1257/aer.102.3.309

Hafez, Y. (2021). *BNM has no immediate plan to issue Central Bank Digital Currency*. https://www.mof.gov.my/portal/en/news/press-citations/bnm-has-no-immediate-plan-to-issue-central-bank-digital-currency-yamani-hafez

Hair, J. F., Black, W. C., Babin, B. J., & Anderson, R. E. (2014). *Multivariate data analysis* (7th ed.). Pearson Education International.

Hair, J. F., Sarstedt, M., Pieper, T. M., & Ringle, C. M. (2012). The Use of Partial Least Squares Structural Equation Modeling in Strategic Management Research : A Review of Past Practices and Recommendations for Future Applications. *Long Range Planning*, *45*(5–6), 320–340. doi:10.1016/j.lrp.2012.09.008

Halim, E. (2021). The Impacts of E-Payment System and Impulsive Buying to Purchase Intention in E-commerce. *2020 International Conference on Information Management and Technology(ICIMTech), May*, 847–852. IEEE. 10.1109/ICIMTech50083.2020.9211154

Harris, J. K., Moreland-Russell, S., Tabak, R. G., Ruhr, L. R., & Maier, R. C. (2014). Communication About Childhood Obesity on Twitter. *American Journal of Public Health*, *104*(7), e62–e69. doi:10.2105/AJPH.2013.301860 PMID:24832138

Hassan, H. E., & Wood, V. R. (2020). Does country culture influence consumers' perceptions toward mobile banking? A comparison between Egypt and the United States. *Telematics and Informatics*, *46*(April 2019), 101312. doi:10.1016/j.tele.2019.101312

Hausman, A. (2000). A multi-method investigation of consumer motivations in impulse buying behavior. *Journal of Consumer Marketing*, *17*(5), 403–426. doi:10.1108/07363760010341045

Havrylchyk, O. (2018). *Regulatory framework for the loan-based crowdfunding platforms*. Ideas. https://ideas.repec.org/p/oec/ecoaaa/1513-en.html

He, D., Leckow, R., Haksar, V., Griffoli, T., Jenkinson, N., Kashima, M., Khiaonarong, T., Rochon, C., & Tourpe, H. (2017). *Fintech and Financial Services:Initial Considerations*. IMF. https://www.imf.org/en/Publications/Staff-Discussion-Notes/Issues/2017/06/16/Fintech-and-Financial-Services-Initial-Considerations-44985

He, D., Leckow, R., Haksar, V., Mancini-Griffoli, T., Jenkinson, N., Kashima, M., Khiaonarong, T., Rochon, C., & Tourpe, H. (2017). *Fintech and Financial Services: Initial Considerations*. International Monetary Fund.

Hellwig, M. (1991). Banking, financial intermediation and corporate finance. *European financial integration, 35*, 63.

Helm, T., Low, A., & Joshua, T. (2019). *The positive impact of technology on the financial services sector in the United Kingdom is unprecedented globally*. UK FinTech— State of the Nation.

Hinson, R., Lensink, R., & Mueller, A. (2019). Transforming agribusiness in developing countries: SDGs and the role of FinTech. *Current Opinion in Environmental Sustainability, 41*, 1–9. doi:10.1016/j.cosust.2019.07.002

Hong Kong Monetary Authority. (2019). *Authorization Of Virtual Banks*. HKMA. https://www.hkma.gov.hk/media/eng/doc/key-functions/banking-stability/guide-authorization/Chapter-9.pdf

Hoornweg, D., & Pope, K. (2016). Population predictions for the world's largest cities in the 21st century Environment and Urbanization. *Sage Journals, 29*(1), 195–216. doi: www.sagepublications.com doi:10.1177/0956247816663557

Horn, M., Oehler, A., & Wendt, S. (2020). FinTech for consumers and retail investors: Opportunities and risks of digital payment and investment services. In Ecological, Societal, and Technological Risks and the Financial Sector (pp. 309–327). Springer.

Howe, J. S., & Morillon, T. G. (2020). Do mergers and acquisitions affect information asymmetry in the banking sector? *Managerial Finance, 46*(12), 1521–1547. doi:10.1108/MF-03-2020-0127

Hsiao, C. (2007). Panel data analysis-advantages and challenges. *Test, 16*(1), 1–22. doi:10.100711749-007-0046-x

Hsiao, M. (2021). Post-purchase behaviour from customer perceived value of mobile payment services. *Journal of Modelling in Management*. doi:10.1108/JM2-11-2020-0293

Huang, R. H., Wang, C. C., & Zhang, O. X. (2022). The development and regulation of robo-advisors in Hong Kong: Empirical and comparative perspectives. *Journal of Corporate Law Studies*, 1–35.

Huang, Y., & Mayer, M. (2022). Digital currencies, monetary sovereignty, and U.S.–China power competition. *Policy and Internet, 14*(March), 324–347. doi:10.1002/poi3.302

Hu, L., & Bentler, P. M. (1999). Cutoff criteria for fit indexes in covariance structure analysis: Conventional criteria versus new alternatives. *Structural Equation Modeling, 6*(1), 1–55. doi:10.1080/10705519909540118

Ighobor, K. (2013, May). *Africa's Youth: a "ticking time bomb" or an opportunity?* Africa Renewal. https://www.un.org/africarenewal/magazine/may-2013/africa%E2%80%99s-youth-%E2%80%9Cticking-time-bomb%E2%80%9D-or-opportunity

Ignatescu, C., & Onufreiciuc, R. (2021). Digital Euro: A (Digital) Symbol of Progress and Integration in Europe. *Logos Universality Mentality Educ. Novelty Sect.: L., 9*(1), 74–82. doi:10.18662/lumenlaw/9.1/58

Im K, M., Pesara, H., Shin Y (2003) Testing for unit roots in heterogeneous panels. *Journal of Econometrics, 115*, 53ñ74.

Iman, N. (2018). Is mobile payment still relevant in the fintech era? *Electronic Commerce Research and Applications*, *30*(May), 72–82. doi:10.1016/j.elerap.2018.05.009

IMF. (2018, September). *The Bali Fintech Agenda*. IMF. https://www.imf.org/en/Publications/Policy-Papers/Issues/2018/10/11/pp101118-bali-fintech-agenda

IMF. (2022). Fast-Moving FinTech Poses Challenge for Regulators. *IMF Blog*. https://blogs.imf.org/2022/04/13/fast-moving-fintech-poses-challenge-for-regulators/

Im, K., Pesaran, M., & Shin, Y. (1997). *Testing for Unit Roots in Heterogeneous Panels. Department of Applied Economics, University of Cambridg Johnston, J. and Dinardo, J. (1997) Econometric Methods*. McGraw-Hill.

International Organization of Securities Commissions. (2017). *IOSCO Research Report on Financial Technologies (Fintech)*. IOSCO. https://www.iosco.org/library/pubdocs/pdf/IOSCOPD554.pdf

Interpol. (2020). *Mobile money and organized crime in Africa*. Interpol. https://enactafrica.org/research/interpol-reports/mobile-money-and-organised-crime-in-africa

Iwamoto, K. (2022, January 2). *Cambodia's digital currency reaches nearly half the population*. https://asia.nikkei.com/Business/Finance/Cambodia-s-digital-currency-reaches-nearly-half-the-population

Jacoby, H. G. (1994). Borrowing constraints and progress through school: Evidence from Peru. *The Review of Economics and Statistics*, *76*(1), 151–160. doi:10.2307/2109833

Jariwala, H. V. (2017). Financial literacy: one step ahead of financial inclusion. *Prestige International Journal of Management and Research, 9/10*(2), 59-65. https://0-searchproquest-com.bibliotecails.tec.mx/docview/2013606469?accountid511643

Jick, T. D. (1979). Mixing Qualitative and Quantitative Methods : Triangulation in Action. *Administrative Science Quarterly*, *24*(4), 602–611. doi:10.2307/2392366

Jinasena, D. N., Spanaki, K., Papadopoulos, T., & Balta, M. E. (2020). Success and Failure Retrospectives of FinTech Projects: A Case Study Approach. *Information Systems Frontiers*. doi:10.100710796-020-10079-4

Jin, T., & Wang, Q. (2019). FinExpert: Domain-specific test generation for fintech systems. *In Proceedings of the 27th ACM Joint Meeting on European Software Engineering Conference and Symposium on the Foundations of Software Engineering*, (pp. 853–862). ACM. 10.1145/3338906.3340441

Johansen, S. T., Selart, M., & Grønhaug, K. (2013). The effects of risk on initial trust formation. *Journal of Applied Social Psychology, 43*(6), 1185–1199. doi:10.1111/jasp.12082

Johnstone, S. (2020). Secondary markets in digital assets: Rethinking regulatory policy in centralized and decentralized environments. *Stan. J. Blockchain L. & Pol'y, 3*, 146.

Kaabachi, S., Ben Mrad, S., & Petrescu, M. (2017). Consumer initial trust toward internet-only banks in France. *International Journal of Bank Marketing, 35*(6), 903–924. doi:10.1108/IJBM-09-2016-0140

Kabaklarli, E., Duran, M. S., & Üçler, Y. T. (2017) The Determinants Of High-Technology Exports: A Panel Data Approach For Selected Oecd Countries. *DIEM : Dubrovnik International Economic Meeting, 3*(1), pp. 888–900.

Kang, J. (2018). Mobile Payment in Fintech Environment: Trends, Security Challenges, and Services. *Human-Centric Computing and Information Sciences, 8*(1), 32. doi:10.118613673-018-0155-4

Kanungo, R. P., & Gupta, S. (2021). Financial inclusion through digitalisation of services for well-being. *Technological Forecasting and Social Change, 167*, 120721. doi:10.1016/j.techfore.2021.120721

Keasey, K., & Veronesi, G. (2008). Lessons from the Northern Rock affair. *Journal of Financial Regulation and Compliance, 16*(1), 8–18. doi:10.1108/13581980810853181

Keister, T., and Sanches, D (2022). Should central banks issue digital currency? *The Review of Economic Studies*. doi:/ rdac017 doi:10.1093/restud

Kempson, E. (2006). *Policy level response to financial exclusion in developed economies: lessons for developing countries*. Paper for Access to Finance: Building Inclusive Financial Systems Conference, World Bank, Washington, D.C.

Kerr, W. R., & Nanda, R. (2015). Financing Innovation. *Annual Review of Financial Economics, 7*(1), 445–462. doi:10.1146/annurev-financial-111914-041825

Khet, K., & Tha, O. (2022). *Mobile money affordances : enabling the way for financial inclusion*. Thirtieth European Conference on Information Systems, Timişoara, Romania.

Kiff, J., Alwazir, J., Davidovic, S., Farias, A., Khan, A., Khiaonarong, T., Malaika, M., Monroe, H., Sugimoto, N., Tourpe, H., & Zhou, P. (2020). A Survey of Research on Retail Central Bank Digital Currency. *IMF Working Papers, 20*(104). doi:10.5089/9781513547787.001

Kilavo, H. J., Mselle, L. I., Rais, R., & Mrutu, S. I. (2022). Reverse Social Engineering to Counter Social Engineering in Mobile Money Theft: A Tanzanian Context. *Journal of Applied Security Research*, 1–13.

Kilponen, J., Jokivuolle, E., Kauko, K., Miettinen, P., & Vanhala, J. (2017). *Central bank digital currency*. www.suomenpankki.fi

Kim, A., & Johnson, K. (2016). Power of consumers using social media: Examining the influences of brand-related user-generated content on Facebook. *Computers in Human Behavior*, *58*, 98–108. doi:10.1016/j.chb.2015.12.047

Kim, D. J. (2012). An investigation of the effect of online consumer trust on expectation, satisfaction, and post-expectation. *Information Systems and e-Business Management*, *10*(2), 219–240. doi:10.100710257-010-0136-2

Kim, D. J., Ferrin, D. L., & Rao, H. R. (2008). A trust-based consumer decision-making model in electronic commerce: The role of trust, perceived risk, and their antecedents. *Decision Support Systems*, *44*(2), 544–564. doi:10.1016/j.dss.2007.07.001

Kitamura, Y. (2022). Can we stabilize the price of a cryptocurrency? Understanding the design of Bitcoin and its potential to compete with Central Bank money. In *Quest for Good Money* (pp. 103–123). Springer. doi:10.1007/978-981-19-5591-4_6

Klein, M., Gross, J., & Sandner, P. (2020). *The digital euro and the role of DLT for central bank digital currencies.* Frankfurt School of Finance & Management GmbH, FSBC Working Paper.

Klein, G., Shtudiner, Z., & Zwilling, M. (2021). Why do peer-to-peer (P2P) lending platforms fail? The gap between P2P lenders' preferences and the platforms' intentions. *Electronic Commerce Research, 0123456789.* doi:10.100710660-021-09489-6

Kling, R. (1996) Computerization and Controversy. Elsevier. doi:10.1016/b978-0-12-415040-9.x5081-7

Knight, E., & Wójcik, D. (2020). FinTech, economy and space: Introduction to the special issue. *Environ. Plan. A Econ. Space*, *52*, 1490–1497.

Koenig-Lewis, N., Marquet, M., Palmer, A., & Zhao, A. (2015). Enjoyment and social influence: Predicting mobile payment adoption. *Service Industries Journal*, *35*(10), 537–554. doi:10.1080/02642069.2015.1043278

Köhler, M. (2015). Which banks are more risky? The impact of business models on bank stability. *Journal of Financial Stability*, *16*, 195–212. doi:10.1016/j.jfs.2014.02.005

Koomson, I., Bukari, C., & Villano, R. A. (2021). Mobile money adoption and response to idiosyncratic shocks: Empirics from five selected countries in sub-Saharan Africa. *Technological Forecasting and Social Change, 167*(July 2020), 120728. doi:10.1016/j.techfore.2021.120728

Kosse, A., & Mattei, I. (2022). *Bank for International Settlements (BIS) Papers No 125 Gaining momentum-Results of the 2021 BIS survey on central bank digital currencies.* https://www.bis.org/publ/bppdf/bispap125.pdf

KPMG. (2022). *Pulse of Fintech H2'21.* https://assets.kpmg/content/dam/kpmg/xx/pdf/2022/02/pulse-of-fintech-h2-21.pdf

Krishna Priya, P., & Anusha, K. (2019). Fintech Issues and Challenges in India. *International Journal of Recent Technology and Engineering (IJRTE). ISSN*, *8*(3), 2277–3878.

Krueger, A. (2007). *What Makes a Terrorist: Economics and the Roots of Terrorism*. Princeton University Press.

Laboure, M., Heinz, G., Singh, S., Stefan, K., Markus, H., & Bank, D. (2021). Cryptocurrencies and CBDC. *The Route Ahead.*, *12*(5), 663–676. doi:10.1111/1758-5899.13017

Ladegaard, I. (2019). Crime displacement in digital drug markets. *The International Journal on Drug Policy*, *63*, 113–121. doi:10.1016/j.drugpo.2018.09.013 PMID:30572247

Lal, T. (2019). Measuring impact of financial inclusion on rural development through cooperatives. *International Journal of Social Economics*, *46*(3), 352–376. doi:10.1108/IJSE-02-2018-0057

Landerer, L. M. (2022). The Anti-Money-Laundering Directive and the ECJ's Jurisdiction on Data Retention: A Flawed Comparison? *Eucrim-the European Criminal Law Associations'. Forum*, *01*, 67–72.

Landis, J. R., & Koch, G. G. (1977). The Measurement of Observer Agreement for Categorical Data. *Biometrics*, *33*(1), 159–174. doi:10.2307/2529310 PMID:843571

Lapina, E. N., Orazaliev, A. A., Kalnaya, A. Y., Kiseleva, I. N., & Oseledko, I. V. (2021). Increasing the availability of financial services as a factor in ensuring socio-economic stability in the region. *Lecture Notes in Networks and Systems*, *206*, 715–724. doi:10.1007/978-3-030-72110-7_78

Larasetiati, M., & Ali, H. (2019). Model of consumer trust: Analysis of perceived usefulness and toward repurchase intention in online travel agent. *Journal of Economics and Finance*, *3*(8), 350–357. doi:10.21276jef.2019.3.8.5

Latour, B. (1987). Science In Action. In Harvard Univerty Press.

Latour, B. (2005). Reassembling the Social: An Introduction to Actor-Network Theory. In Oxford University Press.

Lazonick, W. (2009) What is New, and Permanent, about the" New Economy"? Sustainable Prosperity in the New Economy? Business Organization and High-Tech Employment in the United States. Upjohn Institute for Employment Research.

Lee, D. K. C., Yan, L., & Wang, Y. (2021). A global perspective on central bank digital currency. *China Economic Journal*, *14*(1), 52–66. Advance online publication. doi:10.1080/17538963.2020.1870279

Lee, I., & Shin, Y. J. (2018). Fintech: Ecosystem, business models, investment decisions, and challenges. *Business Horizons*, *61*(1), 35–46. doi:10.1016/j.bushor.2017.09.003

Lee, T., Park, C., & Jun, J. (2014). Two faces of mobile shopping: Self-efficacy and im_pulsivity. *International Journal of E-Business Research*, *10*(1), 15–32. doi:10.4018/ijebr.2014010102

Lee, Y. K. (2021). Impacts of digital technostress and digital technology self-efficacy on fintech usage intention of Chinese gen Z consumers. *Sustainability (Switzerland)*, *13*(9). Advance online publication. doi:10.3390u13095077

Lee, Y., Son, B., Jang, H., Byun, J., Yoon, T., & Lee, J. (2021). Atomic cross-chain settlement model for central banks digital currency. *Information Sciences*, *580*, 838–856. doi:10.1016/j.ins.2021.09.040

Leonard, L. N., & Jones, K. (2021). Trust in C2C electronic commerce: Ten years later. *Journal of Computer Information Systems*, *61*(3), 240–246. doi:10.1080/08874417.2019.1598829

Leong, K. (2018). FinTech (Financial Technology): What is it and how to use technologies to create business value in fintech way? *International Journal of Innovation, Management and Technology*, *9*, 74–78. doi:10.18178/ijimt.2018.9.2.791

Levine, R. (2002). Bank-based or market-based financial systems: Which is better? *Journal of Financial Intermediation*, *11*(4), 398–428. doi:10.1006/jfin.2002.0341

LexisNexis. (2020). *True Cost of Financial Crime Compliance Study: Global Report.* Lexis Nexis. https://risk.lexisnexis.com/insights-resources/research/true-cost-of-financial-crime-compliance-study-global-report#:~:text=This%20is%20not%20without%20cost,%24180.9%20billion%20the%20previous%20year

Liao, G. Y., & Caramichael, J. (2022). *Stablecoins: Growth Potential and Impact on Banking.* Academic Press.

Liébana-Cabanillas, F., Molinillo, S., & Ruiz-Montañez, M. (2019). To use or not to use, that is the question : Analysis of the determining factors for using NFC mobile payment systems in public transportation. *Technological Forecasting and Social Change*, *139*, 266–276. doi:10.1016/j.techfore.2018.11.012

Liftoff. (2021). *Mobile Finance Apps Report: Banking on the Future of Fintech.* https://content.liftoff.io/hubfs/aaa_Reports/2021/2021%20Finance%20Report/Finance%20Report%202021%20-%20EN.pdf?_ga=2.110491333.1392937753.1618499511-196886098.1618499511

Li, J., Wang, J., Wangh, S., & Zhou, Y. (2019). Mobile Payment with Alipay: An Application of Extended Technology Acceptance Model. *IEEE Access: Practical Innovations, Open Solutions*, *7*, 50380–50387. doi:10.1109/ACCESS.2019.2902905

Lin, H. J., Chen, C. C., & Chiu, Y., & Lin, T. Y. (2021). How financial technology (fintech) can improve the business performance of securities firms by using the dynamic data envelopment analysis modified model. *Managerial and Decision Economics*, (April), 1–20. doi:10.1002/mde.3443

Lin, J., Wang, B., Wang, N., & Lu, Y. (2014). Understanding the evolution of consumer trust in mobile commerce: A longitudinal study. *Information Technology Management*, *15*(1), 37–49. doi:10.100710799-013-0172-y

Linneberg, M. S., & Korsgaard, S. (2019). Coding qualitative data : A synthesis guiding the novice data. *Qualitative Research Journal*, *19*(3), 259–270. doi:10.1108/QRJ-12-2018-0012

Lin, P., & Lin, Z. (2013). Buying impulse triggered by digital media. *Service Industries Journal*, *33*(9–10), 892–908. doi:10.1080/02642069.2013.719887

Lin, S., & Lo, L. Y. (2016). Evoking online consumer impulse buying through virtual layout schemes. *Behaviour & Information Technology*, *35*(1), 38–56. doi:10.1080/0144929X.2015.1056546

Liu, W. M., & Ngo, P. T. (2014). Elections, political competition and bank failure. *Journal of Financial Economics*, *112*(2), 251–268. doi:10.1016/j.jfineco.2014.02.005

Liu, X., Wang, Q., Wu, G., & Zhang, C. (2022). Determinants of individuals' intentions to use central bank digital currency: Evidence from China. *Technology Analysis and Strategic Management*, 1–15. doi:10.1080/09537325.2022.2131517

Liu, Y., Li, H., & Hu, F. (2013). Website attributes in urging online impulse purchase: An empirical investigation on consumer perceptions. *Decision Support Systems*, *55*(3), 829–837. doi:10.1016/j.dss.2013.04.001

Li, Z., Zhang, J., Yao, X., & Kou, G. (2021). How to identify early defaults in online lending: A cost-sensitive multi-layer learning framework. *Knowledge-Based Systems*, *221*, 106963. doi:10.1016/j.knosys.2021.106963

Löber, K., & Houben, A. (2018). *Committee on Payments and Market Infrastructures Markets Committee Central bank digital currencies*. https://www.bis.org/cpmi/publ/d174.pdf

Lorenz, E., & Pommet, S. (2021). Mobile money, inclusive finance and enterprise innovativeness: An analysis of East African nations. *Industry and Innovation*, *28*(2), 136–159. doi:10.1080/13662716.2020.1774867

Lskavyan, V. (2020). Banking crisis and bank supervisory accountability. *Journal of Economics and Business*, *107*, 105863. doi:10.1016/j.jeconbus.2019.105863

Luo, S., Sun, Y., Yang, F., & Zhou, G. (2022). Does fintech innovation promote enterprise transformation? Evidence from China. *Technology in Society*, *68*, 101821. doi:10.1016/j.techsoc.2021.101821

Lutfi, A., Al-Okaily, M., Alshirah, M. H., Alshira'h, A. F., Abutaber, T. A., & Almarashdah, M. A. (2021). Digital financial inclusion sustainability in Jordanian context. *Sustainability*, *13*(11), 6312. doi:10.3390u13116312

Luther, W. J. (2016). Bitcoin and the Future of Digital Payments. *The Independent Review, 20*, 397–440.

Luu, H. N., Doan, T. N., & Anh, P. T. H. (2021). Managerial ability and bank failure. *Applied Economics Letters*, *28*(4), 305–309. doi:10.1080/13504851.2020.1752892

Lwoga, E. T., & Lwoga, N. B. (2017). User acceptance of mobile payment: The effects of user-centric security, system characteristics and gender. *The Electronic Journal on Information Systems in Developing Countries*, *81*(1), 1–24. doi:10.1002/j.1681-4835.2017.tb00595.x

Macheel, T. (2021, June 30). *American Express partners with fintech firms to help customers find mortgages*. CNBC. https://www.cnbc.com/2021/06/30/american-express-is-sending-customers-to-fintech-partners-for-mortgages.html

Madir, J. (2021). *FinTech: Law and Regulation*. Edward Elgar Publishing.

Mahalle, A., Yong, J., & Tao, X. (2021). Regulatory challenges and mitigation for account services offered by FinTech. Proceedings of the 2021 IEEE 24th International Conference on Computer Supported Cooperative Work in Design, 2021. CSCWD. www.scopus.com, doi:10.1109/CSCWD49262.2021.9437631

Malik, N., Aseri, M., Singh, P. V., & Srinivasan, K. (2022). Why Bitcoin Will Fail to Scale? *Management Science*, *68*(10), 7323–7349. doi:10.1287/mnsc.2021.4271

Maniff, J. L. (2020). *Motives Matter : Examining Potential Tension in Central Bank Digital Currency Designs*. Federal Reserve Bank of Kansas City.

Mansilla-Fernández, J. M. (2017). Institutions. *Eur. Econ.*, *3*, 41–50.

Markus, M. L., & Mentzer, K. (2014). Foresight for a responsible future with ICT. Information Systems Frontiers. Kluwer Academic Publishers. doi:10.100710796-013-9479-9

Martin, A. (2019). Mobile money platform surveillance. *Surveillance & Society*, *17*(1/2), 213–222. doi:10.24908s.v17i1/2.12924

Mayer., R, Davis, J., & Schoorman, F. (1995). *An Integrative Model of Organizational Trust. Academy of Management Review, 20*(3), 709–734. http://www.jstor.com/stable/258792 .

Mazzocchini, F. J., & Lucarelli, C. (2022). Success or failure in equity crowdfunding? A systematic literature review and research perspectives. *Management Research Review*. doi:10.1108/MRR-09-2021-0672

Mckinsey Global Institute. (2016). *Digital Finance for All: Powering Inclusive Growth in Emerging Economies. September 2016. MGI-Digital-Finance-For-All-Executive-summary-September2016. Ashx (mckinsey.Com)*. McKinsey & Company.

Meaning, J., Dyson, B., Barker, J., & Clayton, E. (2021). Broadening narrow money: Monetary policy with a central bank digital currency. *International Journal of Central Banking*, *17*(2), 1–42. doi:10.2139srn.3180720

Meyers, Z. (2022, July 7). *Why would anyone use a central bank digital currency?* https://www.cer.eu/sites/default/files/insight_ZM_digcurrency_7.6.22.pdf

Mikhalev, I., Struchkov, I., Kiff, J., Burchardi, K., Gross, J., Song, B., Gourav, R., Song, B., & Roy, G. (2022). *CBDC tracker*. https://cbdctracker.org

Mittal, P., & Kaur, A. (2013). E-Governance - A challenge for India. *International Journal of Advanced Research in Computer Engineering and Technology*, *2*(3).

Mi, X., Tang, M., Liao, H., Shen, W., & Lev, B. (2019). The state-of-the-art survey on integrations and applications of the best worst method in decision making: Why, what, what for, and what's next? *Omega*, *87*, 205–225. doi:10.1016/j.omega.2019.01.009

Moghavvemi, S., Xin, T., Wai, S., & Yen, S. (2021). Drivers and barriers of mobile payment adoption: Malaysian merchants ' perspective. *Journal of Retailing and Consumer Services*, *59*, 102364. doi:10.1016/j.jretconser.2020.102364

Mohammad, D., Francisco, R., & Yu, Z. (2020). *CBDC and Monetary Policy*. https://www.banqueducanada.ca/2020/02/note-analytique-person nel-2020-4/

Mohammad, K. (2020). FinTech in COVID-19 and Beyond: What Factors Are Affecting Customers' Choice of FinTech Applications? *Journal of Open Innovation*, *6*(4), 153. doi:10.3390/joitmc6040153

Moradi, S., Naderi, N., & Delangizan, S. (2020). Analyzing Fintech Startups Development Process in Iran. *Journal of Entrepreneurship Development*, *13*, 121–140.

Morales-Resendiz, R., Ponce, J., Picardo, P., Velasco, A., Chen, B., Sanz, L., Guiborg, G., Segendorff, B., Vasquez, J. L., Arroyo, J., Aguirre, I., Haynes, N., Panton, N., Griffiths, M., Pieterz, C., & Hodge, A. (2021). Implementing a retail CBDC: Lessons learned and key insights. *Latin American Journal of Central Banking*, *2*(1), 100022. doi:10.1016/j.latcb.2021.100022

Morgan, J. (2022). Research in International Business and Finance Systemic stablecoin and the defensive case for Central Bank Digital Currency : A critique of the Bank of England ' s framing. *Research in International Business and Finance*, *62*, 101716. doi:10.1016/j.ribaf.2022.101716

Muganyi, T., Yan, L., Yin, Y., Sun, H., Gong, X., & Taghizadeh-Hesary, F. (2022). Fintech, regtech, and financial development: Evidence from China. *Financial Innovation*, *8*(1), 29. doi:10.118640854-021-00313-6

Museba, T. J., Ranganai, E., & Gianfrate, G. (2021). Customer perception of adoption and use of digital financial services and mobile money services in Uganda. *Journal of Enterprising Communities*, *15*(2), 177–203. doi:10.1108/JEC-07-2020-0127

Nadir, M., Pesme, J., & Popovic, A. (2022, December 1). *Is Central Bank Digital Currency the right tool to expandfinancial inclusion?* https://blogs.worldbank.org/allaboutfinance/central-bank-dig ital-currency-right-tool-expand-financial-inclusion

Najaf, K., Schinckus, C., & Chee Yoong, L. (2020). VaR and market value of Fintech companies: An analysis and evidence from global data. *Managerial Finance*, *47*(7), 915–936. doi:10.1108/MF-04-2020-0169

Nakamura, Y. (2016, August 29). New Digital Currency Spikes As Drug Dealers Get More Secrecy. *Bloomberg*. https://www.bloomberg.com/news/articles/2016-08-29/new-digit al-currency-spikes-after-giving-criminals-more-secrecy

Nance, M. T. (2018). The regime that FATF built: An introduction to the Financial Action Task Force. *Crime, Law, and Social Change*, *69*(2), 109–129. doi:10.100710611-017-9747-6

Ndegwa, R. (2014). *Effect of Mobile Money on Non-Performing Loans of Commercial Banks in Kenya*. University of Nairobi.

Nel, J., & Boshoff, C. (2017). Development of application-based mobile-service trust and online trust transfer: An elaboration likelihood model perspective. *Behaviour & Information Technology*, *36*(8), 809–826. doi:10.1080/0144929X.2017.1296493

Nelson, B. (2021, April 15). *The Benefits and Costs of a Central Bank Digital Currency for Monetary Policy*. https://bpi.com/the-benefits-and-costs-of-a-central-bank-digital-currency-for-monetary-policy/

Nemoto, N., & Koreen, M. (2019) *Digital Innovation Can Improve Financial Access for SMEs*. Japan. https://www.rieti.go.jp/en/projects/t20japan/tf9/pb1.html

nerdwallet. (2022). Quicken Loans Mortgage Review 2022. *NerdWallet*. https://www.nerdwallet.com/reviews/mortgages/quicken-loans-mortgage

Neyland, D., & Simakova, E. (2012). Managing electronic waste: A study of market failure. *New Technology, Work and Employment*, *27*(1), 36–51. doi:10.1111/j.1468-005X.2012.00276.x

Ngo, C. N., & McCann, C. R. Jr. (2019). Rethinking rent seeking for technological change and development. *Journal of Evolutionary Economics*, *29*(2), 721–740. doi:10.100700191-018-0591-3

Nguyen, V. H. T., & Boateng, A. (2013). The impact of excess reserves beyond precautionary levels on bank lending channels in China. *Journal of International Financial Markets, Institutions and Money*, *26*, 358–377. doi:10.1016/j.intfin.2013.07.002

Nicoletti, B. (2017). *The Future of FinTech: Integrating Finance and Technology in Financial Services*. Palgrave Macmillan. doi:10.1007/978-3-319-51415-4

Nier, E. W. (2005). Bank stability and transparency. *Journal of Financial Stability*, *1*(3), 342–354. doi:10.1016/j.jfs.2005.02.007

Nikkel, B. (2020). Fintech forensics: Criminal investigation and digital evidence in financial technologies. *Forensic Science International: Digital Investigation*, *33*, 200908. doi:10.1016/j.fsidi.2020.200908

Nilashi, M., Ahmadi, H., Ahani, A., Ravangard, R., & Ibrahim, O. B. (2016). Determining the Importance of Hospital Information System Adoption Factors Using Fuzzy Analytic Network Process (ANP). *Technological Forecasting and Social Change*, *111*, 244–264. doi:10.1016/j.techfore.2016.07.008

Nitescu, D. C., & Murgu, V. (2019). The Economic Growth Catalyzers at the European Level, in the Context of the 2008Financial Crisis. *Amfiteatru Economic*, *21*(50), 241–257. doi:10.24818/EA/2019/50/241

Noreen, M., Ghazali, Z., & Mia, M. S. (2021). The Impact of Perceived Risk and Trust on Adoption of Mobile Money Services: An Empirical Study in Pakistan. *The Journal of Asian Finance. Economics and Business*, *8*(6), 347–355.

Nováková, R. K., & Vávrová, S. (2015). Self-regulation of behaviour in the context of peer pressure and risk behaviour. *Procedia: Social and Behavioral Sciences*, *171*, 158–165. doi:10.1016/j.sbspro.2015.01.102

Ntaryike, D., & Lukong, P. (2016, August 29). Cattle rustling. *Bloomberg*. www.bloomberg.com/news/articles/2016-08-29/cameroon-closes-down-cattle-market-as-militants-turn-to-rustling

Nuño, G. (2018). Monetary policy implications of central bank-issued digital currency. *Banco de Espana Article*, *15*, 18.

Nusair, K., Jin Yoon, H., Naipaul, S., & Parsa, H. (2010). Effect of price discount frames and levels on consumers' perceptions in low-end service industries. *International Journal of Contemporary Hospitality Management*, *22*(6), 814–835. doi:10.1108/09596111011063106

OECD. (2020). Digital Disruption in Banking and Its Impact on Competition. OECD. http://www.oecd.org/daf/competition/ digital-disruption-in-financial-markets.htm

OECD. (2021). *Strengthening Macroprudential Policies in Emerging Asia: Adapting to Green Goals and Fintech*. OECD. doi:10.1787/6f1ed069-

Oh, E. Y., & Zhang, S. (2022). *Informal economy and central bank digital currency*. doi:10.1111/ecin.13105

Opare, E. A., & Kim, K. (2020). A Compendium of Practices for Central Bank Digital Currencies for Multinational Financial Infrastructures. *IEEE Access: Practical Innovations, Open Solutions*, *8*, 110810–110847. doi:10.1109/ACCESS.2020.3001970

Orji, I. J., Kusi-Sarpong, S., Huang, S., & Vazquez-Brust, D. (2020). Evaluating the factors that influence blockchain adoption in the freight logistics industry. *Transportation Research Part E, Logistics and Transportation Review*, *141*, 102025. doi:10.1016/j.tre.2020.102025

Orlikowski, W., Kim, A., Oborn, E., & Sloan, M. I. T. (2018). Trajectory Dynamics in Innovation : Developing and Transforming a Mobile Money Service Across Time and Place. *Organization Science* .

Osakwe, C. N., Ruiz, B., Amegbe, H., Chinje, N. B., Cheah, J. H., & Ramayah, T. (2020). A multi-country study of bank reputation among customers in Africa: Key antecedents and consequences. *Journal of Retailing and Consumer Services*, *56*(May), 102182. Advance online publication. doi:10.1016/j.jretconser.2020.102182

Osakwe, C. N., & Yusuf, T. O. (2021). CSR: A roadmap towards customer loyalty. *Total Quality Management & Business Excellence*, *32*(13–14), 1424–1440. doi:10.1080/14783363.2020.1730174

Osei-Assibey, E. (2015). What drives behavioral intention of mobile money adoption? The case of ancient susu saving operations in Ghana. *International Journal of Social Economics*, *42*(11), 962–979. doi:10.1108/IJSE-09-2013-0198

Ozili, P. K. (2021). Central Bank Digital Currency in Nigeria: Opportunities and Risks. SSRN *Electronic Journal*. doi:10.2139/ssrn.3917936

Ozili, P. K. (2022). Can Central Bank Digital Currency Increase Financial Inclusion? Arguments for and Against. In Big Data Analytics in the Insurance Market (pp. 241–249). Emerald Publishing Limited. doi:10.1108/978-1-80262-637-720221013

Ozili, P. K. (2022). Central bank digital currency research around the world: a review of literature. *Journal of Money Laundering Control*. doi:10.1108/JMLC-11-2021-0126

Ozili, P. K. (2018). Banking stability determinants in Africa. *International Journal of Managerial Finance*, *14*(4), 462–483. doi:10.1108/IJMF-01-2018-0007

Ozili, P. K. (2018). Impact of digital finance on financial inclusion and stability. *Borsa Istanbul Review*, *18*(4), 329–340. doi:10.1016/j.bir.2017.12.003

Ozili, P. K. (2020). 100 Quotes from the Global Financial Crisis: Lessons for the future. In *Uncertainty and Challenges in Contemporary Economic Behaviour*. Emerald Publishing Limited. doi:10.1108/978-1-80043-095-220201014

Ozturkcan, S., Senel, K., & Ozdinc, M. (2022). Framing the Central Bank Digital Currency (CBDC) revolution. *Technology Analysis and Strategic Management*, *0*(0), 1–18. doi:10.1080/09537325.2022.2099261

Pandya, P., & Pandya, K. (2020). An empirical study of compulsive buying behaviour of consumers. *Alochana Chakra Journal*, *9*(6), 4102–4114.

Papadimitri, P., Pasiouras, F., & Tasiou, M. (2021). Financial leverage and performance: The case of financial technology firms. *Applied Economics*, *53*(44), 5103–5121. doi:10.1080/00036846.2021.1915949

Parboteeah, D., Valacich, J., & Wells, J. D. (2009). The influence of website characteristics on a consumer's urge to buy impulsively. *Information Systems Research*, *20*(1), 60–78. doi:10.1287/isre.1070.0157

Parham, D., Roberts, P., & Sun, H. (2001). Information Technology and Australia's Productivity Surge. *Development and Comp Systems*. https://ideas.repec.org/p/wpa/wuwpdc/0110006.html

Parker, J., & Lehmann, D. (2011). When shelf-based scarcity impacts consumer preferences. *Journal of Retailing*, *87*(2), 142–155. doi:10.1016/j.jretai.2011.02.001

Park, H., & Noh, M. (2012). The influence of innovativeness and price sensitivity on purchase intention of smart wear. *Journal of the Korean Society of Clothing and Textiles*, *36*(2), 218–230. doi:10.5850/JKSCT.2012.36.2.218

Passacantando, F. (2021). The Digital Euro: Challenges and Opportunities. *The (Near) Future of Central Bank Digital Currencies*, 113.

Passacantando, F. (2021). *Could a digital currency strengthen the euro?* Luiss School of European Political Economy *Policy Brief* 9.

Patil, P., Dwivedi, Y., & Rana, N. (2018). Digital Payments Adoption: An Analysis of Literature. ILNCS-10595. Cham: Springer International Publishing, 61.

Patton, M. (1990). Qualitative Evaluation and Research method. In *Qualitative Research Practice*. Sage. doi:10.4135/9781848608191.d38

Pelagidis, T., & Kostika, E. (2022). Investigating the role of central banks and cryptoassets. *Economia e Politica Industriale, 49*(3), 481–507. doi:10.100740812-022-00227-z

Perros, T., Bisaga, I., Broad, O., Macon, L., Fennell, P. J., & Tomei, J. (2022). Lost learnings: Breaking the silence of failure in the energy and development sector. *Energy Research and Social Science, 92*(December 2021), 102804. doi:10.1016/j.erss.2022.102804

Peterson, I., & Mallesons, W. (2021, September). Banking Regulation in Australia: Overview. *Practical Law*. https://uk.practicallaw.thomsonreuters.com/w-006-9098?transitionType=Default&contextData=(sc.Default)

Phan, D. H. B., Narayan, P. K., Rahman, R. E., & Hutabarat, A. R. (2019). Do financial technology firms influence bank performance? *Pacific-Basin Finance Journal, 101210*(September). doi:10.1016/j.pacfin.2019.101210

Piron, F. (1991). Defining impulse purchasing. *Advances in Consumer Research. Association for Consumer Research (U. S.), 18*(1), 509–514.

Pizzi, S., Corbo, L., & Caputo, A. (2021). Fintech and SMEs sustainable business models: Reflections and considerations for a circular economy. *Journal of Cleaner Production, 281*, 125217. doi:10.1016/j.jclepro.2020.125217

Pocher, N., & Veneris, A. (2022). Privacy and Transparency in CBDCs: A Regulation-by-Design AML/CFT Scheme. *IEEE eTransactions on Network and Service Management, 19*(2), 1776–1788. doi:10.1109/TNSM.2021.3136984

Ponce, J., Martínez-Jaramillo, S., & Sanz, L. (2020). *Implementing a CBDC: Lessons Learnt and Key Insights Policy Report*. https://www.cemla.org/fintech/docs/2020-Implementing-CBDC.pdf

Popescu, A. (2022). *Cross-Border Central Bank Digital Currencies, Bank Runs and Capital Flows Volatility*. WP/22/83.

PricewaterhouseCoopers. (2017). *Nigeria FinTech Survey 2017*. PWC. https://www.pwc.com/ng/en/pdf/nigeria-fintech-report-2017.pdf

Pruitt, H. (2017). *Predicting bank failure using regulatory accounting data* [Doctoral dissertation, Walden University].

Purwanto, A. (2022). What Is the Role of Customer Behavior for Electronic E-Commerce and Modern Market Visit Intention? [JISMA]. *Journal of Information Systems and Management, 1*(6), 46–57.

PwC. (2021). *PwC CBDC global index*. https://www.pwc.com/gx/en/industries/financial-services/assets/pwc-cbdc-global-index-1st-edition-april-2021.pdf

Racki, J., Patel, P., & DeGroot, D. (2014). Africa 2050: Urbanization. *Global Journal of Emerging Market Economies, 61*(1), 15–34. doi:10.1177/0974910113511191

Ragu-Nathan, T. S., Tarafdar, M., Ragu-Nathan, B. S., & Tu, Q. (2008). The consequences of technostress for end users in organizations: Conceptual development and validation. *Information Systems Research, 19*(4), 417–433. doi:10.1287/isre.1070.0165

Raimi, L., Kah, J. M., & Tariq, M. U. (2022). The Discourse of Blue Economy Definitions, Measurements, and Theories: Implications for Strengthening Academic Research and Industry Practice. In Implications for Entrepreneurship and Enterprise Development in the Blue Economy (pp. 1-17). IGI Global.

Ramos, I., Luna, D., Liébana-cabanillas, F., Sánchez-fernández, J., & Muñoz-leiva, F. (2019). Mobile payment is not all the same : The adoption of mobile payment systems depending on the technology applied. *Technological Forecasting and Social Change, 146*, 931–944. doi:10.1016/j.techfore.2018.09.018

Ranta, V., Aarikka-Stenroos, L., & Väisänen, J. M. (2021). Digital technologies catalyzing business model innovation for circular economy—Multiple case study. *Resources, Conservation and Recycling, 164*(September 2020), 105155. doi:10.1016/j.resconrec.2020.105155

Redman, J. (2016, July 21). Tumbling Bitcoins: A Guide Through the Rinse Cycle. *Bitcoin.com*. https://news.bitcoin.com/tumbling-bitcoins-guide-rinse-cycle/

Reimer, S., & Redhead, M. (2021, May). A New Normal: Countering the Financing of Self-Activating Terrorism in Europe. *RUSI Occasional Chapters.*

Reimer, S., & Redhead, M. (2022, April). Bit by Bit: Impacts of New Technologies on Terrorism Financing Risks. *RUSI Occasional Chapter.*

Reuters. (2017, September 12). Leader of China's $9 billion Ezubao online scam gets life; 26 jailed. *Reuters*. https://www.reuters.com/article/us-china-fraud-idUSKCN1BN0J6

Revels, J., Dewi, T., & Yelena, T. (2010). Understanding consumer intention to use mobile services. [AMJ]. *Australasian Marketing Journal, 18*(2), 74–80. doi:10.1016/j.ausmj.2010.02.002

Rezaei, J. (2015). Best-worst multi-criteria decision-making method. *Omega, 53*, 49–57. doi:10.1016/j.omega.2014.11.009

Rezaei, J. (2016). Best- Worst Multi- Criteria Decision Making Method: Some Properties and a Linear Model. *Omega*, *64*, 126–130. doi:10.1016/j.omega.2015.12.001

Rezaei, J. (2020). A concentration ratio for nonlinear best worst method. *International Journal of Information Technology & Decision Making*, *19*(03), 891–907. doi:10.1142/S0219622020500170

Ridley, N. (2012). *Terrorist Financing: The Failure of Counter Measures*. Edward Elgar.

Rosillo-Díaz, E., Blanco-Encomienda, F. J., & Crespo-Almendros, E. (2020). A cross-cultural analysis of perceived product quality, perceived risk and purchase intention in e-commerce platforms. *Journal of Enterprise Information Management*, *33*(1), 139–160. doi:10.1108/JEIM-06-2019-0150

Sahr, A. (2022). Claims to Sovereignty: MMT as a challenge to money's technical imaginary. In Capital Claims: Power and Global Finance (pp. 88-103). Routledge.

Saldinger, A. (2018). 5 barriers holding back fintech entrepreneurs. *Dervex*. https://www.devex.com/news

Sandner, P., Gross, J., Grale, L., & Schulden, P. (2020). The Digital Programmable Euro, Libra and CBDC: Implications for European Banks. SSRN *Electronic Journal*. doi:10.2139/ssrn.3663142

Sarma, M., & Pais, J. (2008). Financial Inclusion and Development: A Cross Country Analysis. Working Paper: Indian Council for Research in International Economic Relations Tarafdar, M. *et al.* (2011) 'Crossing to the dark side: Examining creators, outcomes, and inhibitors of technostress'. *Communications of the ACM*, *54*(9), 113–120. doi:10.1145/1995376.1995403

Sarmiento, A. (2022). Seven lessons from the e-Peso pilot plan: The possibility of a Central Bank Digital Currency. *Latin American Journal of Central Banking*, *3*(2), 100062. doi:10.1016/j.latcb.2022.100062

Sasongko, D. T., Handayani, P. W., & Satria, R. (2021). Analysis of factors affecting continuance use intention of the electronic money application in Indonesia. *Procedia Computer Science*, *197*, 42–50. doi:10.1016/j.procs.2021.12.116

Schiller, J., & Gross, J. (2021). A model for central bank digital currencies: implications for bank funding and monetary policy. *Beiträge Zur Jahrestagung Des Vereins Für Socialpolitik 2021: Climate Economics*.

Schilling, L., Fernández-Villaverde, J., & Uhlig, H. (2020). *Central Bank Digital Currency: When Price and Bank Stability Collide*. doi:10.3386/w28237

Schueffel, P. (2017). Taming the beast: A scientific definition of fintech. *J. Innov. Manag*, *4*(4), 32–54. doi:10.24840/2183-0606_004.004_0004

Schumpeter, J. (1912). *Theorie der Wirtschaftlichen Entwicklung [Theory of Economic development]*. Duncker und Humblot.

Schwienbacher, A. (2019). Equity crowdfunding: Anything to celebrate? *Venture Capital*, *21*(1), 65–74. doi:10.1080/13691066.2018.1559010

Scott, G. (2021). *Fuzzy Logic. Fintech, Automated Investing*. Investopedia.

Senyo, P. K., & Osabutey, E. L. C. (2020). Unearthing antecedents to financial inclusion through FinTech innovations. *Technovation*, *98*(March), 102155. doi:10.1016/j.technovation.2020.102155

Seo, S., Kim, K., & Jang, J. (2018). Uncertainty avoidance as a moderator for influences on foreign resident dining out behaviors. *International Journal of Contemporary Hospitality Management*, *30*(2), 900–918. doi:10.1108/IJCHM-03-2016-0152

Serbeh, R., Adjei, P. O. W., & Forkuor, D. (2022). Financial inclusion of rural households in the mobile money era: Insights from Ghana. *Development in Practice*, *32*(1), 16–28. doi:10.1080/09614524.2021.1911940

Shen, O., & Yazdanifard, R. (2015). Has mobile payment finally live up to its expectation in replacing cash and credit? *International Journal of Management. Accounting and Economics*, *2*(5), 489–498.

Shen, Y., Hu, W., & Hueng, C. J. (2021). Digital financial inclusion and economic growth: A cross-country study. *Procedia Computer Science*, *187*, 218–223. doi:10.1016/j.procs.2021.04.054

Shiller, R. J. (2013). Capitalism and Financial Innovation. *Financial Analysts Journal*, *69*(1), 21–25. doi:10.2469/faj.v69.n1.4

Shim, Y., & Shin, D. H. (2016). Analyzing China's Fintech Industry from the Perspective of Actor-Network Theory. *Telecommunications Policy*, *40*(2–3), 168–181. doi:10.1016/j.telpol.2015.11.005

Shin, D. H. (2016). Application of actor-network theory to network neutrality in Korea: Socio-ecological understanding of network dynamics. *Telematics and Informatics*, *33*(2), 436–451. doi:10.1016/j.tele.2015.10.002

Shin, H. S. (2009). Reflections on Northern Rock: The bank run that heralded the global financial crisis. *The Journal of Economic Perspectives*, *23*(1), 101–119. doi:10.1257/jep.23.1.101

Shirai, S. (2022, July 12). *Central Bank Digital Currency cast aside as cash reigns king in Japan*. Academic Press.

Siggelkow, N. (2007). Persuasion with case studies. *Academy Of Management Journal*, *50*(1), 20–24. doi:10.5465/amj.2007.24160882

Solberg Söilen, K., & Benhayoun, L. (2022). Household acceptance of central bank digital currency: The role of institutional trust. *International Journal of Bank Marketing*, *40*(1), 172–196. doi:10.1108/IJBM-04-2021-0156

Song, H. G., Chung, N., & Koo, C. (2015). *Impulsive Buying Behavior of Restaurant Products in Social Commerce: A Role of Serendipity and Scarcity Message*. Pacis. https://pacis2015.comp.nus.edu.sg/_proceedings/PACIS_2015_submission_400.pdf

Soudijn, M. R. J. (2019). Using Police Reports to Monitor Money Laundering Developments. Continuity and Change in 12 Years of Dutch Money Laundering Crime Pattern Analyses. [ProQuest Central; Social Science Premium Collection.]. *European Journal on Criminal Policy and Research*, *25*(1), 83–97. doi:10.100710610-018-9379-0

Spiteri Cornish, L. (2020). Why did I buy this? Consumers' post-impulse-consumption experience and its impact on the propensity for future impulse buying behaviour. *Journal of Consumer Behaviour*, *19*(1), 36–46. doi:10.1002/cb.1792

Srite, M., & Karahanna, E. (2006). The role of espoused national cultural values in technology acceptance. *MIS Quarterly: Management Information Systems*, *30*(3), 679–704. doi:10.2307/25148745

Srivastava, S. C., Chandra, S., & Theng, Y. (2010). Evaluating the role of trust in consumer adoption of mobile payment systems: An empirical analysis. *Communications of the Association for Information Systems*, *27*(1), 561–568.

Starnes, S., Kurdyla, M., & Alexander, J. (2016). DeRisking by Banks in Emerging Markets – Effects and Responses for Trade. *IFC EM Compass Note, 24*.

Statista. (2021). *Digital Payments report 2021*. Statista. https://www.statista.com/study/41122/fintech-report-digital-payments/

Sternberg, H., Linan, I., Prockl, G., & Norrman, A. (2021). Tragedy of the facilitated commons: A multiple-case study of failure in systematic horizontal logistics collaboration. *Journal of Supply Chain Management, February 2020*, 30–57. doi:10.1111/jscm.12278

Swiecka, B., Terefenko, P., & Paprotny, D. (2020). Transaction factors' influence on the choice of ´ payment by Polish consumer. *Journal of Retailing and Consumer Services, 58*(102), 264.

Sy, A., Maino, R., Massara, A., Perez-Saiz, H., & Sharma, P. (2019). *FinTech in Sub-Saharan African Countries A Game Changer?* IMF. https://www.imf.org/en/Publications/Departmental-Chapters-Policy-Chapters/Issues/2019/02/13/FinTech-in-Sub-Saharan-African-Countries-A-Game-Changer-46376

Talib, F., Asjad, M., Attri, R., Siddiquee, A.N. (2020). A road map for the implementation of integrated JIT-lean practices in Indian manufacturing industries using the best worst method approach. *J. Ind. Prod. Eng*, 1–17.

Tamirisa, N. T., & Igan, D. O. (2008). Are weak banks leading credit booms? Evidence from emerging Europe. *Comparative Economic Studies*, *50*(4), 599–619. doi:10.1057/ces.2008.35

Tapscott, D., & Tapscott, A. (2016). *Blockchain Revolution*. Penguin.

Tarafdar, M., Gupta, A., & Turel, O. (2015). Introduction to the special issue on "dark side of information technology use. Information Systems Journal. Blackwell Publishing Ltd. doi:10.1111/isj.12076

Tarafdar, M., Pullins, E. B., & Ragu-Nathan, T. S. (2015). Technostress: Negative effect on performance and possible mitigations. *Information Systems Journal, 25*(2), 103–132. doi:10.1111/isj.12042

Tay, L., Tai, H., & Tan, G. (2022). Digital financial inclusion: A gateway to sustainable development. *Heliyon, 8*(6), e09766. doi:10.1016/j.heliyon.2022.e09766 PMID:35785228

Teicher, R. (2018, March 18). *How Uber ghost rides are linked to online money laundering.* The Next Web. https://thenextweb.com/news/uber-ghost-rides-linked-online-money-laundering#:~:text=Laundering%20large%20amounts%20of%20money,operator%20of%20the%20laundering%20scheme

Telci, E. E., Maden, C., & Kantur, D. (2011). The theory of cognitive dissonance: A marketing and management perspective. *Procedia: Social and Behavioral Sciences, 24*, 378–386. doi:10.1016/j.sbspro.2011.09.120

Thakor, A. V., & Boot, A. (Eds.). (2008). *Handbook of financial intermediation and banking.* Elsevier.

The International Association of Insurance Supervisors. (2017). *FinTech Developments in the Insurance Industry.* IAIS. https://www.iaisweb.org/uploads/2022/01/Report_on_FinTech_Developments_in_the_Insurance_Industry.pdf

The World Bank. (2021). *Digital Financial Inclusion.* World Bank. https:/ www.Worldbank.Org/En/Topic/Financialinclusion/Publication/Digital-Financial Inclusion. .

The World Bank. (2022) *World Development Indicators.* DataBank. https://databank.worldbank.org/source/world-development-indicators

Tiron-Tudor, A., Nistor, C. S., êtefĝnescu, C. A., & Zanellato, G. (2019). Encompassing Non-Financial Reporting in A Coercive Framework for Enhancing Social Responsibility: Romanian Listed Companies' Case. *Amfiteatru Economic, 21*(52), 590–606. doi:10.24818/EA/2019/52/590

Tornatzky, L., & Fleischer, M. (1990). *The process of technology innovation.* Lexington Books.

Tressel, M. T., & Verdier, M. T. (2014). *Optimal prudential regulation of banks and the political economy of supervision.* International Monetary Fund. doi:10.5089/9781498338554.001

Tronnier, F., Harborth, D., & Hamm, P. (2022). Investigating privacy concerns and trust in the digital Euro in Germany. *Electronic Commerce Research and Applications, 53*(October 2021). doi:10.1016/j.elerap.2022.101158

Tsagkarakis, M. P., Doumpos, M., & Pasiouras, F. (2021). Capital shortfall: A multicriteria decision support system for the identification of weak banks. *Decision Support Systems*, *145*, 113526. doi:10.1016/j.dss.2021.113526

Tsai, C. H., & Peng, K. J. (2017). The FinTech revolution and financial regulation: The case of online supply-chain financing. *Asian J. Law Soc.*, *4*(1), 109–132. doi:10.1017/als.2016.65

Turel, O., Serenko, A., & Giles, P. (2011). 'Integrating technology addiction and use: An empirical investigation of online auction users', MIS Quarterly: Management. *Information Systems*, *35*(4), 1043–1061. doi:10.2307/41409972

Um, T., Chung, N., & Stienmetz, J. (2022). Factors affecting consumers' impulsive buying behavior in tourism Mobile commerce using SEM and fsQCA. *Journal of Vacation Marketing*, 1–9. doi:10.1177/13567667221090991

UNDESA. (2022). *World Population Prospects 2022*. UN. https://www.un.org/development/desa/pd/sites/www.un.org.development.desa.pd/files/wpp2022_summary_of_results.pdf

UNDP. (2017). *Journey to extremism in Africa: drivers, incentives and the tipping point for recruitment*. UN. https://digitallibrary.un.org/record/3841751?ln=en

United Nations. (2006). *Building Inclusive Financial Sectors for Development*. United Nations.

Vaidyanathan, R., & Aggarwal, P. (2003). Who is the fairest of them all? An attributional approach to price fairness perceptions. *Journal of Business Research*, *56*(6), 453–463. doi:10.1016/S0148-2963(01)00231-4

Van Klyton, A., Tavera-Mesıas, J.F. & Castano-Munoz, W. (2021). Innovation resistance and mobile banking in rural Colombia. *Journal of Rural Studies, 81*, pp. 269-280. doi:. jrurstud.2020.10.035. doi:10.1016/j

Verhagen, T., & van Dolen, W. (2011). The influence of online store beliefs on consumer on line impulse buying: A model and empirical application. *Information & Management*, *48*(8), 320–327. doi:10.1016/j.im.2011.08.001

Verkijika, S. F. (2020). An affective response model for understanding the acceptance of mobile payment systems. *Electronic Commerce Research and Applications, 39*, 100905. doi:10.1016/j.elerap.2019.100905

Vermeulen, P. (2004). Managing product innovation in financial services firms. *European Management Journal*, *22*(1), 43–50. doi:10.1016/j.emj.2003.11.012

Wagner, E., Bruggink, D., & Benevelli, A. (2021). Preparing euro payments for the future: A blueprint for a digital euro. *Journal of Payments Strategy & Systems*, *15*(2), 165–187.

Wagner, J. (2019). Access to Finance and Exports – Comparable Evidence for Small and Medium Enterprises from Industry and Services in 25 European Countries. *Open Economies Review*, *30*(4), 739–757. doi:10.100711079-019-09534-w

Wang, Y., Lucey, B. M., Vigne, S. A., & Yarovaya, L. (2022a). Technological Forecasting & Social Change The Effects of Central Bank Digital Currencies News on Financial Markets. *Technological Forecasting and Social Change*, *180*(May), 121715. doi:10.1016/j.techfore.2022.121715

Wang, Z. G., Xu, R., Lin, H., Wang, R. J., & Ren, J. (2019). Energy Performance Contracting, Risk Factors, and Policy Implications: Identification and Analysis of Risks Based on the Best-Worst Network Method. *Energy*, *170*, 1–13. doi:10.1016/j.energy.2018.12.140

Wass, S. (2017, May 10). Regtech could save banks £2.7bn on AML compliance. *Global Trade Review*. https://www.gtreview.com/news/global/regtech-could-save-banks-2-7bn-yearly-on-aml-compliance/

Watanabe, W. (2007). Prudential regulation and the "credit crunch": Evidence from Japan. *Journal of Money, Credit and Banking*, *39*(2-3), 639–665. doi:10.1111/j.0022-2879.2007.00039.x

Weil, M. M., & Rosen, L. D. (Eds.). (1997). *Technostress : coping with technology @work @ home @play*. Wiley. https://lib.ugent.be/en/catalog/rug01:000826059

Wenker, K. (2022). *Retail Central Bank Digital Currencies (CBDC), Disintermediation and Financial Privacy: The Case of the Bahamian Sand Dollar*. Academic Press.

Wieser, C., Bruhn, M., Kinzinger, J., Ruckteschler, C., & Heitmann, S. (2019). *The Impact of Mobile Money on Poor Rural Households: Experimental Evidence from Uganda*. World Bank. doi:10.1596/1813-9450-8913

Wonglimpiyarat, J. (2018). Challenges and dynamics of FinTech crowd funding: An innovation system approach. *J. High Technol. Manag*, *29*(1), 98–108. doi:10.1016/j.hitech.2018.04.009

Wooldridge, J. M. (2010). *Econometric Analysis of Cross Section and Panel Data* (2nd ed.). The MIT Press. https://mitpress.mit.edu/books/econometric-analysis-cross-section-and-panel-data-second-edition.

World Bank. (2015). *Trafficking and Fragility in West Africa*. World Bank. https://documents1.worldbank.org/curated/en/401851468184741492/pdf/98903-WP-AFR-P148420-Box-393185B-PUBLIC-Trafficking-FINAL.pdf

World Bank. (2020). *How Regulators Respond To FinTech: Evaluating the Different Approaches – Sandboxes and Beyond*. World Bank. https://openknowledge.worldbank.org/handle/10986/33698

World Bank. (2021). *The Global Findex Database 2021*. World Bank. https://www.worldbank.org/en/publication/globalfindex/Report

World Economic Forum. (2015). *Why Africa's Young People Should Turn to Entrepreneurship*. WEF. https://www.weforum.org/agenda/2015/06/africas-young-people-entrepreneurship/

World Economic Forum. (2021, November 20). *4 key cybersecurity threats to new central bank digital currencies*. https://www.weforum.org/agenda/2021/11/4-key-threats-central-bank-digital-currencies/

WorldBank. (2020). The Global Covid-19 FinTech Market Rapid Assessment Study. *World Economic Forum*, 28–32. https://www3.weforum.org/docs/WEF_The_Global_Covid19_FinTech_Market_Rapid_Assessment_Study_2020.pdf

Xing, Y. (2014). China's high-tech exports: The myth and reality. *Asian Economic Papers*, *13*(1), 109–123. doi:10.1162/ASEP_a_00256

Xin, H., Techatassanasoontorn, A. A., & Tan, F. B. (2015). Antecedents of consumer trust in mobile payment adoption. *Journal of Computer Information Systems*, *55*(4), 1–10. doi:10.1080/08874417.2015.11645781

Xu, C., Unger, A., Papastamatelou, J., & Raab, G. (2022). The influence of Internet shopping and use of credit cards on gender differences in compulsive buying. *Journal of Internet and Digital Economics*, *2*(1), 27–45. doi:10.1108/JIDE-11-2021-0017

Xu, J. (2022). Developments and Implications of Central Bank Digital Currency: The Case of China e-CNY. *Asian Economic Policy Review*, *17*(2), 235–250. doi:10.1111/aepr.12396

Yaga, D., Mell, P., Roby, N., & Scarfone, K. (2019). *Blockchain technology overview.* arXiv preprint arXiv:1906.11078.

Yang, F., Tang, J., Men, J., & Zheng, X. (2021). Consumer perceived value and impulse buying behavior on mobile commerce : The moderating effect of social influence. *Journal of Retailing and Consumer Services*, *63*, 102683. doi:10.1016/j.jretconser.2021.102683

Yang, J., & Zhou, G. (2022). A study on the influence mechanism of CBDC on monetary policy: An analysis based on e- CNY. *PLoS One*, *17*(7), 1–27. doi:10.1371/journal.pone.0268471 PMID:35802595

Yang, S., Milner, C., Lancheros, S., & Gunessee, S. (2020). Access to Finance, Technology Investments and Exporting Decisions of Indian Services Firms. *Open Economies Review*, *31*(5), 1009–1036. doi:10.100711079-020-09595-2

Yang, Y., Lau, A. K. W., Lee, P. K. C., Yeung, A. C. L., & Cheng, T. C. E. (2018). Efficacy of China's Strategic Environmental Management in its Institutional Environment. *International Journal of Operations & Production Management*, *39*(1), 138–163. doi:10.1108/IJOPM-11-2017-0695

Yan, T. C., Schulte, P., & Chuen, D. L. K. (2018). *InsurTech and FinTech: Banking and insurance enablement. Handbook of Blockchain* (Vol. 1). Digital Finance, and Inclusion.

Yeh, K. H., Deng, R. H., & Kikuchi, H. (2020). Special Issue on FinTech Security and Privacy. *Future Generation Computer Systems*, *112*, 1172–1173. doi:10.1016/j.future.2020.07.057

Yeo, Y. H.. (2014). The assessment of information and communication technology (ICT) policy in South Korea. In *Lecture Notes in Electrical Engineering* (pp. 1241–1249). Springer Verlag. doi:10.1007/978-3-642-41674-3_172

Yip Hing, W., & Nyen Vui, C. (2021). Malaysian consumers' purchase intention towards online seafood shopping amid pandemic: The moderating role of the Covid-19 risk perception. *International Journal of Business. Marketing and Communication*, *1*(3), 2785–8413.

Yli-Huumo, J., Ko, D., Choi, S., Park, S., & Smolander, K. (2016). Where is current research on blockchain technology? A systematic review. *PLoS One*, *11*(10), e0163477. doi:10.1371/journal.pone.0163477 PMID:27695049

Yong, Y., Chin, L., Gan, L., & Wei, T. (2022). Do E - wallets trigger impulse purchases ? An analysis of Malaysian Gen-Y and Gen-Z consumers. *Journal of Marketing Analytics*. doi:10.1057/s41270-022-00164-9

Yoo, B., Donthu, N., & Lenartowicz, T. (2011). Measuring hofstede's five dimensions of cultural values at the individual level: Development and validation of CVSCALE. *Journal of International Consumer Marketing*, *23*(3–4), 193–210. doi:10.1080/08961530.2011.578059

Yoshino, N., & Morgan, P. J. (2016) *Overview of Financial Inclusion, Regulation, and Education, ADBI Working Papers*. 591. Asian Development Bank Institute. https://ideas.repec.org/p/ris/adbiwp/0591.html

Yuan, Q., & Zhang, Y. (2015). Do banks price litigation risk in debt contracting? Evidence from class action lawsuits. *Journal of Business Finance & Accounting*, *42*(9-10), 1310–1340. doi:10.1111/jbfa.12164

Yusof, N. M., Paul, R. J., & Stergioulas, L. K. (2006).Towards a Framework for Health Information Systems Evaluation. *The 39th Hawaii International Conference on System Science*. IEEE. 10.1109/HICSS.2006.491

Zarate, J. C. (2016, June 23). The Next Terrorist Financiers: Stopping Them Before They Start. *Statement to the Financial Services Committee, Task Force to Investigate Terrorism Financing, U.S. House of Representatives*. https://www.govinfo.gov/content/pkg/CHRG-114hhrg25849/html/CHRG-114hhrg25849.htm

Zellweger-Gutknecht, C., Geva, B., & Grünewald, S. N. (2021). Digital Euro, Monetary Objects, and Price Stability: A Legal Analysis. *Journal of Financial Regulation*, *7*(2), 284s–318. doi:10.1093/jfr/fjab009

Zhang, W., Leng, X., & Liu, S. (2020). Research on mobile impulse purchase intention in the perspective of system users during COVID-19. *Personal and Ubiquitous Computing*.

Zhang, T., & Huang, Z. (2022). Blockchain and central bank digital currency. *ICT Express*, *8*(2), 264–270. doi:10.1016/j.icte.2021.09.014

Zheng, X., Men, J., Yang, F., & Gong, X. (2019). Understanding impulse buying in mobile commerce: An investigation into hedonic and utilitarian browsing. *International Journal of Information Management*, *48*, 151–160. doi:10.1016/j.ijinfomgt.2019.02.010

Zheng, Z., Xie, S., Dai, H., Chen, X., & Wang, H. (2017, June). *An overview of blockchain technology: Architecture, consensus, and future trends. In 2017 IEEE international congress on big data (BigData congress)*. IEEE.

Zhou, H., & Gu, Z. (2015). The Effect of Different Price Presentations on Consumer Impulse Buying Behavior: The Role of Anticipated Regret. *American Journal of Industrial and Business Management*, *05*(01), 27–36. doi:10.4236/ajibm.2015.51004

Zook, M. A., & Blankenship, J. (2018). New spaces of disruption? The failures of Bitcoin and the rhetorical power of algorithmic governance. *Geoforum*, *96*(September), 248–255. doi:10.1016/j.geoforum.2018.08.023

About the Contributors

Sheraz Ahmed works as Associate Professor at the School of Business and Management (LBM). He completed his doctoral degree in economics and business administration majoring in financial economics from Hanken School of Economics in 2009. He has served as co-director of master's degree program in strategic finance and analytics since 2011 and a director since 2021. He currently teaches financial theory, valuation, international financial management and empirical research in finance at LBM. He also supervises post-graduate dissertations in finance and analytics. He is an active researcher and publishes within the themes of international finance, asset pricing, corporate governance, and earnings management.

John Agyekum Addae is a Ph.D. researcher in Economic at LUT University, Finland. He hold double master's degree. Mr. Addae hold double master's degree. He received an MSc. in Development Finance from the University of Ghana and an MSc. in Microfinance from the University of Cape Coast. He is a lecturer in Banking and Finance at Ghana Communication Technology University. John has worked in both academia and industry, including serving as a retail banker at Agricultural Development Bank and participating in projects funded by World Bank, USAID, European Union, and the Government of Ghana. Addae is also a Chartered Banker with a keen interest in Financial Technology, Digital Currencies, Digital Economy, Risk Governance, and Development Finance. Among the journals in which his work has appeared are Journal of Hospitality and Tourism Insights, International Journal of Bank Marketing, and The Learning Organization.

Kwame Simpe Ofori is an Assistant Professor of Finance at International University of GrandBassam. He has taught courses in areas of Finance and Telecommunications Engineering. His research interests lie at the intersection of Technology and Business. He is particularly interested in technology adoption, trust in online systems, the dark side of internet technology, etc. His papers have appeared in Information Technology & People, Marketing Intelligence and Planning, International

Journal of Bank Marketing, Total Quality Management and Business Excellence, Society and Business Review.

* * *

Aidatu Abubakari is now pursuing a doctoral degree in the field of marketing and entrepreneurship at the University of Ghana Business School on the Legon campus of the University of Ghana. She attended the University of Ghana and earned a Master of Philosophy degree in marketing during her time there. Her areas of interest in marketing research include services marketing, electronic marketing, and green marketing. In addition to that, she is a lecturer in marketing at the Lakeside University College in Ghana. Her scholarly articles have been published in international journals such as international marketing review, society and business review, and international journal of productivity and performance management.

Kwami Ahiabenu received a BA (Hons) in Psychology from the University of Ghana in 1998, an MBA (e-commerce) from GIMPA in 2003 and Ph.D. from GTUC/CASS with thesis on technological innovations in the banking sector. He worked with non-profits, private, and government sectors. He served as a member for Postal, Communication, and IT policies for Ghana and provided leadership for the Government of Ghana Assisted PC program. He consulted for several organizations, including GIFEC, NCA, Ministry of Communication on Business Processing Outsourcing. He served as Executive Director of AITEC GHANA, Director and founder of Penplusbytes. He is a board member of Media General and Eban Capital. In 2013, he was awarded Reagan Fascel Fellowship to recognize his work in promoting democracy in Africa. He serves as Tech innovations Expert at Knowledge Innovations and as faculty director. His research interest includes Fintech, digital payments and technological innovations in the banking sector.

Faris Alshubiri, PhD, FHEA, is Full Professor of Finance. Prof. Faris has presented and published more than 60 professional papers, most of them included in Scopus and Web of Science. He is punished in many of top journals and big publishers in the world most of them listed in Scopus and WOS with Impact Factor like: Marine policy (Elsevier), Journal of Business Economics and Management (Vilnius Gediminas Technical University), Financial Innovation (Springer), Journal of Climate Change Strategies and Management (Emerald) , The Review of Socio network Strategies (Springer), International Journal of Engineering Business Management (Sage), international journal of sustainability in higher education(Emerald), Marketing intelligence and planning (Emerald). Sage Open (Sage), Economic Change and Restructuring (Springer), The Journal of Economic Asymmetries((Elsevier),

Future Business Journal (Springer) and Technological and Economic Development of Economy (Vilnius Gediminas Technical University), Asia-Pacific Financial Markets (Springer), Journal of Science and Technology Policy Management (Emerald). Prof. Faris has worked to build a strong citation and he has achieved 1154 citations till now; under H-index 17, i10-iindex 28. Faris Alshubiri – Regional Editor - Middle East: International Journal of emergency services, listed in Scopus, WOS and ABS = 2 of Emerald Publisher and Associate Editor -Vilakshan – XIMB Journal of Management (Emerald Publisher) He received three awards as a best faculty and best researcher in the college of commerce and business administration. He received international award for outstanding scientist finance and accounting for the year (2016) from VENUS International Research Awards. Furthermore, He received international award for best researcher for this year (2020) from CEEMAN (The international association for management development in dynamic societies.

Zelda Arku is a Doctoral candidate with the University of Ghana and an Assistant Lecturer at the Department of Management Studies, University of Mines and Technology, Tarkwa-Ghana where she teaches courses on Management Information Systems, Information Security, Enterprise Resource Planning, Research Methods etc. Her research interest centres on cloud computing, electronic business, information systems security, financial technology, electronic learning, and digital financial inclusion.

Rita Boateng is a Licensed Psychologist in Ghana and a Lecturer at the School of Business and Technology (SOBAT) in Lakeside University College, Ghana (LUCG). She completed her PhD in Psychology (Business Psychology) at the University of Ghana, Legon, and she is currently awaiting her PhD oral defense. She has also obtained Master of Philosophy (MPhil) degree in Industrial/Organisational Psychology (Business Psychology) and a Bachelor of Arts degree in Psychology (First class honours) in the same university. She is presently the Acting Dean of School of Business and Technology (SOBAT) at Lakeside University College, Ghana (LUCG) and a member of the Ghana Psychological Association (GPA). She was also a part time lecturer at Regent University of Science and Technology and a full-time lecturer at Jayee University College. She has a passion for teaching and helping students surmount their academic challenges through supervision and guidance. She has taught Human Resource Management courses as well as Psychology courses at various levels. In addition to her experience at L.U.C.G, Regent University and Jayee University as a lecturer, she has been a teaching/research assistant in the Department of Psychology, University of Ghana, Legon for two academic years. Her research interest is in the area of Humanitarian Work Psychology, Occupational Health Psychology, Women and Work, Cross-Cultural Psychology, and Social and

Organizational Behaviour Issues. As a young scholar, she has published few papers and have presented some papers in reputable national conferences. Ms. Boateng has an impeccable skill in communication, interpersonal relations, organizing, and calming hearts. Her mantra is to have a willing and collaborative spirit in the interest of growth and knowledge generation. She is open to collaboration and willing to assist all colleagues yearning to have cross-national research with Africa in mind.

Stephen Boateng is an Assistant Lecturer with the Department of Management Information Systems, University of Ghana and a Lecturer with Methodist University College. He obtained his BA in Political Science and a Master of Philosophy in Management Information Systems from the University of Ghana. He is an IT consultant for Digital Reach Ltd., on e-learning strategy and content development. He teaches courses on design thinking, software engineering, management information systems, cloud computing, business process modelling, systems analysis, and design, among others. His research interests include e-learning, data security, cloud computing, information systems strategy and financial technology.

Samuel Dorhetso graduated from the Kwame Nkrumah University of Science and Technology (KNUST) in 2003 with a BSc. in Mechanical Engineering, and the University of Ghana Business School in 2011 with an executive MBA in Finance. At present, he is a PhD in Business Administration Candidate of the Open University of Malaysia (OUM) studying at the Accra Institute of Technology (AIT) in Ghana. He is also an economics lecturer at AIT. He has a post graduate certificate in Aero-mechanical Engineering from the Nigerian Air Force, and another in Aircraft and Munitions Maintenance from the United States Air Force. He was commissioned into the Ghana Air Force in 2006 as a Flying Officer (First Lieutenant), but voluntarily resigned in 2011 at the rank of a Flight Lieutenant (Captain). He found Basic Skills Ghana NGO in 2010, and he is a volunteer worker for many other NGOs. On the 26th of August, 2022, he received the best paper award at the 11th Sustainable Education And Development Research Conference (SEDRC 2022) held at the KNUST.

Eli Fianu is a Lecturer and Managing Director of Liscious Services Ltd. He has over seven years' experience as a Lecturer. He also has over seven years' experience in the banking industry and over a decade experience in the telecommunications industry. Dr Eli Fianu has a PhD in Information Systems and Technology from the University of KwaZulu-Natal in South Africa and a MSc in Management Information Systems from Coventry University in the United Kingdom. He has a specialty in Educational Technology. His research interests are in the areas of technology adoption, e-learning, social media, learning analytics and business analytics. He has co-authored several published articles in these areas. Dr Eli Fianu is an advocate of blended learning and strives to conduct research that facilitates the development of effective e-learning models.

Guneet Kaur is a certified credit and securities analyst. She is Msc Fintech graduate (with distinction) from the University of Stirling, Scotland, United Kingdom. Prior to Msc, she has also done MBA from GNDU (gold medal) and has worked as a global client and partner business manager with Singapore-based MNC. Currently, she is working as an Editor (Cryptopedia) at Cointelegraph. She has written various conference papers and has authored a book titled 'The Magic of Compounding'. She was the Finalist of the Women in STEM-Lovelace Colloquium that was held in 2019 at the University of Salford, UK, and Royal Bank of Scotland's Hackathon in 2019. Her expertise includes financial modeling, quantitative analysis, academic research, business valuation, business analysis, data visualization, and financial fraud, and anti-money laundering analysis.

Amir Manzoor holds a PhD in Management Sciences. He is a graduate of NED University, Pakistan, Lahore University of Management Sciences (LUMS), Pakistan and Bangor University, United Kingdom. He has more than 20 years of diverse professional and teaching experience working at many renowned national and internal organizations and higher education institutions. His research interests include E-commerce, Strategic Management, Enterprise Resource Planning (ERP), Project Management, Supply Chain Management, Data Analysis, and Technology applications.

AbdulKarim Mutawakil is a detail-oriented marketing professional with over six years of experience in corporate and community project management. He holds a Bachelor of Science degree in marketing and is currently the alumni Relations Assistant at Lakeside University College, Ghana. He is also a Teaching Assistant at the School of Business and Technology, Lakeside University College, Ghana. He has assisted in teaching numerous courses including tourism marketing, principles of marketing and international marketing. He is also the project lead for Zongo Business Incubator. He is passionate about climate change and has participated in Africa Climate Week and the Conference of Youth on Climate Change. His future research interest is in sustainability marketing.

Jean G. Tompihe teaches in the School of Business and Social Sciences at the International University of Grand Bassam, Côte d'Ivoire. He is Fellow at the Institute for Advanced Study, Princeton University. Given the forthcoming game changer, where the African population is expected to double from 1.2 billion to closer to 2.5 billion by 2050, his research agenda focuses on Africa's demographic dividends, whether they could produce an opportunity for enhanced economic growth or constitute a ticking time bomb.

Devesh Vishwakarma is a certified blockchain developer and a BTech Computer Science and Engineering graduate from Kalinga Institute of Industrial Technology, India. He has worked with multiple organizations helping them with content writing and research and was also a part of building an EdTech startup. Currently, he is working as an Associate Engineer at Deloitte USI, developing an internal product that is involved in helping global clients with Cloud Migration and Database Management.

Index

Recommended Reference Books

IGI Global's reference books can now be purchased from three unique pricing formats:
Print Only, E-Book Only, or Print + E-Book.
Shipping fees may apply.

www.igi-global.com

ISBN: 9781799824022
EISBN: 9781799824046
© 2021; 323 pp.
List Price: US$ **195**

ISBN: 9781799867722
EISBN: 9781799867746
© 2021; 353 pp.
List Price: US$ **225**

ISBN: 9781799867548
EISBN: 9781799867562
© 2021; 420 pp.
List Price: US$ **265**

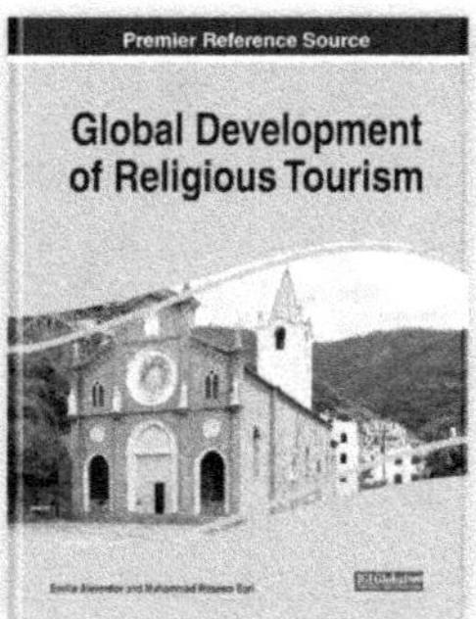

ISBN: 9781799857921
EISBN: 9781799857945
© 2021; 366 pp.
List Price: US$ **195**

ISBN: 9781799850366
EISBN: 9781799850373
© 2021; 297 pp.
List Price: US$ **215**

ISBN: 9781799849124
EISBN: 9781799849131
© 2021; 717 pp.
List Price: US$ **265**

Do you want to stay current on the latest research trends, product announcements, news, and special offers?
Join IGI Global's mailing list to receive customized recommendations, exclusive discounts, and more.
Sign up at: **www.igi-global.com/newsletters.**

Publisher of Timely, Peer-Reviewed Inclusive Research Since 1988

IGI Global PUBLISHER of TIMELY KNOWLEDGE

www.igi-global.com Sign up at www.igi-global.com/newsletters facebook.com/igiglobal twitter.com/igiglobal

Ensure Quality Research is Introduced to the Academic Community

Become an Evaluator for IGI Global Authored Book Projects

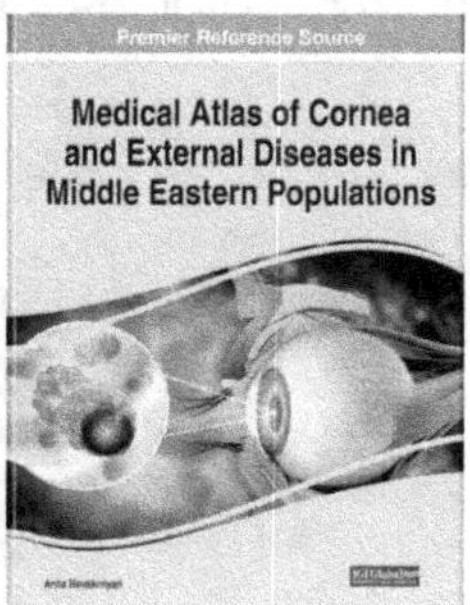

The overall success of an authored book project is dependent on quality and timely manuscript evaluations.

Applications and Inquiries may be sent to:
development@igi-global.com

Applicants must have a doctorate (or equivalent degree) as well as publishing, research, and reviewing experience. Authored Book Evaluators are appointed for one-year terms and are expected to complete at least three evaluations per term. Upon successful completion of this term, evaluators can be considered for an additional term.

If you have a colleague that may be interested in this opportunity, we encourage you to share this information with them.

Easily Identify, Acquire, and Utilize Published
Peer-Reviewed Findings in Support of Your Current Research

IGI Global OnDemand

Purchase Individual IGI Global OnDemand Book Chapters and Journal Articles

For More Information:
www.igi-global.com/e-resources/ondemand/

Browse through 150,000+ Articles and Chapters!

Find specific research related to your current studies and projects that have been contributed by international researchers from prestigious institutions, including:

Massachusetts Institute of Technology
HARVARD UNIVERSITY
COLUMBIA UNIVERSITY IN THE CITY OF NEW YORK
Australian National University

- Accurate and Advanced Search
- Affordably Acquire Research
- Instantly Access Your Content
- Benefit from the InfoSci Platform Features

"It really provides an excellent entry into the research literature of the field. It presents a manageable number of highly relevant sources on topics of interest to a wide range of researchers. The sources are scholarly, but also accessible to 'practitioners'."

- Ms. Lisa Stimatz, MLS, University of North Carolina at Chapel Hill, USA

Interested in Additional Savings?

Subscribe to
IGI Global OnDemand *Plus*

Learn More

Acquire content from over 128,000+ research-focused book chapters and 33,000+ scholarly journal articles for as low as US$ 5 per article/chapter (original retail price for an article/chapter: US$ 37.50).

6,600+ E-BOOKS. ADVANCED RESEARCH. INCLUSIVE & ACCESSIBLE.

IGI Global
PUBLISHER of TIMELY KNOWLEDGE

IGI Global e-Book Collection

- **Flexible Purchasing Options** (Perpetual, Subscription, EBA, etc.)
- Multi-Year Agreements with **No Price Increases** Guaranteed
- **No Additional Charge** for Multi-User Licensing
- No Maintenance, Hosting, or Archiving Fees
- Transformative **Open Access Options** Available

Request More Information, or Recommend the IGI Global e-Book Collection to Your Institution's Librarian

Among Titles Included in the IGI Global e-Book Collection

Research Anthology on Racial Equity, Identity, and Privilege (3 Vols.)
EISBN: 9781668445082
Price: US$ 895

Handbook of Research on Remote Work and Worker Well-Being in the Post-COVID-19 Era
EISBN: 9781799867562
Price: US$ 265

Research Anthology on Big Data Analytics, Architectures, and Applications (4 Vols.)
EISBN: 9781668436639
Price: US$ 1,950

Handbook of Research on Challenging Deficit Thinking for Exceptional Education Improvement
EISBN: 9781799888628
Price: US$ 265

Acquire & Open

When your library acquires an IGI Global e-Book and/or e-Journal Collection, your faculty's published work will be considered for immediate conversion to Open Access *(CC BY License)*, at no additional cost to the library or its faculty *(cost only applies to the e-Collection content being acquired)*, through our popular **Transformative Open Access (Read & Publish) Initiative.**

For More Information or to Request a Free Trial, Contact IGI Global's e-Collections Team: eresources@igi-global.com | 1-866-342-6657 ext. 100 | 717-533-8845 ext. 100

Have Your Work Published and Freely Accessible

Open Access Publishing

With the industry shifting from the more traditional publication models to an open access (OA) publication model, publishers are finding that OA publishing has many benefits that are awarded to authors and editors of published work.

Freely Share Your Research

Higher Discoverability & Citation Impact

Rigorous & Expedited Publishing Process

Increased Advancement & Collaboration

Acquire & Open

When your library acquires an IGI Global e-Book and/or e-Journal Collection, your faculty's published work will be considered for immediate conversion to Open Access *(CC BY License)*, at no additional cost to the library or its faculty *(cost only applies to the e-Collection content being acquired)*, through our popular **Transformative Open Access (Read & Publish) Initiative**.

Provide Up To **100%** OA APC or CPC Funding

Funding to Convert or Start a Journal to **Platinum OA**

Support for Funding an **OA Reference Book**

IGI Global publications are found in a number of prestigious indices, including Web of Science™, Scopus®, Compendex, and PsycINFO®. The selection criteria is very strict and to ensure that journals and books are accepted into the major indexes, IGI Global closely monitors publications against the criteria that the indexes provide to publishers.

WEB OF SCIENCE™ Compendex Scopus®
PsycINFO® IET Inspec

Learn More Here:

For Questions, Contact IGI Global's Open Access Team at openaccessadmin@igi-global.com

IGI Global PUBLISHER of TIMELY KNOWLEDGE www.igi-global.com

Are You Ready to
Publish Your Research?

IGI Global
PUBLISHER of TIMELY KNOWLEDGE

IGI Global offers book authorship and editorship opportunities across 11 subject areas, including business, computer science, education, science and engineering, social sciences, and more!

Benefits of Publishing with IGI Global:

- Free one-on-one editorial and promotional support.
- Expedited publishing timelines that can take your book from start to finish in less than one (1) year.
- Choose from a variety of formats, including Edited and Authored References, Handbooks of Research, Encyclopedias, and Research Insights.
- Utilize IGI Global's eEditorial Discovery® submission system in support of conducting the submission and double-blind peer review process.
- IGI Global maintains a strict adherence to ethical practices due in part to our full membership with the Committee on Publication Ethics (COPE).
- Indexing potential in prestigious indices such as Scopus®, Web of Science™, PsycINFO®, and ERIC – Education Resources Information Center.
- Ability to connect your ORCID iD to your IGI Global publications.
- Earn honorariums and royalties on your full book publications as well as complimentary copies and exclusive discounts.

Join Your Colleagues from Prestigious Institutions, Including:

Australian National University
Massachusetts Institute of Technology
Johns Hopkins University
Harvard University
Tsinghua University
Columbia University in the City of New York

Learn More at: www.igi-global.com/publish

or by Contacting the Acquisitions Department at: acquisition@igi-global.com

www.ingramcontent.com/pod-product-compliance
Lightning Source LLC
LaVergne TN
LVHW061539290926
849162LV00004B/847
9781668463819